PENGUIN BOOKS

THE TIME TRAVELER'S GUIDE TO ELIZABETHAN ENGLAND

Ian Mortimer has BA, PhD, and DLitt degrees in history from Exeter University and an MA in archive studies from University College London. From 1991 to 2003 he worked for Devon Record Office, Reading University, the Royal Commission on Historical Manuscripts, and Exeter University. He was elected a Fellow of the Royal Historical Society in 1998, and was awarded the Alexander Prize (2004) by the Royal Historical Society. He lives with his wife and three children on the edge of Dartmoor, in the southwest of England.

THE
TIME TRAVELER'S
GUIDE TO

Elizabethan England

IAN MORTIMER

PENGUIN BOOKS

PENGUIN BOOKS
Published by the Penguin Group
Penguin Group (USA) LLC
375 Hudson Street
New York, New York 10014

USA | Canada | UK | Ireland | Australia | New Zealand | India | South Africa | China
penguin.com
A Penguin Random House Company

First published in Great Britain by The Bodley Head 2012
First published in the United States of America by Viking Penguin,
a member of Penguin Group (USA) Inc., 2013
Published in Penguin Books 2014

THE LIBRARY OF CONGRESS HAS CATALOGED THE HARDCOVER EDITION AS FOLLOWS:
Mortimer, Ian, 1967–
The time traveler's guide to Elizabethan England / Ian Mortimer.
pages cm
Includes bibliographical references and index.
ISBN 978-0-670-02607-4 (hc.)
ISBN 978-0-14-312563-1 (pbk.)
1. England—Social life and customs—16th century. 2. Great Britain—History—
Elizabeth, 1558–1603. 3. England—Social conditions—16th century. I. Title.
DA355.M687 2013
942.05'5—dc23
2013001566

Printed in the United States of America
1   3   5   7   9   10   8   6   4   2

Book design by Francesca Belanger
Set in Minion Pro

This book is dedicated to my daughter,
Elizabeth Rose Mortimer

But when memory embraces the night
I see those days, long since gone,
like the ancient light of extinguished stars
traveling still, and shining on.

from "Ghosts," *Acumen* 24 (1996), p. 17

ACKNOWLEDGMENTS

I would like to thank heartily the key people who have made this book possible. These are: my agent, Jim Gill; my editor, Jörg Hensgen; and my commissioning editor, Will Sulkin. My thanks are all the more profound as they have supported me since my first book, *The Greatest Traitor*, eleven years ago. Jim took the outline for that off the huge and frighteningly anonymous slush pile; Will agreed to publish it, and Jörg knocked it into shape—and that is pretty much how it's been ever since. I wish Will all the best in his retirement, and hope that he knows I will always be grateful to him for giving me the opportunity to write history in my own way, and for encouraging me from the outset to address a wide range of audiences.

My sincere thanks also go to Dr. Jonathan Barry and Dr. Margaret Pelling, who have supported me and encouraged me for just as long. I am particularly grateful to them for each reading five chapters of this book prior to publication and making suggestions for corrections. I am also very grateful to Professor Nick Groom, who also read a chapter prior to publication. Obviously the fault for any lingering errors is entirely mine—it is impossible to pick up every slip in a book that deals with the whole gamut of life over a forty-five-year reign—but I hope that the steps taken have reduced my errors to a minimum.

I would also like to say thank you to Kay Peddle, who has helped with various aspects of production, not least the illustrations; and to Dr. Barrie Cook, curator of Medieval and Early Modern Coinage at the British Museum, who gave advice about the coins in use in Elizabeth's reign.

Following the publication of this book in the UK, Dr. Steven Gunn alerted me to a handful of minor errors, which have been corrected in this edition. I am very grateful to him for kindly passing on these observations.

Finally I would like to thank my wife, Sophie, who has been remarkably tolerant of my habit of shifting between centuries. History does have a tendency to consume people wholly; I often say that professional historians can work whenever they want—as long as it's all the time. I am grateful to her for being so understanding and supportive. I also appreciate the encouragement that our children, Alexander, Elizabeth, and Oliver, have given me. I hope the whole family takes pride in the publication of this book.

Ian Mortimer
Moretonhampstead,
October 25, 2011, August 1, 2012

CONTENTS

It is a normal morning in London, on Friday, July 16, 1591. In the wide street known as Cheapside the people are about their business, going between the timber-covered market stalls. Traders are calling out, hoping to attract the attention of merchants' wives. Travelers and gentlemen are walking along the recently repaired pavements of the street, going in and out of the goldsmiths' and moneylenders' shops. Servants and housewives are making their way through the market crowds to the Little Conduit near the back gate to the churchyard of St. Paul's Cathedral, some with leather water vessels in their arms, others with casks suspended from a yoke across their shoulders. The morning sun is reflected by the glass in the upper windows of the rich merchants' houses. A maid looks down on those in the street as she cleans her master's bedchamber.

Suddenly there is a great commotion near the market. "Repent, England! Repent!" yells a man at the top of his voice. He is dressed in black, handing out printed leaflets as he strides along. "Repent!" he shouts again and again. "Christ Jesus is come with his fan in his hand to judge the Earth!" This man is no mean fool; he is a prosperous London citizen, Mr. Edmund Coppinger. Another gentleman, Mr. Henry Arthington, also dressed in black, is following him, striding from the alley called Old Change into Cheapside. He too calls out, declaring, "Judgment Day has come upon us all! Men will rise up and kill each other as butchers do swine, for the Lord Jesus has risen." The printed bills they hand out declare that they are intent on a complete reformation of the Church in England. For the illiterate majority in the crowd, they call out their message: "The bishops must be put down! All clergymen should be equal! Queen Elizabeth has forfeited her crown and is worthy to be deprived of her kingdom. Jesus Christ has come again. The reborn Messiah is even now in London, in the form of William Hacket. Every man and woman should acknowledge him as a divine being and lord of all Christendom."

William Hacket himself is still lying in bed, in a house in the parish of St. Mary Somerset. He cuts an unlikely figure as a latter-day messiah. His memory is excellent—he can recall whole sermons and then repeat them in the taverns, adding amusing jokes. He married a woman for her dowry, then spent it and abandoned her. He is well known as a womanizer, but he is even more famous for his uncontrollable and violent temper. Anyone who witnessed his behavior in the service of Mr. Gilbert Hussey will confirm this. When a schoolmaster insulted Mr. Hussey, Hacket met with him in a tavern and pretended to try to smooth over the disagreement. After he had won the schoolmaster's trust, he put a friendly arm around his shoulders. Then, suddenly, he seized the man, threw him to the floor, flung himself on top of him, and bit off his nose. When he held up the piece of flesh, the astonished onlookers entreated him to allow the bleeding schoolmaster to take it quickly to a surgeon so that it might be sewn back on, preventing a horrible disfigurement. Hacket merely laughed, put the nose in his mouth, and swallowed it.

In his bed, Hacket knows what Mr. Coppinger and Mr. Arthington are up to: he himself gave them instructions earlier this morning. They believe he is the reborn Christ largely because he is such a persuasive and fervent character. Together they have been hatching a plot for the last six months to destroy the bishops and undermine the queen's rule. They have spoken to hundreds of people and distributed thousands of pamphlets. What Hacket does not know is that a huge crowd has started to swarm around his two prophesying angels. Some are curious, some are laughing at their proclamations; others want to join them. Most want to see Hacket in person. Such a large crowd is pressing against them that soon Mr. Arthington and Mr. Coppinger are trapped. They seek refuge in a nearby tavern, the Mermaid, and manage to escape by the back door, before returning to the parish of St. Mary Somerset and their slugabed messiah.

News runs through the city. By noon, the city watchmen are marching from house to house. By one o'clock, all three men have been sought out by the authorities and arrested. Within two weeks, two of them are dead. Hacket is tried for high treason, found guilty, and sentenced to death. On July 28, he is dragged on a hurdle to the gallows, hanged while he spits abuse at the hangman, then cut down and beheaded and butchered in the traditional manner, his headless body being cut into four parts, each with a limb attached. Mr. Coppinger dies in prison: the authorities claim he starved himself to death. Mr. Arthington enlists the support of powerful friends on the privy council and thereby saves his life, publishing his renunciation of all the things he has said as part of his penance.[1]

This is an unusual episode, and yet it is evocative of Elizabethan England. Had it taken place two hundred years earlier, Hacket and his gentlemen supporters would have been given a wide berth by the nervous citizens, unused to such sacrilegious uproar. Had it taken place two hundred years later, these events would have been a cause for popular ridicule and a cartoonist's wit. But Elizabeth's England is different. It does not lack self-confidence, but that self-confidence is easily shaken. The seriousness with which the authorities treat the plot, and the ruthless efficiency with which they suppress it, are typical of the time. It is not every day that a man is publicly proclaimed as the risen Christ, and it is extraordinary that well-respected gentlemen believe the messiah to be a violent, philandering, illiterate lout; but it is not at all unusual for Elizabethan people to adopt an extreme religious viewpoint, nor for them to fear the overthrow of the monarch. The last few decades have seen so much change that people simply do not know what to believe or think anymore. They have become used to living with slow-burning crises that might, at any moment, flare up into life-threatening situations.

This picture of Elizabethan England will come as a surprise to some readers. In the twenty-first century we are used to hearing a far more positive view of Elizabeth's "sceptred isle." We refer to the queen herself as Gloriana. We think of the defeat of the Spanish Armada, and Sir Francis Drake circumnavigating the globe in the *Golden Hind*. We think of writers such as Francis Bacon and Sir Walter Raleigh, the poets Edmund Spenser and Sir Philip Sidney, and the playwrights Christopher Marlowe and William Shakespeare. Surely a society that created such architectural masterpieces as Hardwick Hall, Burghley, Longleat, and Wollaton Hall cannot be said to be anything other than triumphal? Surely a small kingdom that sends mariners into battle off the coast of Central America cannot be accused of self-doubt?

The problem is that our view of history diminishes the reality of the past. We concentrate on the historic event as something that *has* happened and in so doing we ignore it as a moment which, at the time, *is* happening. For example, when we hear the word "Armada," we think of an English victory, in which the threatening Spanish ships were scattered and defeated in the Battle of Gravelines, and after which Sir Francis Drake was feted as a hero. Yet at the moment of attack everything was up in the air. As Drake boarded his ship at Plymouth, he would have known that there was a real possibility of the Armada landing successfully and his own ship being sunk. He would have known that a change in the direction of the wind could alter everything—leaving his strategy in jeopardy and his fleet in danger. We can no longer imagine the possibility of the Armada disgorging its troops on English beaches. Our view of the event as a thing of the past restricts our understanding of contemporary doubts, hopes, and reality.

I wrote my first *Time Traveler's Guide* in order to suggest we do not always need to describe the past objectively and distantly. In that book I tried to bring the medieval period closer to the reader, describing what you would find if you could visit fourteenth-century England. Where would you stay? What might you wear? What would you eat? How should you greet people? Given that we know so much about the period, it stands to reason that the historian should be able to answer such questions. There are limits, of course: the historian cannot break through the evidence barrier and actually re-create the past. Moreover, imagining a personal visit is decidedly tricky in some matters of detail. You may well understand why the earl of Essex rebelled against Elizabeth in 1601—but how did he clean his teeth? Did he wear underwear? What did he use for toilet paper? These things aren't so well evidenced. We must exploit what little evidence there is to satisfy, if only partially, our collective spirit of inquiry.

What will strike you first if you visit Elizabethan England? I imagine that, to start with, it will be the smells of the towns and cities. After a few days, however, I suspect it will be the uncertainty of life. You will be appalled to see dead bodies lying in the street during an epidemic of influenza or plague, and the starving beggars in their filthy rags. You will be disconcerted to notice vulnerability even at the top of society. Elizabeth herself is the target of several assassination attempts and uprisings—from a gentry rebellion to her physician supposedly trying to poison her. Uncertainty pervades every aspect of life. People do not know whether the sun goes around the Earth or the Earth goes around the sun; the doctrines of the Church contradict the claims of Copernicus. The rich merchants of London do not know if their ships will be stranded in a North African port, with the crews massacred by Barbary pirates and their cargo stolen. To gauge what Elizabethan life is like, we need to see the panic-stricken men and women who hear that the plague has arrived in the next village. We need to see the farmers in the 1590s, staring at their rain-beaten, blackened corn for the second year in succession. This is the reality for many Elizabethan people: the stark horror that they have nothing to feed their sick and crying children. We need to appreciate that such people, be they Protestant or Catholic, may well connect their starvation with the government's meddling with religious beliefs and traditions. We need to see them looking for something stable in their lives and fixing on the queen herself as a beacon of hope. Do not imagine the proud figure of Queen Elizabeth standing stiff and unruffled in her great jeweled dress on the deck of a serene ship, floating on calm sunlit waters. Rather imagine her struggling to maintain her position on the ship of state in heaving seas, tying herself to the mast, and yelling orders in the storm. This is the real Gloriana—Elizabeth, Queen of England by the grace of God, the pillar of faith and social certainty in the dizzying upheaval of the sixteenth century.

Like all societies, Elizabethan England is full of contradictions. Some practices will impress you as enormously sophisticated and refined; others will strike you with horror. People are still burned alive for certain forms of heresy, and women are burned for killing their husbands. The heads of traitors are still exhibited over the Great Stone Gate in London, left there to rot and be a deterrent to others. Torture is permitted in order to recover information about treasonable plots. The gap between the wealthy and the impoverished is as great as ever, and, as this book will show, society is strictly hierarchical. Humble houses—sometimes whole villages—are destroyed to make room for the parks of the nobility. People still starve to death on the highroads. As for the political situation, a brief note by a government official describes the state of the nation at the start of the reign:

The queen poor, the realm exhausted, the nobility poor and decayed. Want of good captains and soldiers. The people out of order. Justice not executed. All things dear. Excess in meat, drink and apparel. Divisions among ourselves. Wars with France and Scotland. The French king bestriding the realm, having one foot in Calais and the other in Scotland. Steadfast enmity but no friendship abroad.[2]

This description is far removed from the "golden age" interpretation of Elizabeth's reign—but there are at least as many positive contemporary verdicts as there are negative ones. In 1577, Raphael Holinshed publishes a chronicle in which he describes Elizabeth's accession in the following words:

> After all the stormy, tempestuous and blustering windy weather of Queen Mary was overblown, the darksome clouds of discomfort dispersed, the palpable fogs and mist of the most intolerable misery consumed, and the dashing showers of persecution overpast: it pleased God to send England a calm and quiet season, a clear and lovely sunshine, a *quietus est* from former broils of a turbulent estate, and a world of blessings by good Queen Elizabeth.

Obviously Holinshed is addressing a Protestant minority who are literate and wealthy enough to buy an expensive two-volume publication. But we do not need to look through his rose-tinted spectacles to see many national achievements and cheering developments. Elizabeth's reign sees an extraordinary period of wealth creation and artistic endeavor. English explorers, driven by the desire for profit, proceed into the cold waters of Baffin Island and the Arctic Circle north of Russia. Despite the wars with France and Spain, no fighting takes place on home soil, so that for most Englishmen the whole reign is one of peace. In addition to the famous poetry and plays, it is an age of innovation in science, gardening, publishing, theology, history, music, and architecture. Two English sea captains circumnavigate the world—proving to sixteenth-century people that they have at last exceeded the knowledge of the ancient Greeks and Romans. No longer do thinking men claim they can see further than the ancients by virtue of their being "dwarves standing on the shoulders of giants." They have grown to be "giants" themselves.

One of the most striking differences between Elizabethan England and its forerunners lies in the queen herself. Elizabeth's personality and the rule of a woman are two things that make England in 1558–1603 a very different place from the England of Edward III or even that of her father, Henry VIII. More than ever before, the character of the monarch is intrinsically woven into the daily lives of her people. She is without doubt the most powerful Englishwoman in history.[3] It is impossible to write about everyday life in her reign without reference to her. Her choice to steer England away from the Catholicism of her sister, Mary, and to reestablish an independent Church of England, as pioneered by Henry VIII, affects every person in every parish throughout the realm. Even if her subjects accept her religious choices, and never raise their heads above the religious parapet, her decision making touches their lives in numerous ways. The Prayer Book changes, church symbols are torn down, and bishops are replaced. An individual might become persona non grata just because of his or her religious doubts. If ever there was an argument that rulers can change the lives of their subjects, it lies in the impact of the Tudor monarchs. Elizabeth's kingdom is very much *Elizabethan* England.

This book follows my medieval guide, but it does not entirely adopt the same form. It would be tedious to make all the same observations about aspects of daily life that contrast with our own society. Moreover, in writing about Elizabethan England, it would be inappropriate to follow exactly the same formula developed to describe the realm of two hundred years earlier. It is not possible, for example, to relegate religion to a subsection in this book: it has to be a chapter on its own, being integral to the ways Elizabethans live their lives. The England of 1558 has much in common with the kingdom in 1358, but a great deal has changed. As a result, this book is not only concerned with the way Elizabethan England compares with the present day; it also examines how it compares with, or differs from, its medieval roots.

The historian is always a middleman: the facilitator of the reader's understanding of the past. I am no different, even though this book is written in the present tense and based on the premise that the most direct way to learn about something is to see it for yourself. However, in a book like this, my relationship with the evidence is unusual. It goes without saying that literary texts have been important (plays, poetry, travelers' accounts, diaries, contemporary surveys), as have been a wide range of printed records. But making sense of all this evidence as indicative of lived behavior requires the historian to draw on personal experience. As I put it in *The Time Traveler's Guide to Medieval England*, "The key to learning something about the past might be a ruin or an archive but the means whereby we may understand it is—and always will be—ourselves." This goes for the reader's lived experience too. For example, I presume that readers of this book have not seen a bull-baiting contest but yet have enough life experience to imagine what is involved, and thus to know that the Elizabethans' love of this form of entertainment makes them profoundly different from modern English people.

I have been reluctant to include details from outside the period of the reign. Very occasionally I have cited post-1603 evidence, but only in order to illustrate a procedure or practice that certainly existed before 1603. There is more citation of pre-1558 sources: much of Elizabethan England is composed of relics from the late medieval and earlier Tudor periods. This applies obviously to the castles, town walls, streets, and churches; but it also applies to books that were printed for the first time in earlier reigns and which are reread and often reprinted in Elizabethan times. It especially applies to legislation: most of the law is based on medieval precedents, and it goes without saying that all the laws in force at Elizabeth's accession date from an earlier period. It is important to remember that every house and structure that we call "medieval" or "Tudor" because of its date of construction is also Elizabethan. The same applies to many phrases and customs that were in use and practiced before 1558. On this point, readers will note several references to the wonderful Latin phrasebook *Vulgaria* by William Horman, first published in 1519 (I used the 1530 edition). Horman is vividly expressive of the most basic aspects of daily life, so we learn that "unwashed wool that grows between the hind legs of a black sheep is medicinable" and "some women with child have wrong appetite to eat things that be out of rule: as coals." As his purpose was to provide daily Latin in order to encourage the resurgence of the spoken language, we can be confident these examples reflect the experiences of his readers. And while anything written by him about fashionable clothes or religion is, of course, hugely out of date by 1558, what he says about some pregnant women's appetites is as true today as it was in 1519. Bearing in mind these caveats, I have done my best faithfully to represent England as it existed between Elizabeth's accession on November 17, 1558, and her death on March 24, 1603.

Welcome, then, to Elizabethan England, and all its doubts, certainties, changes, traditions, and contradictions. It is a jewel-encrusted muddy kingdom, glittering and starving, hopeful and fearful in equal measure—always on the point of magnificent discoveries and brutal rebellions.

THE
TIME TRAVELER'S
GUIDE TO
Elizabethan England

CHAPTER ONE

The Landscape

Different societies see landscapes differently. You may look at Elizabethan England and see a predominantly green land, characterized by large open fields and woodlands, but an Elizabethan yeoman will describe his homeland to you in terms of cities, towns, ports, great houses, bridges, and roads. In your eyes it may be a sparsely populated land—the average density being less than sixty people per square mile in 1561 (compared with well over a thousand today)—but a contemporary description will mention overcrowding and the problems of population expansion.[1] Describing a landscape is thus a matter of perspective: your priorities affect what you see. Asked to describe their county, most Devonians will mention the great city of Exeter, the ports of Dartmouth, Plymouth, and Barnstaple, and the dozens of market towns. They will generally neglect to mention that the region is dominated by a great moor, Dartmoor, two thousand feet high in places and over two hundred square miles in expanse. There are no roads across this wasteland, only track ways. Elizabethans see it as good for nothing but pasture, tin mining, and the steady water supply it provides by way of the rivers that rise there. Many people are afraid of such moors and forests. They are "the ruthless, vast and gloomy woods . . . by nature made for murders and for rapes," as Shakespeare writes in *Titus Andronicus*. Certainly no one will think of Dartmoor as beautiful. Sixteenth-century artists paint wealthy people, prosperous cities, and food, not landscapes.

The underlying reasons for such differences are not hard to find. In a society in which people still starve to death, an orchard is not a beautiful thing in itself: its beauty lies in the fact that it produces apples and cider. A wide flat field is "finer" than rugged terrain for it can be tilled easily to produce wheat and so represents good white bread. A small thatched cottage, which a modern viewer might consider pretty, will be considered unattractive by an Elizabethan traveler, for cottagers are generally poor and able to offer little in the way of hospitality. Ranges of hills and mountains are obstacles to Elizabethan travelers and very far from picturesque features you go out of your way to see. Hills might feature in an Elizabethan writer's description of a county because of their potential for sheep grazing, but on the whole he will be more concerned with listing all the houses of the gentry, their seats and parks.

It is worth being aware of these differences at the outset. Those things that Elizabethans take for granted are precisely what you will find most striking: the huge open fields, the muddy roads, and the small size of so many laborers' houses. Indeed, it is only at the very end of the Elizabethan period, in the late 1590s, that people start to use the term "landscape" to describe a view. Before this, they do not need such a word, for they do not see a "landscape" as such—only the constituent elements that mean something to them: the woods, fields, rivers, orchards, gardens, bridges, roads, and, above all else, the towns. Shakespeare does not use the word "landscape" at all; he uses the word "country"—a concept in which people and physical things are intimately bound together. Therefore, when you describe the Elizabethan landscape as it appears to you, you are not necessarily describing the "country" as Elizabethan people see it. Every act of seeing is unique—and that is as true for an Elizabethan farmer looking at his growing corn as it is for you now, traveling back to the sixteenth century.

Towns

Stratford-upon-Avon lies in the very heart of England, about ninety-four miles northwest of London. The medieval parish church stands at the southern end of the town, only a few yards from the River Avon, which flows lazily in a gradual curve along the east side. A squat wooden spire stands on top of the church tower. If you look north, you will see the handsome stone bridge of fourteen arches built by Sir Hugh Clopton in the 1490s. Cattle graze in the wide meadow on the far bank; there is a small wooden bridge downstream where the mill looks over the narrowing of the river.

Standing in this part of Stratford in November 1558, at the very start of Elizabeth's reign, you may well think that the town has barely changed since the Middle Ages. If you walk toward the center, most of the buildings you see are medieval. Directly opposite as you leave the churchyard is the stone quadrangle of the college, founded in the 1330s by Stratford's most notable son, John Stratford, archbishop of Canterbury. Passing an orchard and a couple of low, two-story thatched cottages, you come to a muddy corner; turn right into Church Street. Looking ahead, you will see the regular divisions of the tenements. These are substantial timber-framed houses, many of them the full width of sixty feet laid down when the town was planned in the twelfth century.[2] A hundred yards farther along on your right are the almshouses of the medieval Guild of the Holy Cross. These make up a line of timber-framed two-story buildings with unglazed windows, tiled roofs, and jetties that project out above the street at a height of six feet. Beyond is the grammar school and hall of the Guild, a similar long, low building, with whitewashed timbers and wooden struts across the windows. Adjacent is the chapel of the Guild, with its handsome stone tower. Its clock chimes on the hour as you step along the muddy street in the damp autumn air.

Keep walking. On your right, directly across the lane from the chapel, is the most prestigious house in the town: New Place, built by Sir Hugh Clopton—the man who constructed the bridge. It is three stories high and timber-framed, with brick between the timbers, not willow and plasterwork. Five bays wide, it has one large window on either side of the central porch, five windows on the floor above, and five on the floor above that. Each of the top-floor windows is set in a gable looking out across the town. The whole proud edifice is a fitting tribute to a successful businessman. In 1558, Sir Hugh Clopton is the second-most-famous man of Stratford (after the archbishop), and a figure greatly admired by the townsfolk. The boys leaving the grammar school and walking back into the center of the town regard this building as a statement of success. A future pupil, William Shakespeare, will eventually follow in Sir Hugh's footsteps, make his fortune in London, and return to live out his last days in this very house.

As you continue along the street, you come across a few narrower buildings, where the old tenements have been divided to create widths of thirty feet (half a plot), twenty (a third), or just fifteen feet. The narrower houses tend to be taller: three stories, with timber jetties projecting out a foot or so farther at each level. Unlike some towns, however, the houses in Stratford do not shut out the light with their overhanging upper stories. Those market towns that were carefully planned in the Middle Ages have such wide thoroughfares that plenty of light enters the front parlors and workshops. Here in the High Street you will find glovers, tailors, and butchers as well as a couple of wealthy mercers and a wool merchant.[3] Six days a week, they will set up their shop boards in the street and place their wares on them to show to passersby. Most have wooden signs—depicting dragons, lions, uni-corns, cauldrons, barrels—hanging by metal hooks from projecting wooden arms. Note that the symbols painted on the signs are not necessarily related to the trade practiced: a goldsmith's shop may well be called "The Green Dragon" and a glover might work by the sign of "The White Hart." On your right, leading down to the pasture on the riverbank, is Sheep Street, where more wool merchants live and wool and animals are traded. On your left, in Ely Street, swine change hands. Carry on along the High Street for another hundred yards or so and you will come to the main market cross: a covered area where needle-makers, hosiers, and similar craftsmen sell their goods. Beyond is the principal marketplace, Bridge Street. This is more of a long rectangular open space than a street—or, at least, it used to be: the center is now filled with stalls and shops at street level and domestic lodgings on the floors above.

At this point, if you turn right you will see Sir Hugh Clopton's magnifi-cent bridge over a wide, shallow stretch of the river. Turn left and you will find two streets of timber-framed houses. One of these is Wood Street, which leads to the cattle market. The other, leading northwest, is Henley Street. Go along here, and on the right-hand side you'll find the house oc-cupied by the glover John Shakespeare, his wife, Mary, and their firstborn daughter, Joan. Like almost all the other houses in the borough, this has a wattle-and-plaster infill between the beams, with a low roof covering its three bays. This is the house in which their gifted son will be born in April 1564.

At this end of Henley Street you are almost at the edge of town. If you carry on for another hundred yards you will find yourself on the road to Henley-in-Arden. As always on the outskirts of a town, you will smell the noxious fumes of the laystall or midden that serves the nearby residents. John Shakespeare has been known to use part of his own tenement as a laystall, but he also maintains a tanyard at the back of his house, where he prepares the leather for his gloves—and nothing stinks quite as much as a tanyard. A walk around the back of these houses in Henley Street reveals that Mr. Shakespeare is not alone in making practical use of his tenement for refuse disposal. Many of his neighbors do likewise, disposing of fish and animal entrails, feces, vegetable matter, and old rushes from floors in the dumps on the edge of the great field at the back of their property. If you peer into the messy backyards of those whitewashed timber-framed houses, you can also see vegetable gardens, dunghills, orchards of apple, pear, and cherry trees, henhouses, cart houses, and barns—places to dispose of rotten food and places to grow new. You might say that Stratford appears to be as much a town of farmers as of craftsmen. Many of these outhouses are thatched: a marked contrast to the smart tiles of the houses facing the street. Notice that some of the older houses have freestanding kitchen buildings in their gardens; notice too how several gardens have pigs, fed with detritus from the kitchens.

At this point you may wonder again at the medieval aspect of the place. The middens of Stratford stink as much as they did two hundred years ago, and its houses are still predominantly built with timber frames. Many of them are well over a hundred years old. The boundaries and layout of the borough have hardly altered since 1196. The marketplaces have not been moved. What has changed?

The most significant changes are not physically apparent; they are less tangible. For example, Stratford received a charter of incorporation from Edward VI in 1553 and now, five years later, is governed by a bailiff, aldermen, and the most important burgesses. Before 1547, the town was administered by the guild. Now that has been dissolved, and its property has passed to the new town corporation. Although the town in 1558 looks much the same as it did in 1500, it has radically altered in its governance. Moreover, it is not so much a question of what has *changed* as what is *changing*. Most of the medieval houses that still stand in 1558 are hall houses: one or two ground-floor rooms (a hall and a chamber) with packed earth floors, open to the roof, and a hearth in the center of the hall. They do not have chimneys. But just consider what a difference a chimney makes: it allows one heated room to be built on top of another. In this way, a large number of rooms can be built on the same ground as one old hall. No doubt the building that once stood on the patch of John Shakespeare's house was a hall house; its replacement has back-to-back fireplaces and a stack rising through the whole house, giving heat to two downstairs and two upstairs chambers. Another stack rises at the far end, heating the workshop and the chamber above. Many of John's neighbors are still living in single-story houses; but already in November 1558, Stratford, like all the other small towns in England, has started to grow—not outward so much as upward.

You will see exactly how fast Stratford is changing if you return forty years later, in 1598, toward the end of Elizabeth's reign. The church is still there, the roads have not changed, the guild buildings and school have not been substantially altered—but over half the town has been rebuilt. This is partly due to two catastrophic fires in 1594 and 1595, which destroy 120 houses, making about a quarter of the population homeless. There are now many more brick chimneys and consequently many more tall houses. In fact, brick is one of the keys to change. The affordable production of a durable and fireproof chimney material means that two- and three-story houses can be built even in places where stone is scarce and masonry expensive. Walk back down Henley Street, across the marketplace and back into the High Street, and you'll see that the whole skyline has changed. Almost all the houses on your right are now three stories high, displaying much more elegance and symmetry in their timber construction, with more carved woodwork on the beams facing the street. Some of these houses have greased paper or cloth under a lattice in their windows to allow in a little light while keeping out drafts, but some now have glass in the street-facing chambers. Glass, which is very rare in town houses in 1558, becomes available to the reasonably well-off in the 1570s.[4] Not all of the new buildings facing the street will have been constructed with glass windows in mind, for it is still difficult to get hold of in 1598; but most people with disposable income will try to obtain it—importing it in preconstructed frames from Burgundy, Normandy, or Flanders, if they cannot get hold of English glass. Nor will a householder necessarily equip his whole house with glass at once: he might install it in his hall and parlor and leave the other, less important rooms unglazed. In 1558, a chimney is the prime status symbol to show off to the neighbors. In 1598, it is glazing.

A less desirable aspect of the changes being wrought in Stratford is the accommodation of the poor. You might think that barn conversions are a feature of the modern world, but a glimpse at the backyards of some properties will tell you otherwise. Quite a few old barns are let out to paupers who have nowhere else to go. The population of Stratford in 1558 is about fifteen hundred; by 1603 it has swelled to twenty-five hundred.[5] And that latter figure probably does not include all the poor and vagrants in and around the town—one report in 1601 mentions that the corporation is struggling to cope with seven hundred paupers. Now you can see why the well-off are living ostentatiously in handsome, glazed houses: it separates them from the have-nots. You can see why William Shakespeare, the son of the glover, is so proud of having acquired New Place in 1597, with its brick, glazed windows, and chimneys—a far cry from the smelly house where he spent his boyhood (and where his aged father still lives).

What is true for Stratford and its inhabitants also applies to other urban settlements. In 1600, there are twenty-five cathedral cities and 641 market towns in England and Wales.[6] The rebuilding that they are all undergoing makes it impossible to compare them in size, for their populations are changing rapidly. London, for example, has a population of about seventy thousand in 1558 and about two hundred thousand in 1603; it moves from being the sixth-largest city in Europe (after Naples, Venice, Paris, Antwerp, and Lisbon) to being the third (after Naples, with 281,000 inhabitants, and Paris, with 220,000).[7]

The most populous towns and cities in England in 1600.[8]

No.	Place capital letters denote a city; * denotes a port.	Estimated population
1	LONDON*	200,000
2	NORWICH	15,000
3	YORK	12,000
4	BRISTOL*	12,000
5	Newcastle*	10,000
6	EXETER*	8,000
7	Plymouth*	8,000
8	Coventry	6,000
9	SALISBURY	6,000
10	Lynn*	6,000
11	GLOUCESTER*	6,000
12	CHESTER*	6,000
13	Kingston upon Hull*	6,000
14	Ipswich*	5,000
15	CANTERBURY	5,000
16	Colchester	5,000
17	WORCESTER	5,000
18	Great Yarmouth*	5,000
19	OXFORD	5,000
20	Cambridge	5,000

Several points emerge from the above table. First, although Stratford-upon-Avon is not what you would call a large town, with just twenty-five hundred inhabitants in 1600, only twenty towns in England are twice as populous.

Thus we might say that Stratford is truly representative of the majority of towns in England and Wales. Second, only half of the twenty-two English cathedral cities are in the above list. The other eleven—Winchester, Carlisle, Durham, Ely, Lincoln, Hereford, Lichfield, Rochester, Chichester, Peterborough, and Wells—all have fewer than five thousand inhabitants, so you should not assume that a city is a populous place. Third, eleven of the twenty most populous towns are ports (twelve if we include York, which has a modest quay). In fact, the fastest-growing large towns—London, Newcastle, and Plymouth—are all seaports, reminding us that a world of opportunities is opening up to Elizabethans through the island's long coastline and geographical position.[9] Medieval people saw the sea as a barrier or frontier. Under the Tudor monarchs it comes to be recognized as one of the country's greatest natural resources.

The most significant point implicit in the table of populous towns is more subtle. If you compare it with a similar table for medieval England, you will see that it reveals a process of urbanization. The towns on the above list are home to 336,000 people; the twenty largest towns in 1380 had less than half this number. In addition, more people live in the many small market towns than did in previous centuries. Some of these have just five hundred inhabitants, living in a hundred houses clustered around one single main road or square. But dozens more are like Stratford, housing two to three thousand people, with all the professional and administrative functions one associates with a proper town. In 1600, approximately 25 percent of the population lives in a town, compared with about 12 percent in 1380.[10] This is an important development: if one in four people grows up in a town, then English culture is becoming increasingly urban. Society as a whole is less closely tied to the countryside. The self-reliant townsman, with a trade and the ambition to advance his status and living standards, is fast becoming the principal agent of social and cultural change. The system of villenage—the old tradition of peasants being bonded individually and collectively to the lord of the manor, to be bought and sold along with the land—is hardly to be found anywhere.[11]

Like Stratford, many towns retain their medieval street layout. No fewer than 289 of them preserve their medieval walls.[12] Almost all have long lines of timber-framed houses with gables overlooking the streets, interspersed among the medieval churches and old halls. Most have areas where houses with large gardens have something of the "urban farm" appearance: Norwich is said to have so many trees that it may be described as either "a city in an orchard or an orchard in a city."[13] But what will strike you is the number of buildings under construction, their skeletal timber frames open to the elements or their stone fronts surrounded by scaffolding. The old friaries and monasteries are being turned into warehouses or demolished to make way for new housing. In the summer months an English town resembles an enormous building site, as several dozen new houses have their foundations dug, and men stripped to the waist haul dirt up in buckets on pulleys from cellars, or lift heavy oak timbers up to form the joists of a house. Watch them passing up long elm boards to their fellows on the upper floors, talking with the master carpenter, measuring and cutting the frames of the windows and the shutters, and filling the gaps between the timbers with wattle or brick. Everyone is moving into a town, it seems.

Towns are not just for the benefit of the people who live in them. They are also crossroads: places where country life and urban professions, services, and administrations mix, and where agreements can be given legal force. A town like Stratford might have upward of one hundred brewers, but that does not mean the whole town is full of heavy drinkers; rather it indicates that all those who come into town from the hinterland on market days don't have to go thirsty. Similarly a town's surgeons and physicians do not simply administer to urban needs but travel out to the parishes in the surrounding countryside, serving a population that might be several times larger than that of the town itself.[14] Look among the houses and shops of Stratford and you will see the full range of occupations that make up such a settlement: wheelwrights, carpenters, masons, blacksmiths, tinsmiths, tailors, shoemakers, glovers, victualers, butchers, brewers, maltsters, vintners, mercers, lawyers, scriveners, physicians, surgeons, apothecaries, and drapers. Most towns like Stratford will have more than sixty recognized occupations; a large city like Norwich or Bristol may have considerably more than a hundred.

Before leaving Stratford, consider how the seasons affect the appearance of an Elizabethan town. The streets are not paved—very few towns have paving at all—so in April the showers create quagmires, especially at the crossroads, where carts turn, churning up the mud. However much gravel is put down on the main approach roads, it is never enough to be of lasting benefit. In summer the mud dries to cakes of earth and then breaks up, so that the same carts and horses' hooves now kick up dust. The streets are more crowded too, for people mostly travel in summer. The numbers of country dwellers coming to market are supplemented by merchants arriving from the coastal towns with fresh fish for sale. As the season dwindles to autumn, the roads become less busy. On some days the streets will be almost empty as people in the countryside head out into the fields to gather in the harvest, taking baskets of food to sustain them on their long working days. Late autumn sees more rain, and cattle, pigs, and sheep herded into town to be sold before the feast of Martinmas (November 11), when many will be slaughtered and salted for the oncoming season. Looking down the same streets in winter, with the chill air and the smell of wood smoke everywhere, you will see fewer people out and about. The average temperature is about two degrees Celsius colder than what you are used to, with especially cold snaps in the 1570s and 1590s.[15] When snow falls, you wake to see the white blanket across the street—thinner on the edge, where less snow falls because of the overhanging eaves. Houses are decorated with evergreens around the doors. Long icicles hang down from their gutterless roofs, discouraging people from walking too close to the walls. Carts leave wheel tracks, pressing the snow into slush and mud. Many people remain inside their houses, not even opening their shuttered, unglazed windows. The appearance of the whole town thus shifts with the seasons—to a much greater degree than a paved and glazed modern town, where most activities are conducted under cover.

The Countryside

Leaving Stratford-upon-Avon by the long stone bridge, you have a choice of two routes to London. One takes you via Banbury, the other via Oxford (turn right immediately on the far side of the bridge if you prefer the latter). The country here is flat and sparsely populated: the figure of sixty people per square mile given at the start of this chapter is hardly true of this corn-growing region. Parishes here have about thirty people per square mile, on average; but some are as sparse as seventeen.[16] Rather than houses it is the fields that will catch your attention: massive areas of hundreds of acres, or even a thousand, each one divided into smaller units called furlongs. A furlong is divided in turn into between four and a dozen strips of land, each strip being allotted to a tenant of the manor. Between the furlongs are narrow paths of untilled soil, called balks, by which tenants might access their strips with a cart. The contemporary word for this sort of farmland is "champaign country" (from the French *champ,* meaning "field"). The countryside is therefore a giant patchwork of furlongs, each characterized by the direction of the strips and the type of crop that is growing. Some tenants plant wheat on a few of their strips and hardier corn—such as rye, vetches, or barley—on the others. Some rotate the crops they plant: barley this year, wheat the next. Often you will see fields left fallow, or areas left to be grazed by pigs and cattle. Here and there, on the edges of the great fields, you will see small enclosures for livestock (known as "closes" rather than fields). This open-field agriculture dominates the Midlands: Oxfordshire is almost entirely unenclosed in 1600, and no fewer than 125 of the 128 rural parishes in the adjacent county of Berkshire have open fields.[17]

England is not all tilled in this way. In fact, less than a third is tilled at all. About 11.5 million acres of England and Wales are under the plow (29 percent of the total area). Almost as much—about 10 million acres (26 percent)—is untilled heaths, moors, mountains, and marshland. You will be amazed at how much wasteland and "wilderness" there is. In places like Westmorland this is only to be expected: since it is so rugged, and so near the lawless Scottish border, it is not surprising that three quarters of that county is wild. You can say the same for the granite uplands of the southwest: Devon has at least three hundred thousand acres of moor and heath. But even Hampshire has a hundred thousand acres of unfarmed land, and Berkshire sixty thousand acres of waste. On top of this, there are the managed woodlands and natural forests, which account for a further 10 percent of the kingdom, and the pasture, parks, downland, and commons, which collectively occupy another 30 percent. The remaining 5 percent is towns, houses, gardens, churchyards, orchards, roads, rivers, and lakes.[18]

The reason why so much of England is used for grazing is the value of sheep. Obviously sheep are a food source, but an even more important reason for farming them is the value of wool. Many rural communities depend heavily on the wool trade for their income. Huge amounts of money are raised for the government through the imposition of customs duties on wool, woolfells, and fleeces exported to Europe. In 1564–65, cloth and woolens account for 81.6 percent (by value) of all the exports from England—amounting to some £1 million—and the largest proportion of the remaining 18.4 percent is raw wool, followed by woolfells.[19] This is why you will see so many sheep in England: more than eight million of them, twice as many as there are people.²⁰ Having said that, these are not quite the animals with which you are familiar: they are very small. Average weights are gradually rising (through improvements in husbandry), from about twenty-eight pounds per sheep in 1500 to forty-six pounds in 1600, with the largest weighing sixty pounds; still, these are tiny by comparison with modern ewes, which weigh one to two hundred pounds (a modern ram can weigh over 350 pounds).²¹ Much the same can be said for the cattle (about 350 pounds in Elizabethan times, twelve to sixteen hundred pounds today).

The fields, commons, and rivers are the most striking features of the landscape as you travel toward the city of London. But such a journey will also bring many other agricultural practices to your attention. The area of woodland is now rapidly shrinking. One man in Durham has already started his long career felling trees—by 1629, he will have chopped down more than thirty thousand oaks single-handedly.²² As these take more than a century to grow to maturity, this is clearly unsustainable; but many landlords do not regret the permanent loss of their woods because the cleared land can be used for other agricultural purposes. The widespread felling is thus doubly drastic: being permanent, it leads to higher prices of wood, encouraging landlords to fell yet more timber. Add the increase in the population and the extra wood needed for all the extra tools, cupboards, tables, beds, and chests for all the extra people, not to mention the materials needed for the building (and rebuilding) of their houses, and you can see why there is not very much wood left. On top of all this, the wars with France and Spain have led to increased demand for timber—more than six hundred oak trees are needed to build a warship—further adding to the demand for wood.²³ Firewood is thus expensive and in short supply, and many people have started talking about a "fuel famine." The government tries to take action, passing Acts of Parliament in 1558, 1581, and 1585 to prevent wood being used for unnecessary purposes; but demand still massively outstrips supply. The price of timber effectively doubles over the course of the reign.²⁴

Timber felling is not the only substantial change being wrought on the countryside. A second one is enclosure. Many landlords evict their tenants and level their homes, replacing the good arable land with fields for their sheep. Others create deer parks where there used to be villages. Some landowners even deem it necessary to have two parks adjacent to their country seat, one for red deer and one for fallow. In some respects this is an attempt to hold back the pace of change and to re-create a lost "natural world," where men are free to hunt their food in a wooded Elysium. In other respects, it is just a status symbol. But whether done for sheep farming or for hunting, the destruction of arable fields and villages is a profound worry to the families who are evicted. It is equally worrying to the authorities in those towns where the homeless husbandmen go begging. The gradual loss of land to the workingman and his family may fairly be described as the second-greatest single cause of unrest during the reign, second only to religion. By 1600, in some counties, one in six villages that existed in 1450 have been destroyed by enclosure. As we have seen, Oxfordshire and Berkshire are still almost entirely unenclosed, but they are not the norm. Fifty-eight villages have disappeared in Warwickshire, sixty in Leicestershire.[25]

Not all of England's landscape is the same. Large open fields dominate the heart of the kingdom, from Yorkshire down to the south coast, but they are not found along the Welsh border, or in the northwest, East Anglia, or Kent, where enclosed field systems are the norm. Similarly you are unlikely to come across large open fields anywhere farther west than Braunton, in North Devon. The villages in these regions are also different. Rather than being nucleated—gathered closely around a church, as they are in open-field farming counties—the houses are more spread out, often quite isolated from the center of the community.

Different types of corn are grown in the various regions. Oxfordshire is mainly champaign country, growing high-quality wheat. Go to Norfolk, however, and you will find more rye in the fields. In Wiltshire, wheat and barley are equally popular. Farther west, barley thrives better in the wet conditions. In Lancashire and the north, oats are the most common crop. In Yorkshire, three times as much rye is grown as wheat. In Kent—the garden of England—there are more orchards than anywhere else, producing the finest apples and cherries. Indeed, Kent is particularly well provisioned, for the Kentish inheritance system of *gavelkind* means that yeomen's estates are divided equally between their sons. Thus large estates are often broken up and turned into smaller units, and these are carefully tended by the next generation of yeomen, who are owner-occupiers and more efficient in their use of land.

Another rapidly changing area of the countryside is its perimeter—the coast. Ports have existed since Roman times, of course, but changing attitudes to the sea are observable in the way people are now prepared to live on the coast in smaller communities. The dangers of the early Middle Ages, when any coastal community was prey to Norse and Danish marauders, or Irish and Scots pirates, are long gone. People across England have started to build much closer to the sea, and fishing villages have sprung up all round the coast.

Any village is much more than just a series of houses. There are the communal structures of the church and church house. All across the surrounding parish there are barns, byres, corn lofts, henhouses, stables, cart houses, and mills. Watermills are far more common than windmills, but you will find a good many of the latter in the southeast, situated on the summits of hills. Marked out with flags on top of them, they are otherwise largely unchanged from the windmills of the late Middle Ages. They have cloth-covered sails and may be two or three stories high; but the most remarkable thing about them is that they are built on a pivot, so the whole building can be turned to face the direction of the wind.[26] In most villages you will also come across sawpits, timber piles, dung heaps, haycocks, beehives, and, of course, gardens. A statute of 1589 decrees that every new house is to be provided with four acres of land: this is the minimum thought to be appropriate for the needs of a family. All domestic buildings are positioned so as to avoid frost pockets and flooding, with further provision for the best juxtaposition of buildings. "A hay house near a stable breedeth peril," declares William Horman, indicating just how much thought you need to put into the location of your barns and outhouses.

However much thought goes into the planning of a village, the simple fact of people living in close proximity leads to sanitation problems. Many villages have common drains or sewers which regularly are blocked by feces and detritus. Walk through Ingatestone in Essex in the 1560s, for example, and you will find that people have built privies over the common gutter or sewer. In 1562 the manor court has to forbid people from leaving dead pigs, dogs, and other carcasses in the lanes. In 1564 a local man is ordered to remove a dunghill he has created in a public place, to cease leaving dung and the gore of slaughtered animals on the highway, and to stop doing things that block the common drain and make terrible stinking odors. That same year a general order is passed to prevent villagers building "jakes" or privies above the common gutter, because of the stench thus created. Further orders to that effect are made in 1565 and 1569. But do not let these incidents give you the impression that Ingatestone is a particularly noisome place; rather these entries in the manor-court roll indicate that the manorial officers are particularly sensitive to the fact that their community is built alongside the main highway between London and Chelmsford, and the lord of the manor, Sir William Petre, has no wish to be associated with a village that stinks. Sir William's own house, Ingatestone Hall, has one of the most highly developed drainage systems in the country. Mind you, in Chelmsford you regularly find people urinating on the market cross; and in nearby Moulsham various people have been known to empty their chamber pots in the garden of a house known as the Friary, much to the annoyance of the inhabitants.[27]

London

London is not like any other city or town in England. As we have already noted, it is vastly more populous and geographically larger than anywhere else in the kingdom. Its social organization is also different: it is far more cosmopolitan, and its role in the government of the realm, including that of Westminster, is unique. Even at the start of the reign, when its population is about seventy thousand, the taxable wealth of its citizens is ten times that of the second-largest city, Norwich, which has about 10,600 inhabitants.[28] It is thus not only more populous, it is proportionally more prosperous. By 1603, when London's population has reached two hundred thousand people, there is simply no comparison. But forget statistics: long before you reach the city, the tangible social differences will strike you. Just look at the large numbers of people you meet on the highway. Traveling along the old Roman road known as Watling Street, you will come across messengers in their riding gear and farmers driving their animals to the city's suburbs, physicians riding out of the city to treat patients in the country, and foreign travelers in their carriages on the way to Oxford. So much wealth and variety of life is compacted into the city that in 1599 the Swiss traveler Thomas Platter declares: "London is not in England but England is in London."[29] Most Londoners would agree. The historian John Stow describes it in his great *Survey of London* as "the fairest, largest, richest and best inhabited city in the world."

All cities are places of contrast—and you will be harshly reminded of this when you get to the junction of Watling Street and the long road that is, in more recent times, Oxford Street. This point is known as Tyburn; here stand the gallows for hanging thieves. Executions normally involve several people being hanged at once. The crowds from the city come to watch the killing as if it were a great entertainment. Afterward the naked bodies may be left turning in the breeze for a day or two. When they have gone, and the gallows are ominously empty, a haunting atmosphere remains. As the leaves of the tall elm trees that grow here rustle in the wind, you cannot help but contemplate this ancient place of death.

Turn east. In the distance you can see the city. If you make this journey on the day of Elizabeth I's accession, November 17, 1558, you will hear the church bells of all the parishes in the city and the surrounding villages ringing out across the fields. The road from here into London is more or less straight, leading from Tyburn to Newgate, about two and three-quarters miles away. In the distance, towering above the city, stands the immensely tall medieval spire of St. Paul's Cathedral, more than five hundred feet high. If you stand here three years later, on June 3, 1561, you might see a bolt of lightning strike the cathedral spire and set fire to the roof. The spire collapses, taking with it the bells and the lead of the roof, leaving just the tower.[30] One of the glories of the medieval cathedral builders is left like a smile with a broken tooth. The church itself is reroofed, but the spire is never rebuilt: a visible symbol to Londoners and visitors of the uncertainty of the times.

The road along which you are traveling is bordered by fields on both sides until the crossroads with St. Martin's Lane and Tottenham Court Road. Beyond this junction, behind a large copse of trees, is the church of St. Giles in the Fields. Farther on the road turns into a street, with about a dozen houses on each side. The next turning on the right is Drury Lane, which leads between the fields to the Aldwych and Fleet Street. If you don't take this but keep on going straight, a moated building called Southampton House appears on your left. The road turns slightly and enters the village of Holborn. From here to the city walls the street is lined with houses on both sides. This is where several of the Inns of Court are situated—Gray's Inn, Bath Inn, and Furnival's Inn on your left; Clement's Inn, Lincoln's Inn, Staple Inn, Barnard's Inn, and Thavie's Inn on your right. In these places law students live and study in close proximity to Chancery Lane. The parish church of St. Andrew's Holborn is next, on the right, and facing it is the imposing medieval residence of the bishop of Ely. After that you pass the turning into Shoe Lane, cross the bridge over the Fleet River (Holborn

Bridge) and find yourself in the sprawling mass of houses that have erupted from the city. Still you have not reached the city wall, although you can see it ahead: eighteen feet high, with the crenellated gatehouse of Newgate guarding the entrance. But you are already within the jurisdiction of the lord mayor and sheriffs of London.

Return this way at the end of the reign and you will see the city has spread even farther west. Although the queen has it proclaimed in 1580 that there should be no development of the suburbs, London carries on expanding. In 1593 the government passes an act prohibiting any new housing within three miles of the city; this too only slightly slows development. In 1602 the queen issues orders that all unauthorized developments in the suburbs are to be removed, but the spread of housing cannot be stopped: the houses either side of the main road through St. Giles and Holborn are one continuous stretch by 1603.[31] Within twenty years of Elizabeth's death, Drury Lane will have been entirely developed, with 897 houses along it.

Suppose you do not rush straight into London this way. Let us assume that, at Tyburn, you turn right along the country lane that leads south, alongside the queen's private hunting ground, called Hyde Park. This brings you down to a junction with a road to the city known by Londoners as "the Way to Reading." One day, in the next century, this will be Piccadilly, lined with aristocratic houses. For now, though, it is an unmade track between the fields. If you come this way on a fine day, you will see washerwomen laying out clothes, bed linen, and tablecloths on the grass to dry. But it is not to see the washerwomen that you should come this way: rather it is to admire the palaces. If you turn off and follow the track that will later become Haymarket, this leads you down to the tall medieval cross at Charing Cross. From here you will see the sparkling Thames straight ahead and, along its bank to your right, the royal palaces of Whitehall and Westminster.

What will you make of the nearer palace, Whitehall? None of the buildings will be known to you; the only one standing in modern times (the Banqueting House) has not yet been built, so it will appear as an unintelligible mass of houses and roofs. It lacks all harmony or structural unity. Although the full scale of the twenty-three and a half acres of building that will one day come to be known as "the largest and ugliest palace in Europe" has not yet materialized, it will probably leave you with that same impression. Do not get me wrong: these buildings are lavish in the extreme, with great care and attention spent on their construction and no expense spared on their internal decoration. But the whole palace is just "a heap of houses," as one French visitor later puts it.[32]

Ahead there is the gatehouse of the old Palace of Westminster. Here, beside the great abbey church, is the old hall of William II, which is now used by the offices of Chancery. The other buildings of the medieval royal palace that were not destroyed in the fire of 1512 have similarly been transformed into bureaucratic offices or halls of government. The great royal chapel of St. Stephen is now the place where the House of Commons meets. Members of the House of Lords convene in the old Queen's Chamber. However, as Elizabeth summons only ten parliaments, and these sit only for a total of about two and a half years of her forty-five-year reign, these huge rooms are normally left cold and empty. That is true of most of the royal palaces in Elizabeth's reign. If you go upriver and visit Hampton Court Palace, you will find that the walls are bare whitewashed plaster with empty wooden frames, for the tapestries are taken down when the queen is not in residence. Rather than servants scurrying about, carrying food for a feast or logs for a hearth, you will see dust blowing across the empty courtyards.

The Strand is the great street that connects Westminster and Whitehall to the city of London itself. Every morning you will see hundreds of lawyers and clerks walking along it from the city and returning in the evening. But it is much more than just a street: it is where many of the most magnificent houses in London are situated. At the Whitehall end, just north of Charing Cross, is the royal mews, where the queen's hunting falcons and her horses and carriages are kept. Beyond, backing onto the river, are Hungerford House, York Place, Durham Place, the Savoy Palace, and Arundel Place—substantial mansions that are the homes of statesmen and bishops. The greatest lords have always preferred this area, because it is quieter than the city itself, the air is cleaner, there is plenty of space for the servants' quarters, and, most of all, the houses have river access. From here the lords and their guests can simply take a barge to their destination; they do not have to travel by road or risk the attention of the mob.

At the heart of London is the Thames. It is a major asset to those who live here. As the alleys and lanes of the city are so dank, dark, and dangerous, and the streets so congested, many people cut through between the houses to the stairs down to the river, where they hire a wherry to take them upstream or down. Upstream from London Bridge you'll find the wharf at Vintry, next to Queenhithe, with three cranes (Three Cranes Wharf) for lifting cargo that needs to be transported upriver, such as tuns of wine and timber. You will see hundreds of boats moored here of an evening. But far more important is the main port of London. This is made up of the twenty or so quays and wharves on the north bank of the river between London Bridge and the Tower of London, where deep-water ships can draw up and where cranes are able to hoist the goods ashore. Galley Quay, nearest the Tower, is a general lading place, but most of the others have designated purposes. Old Wool Quay is for wool and fells; Beare Quay is for traders coming from and going to Portugal; Sabbes Quay is for traders of pitch, tar, and soap; Gibson's Quay is for lead and tin; Somers Quay is for Flemish merchants; and so on. So many vessels are moored here that the Elizabethan writer and schoolmaster William Camden compares the wharves to wooded groves, "shaded with masts and sails." In 1599 Thomas Platter notes that there is one large boat, nose to stern, all the way from St. Katherine's Wharf (just to the east of the Tower of London) to London Bridge: one hundred vessels in all.[33]

Although the majority of visitors to the city remark on the large numbers of swans on the Thames, you will probably be more impressed with the numbers of boats. These range from dung boats to thousands of wherries and one glass boat: the royal barge. The river itself is wider and shallower than in modern times, with no high embankments. But one thing goes for all visitors: *everyone* talks about London Bridge. This magnificent ancient structure of twenty arches—over eight hundred feet long, sixty feet high, and almost thirty feet wide—towers above the water. It is built on huge "starlings": low, flat pillars of stone, which are shaped like boats. These serve as both foundations and cutwaters; they also impede the flow of tidal water under the bridge. When the tide is going out it is impossible to row upstream. Similarly, it is dangerous to "shoot the bridge" and risk yourself in the turbulent water when heading downstream. The starlings also act collectively as a form of weir, slowing the flow of the river, so that it sometimes freezes in very cold weather. In the winter of 1564–65, the ice is thick enough for some boys to play a football match on it. Everyone enjoys that occasion, even the queen, who leads her courtiers out onto the frozen river to shoot arrows for sport.

The impressive bulk of London Bridge is greatly enhanced by the shops and four-story houses constructed along it. These are the homes of prosperous merchants, so the bridge has all the appearance of a fine street. Toward the north end is a gatehouse, the New Stone Gate. Six arches from the south end is the drawbridge. This originally had two purposes: one was to allow larger ships access to the river beyond the bridge; the other was the defense of the city. A second gatehouse stands just to the north of this drawbridge, emphasizing the latter purpose. However, the drawbridge has not been raised for many years; nor will it ever be used again. In 1577 the dilapidated drawbridge tower is taken down to be replaced by Nonsuch House: a four-story timber-framed house prefabricated in the Low Countries, shipped to London, and erected in 1579. Built over the seventh and eight arches, this magnificent, brightly painted building straddles the entire bridge and allows traffic to pass through its center by way of a great passageway. At the south end there is a third gatehouse, the Great Stone Gate, with drum towers of four stories. After the drawbridge tower is removed, the Great Stone Gate is where traitors' heads are displayed. Even after they have rotted, the skulls are left on spikes as a reminder of the fate that befalls those who dare oppose the monarch. At the end of the century, you can still see more than thirty skulls there. London Bridge is more than just a bridge: it is a symbol of London and a statement of royal authority.

There are many other landmarks to visit. The Tower dominates the eastern side of the city; you might be interested to see the medieval palace in the inner bailey, which still survives in Elizabeth's reign. The fifteenth-century Guildhall is another important building which you might recognize: it houses the administration of the twenty-six wards of the city of London.[34] Many locals will direct you to London Stone on your sightseeing journey: a large menhir standing in the middle of Candlewick Street (much larger than the fragment that survives in modern times in a nearby wall). For many people, this stone is the heart of London; they will tell you that it was erected by Brutus, the legendary founder of Britain. Here they swear oaths, agree deals, and listen to official proclamations. Other sightseeing destinations will be completely unfamiliar to you, however. The cathedral, for example, was completed in the fourteenth century, and despite the loss of its dramatic spire, it is still worth visiting for its medieval antiquities, such as the Rose Window and the tomb of John of Gaunt. The medieval city walls are also intact, having been extensively repaired with brick in 1477.[35] The ancient gates of Ludgate, Newgate, Cripplegate, Bishopsgate, Aldgate, Aldersgate, and Moorgate similarly still stand. Baynard's Castle is located at the western extreme of the ancient city walls, mirroring the Tower in the east. It is not a castle as such but a palatial fifteenth-century house built round two large quadrangles, one with hexagonal towers at each corner. Another unfamiliar landmark is Paul's Cross, the elevated octagonal preaching place with a lead roof in the northeast corner of the churchyard of St. Paul's Cathedral. Three days after Queen Elizabeth's accession in November 1558, her chaplain preaches here. Sermons by him and other authorized preachers over the subsequent months attract thousands of Londoners and visitors who gather eager to learn how the Church is being reformed by their new monarch. It can also be a place of rioting when a preacher upsets his audience. On one occasion in the last reign, a dagger was thrown at a bishop preaching here. It stuck quivering in the timber beside him.

Say what you want about the palaces and castles, and the landmarks of London Stone, St. Paul's, and London Bridge, the real soul of London is in the streets. You will pass through alleys so narrow and dark with overhanging houses, stinking so strongly of the privies emptying into cellars, that you will wonder how people can bear to live in such an environment. Yet you may turn a corner and suddenly find yourself on a wide street with smart houses of four or five stories, with brightly painted timbers and glass in all the windows. The Venetian Alessandro Magno is impressed on his visit to the city in 1562, remarking, "The houses have many windows in which they put glass clear as crystal"—which is quite a compliment, coming from a man whose home city is one of the great centers of glassmaking.[36] In some narrow lanes you will find the clay of the street is damp all year round; in other areas the city authorities regularly place gravel down to provide a road surface. In July 1561 Henry Machyn records that the whole way through the city—from the Charterhouse, through Smithfield, under Newgate, and along Cheapside and Cornhill to Aldgate, and on to Whitechapel—is "newly gravelled with sand," ready for the queen's progress.[37] Most of the approach roads to the main gates to the city are paved for a short distance both inside and the outside the walls, as are the Strand and Holborn High Street.[38]

On market days you will find it almost impossible at times to make your way along some thoroughfares. You won't find so many people in one place anywhere else in England. The city engages all your senses: it is visible, audible, and you can smell it. In Lothbury, in the north of the city, you hear the rasping on the lathe, the clanging, banging, and hissing where the

metalworkers operate. In the markets you hear the yells of the street ven-
dors. There are criers in the street delivering news and public announcements. A woman in an apron walks past calling, "Who will buy my fine
sausage?" Another approaches you with a basket on her head, calling, "Hot
pudding pies, hot!" Stand still for any length of time and you will hear
"Come buy my glasses, glasses, fine glasses," from a woman walking along
selling drinking goblets, or "Rosemary and bays, rosemary and bays," from
another, carrying a basket of herbs. At dusk, as the markets are being
cleared away, the lighters walk between the houses calling, "Maids, hang
out your lights."[39] Passing the prisons of Newgate and Ludgate, you can
hear the poor crying out through the grilles in the walls: "Bread and meat
for the poor prisoners, for Christ Jesus's sake!"[40]

Alongside all this activity, it is the speed of change that makes London
unique. John Stow, describing the city in 1598, mentions the long street to
the east of the Tower, which has become home for thousands of mariners;
fifty years earlier, no one lived there. He is no less aware of the expansion to
the north of the city: the lines of houses which now stand where windmills
were situated at the start of the reign. All over the city, old houses are being
rebuilt. You might think that the authorities would take the opportunity to
widen the narrow alleys and make the city more splendid. But, despite London's wealth, they cannot afford to do so. As the population of the city expands, the value of each house increases, and so every square foot of space
commands a higher premium. Hence you see many houses rebuilt as six- or
seven-story buildings, even though there is nothing more solid than timber
to support them.[41] Like all the other towns and cities in the country, London is growing upward as well as outward.

Given that the roots of London's wealth and exponential growth lie in
trade, it is appropriate to end this brief description of the city with a word
or two about the commercial centers. As you may have gathered from the
street names already mentioned, many markets are held in the streets.
Bread Street is termed thus because it originally housed the bread market.
Fish Street, Milk Street, Hosier Lane, Cordwainer Street, and many dozens
of others are similarly named after the trades carried on in each location.
But there is no place where all these trades can come together except the
one great communal gathering place, St. Paul's. As you can imagine, a cathedral does not make an ideal place to trade; it is especially unsuitable for
selling fish (although this does happen from time to time).[42] Sir Thomas

Gresham, the wealthy merchant and financier, is the man who decides to do something about this. He persuades the Corporation of the city to buy up eighty houses on Cornhill and sell them for the building materials alone, thus ensuring the demolition of the houses. The city loses out to the tune of more than £3,000, but in return Sir Thomas, at his own expense, builds the Royal Exchange in 1566–67. This is a three-story structure of stone enclosing a paved quadrangle, based on the Bourse in Antwerp. The city's merchants meet in the cloisters on the ground floor, while upstairs (known as "the Pawn") there are shops. Milliners, haberdashers, armorers, apothecaries, booksellers, goldsmiths, and glass-sellers all find it a profitable place to trade. It is London's first purpose-built shopping center.

No description of the city of London would be complete without some reference to Cheapside. If any street in the city deserves to be called London's High Street, this is the one. It is the main marketplace, the widest street, the location for the lord mayor's pageant and the main showplace for royal processions. If you leave the Royal Exchange and walk westward from Cornhill, and through Poultry, you will soon reach it. The great hall of the Mercers' Company can be found here. It is also the location of the Great Conduit, the large stone fountain where housewives, servants, and water carriers alike queue up to fill their pails and water vessels. Ahead of you is the Standard: another public water fountain adjacent to a column surmounted by a cross. The Standard is also the place where the city authorities demonstrate their power: here you can witness the cutting off of hands for causing an affray. One row of fourteen shops and houses on your left will undoubtedly catch your attention. Running along Cheapside between Bread Street and Friday Street, these are the most handsome houses in the whole city: four stories high and covered in gold. As the name indicates, the houses in Goldsmith's Row are mostly owned by bankers and goldsmiths. They are faced, in the middle of the street, by the huge Cheapside Cross— one of the great three-tiered medieval crosses erected by Edward I to commemorate his late queen, Eleanor. The cross is much abused these days, and in 1581 the lowest tier of statues is badly vandalized by youths; the statue of the Virgin is pulled out of position and won't be restored for another fourteen years. Continue on a little farther and you come to West Cheap, where the market takes place and where the Little Conduit supplies water to the northern part of the city. Finally you come to St. Paul's and Paternoster Row, where the booksellers and stationers have their stalls. If you carry on westward, you can leave the city by way of Newgate, and if you head along the road to the gallows at Tyburn and the road to Oxford, you will eventually return to Stratford.

Along Cheapside, you might notice a tavern on your left: the Mermaid. It is here that Mr. Edmund Coppinger and Mr. Henry Arthington seek shelter from the London crowds in 1591. It also happens to be a drinking haunt of William Shakespeare of Stratford.[43] In this street wealth rubs shoulders with poverty while philanthropy watches on. City dwellers meet country folk. It is a place of announcements, public demonstrations, and business. For the goldsmiths who live here, and the rich merchants who attend meetings at Mercers' Hall, it is a place of professional achievement and pride. For the chronicler John Stow, it is a place of antiquity and great dignity. For the well-dressed, it is an opportunity to show off. For Mr. Coppinger and Mr. Arthington, it is a place of reckoning. And for the poet from Stratford, it is a chance to observe it all, with a "pot of good double beer" in his hand.

CHAPTER TWO

The People

Population

Population growth is one of the biggest topics of conversation in the Elizabethan age. From Cornwall to Kent you will hear remarks on the burgeoning numbers. Townspeople see the new housing spreading out beyond the town walls; country dwellers are suspicious of the numbers of paupers on the roads. But how fast is the population expanding? How can one tell?

Statistics are rarely collated in Elizabethan England, and it is very unlikely that you will find anyone who has a good idea of the actual population. It is ironic but it is considerably easier for historians in the modern world to measure sixteenth-century population fluctuations than it is for those alive at the time. Today we know that contemporary impressions of population expansion are correct. At the end of the reign, England has a population of about 4.11 million—an increase of 30 percent from the 3.16 million at the beginning. These are startling figures; the country will see nothing like it until the even greater population expansion at the end of the eighteenth century.[1] It is even more shocking when you realize that the population has been well below three million for the previous two centuries, having never properly recovered from the Black Death of 1348–49. It is not surprising, therefore, that contemporaries feel that their numbers are increasing significantly.

Why is this happening? In 1594 in Kent, William Lambarde offers this explanation: "Nowadays not only young folks of all sorts but churchmen also of each degree do marry and multiply at liberty, which was not wont to be, and . . . we have not, God be thanked, been touched with any extreme mortality, either by sword or sickness, that might abate the overgrown number of us."[2] Richard Carew, writing in Cornwall a few years later, agrees, associating the increase with the relaxation of the rules against priests marrying, people marrying younger than they did in earlier ages, and a long absence of wars and plague.[3] But as you might expect, the real reasons lie far deeper than these gentlemen's intelligent guesses. Wars do not make much of a dent in the population for the simple reason that they do not reduce the number of fertile women at home. The market for husbands is limited not by romantic ideals of the perfect man but by the availability of men of adequate quality and means; and even the loss of eight thousand men in war (1 percent of the adult male population) results in only a very slight lowering of standards—it doesn't create a host of permanently grieving brides. If you want to know the real reason for the population expansion, look for it in the availability of food and its effect on marriage and fertility. To put it simply, if there is an abundance of food, then its price drops and people's health, welfare, and security improve. More people marry who might not have married in leaner times. Confident of feeding a family, a servant will leave his employer, begin a trade, set up his own household, marry, and take care of his wife and children. Obviously, if food is scarce and expensive, then such a move is potentially fatal. It is the availability of food across the whole country at an affordable price for the marginal families that is thus the cause of population expansion.[4]

Age

Although the total size of the population is rapidly increasing, its structure is hardly any different from that of the Middle Ages. As you walk down an Elizabethan street, you will see the same high proportion of young people as in the fourteenth century. In twenty-first-century England, the number of under-sixteen-year-olds is more or less equal to the number of over-sixties: 20 percent of the population compared with 21 percent. In Elizabethan England, boys and girls under sixteen account for 36 percent of the entire population, and over-sixties for just 7.3 percent. There are thus five times as many children in relation to old people as there are in the modern world. The effect on the social makeup is striking: the median age is twenty-two years, so half the population is aged twenty-two or under; in the modern world, the median age is almost forty. What is more, the men *look* younger too: the age at which beards naturally begin to grow is considerably later than in the modern world—most men have no more than a few hairs by the age of twenty-two.[5] Men look more like boys and behave more like reckless youths—with all the greater energy, violence, eagerness, and selfishness that you would expect.

All this raises the question of what it is like to be old in Elizabethan England. Thomas Whithorne describes his age of forty as "the first part of the old man's age."[6] William Harrison declares, "Women through bearing of children do after forty begin to wrinkle apace."[7] As with so many things, it is a matter of perspective. It goes without saying that a person of forty-five seems "old" to a person of fifteen. But to be over sixty in Elizabethan times is as common as being over seventy-five in the twenty-first century. Life expectancy at birth fluctuates between twenty-eight in the early 1560s and forty-one in the early 1580s; not until the late nineteenth century will it exceed this latter figure. Most people simply do not reach "old age" in the modern sense—they never get the chance. In Stratford in the 1560s, there are on average sixty-three children baptized every year—and forty-three children buried.[8] Child mortality is greater in towns because of the spread of diseases, but even in rural areas, 21 percent of children die before they reach their tenth birthday, two-thirds of them in their first year of life.[9]

If you reach fifty, you are one of the lucky ones. This is the age at which Elizabethans start to describe one another as "old."[10] That doesn't mean people of fifty are frail; if you live to thirty, you may well live to sixty.[11] At fifty you will be expected to work just as hard as you always did, and men up to sixty are expected to fight in the militia. At fifty many of your generation will be dead, and even if you do not feel old you are certainly old-fashioned in your tastes and habits. Men grow physically weaker. A woman may acquire a reputation as a "wise woman" from about the age of fifty. At sixty, you are definitely regarded as old.

Many factors influence survival beyond sixty. Wealth is one—poor people die younger, given the cost of fuel, food, and medical help. The countess of Desmond, Katherine Fitzgerald, is said to have walked to London with her ninety-year-old daughter in 1587, and will supposedly die after falling out of a nut tree early in the next reign, at the age of 140. She is indeed an old lady but hardly any more than a hundred, if the truth be told.[12] But wealth in itself is not a guarantee of long life. In Norwich in 1570 there are five paupers in their nineties and two who claim to be over a hundred.[13] Richard Carew declares that in Cornwall "eighty or ninety years is ordinary in every place. . . . One Polzew, lately living, reached unto 130, a kinsman of his to 106."[14] Whether you believe these extremes or not, it is evident that Elizabethan people *can* live to be centenarians.

Social Order

William Harrison is of the opinion that there are four sorts of men in England: gentlemen, prosperous townsmen, countrymen (yeomen, husbandmen, and laborers), and artificers (craftsmen). His contemporary Thomas Wilson, who also writes a description of England a few years later, states that there are five types: nobles, townsmen, yeomen, artisans, and countrymen; and he further divides these groupings into smaller sections, according to title, income, and land ownership.[15] From this alone you can see that the social order is not simple. Some knights are richer than lords, a rich husbandman can be more respectable than a poor yeoman, and a spinster born into an ancient gentry family with a coat of arms might look down on a merchant with ten times as much income. Class distinctions in England are a little like the age brackets of "young" and "old"—self-perception does not always agree with general perception, and only the extremes can be described without fear of contradiction. One thing is certain: the queen is without peer at the top of the whole pile—in terms of social respectability, wealth, authority, and divine grace.

Queen Elizabeth

The Swiss visitor Thomas Platter writes of the queen in 1599:

> The English esteem her not only as their queen but as their God, for which reason three things are prohibited on pain of death. Firstly none may inquire whether she is still a virgin, for they hold her too holy to admit of doubt. Secondly no one may question her government or estates, so completely is she trusted. And lastly it is forbidden on pain of death to make enquiries as to who is to succeed her on her decease, for fear that if it were known, this person in his lust for government might plot against the queen's life. For they love their queen and fear her mightily, for she has ruled her kingdom for so long and kept the peace against all schemers; nor can she bear any other person besides herself to be popular with the people.[16]

It is a revealing description in many ways. Platter stresses how much the people *love* their queen, and at the same time how much they *fear* her. Her status is compared to that of a divine being, and yet there is evidence of the queen's insecurity: not only is she unable to bear the thought of anyone else being more popular than she, but she will not tolerate discussion of her successor in case it leads to a threat to her life. Her position is delicate, occupying seemingly contradictory positions.

Elizabeth is the second regnant queen of England, following her half-sister Mary who reigned from 1553 to 1558. Her kingdom includes Wales, the Channel Islands, large parts of Ireland (despite a rebellion there in 1593), and, later in the reign, a few short-lived settlements on the North American continent. It does not include Scotland, which is still independent. She still calls herself queen of France in her title, in pursuit of a claim first made by her ancestor Edward III; but this is merely formulaic. Far more controversial is the matter of her sex. Traditionally, monarchs are assumed to be male and expected to perform two basic functions: to lead the kingdom in battle, and to exercise the law fairly and justly. A queen is traditionally expected to be a king's consort: to provide him with heirs, obey him, and implore him to show mercy when he bestrides his vanquished enemies as a conquering hero. A regnant queen is thus doubly challenged: she is in a position neither to be a king nor to be a traditional queen. She cannot lead an army into battle; nor is the exercise of law a straightforward issue, for women are barred from holding any legal office. It is a paradox that a woman can hold the very highest office, that of sovereign, but none of the lesser ones—and thus is barred by her sex from professionally interpreting her own laws.

The legal position of a queen regnant is not the only problem. Elizabeth is queen of England "by the grace of God," and her divine selection itself creates further anomalies, for it gives her spiritual authority over her subjects. The queen is the Supreme Governor of the Church of England, and appoints all the archbishops and bishops in England and Wales; but as a woman, she is barred from holding any religious office within the Church. How, then, can she interpret the word of God? If you consider her ecclesiastical and legal position, it appears that to be a successful queen in the sixteenth century requires the most extraordinary array of skills: she has to overcome many social prejudices in addition to ruling well.

Fortunately, Elizabeth has all the qualities one could hope for. As she says of herself: "I am your anointed queen. I will never be by violence constrained to do anything. I thank God I am endued with such qualities that if I were turned out of the realm in my petticoat I would be able to live in any place in Christendom." At a time when most people cannot even read, she can write in Latin and Greek as well as in French, English, and Italian. Late in life, when on the receiving end of a bombastic speech in Latin by the Polish ambassador, she does not call for a translator but leaves the diplomat stunned by replying—in fluent Latin. Her bravery and her coolness under pressure are striking. During her half-sister Mary's reign she is the "second person" in the realm (to quote her own phrase), and suspected of being complicit in Thomas Wyatt's plot to assassinate Mary. She never forgets the subsequent experience of being locked in the Tower: she knows what it is to be a suspect and a prisoner. It is laudable, therefore, that, whereas her father tended to execute people who disagreed with him, Elizabeth listens to them. She is politically confident, and willing to upbraid even her long-standing principal secretary, Sir William Cecil, when he compromises on her diplomatic ambitions. Similarly she has no qualms about telling Parliament that its members are not at liberty to discuss certain matters—such as the royal succession. Even the archbishop of Canterbury can expect the occasional dressing-down from her.[17] She is peace-loving and inclined to seek agreement wherever possible, while not failing to support military engagement if that is in the nation's interest. Her logic is quite ruthless: she will opt for an aggressive foreign policy if that seems the best course.

Not only does the queen claim to love England in her speeches, she demonstrates it in her actions. She has a portrait painted showing her standing on a map of England; another depicts her with her victorious warships in the background after the defeat of the Armada. Her political responsibilities are more exclusively English than those of her predecessors; the kingdom's very last Continental possession, Calais, is lost a few months before her accession. Thus the kingdom of England in 1558 is more independent from Europe than it has been since Saxon times.[18] In addition, the break from Rome means that England is no longer part of a wider Catholic Church. So Elizabeth is cut off from Europe politically, territorially, and spiritually. She is cut off dynastically too. Unlike medieval kings, whose mothers were normally from Continental ruling houses, Elizabeth's father was of predominantly English stock; only two of his eight great-grandparents were born on the Continent and one born in Wales. Her mother, Anne Boleyn, was entirely English—all eight of Anne's great-grandparents were born in England—so Elizabeth's Englishness contrasts with the Continental character of her half-sister Mary, whose mother was Aragonese and whose husband Castilian. It is easy for Englishmen and women to see in Elizabeth someone like themselves. By birth, she is one of them.

There are very few weaknesses in her character. Given her enormous political responsibilities, she can hardly be condemned for being secretive and manipulative. Similarly it is difficult to blame her for her determination to take personal responsibility for political decisions, and for wanting to influence most aspects of government. She is, after all, the queen: ruling is not just her job, it is the reason for her existence. Her only significant shortcomings are a certain stubbornness, which makes life difficult for her advisers and councilors, and a sense of insecurity, arising from her experiences as "second person" in her youth, which makes her react sharply against anyone who questions her authority. She strongly identifies herself with the figure of Richard II—a king who was deposed and murdered—so much so that, in 1599, she personally accuses the lawyer John Hayward of sedition for daring to write a book about Henry IV, the king who deposed Richard II. Hayward is accordingly locked up in the Tower for the rest of her reign.[19] It could have been worse. In 1579 John Stubbs writes a pamphlet entitled *The Discoverie of a Gaping Gulf* in order to draw attention to the dangers of a marriage between Elizabeth and the duke of Anjou, the heir to the French throne. The queen has Stubbs arrested and orders his right hand to be cut off—and that of his publisher too. When her cousin Lady Catherine Grey (sister of Lady Jane Grey) becomes pregnant, having married Lord Hertford in secret, she has the newlyweds locked up in the Tower, fines Lord Hertford the colossal sum of £15,000 for seducing a virgin of the royal blood, and has their children declared officially illegitimate (although she has no authority to do so). As her godson Sir John Harington declares after her death, "When she smiled, it was pure sunshine that everyone did choose to bask in, if they could; but anon came a storm from a sudden gathering of clouds and the thunder fell in wondrous manner on all alike."[20] Clearly, crossing Queen Elizabeth is something you do at your peril.

This helps to explain why some Elizabethan people do not have a glowing opinion of their queen. As we will see in the next chapter, her personality is the key to the religious changes of the age, which are the most fundamental that England has ever seen. Puritans as well as Catholics despise her. Parliament is threatened by her willfulness—she has very little time for parliamentary privileges and no respect for MPs' freedom of speech. There are a number of revolts against her, some led by Catholics and others by members of the nobility who do not have faith in her leadership. Several northern lords take up arms in 1569 (the Northern Rebellion). Assassination attempts are thwarted in 1571 (the Ridolfi Plot), 1581 (Anthony Tyrrell's plot), 1583 (two plots: the Throgmorton Plot and the Somerville Plot), 1584 (Dr. Parry's plot), and 1586 (the Babington Plot). One of her physicians, Dr. Rodrigo Lopez, is hanged for trying to poison her in 1594. The earl of Essex is sentenced to death for plotting against her in 1601. In addition, seditious rumormongers are to be found in every town. In 1576, Mary Cleere of Ingatestone, Essex, is burned at the stake for high treason: she has declared that the queen is baseborn and therefore not rightly queen, and that a woman cannot make knights.[21] Other people whisper about the queen's virginity, circulating the rumor that Elizabeth has given birth to children by Robert Dudley in secret and has had them killed and burned.[22] Her status as a paragon of virtue is by no means universally acknowledged by her contemporaries.

How does Elizabeth actually govern? This subject would keep you entertained for hours if you could be a fly on the walls of the royal palaces—for instance, watching the nuances of her favor, displayed with a terse quip or a shrug of the shoulder, a smile or a cold stare. However, for present purposes, it is sufficient to be aware of five elements to her governance: the five "P"s—the privy council, patronage, the royal presence, the royal purse, and Parliament.

Elizabeth's preferred method of governing is through her privy council. In the first half of the reign, this body consists of nineteen men and sits three or four times a week, conducting most routine business on Elizabeth's behalf and directing extraordinary business in accordance with her instructions. In the 1590s she reduces their number to fourteen, and sometimes just ten or eleven, and asks them to meet every day. Routine business includes orders for the army and navy, diplomatic instructions, directions to the clergy, sheriffs, and local officials, appointments of justices of the peace, and hearing petitions. The privy council also sits as a court of trial, the Star Chamber, in which role it exercises the monarch's judgment. Other roles include advising the queen on policy and exercising her power of patronage.

Elizabeth is acutely aware of the dangers of so much power being vested in a group of privy councilors; thus she manipulates them in a number of ways. She does not let any one man monopolize her use of patronage or control access to her presence. She plays one councilor off against another in a policy of "divide and rule"—for instance, she encourages her favorite, Robert Dudley, to act as a foil to Sir William Cecil, her principal secretary, so that neither man can become too powerful. At times she acts without consulting the whole privy council. When she does not wish anyone to interfere with her Dutch policy in the 1580s, she does not share with her councilors the news she hears from her overseas representatives, nor does she reveal to them her response.[23]

Elizabeth uses her physical presence to demonstrate her royalty. She does this in all the usual places—such as her palaces and in Parliament—but she also does it in public. She shows herself off in processions through the city of London, following the example of her half-sister Mary, thereby encouraging the adulation of the people.[24] She demonstrates her royal status by summoning dignitaries to wait on her on specific occasions. Most famously, she goes on long progresses through the country. You will often see her staying in the great houses of courtiers, or traveling between them in long processions of riders, carriages, wagons, and carts. Some claim that this is because she loves the countryside, or that she wants to save money by staying with other people; but these are whimsical explanations. She can see the countryside easily enough from most of her palaces. As for the expense, although these progresses do not cost the royal purse as much as they cost the men who entertain her majesty, they are not mere money-saving measures. The real reason for her progresses is that she wants the people to see her. Although she never goes to the north or the southwest, where the pro-Catholic gentry are hostile, she uses her presence to reinforce her queenship and Englishness in the eyes of the people.

Elizabeth also governs through her control of money. In 1600, the royal estates yield £123,587. In addition, she receives clerical levies and "first fruits"—a tax of the whole first year's income from an ecclesiastical position, payable within two years of the incumbent's taking office. Then there is her "extraordinary" income: money granted to her by Parliament or due on customs and sales of assets. The whole royal revenue, including the receipts from the royal estates, therefore amounts to about £300,000.[25] This sounds like a huge sum in an age when a master craftsman earns a shilling per day and a laborer just 4 pence—except that the queen has to pay for the entire government of the realm. Over a third of the entire budget is spent on food for the royal household and the court, including stabling and provision for the horses. Wages and salaries of the royal officials amount to £73,167. Elizabeth's personal jewels, clothes, coaches, and barges cost a further £20,000. She gives away no less than £2,000 in alms, and another £4,000 in gifts to visitors and dignitaries. It is estimated that her processions, shows, pageants, and triumphs cost £5,000 per annum, and maintenance of the royal castles, palaces, houses, and ships requires a further £50,000.[26] On top of all this there is the cost of war. When you consider that the war in Ireland in the years 1599–1603 costs £1.131 million, you can see that it is very difficult to make ends meet. But Elizabeth manages her budgets so well that the national debt is a mere £300,000 when she dies.[27]

As mentioned above, Elizabeth is no great fan of Parliament. She cannot control the elections of MPs and so it is in Parliament that she has to face her largest body of critics. Consequently, she only summons Parliament ten times in the course of her forty-five-year reign (most monarchs before her summoned it once a year). However, although she cannot control who is elected, she can control almost everything else. She addresses MPs directly, with great effect. She stipulates what Parliament may and may not discuss and bans an MP from the House of Commons for introducing legislation that is not to her liking.[28] She influences MPs individually by threatening to withhold appointments and patronage. She appoints the Speaker of the House of Commons, and through him controls the debates. And if she so wishes, she can simply dismiss Parliament. Although in theory the queen runs the country in collaboration with the privy council and Parliament, in reality it is governed in line with Elizabeth's wishes.

The Nobility

In the Middle Ages kings constantly had to watch out for great lords waiting in the wings. These could be the king's own cousins; sometimes they even were his brothers or sons. Elizabeth does not have this problem. Her grandfather Henry VII had no brothers or cousins. He had just two daughters and one surviving son, Henry VIII, who in turn sired two daughters and one legitimate son, Edward VI. As the last surviving child of Henry VIII, Elizabeth is in the extremely fortunate position that she does not have to contend with powerful royal dukes. There is no obvious heir champing at the bit—and that is just how she wants things to remain.[29] She consistently refuses to name a successor, even when Parliament demands that she do so. In her first parliament she declares that she will die a virgin and, despite being tempted on more than one occasion to change her mind, she remains unmarried. She knows that, if she were to acknowledge her eldest aunt's granddaughter, Mary, the Catholic queen of Scots, as her heir, she would only make herself a bigger target for Catholic assassins. When asked to declare her will on the succession, she responds: "Do you think I could love my own winding sheet?" As for her other cousins, she has no qualms about locking up Lady Catherine Grey, as noted above.

Elizabeth has very few over-mighty lords to deal with too. After the Catholic duke of Norfolk is executed for treason in June 1572 (for his part in the Ridolfi Plot), there are no more dukes in England. Like her grandfather Henry VII, Elizabeth has a policy of not creating any new marquesses or viscounts, and she creates very few barons and even fewer earls. The reason is to limit the power of her subjects and thus strengthen the authority of her government. Even the bishops, who used to exercise political opposition to kings in the old days, are politically weak. They are no longer servants of the Roman Church, independent of the king of England, but serve the monarch in her role as Supreme Governor of the Church of England. Rather than challenging the queen, they find themselves having to preach "the doctrine of the godly prince"—or, in this case, the godly princess.[30] Elizabethan England is thus devoid of private armies, royal dukes, and political bishops. Those considering revolt against Elizabeth have no one to turn to for leadership.

Elizabeth's careful policy means that there is something of a scarcity of noblemen in England. After the execution of the duke of Norfolk, the highest rank in the peerage is that of marquess; never a common title: there is just one in 1600 (the marquess of Winchester), plus a dowager marchioness (the widow of the last marquess of Northampton, William Parr, who dies in 1571). Third highest in rank are the earls; there are eighteen of these in 1600.[31] Next come the two viscounts, Lord Montagu and Lord Howard of Bindon.[32] The lowest rank is the baronage: there are thirty-seven barons in all.[33] In total, just fifty-seven peers are summoned to Parliament at the start of the reign and fifty-five at the end (underage heirs are not summoned). Collectively they are all peers of the realm, but the equality suggested by that word "peers" is misleading. Even within each class of title there is a hierarchy, the older titles taking precedence over the more recent ones. There are huge discrepancies of wealth too. Only two or three lords have an income of £10,000 per year; most have over £800, some as little as £300.[34] Thomas Wilson estimates that the earls and the marquess have an average income of £5,000 per year and the barons and viscounts about £3,000.[35] As you will see, the very idea of "equality" is something that Elizabethans reckon relates to men only when they stand before God on Judgment Day. Here on Earth, there is no such thing.

Income does not equate to spending power—not when you are a peer of the realm and can borrow money. Take the example of the young Henry Percy, ninth earl of Northumberland. His father, the eighth earl, has a good income in 1582 (£4,595), but after he dies in 1585, a large part of the estate is apportioned to provide an income for his widow, the dowager countess, leaving young Henry with "just" £3,363. The problem is that Henry proceeds to spend twice that. In his own words: "Hawks, hounds, horses, dice, cards, apparel, mistresses; all other riot of expense that follow them were so far afoot and in excess as I knew not where I was or what I did until, out of my means of £3,000 yearly, I had made shift in one year and a half to be £15,000 in debt."[36] Fortunately for Henry, one of the privileges of being a nobleman is that he cannot be imprisoned for debt, so he is at least clear of that worry. Other privileges include the right to be judged by his peers, paying very little tax, and freedom from torture.[37] Having said this, with Elizabeth on the throne, it is probably best not to rely upon these privileges too heavily. The queen is not like her tyrannical father, Henry VIII, who would get around a lord's right to be judged by his peers by having the offending man summarily executed; however, not many courts will defy the queen's wrath. Several peers of the realm spend years imprisoned in the Tower before they even come to trial.

The Gentry

Rich and privileged as the nobility are, it is the gentry who own and run England. They are the five hundred or so knights with country estates, and approximately fifteen thousand other gentlemen with an income from land sufficient to guarantee they do not have to work for a living.[38] In this group you have the greatest disparities of wealth—from knights as rich as Sir John

Harington (later Lord Harington) and Sir Nicholas Bacon, with incomes of £4,000 or more per year, down to local gentlemen with a thousand acres let out to tenant farmers for not much more than £100. Thomas Wilson declares that to be a gentleman, one should have £500 per year in the south of England and £300 in the north.[39] The relationship of wealth to status is thus complicated. Some people see them as completely separate issues: they think that having a coat of arms is the crucial factor denoting gentlemanly status, armigerous men being descended from knights and thus having the right to call themselves "esquire." It is not surprising, therefore, that families in every county are claiming coats of arms, whether they truly are entitled to them or not. Heralds (officers of the College of Arms) make regular visitations of the counties to examine these claims. Talk about hierarchy: at a time when there is no national police force, there is a national organization devoted to policing the right to bear a coat of arms.

You begin to get a sense of the extent of the gentry's dominant position when you compare their total wealth with that of the nobility. All the earls, barons, and other lords have a combined income of approximately £220,000 in 1600. The income of the gentry is at least ten times as much, if not twenty times. And wealth is not the limit of their influence. They control the rural population through governing them, employing them as servants, and directing the majority who are their tenants. There are fourteen hundred justices of the peace (JPs), who sit as magistrates in each county, and all are drawn from the ranks of the gentry. In the absence of a standing army, the defense of the realm is overseen by the deputy lieutenants of each county, who have authority over the "trained bands" or militia. Again, these men are drawn from the ranks of the gentry. In Sir Walter Raleigh's words, "The gentry are the garrisons of good order throughout the realm." Small wonder, then, that Elizabeth takes such care over the lists of justices of the peace. She pores over them and pretends she is personally acquainted with every gentleman in the kingdom. Some courtiers snigger at this behind her back; but, in truth, she does know a great number of them because of her progresses through the country. Displease the queen and you can bet she will remember your name when it comes to scrutinizing those lists.

The other area in which the gentry have a large say in running the country is in Parliament. They exert influence in two ways. First, they take a major role in electing the seventy-four "knights of the shire" who form approximately one-third of the House of Commons. Second, a large number of gentlemen are sent to Parliament as representatives of boroughs, through the patronage of wealthy landowners. The duke of Norfolk, for instance, sends eighteen gentlemen to the House of Commons as representatives of boroughs where he is the major landowner.[40] The gentry's representation extends to urban areas too. You might have thought that the larger towns would want to be represented by merchants and traders, but often a community will choose a member of the gentry, on the basis that he will have more influence over his fellow MPs.

Professions

There are three distinct professions or vocations in England: the law, the Church, and medicine. All three have an extended period of training, and require considerable investment. All three are the subjects of university degrees and can generate a healthy income. Schoolmasters are not considered wholly "professional" because they do not need a degree and they are not normally paid more than tradesmen. Similarly, although music can be studied at a university, it does not make men rich, so musicians are not considered "professional" either. Even writing books is not generally considered a "professional" activity. There are no publishers paying royalties, alas, so one needs to have an income in order to be able to write in the first place. Shakespeare is one of the very few writers who manages to elevate himself from a relatively humble level to the status of a gentleman. It is a salutary thought that, although he manages to acquire sufficient wealth to buy New Place in Stratford and a significant portion of the rectorial tithes of the parish, one of the heralds dismisses his newly acquired coat of arms as that of "Shakespeare the Player."[41]

It is the Church and the law that offer the greatest opportunities to an ambitious man. If you rise through the ranks of the clergy to become archbishop of Canterbury, you will have not only a seat in the House of Lords but an income of £2,682 per year. Those who profess the law can do even better. When Sir Nicholas Bacon dies, he leaves £4,450 of cash and silver, plus an income from land of about £4,000 per year. Sir Edward Coke is reputed to have an income of between £12,000 and £14,000, making him one of the richest men of the century; and Sir John Popham is not far behind with £10,000 per year.[42] Obviously not many lawyers earn in the thousands, but most make a decent living, in the region of £100 per year.

Medicine is the least rewarded of the three professions, both financially and in social distinction. Elizabeth does not bestow a knighthood on any of her physicians or surgeons.[43] Most wealthy Elizabethans do not pay their medical practitioners anywhere near as much as their lawyers. It is perhaps not surprising. Faced with a legal issue, an Elizabethan lawyer will serve you just as well as his modern counterpart. You would be unwise to place that much confidence in an Elizabethan physician.

Merchants, Traders, and Townsmen

Civic society too is hierarchical: another great spectrum of wealth, social status, and authority. At one extreme you have the richest London merchants, some of whom have capital worth £50,000 at the start of the reign and twice that much at the end.[44] These men tend to have significant political roles, becoming an alderman (the chief representative of one of the twenty-six London wards), lord mayor, or the master of a livery company. They have considerable influence; several wealthy London merchants are knighted. It is commonly said that most aldermen have goods to the value of £20,000.[45] At the other end of the social scale, there are merchants who are destitute, and shopkeepers and artificers who struggle to earn £8 per year.

In most large towns about half the population have no goods or assets of any significant value. The larger provincial towns and cities in particular are dominated by a few merchant families who own virtually all the wealth. In Exeter, for instance, 2 percent of the population own 40 percent of the taxable property, and just 7 percent own two-thirds of it.[46] On top of this, life expectancy is shorter, people marry later and have fewer children, and a greater proportion of their children die young. Why, then, do the other 93 percent not simply leave? One answer to this is obvious: where else would they go? These people rely heavily on their fellow townsmen to defend their reputations and to protect each other physically. Many have responsibilities to their friends and kin in the city. Leaving your hometown is not something you do without considerable preparation or in a state of desperation.

There are other reasons why people choose to live in urban areas. When a rich merchant becomes pre-eminent, he looks to move out to a country estate and to set himself up as a country gentleman; therefore no English merchant family dominates a large town for long.[47] New families and indi-

viduals rise up, competing to take the place of those that have left. Hugh
Clopton and William Shakespeare are both good examples of men who
move to London, make their fortunes, and return to their place of birth.
You will find much the same in cities such as Exeter and Coventry: the
mayors and aldermen are often sons of country yeomen who have come to
make their fortune. Don't think the urban rich are all born rich. The
wealthy 7 percent is not a static cohort in any city or town.

For the less well-off, a city or town offers a certain reliability of income.
Take Exeter, for example, which has a population of about 8,000. About 30
percent of these are dependents under the age of fifteen, which leaves a population of adults and working youths of 5,600. About 880 of these are servants. Another 2,000 are women—480 widows, 80 independent single
women, and 1,440 dependent wives.[48] That leaves about 2,720 independent
adult males. In theory, a man needs to become a freeman of the city in order to run a business. To do this, he has to be the son of a freeman, serve an
apprenticeship, or pay a hefty fine of £1–£5 (depending on his circumstances). How many of those 2,720 men qualify? If you examine the rolls
held in Exeter's Guildhall, you will see that 1,192 individuals are admitted to
the freedom of the city over the period Michaelmas (September 29) 1558 to
Michaelmas 1603.[49] Given that most men gain their freedom in their early
to mid-twenties, they can expect to be freemen for about another thirty-five
years. Thus, in any year, about 930 of those 2,720 men are freemen of the
city. In addition, there are the professionals—clergy, lawyers, and medical
men—and the schoolmasters, whose authority to practice is normally based
on a university degree or a license granted by the bishop. These people
might not own a significant portion of the wealth of the city, but they all
have a considerable stake in its good management. The freemen themselves
take a part in this, by electing the twenty-four aldermen who run the city.
The huge inequalities of wealth thus distort our image of the satisfaction of
the citizens at the time. A barber or a butcher in Elizabethan Exeter is not
necessarily preoccupied with the discrepancies of wealth around him—no
more than his modern equivalent is today—if he is earning enough to keep
his family clothed and fed.

Admissions to the freedom of Exeter, 1558–1603

	Trade	Nos.
1	Mercer / merchant	171
2	Tailor	95
3	Tucker	57
4	Weaver	55
5	Cordwainer	40
6	Baker	32
7=	Gentleman	24
7=	Victualer	24
9	Butcher	22
10=	Brewer	19
10=	Haberdasher	19
12=	Barber	18
12=	Glover	18
12=	Smith	18
15	Goldsmith	17
16	Carpenter	16
17=	Felt-maker	14
17=	Joiner	14
17=	Saddler	14
20	Hellier (roofer)	13
21	Draper	12
22	Cutler	11
23	Skinner	10
24	Chapman	9
25=	Apothecary	8
25=	Stationer	8
27	Mason	7
28=	Barrel-bearer	6
28=	Clothier	6
28=	Cooper	6
28=	Currier	6
32=	Chandler	5
32=	Cook	5
32=	Fletcher	5
32=	Hatter	5
32=	Innkeeper	5
32=	Ironmonger	5
32=	Silkman / silk weaver	5
39=	Capper	4
39=	Cobbler	4

	Trade	Nos.
39=	Glazier	4
39=	Laborer	4
39=	Tinker	4
44=	Clergyman	3
44=	Clerk	3
44=	Dyer	3
44=	Pewterer	3
44=	Physician	3
44=	Plumber	3
44=	Vintner	3
51=	Basket-maker	2
51=	Brazier	2
51=	Carrier	2
51=	Furrier	2
51=	Gunner	2
51=	Hosier	2
51=	Lawyer	2
51=	Leather-dresser	2
51=	Locksmith	2
51=	Ostler	2
51=	Scrivener	2
51=	Sleighmaker	2
51=	Stainer	2
51=	Surgeon	2
51=	Yeoman	2
66=	Bookbinder	1
66=	Bowyer	1
66=	Carman (driver of horse-drawn vehicle)	1
66=	Costermonger (greengrocer)	1
66=	Grocer	1
66=	Hardwareman	1
66=	Hooper	1
66=	Lantern-maker	1
66=	Mariner	1
66=	Miller	1
66=	Milliner	1
66=	Needlemaker	1
66=	Notary public	1
66=	Parchment-maker	1
66=	Point-maker	1
66=	Retailer	1

Trade		Nos.
66=	Shuttle maker	1
66=	Tanner	1
66=	Virginals-maker	1
	Other[50]	8
	Trade unknown	270
	Total	1,192

What about those men who are not freemen or professionals? Some are still young, with few financial responsibilities. They may be apprentices or journeymen working to save enough money to pay the fines to become freemen. Only about 10 percent of all those becoming freemen of Exeter do so simply through the easy route of succession from their fathers. The remainder earn their positions. Those who are not freemen are employees, laborers, and unskilled workers. Some are described by their contemporaries as "poor," owning nothing except the clothes they stand up in. A number of those are truly destitute or are itinerant beggars looking for food (we will meet them later). Nevertheless, in a town they do at least have a chance of finding employment or a meal. Merchants are not the only ones who look at a city as a place of opportunity.

Yeomen, Husbandmen, and Countrymen

Rural areas have just as much disparity of wealth as towns. At one extreme you have the very rich, the gentry in their manor houses and stately homes, with the large incomes noted above. At the other end you have itinerant beggars and local paupers. In between you have a range of yeomen, husbandmen, rural craftsmen, and laborers.

Yeomen are the successors of the medieval franklins. They are "free men"—not in the sense that they have the freedom of a city but because they are "free" from the bonds of servitude that applied to the villenage in the Middle Ages. In William Harrison's understanding, they are "forty-shilling freeholders": the rents of the land they own bring in £2 or more per year, giving them the right to vote in a parliamentary election. But who is a yeoman, who a gentleman, and who a husbandman is a very confused issue. Some "yeomen" could buy out quite a few local "gentlemen." As a rule of thumb, apply the following gradations and be prepared to modify them when someone takes umbrage:

- A gentleman owns land but does not farm it: he lets it to others through copyhold (if it forms part of a manor) or by lease (if it is freehold land).
- A yeoman does farm land, and might own the freehold of some of it; but he normally leases a substantial acreage. He employs laborers to help him.
- A husbandman farms land but does not own it—normally he rents it. He may also employ helpers, especially at harvest time; but he tends to be poorer than a yeoman.

One of the reasons why some yeomen become wealthy is that, being workers, they have little reason to spend their income in an ostentatious manner—unless they want to pretend they are gentlemen. Another is that they are better positioned to exploit the land for profit. Fixed rents—by way of long leases—and the increasing value of wool underpin the wealth of many yeomen. Some husbandmen also benefit from these conditions: their thriftiness, low rents, and the rising value of their produce allow them to make a considerable amount of money. William Dynes of Godalming, Surrey, describes himself as a husbandman despite having goods to the value of £272 in 1601.[51] Similarly Edward Streate, husbandman of Lambourn, Berkshire, leaves goods worth £97 to his widow in 1599 (the average is about £40).[52]

There are others who make their living on the land. An agricultural laborer works in the fields on behalf of a yeoman or husbandman. You will often hear the words "cottager" and "artificer." A cottager is someone who, unsurprisingly, lives in a cottage and has very little or no land except a garden. He may also have rights to graze a couple of cattle and a horse or two on the common, and to collect firewood from the manorial woods. "Artificer" is the Elizabethan word for a craftsman. Rural areas have a great demand for a wide range of locally manufactured products, and as you journey around the country you are bound to come across basket-makers, hurdle-makers, fishing-net makers, charcoal burners, thatchers, knife-grinders, and woodsmen, as well as farriers, blacksmiths, millers, brewers, carpenters, wheelwrights, and cartwrights. Many of these people are laborers, cottagers, and artificers all in one—plying a mixture of trades, laboring at harvest time, and growing their own vegetables and fruit in order to sustain themselves and their families.

The Poor

In 1570 the civic authorities in Norwich take a census of the city's poor. When complete there are 2,359 names on the list: about a quarter of the whole population (about 10,625 in that year).[53] Not everyone included is unemployed or homeless; although three hundred of them are accommodated in parish poorhouses, hospital buildings, old city gatehouses, or church houses, most are living in their own homes, whether these be rented or owned. Quite a few have a means of making a little money, but others are wholly impoverished. Some are disabled, some mentally unstable or "lunatic"; some in extreme old age. What they all have in common is that they are likely to be a burden on the community.

The poor are an unavoidable feature of Elizabethan life. In 1577 William Harrison estimates that there are ten thousand vagrants on the roads, not including the resident poor in towns and villages. In 1582 William Lambarde remarks on the increasing number of vagabonds in Kent; and in 1593 he laments that the county is "overspread not only with unpunished swarms of idle rogues and of counterfeit soldiers but also with numbers of poor and weak but unpitied servitors."[54] It is the same at the western end of the country. In 1600 Richard Carew writes that of the poor "few shires can show more or own fewer than Cornwall."[55] He blames Ireland for sending over so many vagrants to beg in the county. The following year, Stratford-upon-Avon complains of seven hundred paupers in the town; and in 1602 a judge declares that there are thirty thousand "idle persons and masterless men" living in London.[56] Thus, whether we are talking about the urban poor or gangs of young vagrants on the roads, poverty brings us face-to-face with the harsher side of Elizabethan life.

Let us begin with the resident poor, and consider those in Norwich. No fewer than 926 of them (40 percent) are children below the age of sixteen. For them this is a sad world: they have a significantly diminished chance of surviving to adulthood, let alone gaining an apprenticeship and a place in the community. Poorly fed, weak, and suffering from ailments such as scurvy and scald head, such children will find few masters to employ them. Of the 1,433 poor adults, about two-thirds are women, and about a quarter of these are over the age of sixty. You may think that there are more women than men because women live longer and they are widows. It comes as somewhat of a shock to realize there are just as many women who have been abandoned by their husbands. Margaret Matheu, for example, is a born-and-bred Norwich woman aged thirty-two years. Her husband, Thomas Matheu, left the city three years ago, and she has no idea where he is. He could be dead for all she knows; but she cannot remarry while he might yet be alive. She rents a room from William Joy, receives no alms (parish charity), and is described as "very poor," having nothing but a few pennies per week for spinning "white warp" (yarn).[57] In a similar state is Alice Reade, forty, whose husband justified his abandoning her by claiming that he was already married to someone else and therefore their marriage was invalid. He left her with three children and a baby at her breast.[58] She rents a room and lives from spinning; her nine-year-old son also spins, as does her fourteen-year-old daughter. They receive no alms and are "very poor." Perhaps even more lamentable is Helen, the wife of John Williams; she is heavily pregnant, about to give birth, and cannot work. Her husband has disappeared off to Cambridge and left her with no money.[59]

If you want to see what it is really like to be poor in an Elizabethan city, visit the property called Shipdams in the Norwich parish of St. Martin at the Bale. It is a large old house, the rooms tenanted by a number of destitute people. In one you have Richard Starkyn, sixty-six, an unemployed cobbler, and his seventy-six-year-old wife, Elizabeth, who is too sick to work. They have alms of just 2 pence per week and are "very poor." In the next room you have Cecily Barwic, fifty-four, a widow who spins white warp and is also "very poor." Then there is Margaret Harrison, sixty, who lives by knitting and helping to wash dirty laundry and looks after her nine-year-old son, who also knits every day. In the room next to her lives Agnes, sixty-eight, whose husband, Thomas Gose, is in the hospital; she spins white warp for a living, receives 1½ pence per week in alms, and is "very poor." In the next room there is Agnes's daughter Margaret, twenty-eight, the wife of Thomas Collins, hatter, who has abandoned her and gone to London and sends no help to her in her poverty; she knits to keep herself and her two daughters. They receive no alms, and when the inspector visits he finds a prostitute in their bed. In the next room there is Christopher Smythe, forty, an unemployed hatter with only one leg, and his wife, Dorothy, thirty-eight, who spins white warp, and their two daughters, who are both learning to spin with Widow Mallerd; they receive 3 pence alms per week between them. Next is Robert Haygat, forty, an unemployed brewer, and his wife, Margery, twenty-five, who has a breastfed baby and spins white warp;

they receive no alms and are "very poor." Finally in this property there are three old widows: Katherine Mallerd, sixty-nine, who teaches Christopher Smythe's daughters to spin, receives no alms, and is "very poor"; Alice Colton, eighty, who spins but is lame in her hand, receives no alms, and is "very poor"; and Eme Stowe, eighty, who is lame in one arm, receives 2 pence per week in alms but has to look after her daughter's eleven-year-old illegitimate son. The two of them go about the streets begging together. That is what the urban poor are like: old, lame, sick, impotent, abandoned, and desperate. They have all developed strategies for survival—from keeping younger people in the household to prostitution and laundry help. You might notice a blind man in his fifties being led around the streets of Norwich by a twelve-year-old boy, an orphan, whom he provides with food. Some women make 2 shillings per week from caring for the sick and dying. This is a dangerous occupation, especially if the sufferers have an infectious disease such as smallpox or plague. But if as much as 6 shillings is on offer for a week's attendance on a plague victim, poor women willingly take on the task.[60]

Whereas the resident poor are mostly women, three-quarters of the itinerant poor are single men. They are inevitably much younger: two-thirds are below the age of twenty-five. One group of twenty beggars in Crompton, Lancashire, in 1597 includes twelve boys under the age of fifteen and three under the age of five. The cause of their begging is the famine of 1594–97; their parents have probably starved to death. Alternatively, look at poor Alice Morrice at about the same time. Born at Borden, Kent, she is sent at about the age of ten to be a servant in the house of her uncle. All is well until her father dies and her uncle throws her out. Orphaned, with only a small amount of money left to her by her father, she goes from town to town. When the money has all gone, she can do nothing but join those who beg or steal.[61] The Devon parish of Morebath sees several "poor walking women" give birth in outhouses and barns in the early 1560s.[62] In London in 1583, "the poor lie in the streets upon pallets of straw . . . or else in the mire and dirt . . . [and] are suffered to die in the streets like dogs or beasts without any mercy or compassion."[63]

The fundamental problem is that of population expansion. The number of people in England has been increasing since the second decade of the century, when it was 2.4 million.[64] As we have seen, by 1600 it has risen to 4.11 million; yet no provision has been made for the extra people. With the land clearances making way for sheep-grazing and parkland, there is now even less agricultural land to support them. When you also consider the harvest failures and the downturns in certain industries, you can see why there are so many beggars on the highways. Walk into Canterbury, Faversham, and Maidstone and talk to the poor there. Some have traveled several hundred miles, coming from Lancashire, Yorkshire, Cumberland, and Cheshire. They have not traveled from the northern towns but from rural areas, where their crops have died and they have been unable to pay their ever-increasing rents, with the result that they have been evicted. They have gone south hoping for a better life.[65] But when they get there, they are treated like outcasts.

Unless you dress well, you yourself are likely to be treated as a vagrant wherever you go. Property owners are scared of strangers. They deliberately conflate them with the "Egyptians" or Gypsies who have been traveling in England for decades. Although Gypsies form a small percentage of the itinerant poor, they are a potent symbol of why such people are considered undesirable. Gypsies are considered synonymous with thieves: it is said that they travel eighty in a band and break up into groups of five or six to go searching for food and things to steal.[66] In reality, they travel in small family groups, but people are not interested in the mitigating circumstances. The Egyptians Act of 1530 declares that, as Gypsies have no means of making a living except palmistry, telling fortunes, and robbery, they must abjure the realm. This law is confirmed by Elizabeth in 1563 in "An Act for further Punishment of Vagabonds calling themselves Egyptians."[67] This states that anyone even found in the company of Gypsies may be hanged.

It is in this context that the lawmakers turn their attention to other itinerants. A whole genre of literature springs up on the topic. The books are sensational: they purport to offer insights into the criminal world that lurks in every town and describe in detail the sinful, filthy miscreants and their strategies for thieving and murdering the good citizens. The hatred that once applied just to the bands of Gypsies is now transferred to the roaming dispossessed and starving youths. In 1572, Parliament passes "An Act for the Punishment of Vagabonds and for the Relief of the Poor and Impotent."[68] This states that "a vagabond above the age of fourteen years shall be . . . grievously whipped and burned through the gristle of the right ear with a hot iron of the compass of an inch unless some credible person will take him into service for a year." Additionally, a youth of eighteen who lapses into an itinerant lifestyle having previously been caught is to be hanged as a felon. Oh, merry, merry England! In 1589 things take a dramatic turn when—illogical though it may seem—the government prohibits anyone giving accommodation to these unfortunate people.[69] This means that now only one family may legally inhabit a household, and the manor courts soon start to search for the "inmate" poor. In 1600, in Moulsham, Essex, eight tenants are presented to the manor court for harboring poor people. Three of them have sheltered a pauper and his wife for several months; one has given accommodation to two poor couples for six months; the others have all sheltered poor widows as well as couples. Some of the poor have been living in Moulsham for years. Nevertheless, the tenants are ordered to evict their inmates immediately or pay a fine of £1.[70] Clearly these couples and widows are far from the crowds of young males roaming and stealing. But they are poor, and the people of Moulsham fear that the financial responsibility for looking after the paupers will fall on them. Therefore they want these strangers thrown out—for the double crime of having no money and no home.

Surely Elizabethan England, with all its wit and political application, can do better than this? Eventually it does. Certain towns—Norwich is among them—start to make provision for their resident poor. Licenses are occasionally issued to allow the genuinely needy to beg legally. There is also a growing recognition that the root of the problem is not the desire to be a vagrant but poverty. It is a slow process, however. The first Elizabethan Poor Law is passed in 1563: it forces villagers and townspeople to pay toward the upkeep of the local poor, with those who refuse being handed over to JPs. In 1576 another act orders civic authorities to keep a stock of capital items so the poor might be set to work, and in this way pay for their upkeep. Finally in 1597 Elizabeth's government passes "An Act for the Relief of the Poor."[71] This piece of legislation is not as famous as the defeat of the Spanish Armada but it is just as significant, for it establishes the means by which poor people in England are looked after for the next 237 years. From now on, overseers are to be appointed in every parish, who are to see to all the children that cannot be cared for by their parents, placing them as apprentices where appropriate. In addition, the overseers are to manage a supply of work for all those who cannot maintain themselves. And they are to tax the parishioners to provide for the poor. Note the word "tax"—from this moment on, looking after the poor is a matter of secular social responsibility, paid for by local taxation; it is no longer an act of religious charity designed to improve the standing of the donor's soul and send the rich man to Heaven. It is no longer a matter of choice. A second act repeals all the earlier legislation for the punishment of vagabonds, and practices such as cutting holes in people's ears cease. A third act allows for hospitals or workhouses to be established for the accommodation of the poor. Workhouses might be spoken about with some horror in the modern world, but they mark a positive step away from the practice of evicting the homeless repeatedly until they are forced into felony and hanged. The Act of 1597, revised and reissued in 1601, does not solve all the problems overnight, but it leads to a long-term solution. And it saves lives. If you hear it being proclaimed, it is worth pausing and reflecting that, partly because of it, the English will never again starve to death in their thousands because of a harvest failure.

Women

Most Elizabethan men will shake their heads in disbelief if you suggest the idea of the equality of the sexes. No two *men* are born equal—some are born rich, some poor; the elder of two brothers will succeed to his father's estates, not the younger—so why should *men and women* be treated equally? Religious commentators point out that God created men and women in unequal strength and size—men being on average five feet seven inches (172 centimeters) and women five two and a quarter (158 centimeters).[72] The London physician Simon Forman makes a list of seventy diseases that occur in women and not in men and states that they are a punishment for Eve tempting Adam to eat the forbidden fruit.[73] The more you look at Elizabethan society, the more you realize that the very idea of the equality of the sexes is a product of a secular, safe, and democratic society. Elizabethan England is none of these things: it is religiously charged, inherently violent, and far from democratic.

A woman cannot vote in a parliamentary or a mayoral election. She cannot be a JP, a lawyer, a mayor, or an alderman. One of the very few official roles open to her is that of churchwarden—but that is an onerous, unpaid position, and very few women seek it.[74] The only professional role she may act in officially is that of a licensed surgeon—but it is exceptionally rare that a woman acquires such a license. Mary Cornellys of Bodmin receives a license to practice surgery throughout the diocese of Exeter in 1568, but she is the only female who does so for the whole reign.[75] Although women can and do obtain licenses to practice midwifery, this is as much a method of social control as enabling them to be recognized professionally, making sure babies are baptized into the Church of England.[76] As for other trades, a woman is not freely able to do business in a town, as she is barred from being a freeman; she has to start a trade in conjunction with her husband. If they set up a business together, and he is a freeman, she will be allowed to continue his trade after his death—but even this concession is made largely so she can support her deceased husband's children.

Other than the above prohibitions, a woman may travel, pray, write, and generally go about her affairs just as freely as a man—as long as she is not married.

The legal implications of marriage provide a second layer of restrictions. Authority in any household is vested in the head of that household: where it is a man, his wife or daughter automatically falls under his authority. All property is vested in him, so a wife's possessions are legally her husband's property, not her own. If a woman owns or inherits freehold property in her own right, then the right to enjoy the income from it automatically transfers to her husband; he can keep taking the income even after her death (as long as she has given him children). If a married woman wishes to dispose of anything she owns, she has to ask her husband's permission. A married woman is not allowed to enter a legal contract without her husband's consent. She cannot do or say anything contrary to her husband's interests. She cannot even draw up a last will and testament without her husband's permission. She is not allowed to let anyone from outside the family into the home without his permission. She can be chastised or beaten with impunity by her husband as long as he does not actually kill her. It is said that a man may legally beat "an outlaw, a traitor, a pagan, his villein and his wife"—and that list suggests the low status a married woman occupies in the eyes of the law.[77] And many men do beat their wives, whether because of a violent nature, a disagreement, or an act of disobedience. In 1600, Simon Forman suspects that his wife is having an affair. He believes she has lied about her whereabouts, and when he confronts her, she shouts back "with howling and weeping." He notes in his diary that she would not be quiet until he had hit her two or three times.[78] Few Elizabethan men feel shame about striking their wives in such circumstances. When the reason is disobedience or adultery, other women may even approve of the beating.

So why do women marry? After all, the legal situation is grim, you give up your property, you have to take on a load of chores—such as cleaning clothes, linen, and bedding, which Elizabethan men *never* do—and run the risk of dying in childbirth. The question, of course, presupposes you have a choice. Normally you don't. You get married because it is what your father and mother want you to do and what is expected of you. Moreover, unless someone is prepared to look after you indefinitely, the alternative to marriage might be poverty and starvation.

But think of marriage in a different way. You give up few or no rights if you move from the authority of your father to that of your husband. In fact, you may gain considerably, for you are able to take advantage of your husband's position in society, becoming his deputy. While you were a child in your father's household, your mother or stepmother filled that role and commanded you and any servants; now you assume that position of authority yourself. As a married woman you organize the household, govern the behavior of the servants and children, and place the orders for supplies. There are no rivals to your authority—Elizabethan households are all built around the single married couple, and it is rare for them to contain a parent of one of the married partners or other in-laws; fewer than 10 percent do.[79] It is very much a nuclear family, with children, servants, and apprentices revolving around husband and wife.[80] Finally, the heavy legal bias in favor of men means that your husband is also legally responsible for all your debts. And if he throws you out, he can be compelled to take you back again: a husband has responsibilities toward his wife that he can't shirk or neglect without doing significant damage to his position in society. Thus a woman often gains from marriage, even though it places her in a role that is legally subservient to her husband.

Marriage, then, is a weighty decision on which your future happiness depends. Most wealthy people's marriages are carefully arranged between the families. The dowry—a payment from the father of the bride to the husband—is an important feature of betrothals. Where a bride comes with a few hundred acres, it may be the land that persuades the husband to go to the altar, not her feminine charms. For this reason, it can usually be expected that a man will not be faithful to his wife. Or as one contemporary puts it: "They that marry where they do not love will love where they do not marry."[81] For the less well-off, things may be just as businesslike: "Easy agreement followeth where women be married not for love but for good," says William Horman.[82] Watch out for the man who will marry you for your dowry, spend it, and then abandon you—like William Hacket at the start of this book. At the bottom end of the scale, marrying a man who might leave you, or cannot keep you, is very dangerous. It might lead to poverty and starvation as well as misery. Having said that, there are many marriages that prove to be long, faithful, rewarding, and loving, and many more lives are enriched by marriage than ruined by it.

At what age should you marry? On the whole, girls are not considered old enough for cohabitation until they reach sixteen, although in certain circumstances they can be married at a younger age. In *Romeo and Juliet*, Capulet declares of Juliet, "My child is yet a stranger in the world—she hath not seen the change of fourteen years; let two more summers wither in their pride ere we may think her ripe to be a bride."[83] And this sense of "ripeness" is echoed in the arrangements for a child bride, Margaret, Lady Rowecliffe, and her husband "not to lie together til she came to the age of sixteen years."[84] Even this is still very young for a bride to be led to the altar. On average, men are twenty-eight and women twenty-six when they marry—although the wealthier your parents are, the earlier these things are arranged.[85] Those marrying with a license from the bishop (rather than by banns) tend either to be people from more prosperous families or couples marrying for reasons of urgency (such as bridal pregnancy); they marry on average at the age of twenty-six and twenty-three respectively. Noblemen and women marry younger still, at twenty-four and nineteen.[86] The notion is that they need to marry and produce a rightful heir as quickly as possible to provide a political alliance between two families.

Given all this, you will be surprised to see that many brides and bridegrooms are much older, in their thirties and forties or beyond. The reason for the discrepancy is that the ages given above are for *first* marriages. When life is so precarious, many women find themselves widowed in their twenties. And the chances of dying in childbirth mean there are many young widowers too. Where a man has children by his dead wife, he needs to remarry quickly—not just to satisfy his sexual needs but to help with the care of his children. The same goes for a widowed mother: whatever ages her children are, it is difficult for a woman to earn enough money by herself to provide food for a family. Thus remarriage becomes an important survival strategy—another reason why people "marry for good, not for love." In all, 25 to 30 percent of all marriages are remarriages.[87] When food is scarce and expensive, older people marry in greater numbers, to pool their resources. This leads some people to marry in their sixties and seventies; they may also take younger spouses who are in need of food but more able. In Norwich, there are seven men with wives thirty to thirty-nine years younger, and six with wives more than forty years younger. For similar reasons, older women marry younger men: twenty-one poor women in Norwich in 1570 have husbands ten to nineteen years younger, fifteen have husbands twenty to twenty-nine years younger, and two have husbands more than thirty years younger (one husband being more than forty years younger).[88] Thus marriage, in all its degrees and purposes, is far too serious a matter to be left to the vagaries of affection, for both men and women. If you are a woman with no income and no family to keep you, or if you are disabled or have children who need feeding, then giving up legal rights to a husband is a small price to pay.

On a positive note, foreign visitors often remark that in England women have more freedom than anywhere else in Europe. This is what the Swiss Thomas Platter writes about Englishwomen in 1599:

> Now the women-folk of England, who have mostly blue-gray eyes and are fair and pretty, have far more liberty than in other lands, and know just how to make good use of it for they often stroll out or drive by coach in very gorgeous clothes, and the men must put up with such ways, and may not punish them for it, indeed the good wives often beat their men, and if this is discovered, the nearest neighbor is placed on a cart and paraded through the whole town as a laughing-stock for the victim, as a punishment—he is informed—for not having come to his neighbor's assistance when his wife was beating him. . . . And there is a proverb about England, which runs: England is a paradise for women, a prison for servants and a hell for horses.[89]

Platter is partly quoting (and thus agreeing with) the duke of Württemberg's secretary who visits England in 1592 and writes that "The women have much more liberty than perhaps in any other place."⁹⁰ The Venetian Alessandro Magno provides a Mediterranean perspective on this unusual liberty in his comment that

> Englishwomen have great freedom to go out of the home without menfolk. . . . Many of the young women gather outside Moorgate and play with young lads, even though they do not know them. Often during these games the women are thrown to the ground by the young men who only allow them to get up after they have kissed them. They kiss each other a lot.⁹¹

Emanuel van Meteren likewise declares in 1575:

> Although the women there are entirely in the power of their husbands, except for their lives, yet they are not kept as strictly as they are in Spain or elsewhere. Nor are they shut up but have the free management of the house or housekeeping, after the fashion of those of the Netherlands and other neighboring countries. They go to market to buy what they like best to eat. They are well-dressed, fond of taking it easy, and commonly leave the care of household matters and drudgery to their servants. They sit before their doors decked out in fine clothes in order to see and be seen by the passers-by. In all banquets and feasts they are shown the greatest honor; they are placed at the upper end of the table where they are served first; at the lower end they help the men. All the rest of their time they employ in walking and riding, in playing at cards or otherwise, in visiting their friends and keeping company, conversing with their equals (whom they term "gossips") and their neighbors, and making merry with them at childbirths, christenings, churchings and funerals; and all this with the permission and knowledge of their husbands, as such is the custom. Although the husbands often recommend to them the pains, industry and care of the German or Dutch women, who do what men ought to do both in the house and in the shops, for which services in England men are employed, nevertheless the women usually persist in retaining their customs. This is why England is called "The Paradise of Married Women." The girls who are not yet married are kept much more rigorously and strictly than in the Low Countries.⁹²

If you look in the London taverns and alehouses, you will see women there—sometimes in greater numbers than the men. Women help their husbands run such establishments, acting as "alewives" and brewsters, and if they are widowed they will often run them single-handedly. It is unusual to see a woman in a tavern or alehouse by herself (unless she is an alewife), and lone female customers in such premises will be assumed to be either drunkards or immoral, or both; but groups of women and women with their husbands form a significant proportion of any tavern's clientele.[93]

The one area in which some women can claim a degree of parity is in literature. The educated ladies of Elizabethan England are making their biggest impression through translations, for noble and gentry families choose to educate their daughters in languages and music above all other things. The daughters of Sir Anthony Cooke are the foremost among these. The formidable Anne, who marries Sir Nicholas Bacon, publishes a translation from the Latin of no less a work than John Jewel's *Apologie of the Church of England* in 1564. Her sister, Mildred, the wife of Sir William Cecil, can speak Greek as fluently as English and translates several works. Another of Sir Anthony's daughters, Elizabeth, Lady Russell, publishes her translation from the French of *A Way of Reconciliation Touching the True Nature and Substance of the Body and Blood of Christ in the Sacrament*; and a fourth daughter, Katherine, is renowned for her ability to translate from the Greek, Latin, and Hebrew. Other families also produce female scholars. Mary Bassett, granddaughter of Sir Thomas More, is well versed in the classics and translates works by Eusebius, Socrates, and several other ancient writers, not to mention a book by her grandfather. Jane, Lady Lumley, publishes a translation of Euripides. Margaret Tyler publishes *The Mirror of Princely Deeds and Knighthood* (1578), translated from the Spanish. And so on. The educated ladies of Elizabethan England are far freer to reveal the fruits of their intellect than were their mothers and grandmothers.

Alongside translation you will come across published volumes of original writings by Elizabethan women. In 1582 Thomas Bentley brings out two volumes called *The Monument of Matrones,* an anthology of religious writing by women for women. It is an extraordinary publication: religion, of all things, is an area in which men presume dominance. Yet many women confidently put forward original lines of theological thinking in this work:

Dorcas Martin, the wife of the Lord Mayor, writes a piece in which a *woman* is catechizing her daughter, even though this is normally the role of a clergyman. Frances Neville, Lady Bergavenny, composes her "Praiers in Prose and Verse" for the same volume. Anne Wheathill and Elizabeth Grymeston are examples of less aristocratic ladies who write of their faith. In 1584 Anne publishes *A Handful of Wholesome (Though Homely) Herbs*, being a collection of forty-nine prayers; Elizabeth dies just before her *Miscelanea: Meditations, Memoratives* (1604) appears in print. Most remarkable of all these pioneering female religious writers is Anne Locke. Just before the start of the reign, she leaves her husband in London and sets off with two infant children to Geneva to translate the sermons of the French Protestant theologian Jean Calvin; two books of translations follow. In a telling line from the preface to her second book she reasons that, because she is a woman, great things are denied her; yet that makes it all the more important for her to accomplish what little she is permitted to do.[94]

The fullest exposition of this new female freedom to write and publish is to be found in poetry. The first published volume of verse by an Englishwoman is Isabella Whitney's *The copy of a letter lately written by a gentlewoman in meter to her unconstant lover* (1566–7). This is followed by her *A sweet nosegay, or pleasant posie, containing a hundred and ten philosophical flowers* (1573). Remarkably, Isabella is not actually of gentle birth but a Cheshire lass who comes to London, works as a servant, and teaches herself to write. Her wit is straightforward and honest, and thus all the more powerful. Consider her "philosophical flower" number 65:

> The lover's tears will soon appease
> His lady's angry mood
> But men will not be pacified
> If women weep a flood.

As a poet, Isabella is followed by Anne Dowriche, whose *The French History: That is, a lamentable discourse of three of the chief . . . broiles that haue happened in France for the Gospell of Iesus Christ* (1589) is a long and complex historical poem. The third published female poet is Elizabeth Melville, who brings out *A godly dreame* in 1603, and the fourth the remarkable Emilia Lanier, who is hard at work on *Salve Deus Rex Iudaeorum*, which will eventually appear in 1611. Clearly written for a female readership, and dedicated to Queen Elizabeth, this collection argues forcefully in favor of women:

> It pleased our Lord and Savior Jesus Christ, without the assistance of man, being free from original and all other sins, from the time of his conception till the hour of his death, to be begotten of a woman, born of a woman, nourished of a woman, obedient to a woman; and that he healed women, pardoned women, comforted women . . . after his resurrection appeared first to a woman, and sent a woman to declare his most glorious resurrection to the rest of his Disciples.[95]

The title poem describes Christ's passion from the point of view of the female witnesses of the crucifixion. Lanier points out that it was men who crucified Christ and Pilate's wife who tried to stop the execution. Elsewhere, she gives "Eve's apology"—an argument that the original sin of eating the forbidden fruit wasn't Eve's fault alone:

> But surely Adam cannot be excused;
> Her fault, though great: yet he was most to blame;
> What weakness offered, strength might have refused,
> Being lord of all, the greater was his shame:
> Although the serpent's craft had her abused
> God's holy word ought all his actions frame,
> For he was lord and King of all the Earth
> Before poor Eve had either life or breath.

This is a witty and imaginative piece of work, sustained for two hundred stanzas. But what is astonishing about it is the boldness of Lanier's stance. She clearly rejects the idea that women are inferior to men; rather, she seems to suggest that women, being in a mystical union with Christ, are in fact *superior*. Thus women are starting to use their position as published writers to rail against their secondary status in society. It will take another three hundred years to make any significant progress against patriarchy, but the roots of feminism can be found in the public voice that women acquire in the reign of Queen Elizabeth. They can be seen in Anne Locke making her way to Geneva to take part in the Calvinist Reformation; they are apparent in Isabella Whitney's self-confidence in publishing her witty rhymes; and they are evident in the ruthless yet graceful logic of Emilia Lanier.

Even though Elizabeth herself does nothing directly to advance the cause of women, she clearly inspires her female contemporaries. In legal terms, nothing changes; but under her rule, women begin to enjoy social freedoms that they have never enjoyed in the past, and a few brave souls gain public respect—not as the wives of great men, but on account of their own intellectual and creative brilliance.

CHAPTER THREE

Religion

Given the split with Rome and the establishment of a national Church, you might think that society is becoming more secular in the sixteenth century. If you look around you, there are plenty of things to suggest that this is happening. The dissolution of the monasteries has resulted in a reduction in the numbers of priests and churches. Huge amounts of ecclesiastical property have been confiscated. The monarch—a secular individual—is the head of the Church. Saints' cults are outlawed, their statues smashed, and their altars removed. All the chantries have been abolished—there are to be no more Masses sung for the dead who built the chapels—and the practice of laying wax or wooden images of human limbs and animals on altars and praying for their recovery is outlawed. Church ales (brewed to raise money for church funds) are discouraged and wakes for the dead are abolished. Most religious processions and fraternities are banned, as are religious indulgences. Even rosary beads are made illegal.

These prohibitions are not aimed at religion itself but at Roman Catholicism, which is widely considered as unfit for purpose. In fact, society is becoming *more* religious, not less. Naturally, the population occupies a spectrum of religious positions, but if you talk to those at the more spiritual end, you will see that they wish to commune with God more directly, without the distractions of so many statues, images, and decorations, and certainly without the moneymaking and political interventions of the papacy. Yes, there is a secular element to the nationalism of the Church of England, but this is largely a by-product of the desire to eliminate anything that comes between the humble Christian and God. It is this desire that creates the reforming zeal of Elizabeth's ministers and their brand of Anglicanism. A heightened form of this passion gives rise to Puritanism and Calvinism. Conversely, for traditionalists, the sense that their spiritual values are under attack from these fanatics reinforces their commitment to the Catholic cause and their resistance to Anglicanism, Puritanism, and Calvinism. Although most people are not prepared to risk their lives for the sake of a religious viewpoint, some are. They would rather die than deny what they believe to be the truth.

For this reason, it would be deeply unwise to set off into Elizabethan England without knowing something of its religion. Religion touches upon every aspect of Elizabethan life. Not only that, orthodox faith changes so rapidly that you need to know what is acceptable at any given time. In Mary's reign, no fewer than 283 men and women are burned at the stake for maintaining their Protestant beliefs—many of which would be called orthodox in Elizabeth's reign. Although Elizabeth's government does not burn as many people as Mary's, proscribed views are still enough to get you killed. What is orthodox in 1558 is sufficient to have you hanged in 1570. This is something to ponder on: the religious changes of the sixteenth century are far more profound, far-reaching, and rapid than those of the twentieth century, which we think of as a century of great change.

Atheism

You might think that, if you have no religion, no one will bother you. After all, the rivalry is between Catholics and Protestants—surely you can simply rise above the controversy? There you would be wrong. The atheist is the enemy of all, being utterly godless and therefore outside the scope of Elizabethan morality. As Francis Bacon writes in his essay "On Atheism": "They that deny God destroy a man's nobility; for certainly man is of kin to the beasts by his body; and, if he be not kin to God by his spirit, he is a base and ignoble creature."

The question is very much a sixteenth-century one. Prior to the Reformation there is no discussion about the existence of God. Not believing in God is like not believing in trees. Most people simply cannot conceive of a line dividing the metaphysical and the physical. To them the two are indivisibly linked: Creation cannot exist without its Creator. However, from the middle of the century, certain people start to be labeled "atheists" by their enemies. Some even admit themselves to being *nulla fidians* or "nothing believers." Then, in 1583, Philip Stubbes writes his *Anatomy of Abuses,* which defines atheists as people who "deny there is any God."[1] Atheism as we know it is born.

Two groups of people lead the way in separating the physical and the metaphysical. First, there are the political philosophers influenced by Niccolò Machiavelli, whose book *The Prince* makes no appeal to morality or divine intervention but is simply a study in how to control a state—as if

God does not exist. Second, there are the physicians and surgeons who make a distinction between the physical and the metaphysical when considering certain diseases and ailments. William Bullein, who is both a clergyman and a physician, writes of a fictional medical man in 1564: "I am neither Catholic, Papist, Protestant or Anabaptist, I assure you." To this his plague-ridden patient replies: "What do you honor? The sun, the moon, or the stars, beast, stone or fowl, fish or tree?" The physician answers: "No forsooth. I do none of them all. To be plain, I am *nulla fidian* and there are many of our sect."[2]

Bullein himself is not an atheist. For a start, if God does not exist, then the ability of physicians to effect cures is entirely dependent on their knowledge of the human body, and that is clearly limited. It is far better for a physician to maintain that he is God's instrument and that the Almighty cures people through him. For reasons of human compassion, many physicians genuinely *want* to perform such medical miracles. In addition, developments in medical philosophy toward the end of the century suggest that medicines might be found in nature for every human ailment, thus revealing the hand of a benevolent Creator. Last but not least, there is the plain fact that, given the choice, most gravely ill patients would prefer a priest to come to their bedside than a physician, having more faith in the redemptive power of the Almighty than in the curative abilities of physicians. The philosophical position of the *nulla fidians* is simply inadequate when it comes to helping sick and dying people: both physicians and patients need to believe in an interventionist God.[3]

The word "atheist" also means "against God," and in this sense it comes to be used in the late sixteenth century as a method of smearing a person's reputation. If a person can be shown to be acting "against God," then he is effectively excommunicated, having placed himself in enmity to all God-fearing people. Catholics argue that Protestants act in ways that are "against God" and denounce them as atheists—even though the Protestant position is driven by a commitment to a simpler, more direct relationship with God. In 1565–66, the physician John Caius is accused of atheism by members of his college at Cambridge University. In 1592 Sir Walter Raleigh is accused of presiding over a school of atheism in which "both Moses and our Savior, and the Old and New Testaments, are jested at, and the scholars taught, among other things to spell 'God' backward." In October 1596 the Church of Scotland minister David Black declares that Queen Elizabeth herself is an atheist and the religion professed in England nothing but a show.[4] Such accusations are all propaganda. Dr. Caius is a humanist but not an unbeliever; his accusers simply don't like the autocratic way in which he rules the college. Raleigh does entertain some challenging philosophical points of view, but his own writings reveal him to be an Anglican conformist.[5] As for Elizabeth, although she dismisses theologians as "ropes of sand," her own commitment to religious reform suggests that her personal faith is strong. She retains her father's title of "Defender of the Faith" and maintains that she rules by the grace of God.

There is one man who does profess himself to be an atheist, but he is hardly typical. This is the charismatic and unorthodox Christopher Marlowe, the playwright and poet. The earliest indications of Marlowe's atheism are to be noted in 1587, when a fellow undergraduate at Cambridge, Mr. Fineux, claims that Marlowe inducted him into atheism. However, Fineux clarifies this by adding that he occasionally goes out at midnight into a wood and prays heartily that the devil might come. This clearly is not atheism as we know it but being "against God"—or devil-worship. Over the years, Marlowe encourages people to associate him with atheism. In his play *The Jew of Malta* he has the ghost of Machiavelli declare, "I count religion but a childish toy / And hold there is no sin but ignorance." In 1592 Robert Greene accuses him of declaring, "There is no God," and of embracing "Machiavellian policy" and "diabolical atheism." One Richard Cholmeley confesses that he was converted to atheism by Marlowe, who "is able to show more sound reasons for atheism than any divine in England is able to give to prove divinity." Another informant claims that it is Marlowe's custom "to jest at the divine scriptures, gibe at prayers and strive in argument to frustrate and confute what hath been spoken or written by prophets and such holy men"; he accuses him of joking that St. John the Baptist was Christ's homosexual lover.[6] Given that men can be hanged for homosexual acts in Elizabethan England (in line with the Punishment of Buggery Act of 1563), and that heretics are burned alive, a man who jokes that Christ is a sodomite is putting his life at risk. Marlowe does not exactly help himself by declaring, "All they that love not tobacco and boys are fools."[7] The government orders him to be arrested on account of his indiscretions, but before he can be brought in for questioning, he is stabbed to death in a house in Deptford in 1593, in an argument over a supper bill.

The Elizabethan Settlement of 1559

One of the popular misunderstandings of Elizabethan England is that, at the very moment when Mary I dies, on November 17, 1558, England suddenly ceases to be a Catholic kingdom, just as if a candle has been snuffed out. As you will see, it isn't like that. Unlike Henry VIII's reforms, which are suddenly imposed on the people by the king's will and upheld by violence, Elizabeth's Church is the result of a series of long debates and compromises in Parliament, which are made palatable to the majority principally by their very Englishness. Indeed, the whole process of discussion is probably the reason that the Church of England proves so enduring. England remains a Protestant country not because of Henry VIII and his marital difficulties but because of the resolution of Elizabeth and her government to establish a new independent Church of England which is acceptable both to the majority of Englishmen and to the queen herself.

At the start of her reign, everyone is full of curiosity, expectation, and nervous apprehension concerning Elizabeth's religion. Eighteen days after becoming queen, on December 5, 1558, she issues a summons for Parliament to assemble on January 23, 1559. The days tick by. The Venetian ambassador, Il Schifanoya, listens for any hint about the likely religious developments. On December 17 he writes home in alarm, saying, "At court, when the queen is present, a priest officiates who says certain prayers with the litanies in English after the fashion of King Edward. I pray God to grant that worse may not happen."[8] Elizabeth's appointment of a Protestant to be the first preacher at St. Paul's Cross in London causes the Catholics further concern. So does the appointment of seven new members to the privy council—all Protestants. She allows her late sister to be buried according to the Catholic rite in Westminster Abbey in mid-December, which gives the Catholics some hope; but then on December 31 Il Schifanoya hears terrible news. He writes:

> Until now I have believed that the matters of religion would continue in the accustomed manner, her majesty having promised this with her own mouth many times; but now I have lost faith and I see that little by little they are returning to the bad use. On Christmas Day the bishop of Carlisle sang high Mass and her majesty sent to tell him that he was not to elevate the host; to which the good bishop replied that thus he

had learned the Mass and that she must pardon him as he could not do otherwise. So, the gospel being ended, her majesty rose and departed.[9]

The queen's premature departure from Mass leaves little doubt that the kingdom is set to leave the Church of Rome again. On January 12 Elizabeth takes a barge to the Tower, and on January 14, in accordance with royal custom, she makes her way through the streets of London to Westminster Abbey, where she is to be crowned on the following day. On the day itself there are a number of pageants held on Cornhill, in Gracechurch Street, in Soper Lane, and in Fleet Street. Over the next two days there are celebratory jousts at Whitehall. But beneath this veneer of pageantry, the country is on tenterhooks.

It is fair to say that many people just want things to continue as they are. When the news of Elizabeth's accession reaches Much Wenlock in Shropshire, on November 25, the Feast of St. Catherine, the sheriff informs the vicar, who makes the pronouncement in a loud voice, exhorting all to pray for "Queen Elizabeth, by the grace of God, queen of England, France and Ireland, Defender of the Faith." Then, after a suitable anthem, he goes to the altar and says a Catholic Mass.[10] The congregation have no great desire to see all their time-honored traditions shifted once more. There are also many of whom it may be said "they love a pot of ale better than a pulpit," especially in rural areas.[11] But there is a real hunger for change among the more literate townsfolk. Ever since the Bible was first printed in English, in 1526, men and women have been studying it in detail. They have been instructing themselves in the teachings of Christ and interpreting the lessons of the Old Testament without the intervention of priests. Increasingly over the years, such self-taught interpretations have clashed with the time-honored interpretations of the Church, and there is a profound frustration at the Church's refusal to change its views. People look at all the trappings of official religion and question how much religious practice is actually rooted in the Bible. Very little, they conclude. The Reformation of the Church under Henry VIII has encouraged them to think more freely: if Henry could abolish the monasteries, why not remove the whole paraphernalia of Catholic ritual? These things are just symbols, they argue—mere fripperies by comparison with the serious business of prayer. A few more fervent and courageous thinkers go further. Why should the monarch have the right to interfere in matters of religion? Why cannot the state and the

Church be separate? Why should there be a hierarchy of bishops and arch-bishops? Why not have just simple priests serving their communities in a humble way, as the apostles did in the New Testament?

Elizabeth's very existence is the result of Henry's split with Rome. It was for her mother, Anne Boleyn, that her father divorced his first wife, then broke from Roman Catholicism and had himself proclaimed Supreme Head of the Church in 1534. Elizabeth is the living product of that religious break. Therefore she is bound to associate herself more with the reformers than with the traditionalists. There is also the political element to consider. As she herself aptly puts it in a later speech to Parliament: "One matter toucheth me so near as I may not overskip: religion, *the ground on which all other matters ought to take root. . . .*"[12] Religion is the basis of most people's understanding of how the world works—from Creation through to the health of the individual—and as the Church intrudes into almost every walk of life, it is hugely important to incorporate its authority within that of the Crown. Elizabeth herself has personal preferences, such as that the clergy should remain unmarried and celibate, and that both the extravagant religious vestments and church music should be retained; she has no time for the Calvinist reformers who would abolish the ecclesiastical hierarchy. But these are minor issues compared with her principal objective: that, as queen of England, she should be the Supreme Head of the Church, like her father. It is the *combination* of spiritual and secular authority that delivers absolute authority, giving the monarch's political rule divine approval.

Parliament meets on January 25, 1559. The debates are fervent from the start. On February 4 the queen recalls her ambassador to the papal court. Five days later a bill is placed before Parliament recognizing the queen as Supreme Head of the Church. Then words really start to fly. But the first Supremacy Bill is turned down. So is the next. A third is introduced. Meanwhile the clergy—who have not been invited to attend this Parliament—are discussing religious reform separately, in Convocation. They reaffirm their belief in transubstantiation, papal supremacy, and the key pillars of Roman Catholicism. On March 31, Sir Nicholas Bacon accuses the Catholic proponents of contempt for the Crown and locks two of them up in the Tower. In this heated atmosphere, the Church of England is hammered into shape. The final form of the Supremacy Act, passed on April 29 by the narrow majority of three votes, carries the compromise that the queen is not

Supreme Head of the Church (because she is a woman) but its Supreme Governor. All the religious legislation of the previous reign is repealed. The Act of Uniformity (passed on the same day) reestablishes the Prayer Book of Edward VI as the authorized version. All officeholders—clergymen, judges, JPs, mayors, royal officials, and university graduates—are required to swear an oath acknowledging Elizabeth as Supreme Governor of the Church. Refusal to do so results in loss of office. Anyone writing, teaching, or preaching that Elizabeth should be subject to the authority of a foreign power (including the pope) is to lose all his or her property and movable possessions. Repeated offenses will be judged high treason and incur the death penalty. Henceforth it is compulsory to attend Church of England services every Sunday and holy day, and those who fail—recusants, as they are known—are to be fined a shilling for each Sunday they fail to attend.

All in all, the queen succeeds in passing most of her agenda for reform. She has to allow the clergy to marry "for the avoiding of fornication," but she makes up for this by insisting that they only marry discreet, honest, and sober women who have been approved of by a bishop. She manages to retain the vestments and music of the Church, and much of its symbolism. And she succeeds in resisting the Calvinists, who would like to abolish the bishops. Most of all, she retains absolute authority over the Church, pointing out carefully that, although her title as Supreme Governor differs from that borne by her father, she fully intends to exercise all the rights that he had. No one gets exactly what he wants out of the Settlement of 1559—everyone makes compromises—but Elizabeth makes fewer compromises than anyone else.

The Establishment of Protestant England, 1559–1569

If you visit England in the 1560s, you are most likely to be struck by how easily people accept the Settlement of 1559. Throughout England, the saints' cults and altars are dismantled and religious processions halted. Texts that defend and celebrate the new religion are published. Matthew Parker, archbishop of Canterbury, brings out his *Book of Homilies* in 1562, outlining a moral code for Protestant England and stressing both the heinousness of rebellion and the immorality of excessive dress. In the same year, the newly appointed bishop of Salisbury, John Jewel, publishes a justification for the Church of England in Latin, entitled *Apologia ecclesiae Anglicanae*. Translated (as we have seen) into English by Anne Bacon in 1564, it grounds Anglicanism in the teachings of Christ, the apostles, and the early Fathers of the Christian Church. A third hugely influential book appears in 1563—*Foxe's Book of Martyrs*.[13] This massive history of the Christian martyrs gives special weight to the persecution and suffering of English Protestants, and implies that the English are God's chosen people for putting down the antichrist (the pope). The book is an enormous asset to Elizabeth in her propaganda war against Catholicism. And propaganda is the key. Elizabeth makes sure all history books praise her and Protestantism, and reflect Mary's reign in a negative light.[14]

The Parliament of 1563 confirms the reforms of 1559 and extends them. It is agreed that there should be a Bible in Welsh (a task that takes twenty-five years to complete). The list of those who are to swear the Oath of Supremacy is extended to include schoolmasters, MPs, lawyers, and sheriffs, and harsher penalties for those claiming the superiority of the pope are introduced. But there are those who want to see the reforms go further and who submit a bill to abolish ecclesiastical vestments and do away with many other symbols, such as wedding rings, the sign of the cross in the baptism service, and church organs. They are very nearly successful, being defeated by just one vote.

Although the Church of England is firmly established by the mid-1560s, not everyone is a willing, orthodox Protestant. A year after the 1563 Parliament, half of all the JPs in the country still have not sworn the Oath of Supremacy. It is possible to be a Catholic recusant without too much trouble—if you can afford the 12 pence fine every Sunday—and the English government is still relatively tolerant of religious deviation in the 1560s. Yes, there are searches for seditious and heretical writings—even the house of the writer John Stow is ransacked in the search for "Popish" texts, and he is saved from arrest only through the intervention of powerful supporters within the government. Certain people are placed under house arrest for harboring Catholic agitators. Suspected Catholics are denied political roles and stripped of their offices; but it is not a treasonable act simply to *be* a Catholic.

Things become much more serious as a result of the events of 1569–70. In November 1569 the Northern Rebellion takes place. The earls of Westmorland and Northumberland gather an army and march into Durham, where they openly celebrate Mass in the Catholic fashion. That same month, they write to the pope asking him to justify their rebellion by excommunicating Elizabeth. Accordingly, on February 5, 1570, Pope Pius V takes the dramatic step of commencing heresy proceedings against the queen of England. On the 13th she is found guilty—and on the 25th a papal bull is issued excommunicating and deposing her.

Confrontation with Catholicism, 1570–1603

You may feel that all this has got nothing to do with you, that it is just other people's religion. However, it is essential that you understand the religious conflict—ignorance is no defense if you are deemed to be too friendly to Catholics. Whatever your faith, you cannot turn a blind eye to the papal bull of 1570, which requires all good Catholics to turn against their monarch—and thus forces them to choose between their loyalty to Elizabeth and their allegiance to the Roman Church. Nor can you afford to be ignorant of the establishment of the first English seminary college at Douai, in France, in 1568. This college and others set up later at Rome (1579), Valladolid (1589), and Seville (1592) teach theology to youths from respectable English Catholic families along the lines set out by the Jesuits, so they can return to England, minister to existing Catholics, and convert others. The government and senior clergy are alarmed. Bishop John Jewel rails at the pope from his pulpit, pouring scorn on Catholicism. The privy council orders the ports to be watched against incoming papal messengers; the importation of books is carefully monitored to guard against seditious tracts. In this atmosphere, Parliament meets on April 2, 1571, and makes a number of key resolutions. A new act is passed making it high treason to claim that the queen is "a heretic, schismatic, tyrant, infidel or usurper." It also becomes illegal to proclaim that any particular person ought to be heir to the throne. A second act forbids the importation of bulls from Rome, as well as crucifixes and rosary beads. A third confiscates the property of anyone leaving the country without the queen's permission and staying abroad for six months, thereby removing the wealth of many émigré Catholic families. The twelfth act of this Parliament legally binds all the clergy to observe the doctrines laid out in the Thirty-Nine Articles of 1563. A separate order directs all cathedrals and members of the higher clergy to obtain a copy of *Foxe's Book of Martyrs* and to make it available for visitors to read. The fight against Catholicism has started.

If you are a Catholic, life becomes increasingly hard at roughly ten-year intervals. The Settlement of 1559 is bad enough, and if the situation gets worse in 1570, in 1580 it becomes almost unbearable. In this year, Catholic scholars from the college at Douai set up an illegal printing press at Stonor Park in Oxfordshire, thereby avoiding the censors who patrol the ports. Also in 1580, Jesuits arrive on a mission "to preserve and augment the faith of the Catholics in England." Over a hundred of these disciplined, militant Catholic priests are in the kingdom by the end of the year, living undercover and stirring up conspiracies. Consequently Parliament is summoned and "An Act to retain the Queen's Majesty's Subjects in their due Obedience" is passed in 1581. Anyone trying to persuade people to join the Catholic Church is to be held guilty of high treason and executed. Anyone missing a church service is now to be fined £20 per month. Offenders who fail to attend for a whole year must additionally submit a bond for £200 to guarantee their good behavior. Saying Mass becomes punishable by a fine of 200 marks (£133 6 shillings 8 pence) and a year's imprisonment; even just *hearing* Mass will get you a fine of 100 marks (£66 13 shillings 4 pence) and a year in prison. Anyone maintaining a schoolmaster who does not attend church is liable to pay a fine of £10 per month.[15] A second act makes it illegal to say anything derogatory about the queen. Many people are taken to the assizes as a result.

The bitterness deepens. A leading Jesuit, Edmund Campion, confirms that Catholics should not attend Anglican services (even though many Catholic sympathizers do so).[16] In 1581 Campion is caught, tortured on the rack, and led through the streets of London with a sign on him saying, "This is Campion, the seducer of the People," before he is publicly executed. Another Catholic, Anthony Tyrrell, is arrested for plotting to kill the queen in 1581: he too is tortured on the rack. John Payne, a graduate of the Douai college, is arrested for the same reason, tortured on the rack, and hanged the following year. The abhorrence felt in Rome is expressed in a book by Robert Parsons, *De Persecutione Anglicana* (1582), which depicts the Catholic suffering and deepens the hatred for English Protestants across Europe.[17] But every year the religious crisis seems to get worse. Every year there is at least one Catholic attempt to assassinate the queen.

The year 1585 is a watershed. War breaks out with Spain. More worryingly, a Catholic agent called Gilbert Gifford is arrested at Rye, Sussex, and confesses to being part of a plot against Elizabeth. Sir Francis Walsingham offers to save Gifford's life if he acts as a double agent; Gifford agrees and provides Walsingham with the information that leads to the uncovering of Anthony Babington's conspiracy to kill Elizabeth and deliver the throne to Mary, queen of Scots, so Catholicism can be restored. All those involved are caught, tortured, and executed; in 1587 Mary herself is tried and beheaded. By this time, plans are already in place for the Spanish Armada to sail and conquer England. After the destruction of the Armada in 1588, treatment of Catholics worsens further. In 1591 commissions are established in every county to examine people's beliefs and test their church attendance. Finally, in 1593, the most extreme anti-Catholic act of all is passed. Those not attending church for a month are to be imprisoned. Catholics are not allowed to travel more than five miles from their homes—on pain of forfeiting all their property and estates. They must register with the local authorities and obtain a license if they wish to go anywhere.[18]

We have come a long way from 1564, when half of the JPs hesitate to swear the Oath of Supremacy. Just thirty-five years see Catholicism change from being the respectable norm to the religion of a persecuted minority. Between 1571 and the end of the reign, at least 180 Catholics are executed as traitors—perhaps more than 250.[19] If you are a Catholic in the last years of the reign, you can expect to celebrate Mass in secret, late at night or very early in the morning, in the houses of the gentry. No doubt you will experience that frightening moment when a stranger knocks insistently on the door and you look at the terrified faces of those around you, wondering whether you have been discovered. You may find out what it is like to hide in a priest hole—a small, secret chamber in a wall or beneath a floor—while the authorities search the house. Father William Weston, a Jesuit priest educated at Douai, describes just such an experience in 1585:

A house where I used secretly to be given hospitality was visited once by certain Catholics, who gave a satisfactory account of themselves, both to me and to the head of the family, and said that they wished to hear Mass. After the end of Mass, when the people had left, I stayed on as usual and went upstairs to the room where I kept my books and resumed my work. Not quite two hours later the house was surrounded by a large mob of men. Whether they came on information or on chance, I do not know. But the servant rushed up to my room—I was still there—and warned me of the danger. She made me come downstairs at once and showed me a hiding place underground; Catholic houses have several places like this, otherwise there would be no security. I got down into it, taking my breviary with me—it was all I had near me at the time, and to loiter would have been dangerous. In the meantime the heretics had already made their way into the house and were examining the remoter parts. From my cave-like hide I could follow their movements by the noise and uproar they raised. Step by step they drew closer, and when they entered my room the sight of my books was an added incentive to their search. In that room also there was a secret passageway for which they demanded the key, and, as they opened the door giving on to it, they were standing immediately above my head. I could hear practically every word they said. "Here, look!" they called out, "a chalice! And a missal!" The things were, in fact, there. There had been no time to hide them and, in any case, it would have been impossible. Then they demanded a hammer and other tools to break through the wall and paneling. They were certain now that I could not be far away.

Meanwhile I was praying fervently to God that He would avert the danger. At the same time I reflected that it would be better to surrender myself into the enemy's hands than be dragged out ignominiously. I believed that some Judas had given information and betrayed me but, to cover up the traitor, they wanted my discovery to appear accidental, and not the result of treachery.

While I was reflecting in this way, one of the men, either by mistake or on purpose, or at the prompting of a good angel, shouted out: why waste time getting hammers and hatchets? There's not enough space here for a man. Look at the corners: you can see where everything leads to. There can't be a hiding place here. . . .

The whole of that day I lay in hiding, and the night and day following it as well, almost till sunset. The cellar was dark, dank and cold, and so narrow that I was forced to stand the entire time. Also I had to stay completely quiet, without coughing or making the smallest noise. If they failed to find me, I thought they would probably surround the house and cut off my escape. During those long hours not a servant came to open the door and this confirmed my suspicion that the enemy was still in possession of the house. . . . The servant who had shut me in this place had been taken off to prison; those left behind did not know of it and had no idea what had happened to me.[20]

Father Weston is eventually caught in August 1586 and imprisoned with a number of other Catholics in Wisbech Castle. In 1599 he is transferred to the Tower of London, and only released after Elizabeth's death, whereupon he is sent into exile.

The Tower is the most feared place of confinement for Catholics. Seven types of torture are used there to extract confessions from Jesuits and seminary priests like Weston. Another English Catholic internee, Edward Rishton, describes them as follows:

1. The first is the Pit: a subterranean cave, twenty feet deep and entirely without light;
2. The second is a cell or dungeon, so small as to be incapable of allowing a person to stand erect. From its effect on its inmates it is called the "Little Ease";
3. The third is the rack, on which, by means of wooden rollers and other machinery the limbs of the sufferer are drawn in opposite directions;
4. The fourth, I believe from the inventor, is called The Scavenger's Daughter. It consists of an iron ring that brings the head, hands and feet together until they form a circle;
5. The fifth is the iron gauntlet, which encloses the hand with the most excruciating pain;
6. The sixth consists of chains or manacles, attached to the arms;
7. The seventh consists of fetters, by which the feet are contained.[21]

In view of all this, it is quite surprising that William Harrison can blithely state in his *Description of England*:

To use torment also or question by pain and torture in these common cases with us is greatly abhorred, since we are found always to be such as despise death and yet abhor to be tormented, choosing rather frankly to open our minds than to yield our bodies unto such servile hauling and tearings as are used in other countries.[22]

Clearly there is a huge gulf between the complacency of a Protestant writer in 1577 and the experiences of Catholic priests in the 1580s and 1590s.

Few Catholics have left firsthand accounts of being tortured. However, one compelling narrative is that of Father John Gerard, who is taken to the Tower in 1597.

We went to the torture room in a kind of solemn procession, the attendants walking ahead with lighted candles. The chamber was underground and dark, particularly near the entrance. It was a vast place and every device and instrument of human torture was there. They pointed out some of them to me and said I would try them all. Then they asked me again whether I would confess.

"I cannot," I said.

I fell on my knees for a moment's prayer. Then they took me to a big upright pillar, one of the wooden posts that supported the roof of this huge underground chamber. Driven into the top of it were iron staples for supporting heavy weights. Then they put my wrists into iron gauntlets and ordered me to climb two or three wicker steps. My arms were lifted up and an iron bar was passed through the rings of one gauntlet, through the staple, and through the rings of the second gauntlet. This done, they fastened the bar with a pin to prevent it slipping, and then, removing the wicker steps one by one from beneath my feet, they left me hanging by my hands and arms fastened above my head. The tips of my toes, however, still touched the ground and they had to dig away the earth from under them. . . .

Hanging like this, I began to pray. The gentlemen standing around me asked whether I was willing to confess now.

"I cannot and I will not," I answered.

But I could hardly utter the words, such a gripping pain came over me. It was worst in my chest and belly, my hands and arms. All the blood in my body seemed to rush up into my arms and hands, and I thought that blood was oozing from the ends of my fingers and the pores of my skin. But it was only a sensation caused by my flesh swelling above the irons holding them. The pain was so intense that I thought I could not possibly endure it, and, added to it, I had an inward temptation. Yet I did not feel any inclination or wish to give them the information they wanted. The Lord saw my weakness with the eyes of His mercy, and did not permit me to be tempted beyond my strength. With the temptation He sent me relief. Seeing my agony and the struggle going on in my mind, He gave me this most merciful thought: *the*

*utmost and worst they can do is to kill you, and you have often wanted
to give your life for your Lord God. The Lord God sees all you are
enduring—He can do all things. You are in God's keeping.* With these
thoughts, God in His infinite goodness and mercy gave me the grace of
resignation, and with a desire to die and a hope (I admit) that I would,
I offered Him myself to do with me as He wished. From that moment
the conflict in my soul ceased, and even the physical pain seemed
much more bearable than before, though it must, in fact, I am sure,
have been greater with the growing strain and the weariness of my
body....

Sometime after one o'clock, I think, I fell into a faint. How long I
was unconscious I don't know, but I do not think it was long, for the
men held my body up or put the wicker steps under my feet until I
came to. Then they heard me pray and immediately let me down again.
They did this every time I fainted—eight or nine times that day—
before it struck five.[23]

Confrontation with Puritanism, 1570–1603

You need to bear in mind that the religious divide in England is not just a
two-way battle between Anglicans and Catholics. In most respects, Anglicanism is a middle way, a series of compromises between the two extremes
of Roman Catholicism and more radical Protestant positions such as Calvinism and Puritanism. Although there is as much conflict with Puritans
as with Catholics, there is an important difference. The pope and England's
Catholic enemies pose a political threat; the conflict with Puritanism remains almost entirely religious.

The narrow defeat in 1563 of the bill to abolish religious vestments and
symbols does not mean that all those who would have a "purer" form of
worship simply acquiesce and start supporting the orthodox line from
Westminster. Discontent simmers away throughout the 1560s. The triumph
in Scotland of John Knox and his Presbyterianism—based on the ideas of
Jean Calvin—encourages some people to think that such radical agendas
should be adopted in England too. They find a leader in Dr. Thomas Cartwright, professor of divinity at Cambridge, who uses his position to preach
that the current system of church administration has no basis in the scriptures. He advocates abolishing archbishops, archdeacons, and most of the

higher clergy, and returning bishops to their original function of preaching and teaching, while deacons should minister to the poor. Such radical views incur the anger of John Whitgift, who becomes vice-chancellor of the university in 1570. Cartwright is deprived of his professorial chair; in 1574, he is driven into exile when he hears that orders for his arrest have been issued.

With a cause célèbre like this, Puritanism finds a new focus and gains vitality. It has a number of influential supporters, such as the queen's favorite, Robert Dudley, earl of Leicester, who is an advocate of preaching (which the queen is not) and even subscribes to some Calvinist ideas. At a lower social level, among the gentry, Puritans argue that Elizabeth remains too close to the Catholics. In 1574 a gentleman from Essex, Thomas Bedell, declares, "They are not papists who say that the queen is a papist but rather divers others who call themselves puritans."[24] Bedell is fined £100 for this remark, even after withdrawing it and repenting (by which he saves himself a few hours in the pillory and the loss of both of his ears). Most Puritans would agree with Bedell; it is just that saying such things is beyond the pale.

Herein lies the problem for the Puritans. They are religious thinkers who question the current state of the Church; yet for the queen all such doubt is treasonable. She has made her mind up on religion, and wants to maintain the Settlement of 1559 as far as possible. When Puritan preachers continue to raise questions in people's minds, the queen takes action: one or two preachers in each diocese will be sufficient, she declares, and they will have to be authorized by her.

For Puritans, like Catholics, the most difficult years of Elizabeth's rule are the last. Robert Dudley, earl of Leicester, dies in 1588, and although the queen weeps for him, his death allows her to take sterner measures against his friends. The Puritans respond in the same year with a series of pamphlets, signed by "Martin Marprelate," which lampoons the ecclesiastical hierarchy. The printer John Penry is forced to flee to Scotland, but is caught on a visit to London and hanged. In 1593, the theologian Richard Hooker publishes *Of the Laws of Ecclesiastical Polity*, which gives the Church of England a stronger theological basis than that provided by John Jewel thirty years earlier and heavily criticizes Puritanism. The queen is most satisfied. Resigned to a lack of reform in the Church, the Puritans bide their time for the rest of the reign, before emerging as a powerful force in the seventeenth century.[25]

How to Survive in a Religious World

As you can see, religion is a matter of life and death in Elizabethan England. If you want to avoid unwelcome attention, observe the routine details of orthodox religion. Kneel and say prayers when you rise in the morning, before dinner, in the evening, and at bedtime (remember, your servants may well be listening). Do not forget to say grace at dinner. Attend church regularly—every Sunday and every holy day—and, if in London, attend the sermons preached at St. Paul's Cross from time to time.[26] Pay attention to your Bible and other religious works: Sir William Cecil exhorts his son to read the whole psalter once a month.[27] Avoid arguments with your neighbors lest they inform on you and report you for sedition or, worse, heresy. Do not predict the future or make "fantastic prophecies" which could bring you into conflict with the authorities. In short, unless you are prepared to be tortured and die for your beliefs, keep your head down. Take the Portuguese Jews of London as an example. Although all the Jews were expelled from England in the Middle Ages, a small Portuguese Jewish community of eighty to ninety people quietly lives in the city, largely untroubled by the authorities.[28]

Whatever you do, don't join any of the more extreme Protestant sects that come from the Continent. In particular, the radical reformers called Anabaptists, who refuse to accept civil government or infant baptism, are persecuted. In England, Catholics are not burned as heretics, but Anabaptists are. In 1575 a community of Dutch Anabaptists is discovered living near Aldgate, in London. They are tried. Five recant, fifteen are returned to the Low Countries, and five are sentenced to death. For two of them, the authorities relight the bonfires of religion: they are burned alive at the stake "in great horror, with roaring and crying."[29]

For the love of God.

CHAPTER FOUR

Character

O scar Wilde once quipped, "The old believe everything, the middle-aged suspect everything and the young know everything." Apply that remark to Elizabethan England and you will begin to understand the bold, abrasive character of the people. It is the self-confidence of youth that gives Elizabethan society much of its arrogance and determination. Hand a man in his twenties command of a ship and the chance to make himself rich, and, despite the difficulties of navigation and the huge dangers that beset him when a thousand miles from land, you may well see him sail round the world. Give a similar man a commission to keep the peace and constables to enforce local justice and you will see the disruptive elements of society ruthlessly put down. To control such self-righteous individuals requires older men to show no less self-confidence—and a will as strong as that of the queen herself.

That, of course, is a simplification of things. Elizabethan people aren't determined in an unquestioning sort of way. It is precisely the level to which Elizabethans *do* question their place in the world that sets them apart from their medieval forebears. From the top of society to the barely literate, individuals are reorienting their conception of God, the world, and themselves. In the medieval worldview, the most important subject in a person's life is not the individual himself but God; most medieval autobiographies are personal reflections on the divine will and the sinful life of the author, not a boastful list of personal achievements. In Elizabethan England, the focus begins to shift to the individual: the responsibility for a man's achievements is increasingly attributed to the person himself. God is more of a facilitator than the architect of his successes and failures.

One of the clearest manifestations of how this growing individualism permeates the lives of ordinary people can be found in personal writing. There is practically no such thing as a diary in 1500; people write chronicles about major events, which are structured predominantly to reflect the will of God. But by 1558 the old tradition of the chronicle is beginning to give way to a new literary genre. The "cronacle" of Henry Machyn is a good example. Henry arrives in London from Leicestershire in the early sixteenth century with his brother Christopher, both hoping to make their fortunes in the time-honored fashion. They serve apprenticeships and become members of the Merchant Taylors' Company. They do moderately well. Henry teaches himself to read and becomes the clerk of Little Trinity Parish. This is when he starts writing his "cronacle." He thinks he is continuing the old tradition of Londoners recording the major events of their city; but because he is personally so deeply involved in the life of the city, he actually records what is going on around him, day by day. He describes the processions he witnesses, he lists the executions of those he sees being carted off to Tyburn, and the deaths he records are those of his friends and clients. Unwittingly, Henry has started to write a diary. Although he hardly ever mentions himself or his family by name, his "cronacle" is about *his* life. Coincidentally, in the same years as Henry is writing one of the very first diaries, Edward VI is doing the same thing. Although still only a boy, Edward writes a chronicle of the events going on around him, and, of course, as he is the king, everything he is aware of concerns him personally. By the end of Elizabeth's reign many people are writing diaries and autobiographies, pioneering the personal narratives that are still with us today.

Another character trait that will strike you is the depth of people's courage. When you look at an oceangoing vessel moored in London, Plymouth, or Bristol—no more than a hundred feet from stern to prow—it is hard to believe that anyone dares to set off in one of them. Yet men do, knowing they might face waves thirty or forty feet high, which can easily capsize a ship and smash it to pieces. Tens of thousands of boys and young men sail with the likes of Frobisher, Drake, and Raleigh. Nor are these pioneering sea captains themselves any less bold. Consider the case of Sir Richard Grenville, captain of the *Revenge*. In 1591, after fighting for a whole day single-handedly against a Spanish fleet, with forty men dead on deck, no gunpowder left, gaping holes in the side of his ship, and six feet of water in the hold, you might think he would surrender. Nothing of the sort: Sir Richard vows to fight on, to the death.

Violence and Cruelty

Violence is endemic throughout the kingdom. "The English are universally partial to novelty, hostile to foreigners and not very friendly among themselves," writes the Venetian Michiel Soriano in 1559, adding, "They attempt to do everything that comes into their heads, just as if all that the imagination suggests could be easily executed; hence more insurrections have broken out in this country than in all the rest of the world."[1] It is true that at the top end of society fewer lords take arms and fight than in the past. Even though they are in command of armies, they themselves have become more gentrified—more "gentle." They rarely even fight duels. At the bottom end, however, murder, rape, and robbery are as common as they were two hundred years earlier. Fights often break out in alehouses, with the inevitable result that someone draws a knife and stabs his assailant. Killing a man in self-defense is legal under a law of 1532, but most people caught up in a fight will not hang around to stand trial; they will take flight and evade justice.[2] Over and over again you will find instances of hotheadedness resulting in murder, violent affray being seemingly more common than logical argument. You will also come across calculated killings. Rather than face the humiliation of being named by a maidservant as the father of an illegitimate child, or being accused of rape, some men will murder the pregnant girl before she gives birth. A tailor of Maldon, for instance, kills a girl whom he has impregnated by beating her around the belly, trying to induce a miscarriage; he is hanged for it. You will hear rare but true accounts of starving vagabonds breaking into houses and smashing the skulls of the occupants with an ax, just so they can look for food. Then there are the unprovoked, cold-blooded murders. A London painter-stainer, wishing to relieve a Barking widow of £8 12 shillings, persuades one of the widow's maidservants to steal it for him, and when she brings him the money, he breaks the girl's neck.[3]

Some of the extreme cruelty that we usually associate with the medieval world is in reality more common in Elizabeth's reign. Medieval English kings used to pride themselves on the fact that they did not employ torture except in extraordinary circumstances. As we have seen in the last chapter, Elizabethan society has no such qualms: torture is not just accepted as a necessary evil but officially recognized as an instrument of government. It is used against women as well as men. When Margaret Ward helps a Catholic priest to escape from prison in 1588, she is kept in irons for eight days and suspended by her hands for long periods before being taken to Tyburn and executed. Unlike their medieval ancestors, Elizabethans maim and hang people for vagrancy and burn them for heresy (as we have seen in the case of the Anabaptists). Whether these punishments are more barbaric than being hanged, disemboweled, and quartered is debatable; but both suggest strongly that Elizabethans are no soft touch.

You do occasionally come across official acts of mercy, but they are rare. Some women condemned to death for witchcraft are let off by sheriffs unwilling to kill them for such dubious crimes.[4] More commonly, when children under the age of fourteen are found guilty of theft, they are sentenced to hang but then shown mercy; they are flogged instead. Perhaps it is also worth noting that the cruelest method of execution—being boiled alive—has been repealed as the statutory punishment for poisoning. Nevertheless it is a salutary thought that this punishment was only recently introduced by Henry VIII. It was enacted at least twice in his reign, the last victim being a young woman, Margaret Davy, who was boiled alive in 1542 for poisoning her employer.

Violence and cruelty permeate all areas of life in Elizabethan England. At home it is a father's duty to whip his sons in order to instill in them respect for authority. Similarly, at school a schoolmaster will see it as part of his duty to beat his pupils with a birch, or to rap their hands with a wooden rod. When schooldays are over, the boys will fight in the street, preparing for the disputes of later years, in the tavern, or aboard ship. Young men are trained to serve in the militia, to defend the shores in case of invasion, and that training further sharpens their readiness to draw blood. Thus the Elizabethan character is an amalgam of rashness, boldness, resolution, and violence—all mixed in a heady brew of destructive intolerance. And this behavior in turn feeds back into the harsh rhetoric and pitiless sentiments of society. Enemies of the state, such as Mary, queen of Scots, are regularly described as "enemies of God and friends of Antichrist." When the news that Mary has been beheaded arrives in London on February 9, 1587, church bells ring out, bonfires are lit, and there is feasting and dancing in the streets for a week. The killing allows Elizabethan society a savage release which, to the modern visitor, has more in common with tribal warfare than with civilized society.

Bribery and Corruption

As you have probably gathered by now, there is no equality of opportunity in Elizabethan England. It is taken for granted that everything is hierarchical. Cast your mind back to the beginning of this book and the story of William Hacket, the man who was proclaimed the risen Christ. His two supporters suffer very different fates: one dies in prison and the other is released thanks to his having friends on the privy council. That a man in office might intervene to save a personal friend is considered normal; you might think it corrupt, but the whole of society is a network of people helping each other to get by, and that includes helping to get men out of prison. Therefore, it is not stretching things to say that your life might depend on whom you know.

If you don't know the right people, there is only one other option open to you: bribery. The practice of paying men to deviate from the line of duty is probably as common as paying them wages to stick to it. Sheriffs and magistrates are notoriously open to bribes—and if they are not bribed, they are regularly found extorting sums of money from those they have arrested. Even the election of fellows to university colleges is open to bribery, so much so that an Act of Parliament has to be passed in 1589 to ensure that fellows have some academic merit, not just deep pockets. Bribery is practiced all the way to the top of society. Sir William Cecil has to swear an oath as the queen's principal secretary not to accept any bribes or presents in the performance of his office. Other members of the privy council have fewer scruples. When members of the Vintners' Company try to stop legislation that would restrict their business, they give out presents and hold lavish dinners for their friends in Parliament. Sir William Cecil does not accept any such presents, of course; he is far too circumspect. And the Vintners know better than to try and tempt him. Instead they present his wife with high-quality table linen worth £40.[5]

The whole system of patronage and bribery is likely to leave you feeling that everybody is corrupt. But you will have to get used to it: the state itself adopts similar methods. Perhaps the best example of this is "dead-pay" in the army. When an army is gathered, for example at Leith in 1560, not all the troops receiving pay actually exist: many of them are dead men whose notional presence allows the captains to overcharge the government. At Leith the government is paying the wages of eight thousand soldiers, but in fact there are only five thousand men in the army. The remainder is dead-pay, which goes straight into the captains' pockets. You might think that this is even worse than bribery and nepotism. Nevertheless, in 1562 it becomes official government practice when it is proposed that for every ninety-five soldiers provided, the government will pay for one hundred. Corruption or not, the privy council agrees—on the condition that no more than 8 percent of the wages bill should go on dead-pay.[6]

Wit

If you're in need of some lightheartedness to cope with all this pride and violence, you will find it in the rapid, clever banter of the London play-wrights. You will hear it in the ribald ballads sung or recited in the ale-houses and taverns, mocking those in positions of authority. The plain sarcasm of medieval humor has diminished, replaced by a wit that is wry, intelligent, and heavy with irony. Puns are all the rage, as are quips, satires, and wordplay. So too are practical jokes. Gamaliel Ratsey, a highwayman condemned to hang at Bedford, is at the very moment of death, with the rope around his neck, when he indicates he has something important to say to the sheriff. In front of the crowd, he is let down from the gallows and allowed to speak to the official, who patiently waits as Gamaliel says his piece, which is lengthy. It begins to rain. In fact, it starts to pour. After a few minutes, Gamaliel admits he has nothing to say: he just noticed a storm cloud coming and wanted to see the sheriff and the crowd get thoroughly drenched. Wit on the gallows is noted in several other cases. As George Brooke listens to his executioner and the sheriff argue over who should have his damask gown, he asks them when he should lay his head on the block, adding that he does not know because he has never been beheaded before.

Perhaps the sole requirement of a nation's good humor is that it should be sufficient for its citizens. If so, there is no doubt that English people are well served, for they do love their own wit. "No country's mirth is better than our own," writes Ben Jonson. The queen herself is known for her sense of humor. One day the earl of Oxford breaks wind as he bows down in front of her. Mortified, he leaves court immediately and does not return for seven years. When he finally does come back, the queen greets him cheerfully with the quip "My lord, I had forgotten the fart." One could go on citing examples—and it is hard to resist. "Virtue is like a rich stone, best plain set," smirks Francis Bacon. He also remarks, "Laws are like cobwebs: the small flies are caught and the great ones break through." Sir John Harington, a courtier and the inventor of the water closet, quips: "Treason doth never prosper; what's the reason? For if it prosper, none dare call it treason." Everyone knows the famous poem "The Passionate Shepherd to His Love" by Christopher Marlowe, which begins, "Come live with me and be my love, and we will all the pleasures prove. . . ." In his rejoinder, "The Nymph's Reply to the Passionate Shepherd," Sir Walter Raleigh writes:

> If all the world and love were young,
> And truth in every shepherd's tongue,
> These pretty pleasures might me move
> To live with thee and be thy love.

And so on. Let one more example suffice, for quickness of wit on the spur of the moment. John Manningham of the Middle Temple records in his journal for March 13, 1602, a performance of Shakespeare's play *Richard the Third*, in which Richard Burbage plays the title role. A female member of the audience grows so smitten with Burbage that she urges him to come to her that same night. She tells him to knock on her door and announce himself as "Richard the Third." Shakespeare overhears their conversation, and goes to the lady's chamber first. When the appointed hour arrives Burbage knocks on the door and announces that "Richard the Third" has arrived— only to hear Shakespeare reply from within: "William the Conqueror came before Richard the Third."[7]

Literacy and Printing

Formal education is one of the things that changes rapidly in the sixteenth century. The Tudor monarchs have a huge need for literate men to fill bureaucratic offices, taking on everything from corresponding with foreign agents to the production of baptism, marriage, and burial registers for every parish in the country. With such a high value placed on literacy, people increasingly recognize that there are financial advantages to educating their sons. But more important, the increasing availability of books in English encourages many people to teach themselves to read, including women. While books produced in the previous century were predominantly scholarly in subject matter and mostly written in Latin, in the sixteenth century, recipes for meals, medicines, and means of cleaning can be found in volumes such as *The Good Houswives Treasurie* (1588) and Thomas Dawson's *The Good Huswife's Jewell* (1596). If you want to know which herbs to pick to cure an ailment, you can find the answer in a book; likewise if you want to learn about the history of London or the common law or how to fire a cannon. Thomas Tusser's *Five hundred pointes of good husbandrie* is a good example: it is the essential guide for anyone trying to profit from agriculture. First published in 1573, it is in its thirteenth edition by 1600. There are therefore practical and financial reasons to learn to read in Elizabethan England.

Printing is often described as one of the greatest inventions in human history. It certainly sets the Elizabethan world apart from the medieval. But it is the mass production of books in English that prompts the shift to a more literary culture, not printing itself. Books produced in the fifteenth century were intended to be as fine and desirable as illuminated manuscripts; they were produced in relatively short print runs and were very expensive as a result. They also were predominantly scholarly in subject matter and mostly written in Latin. These could never have induced a revolution in reading. It is the availability of self-help books in English from the 1540s, as well as controversial texts on religion and new works of literature, that induces a revolution in reading.

One book above all others transforms reading: the English Bible. The Bible in the vernacular is the ultimate self-help book, allowing the reader to consider the word of God and its meanings for himself or herself; thus it is the most desired of all books in the sixteenth century. Most copies of William Tyndale's first edition of his translation of the Bible (1526) are destroyed by the authorities as soon as they are printed, but the first authorized translation, "the Great Bible" (1539), quickly becomes a prized possession. The same can be said of the Geneva Bible (1560) and the Bishops' Bible (1568). If you travel through England in 1600, almost every self-respecting yeoman has a Bible in the vernacular, and often a psalter, a prayerbook, or an almanac as well.[8] The desire to read thus takes over from education: people start to teach themselves. As a result, male literacy increases from about 10 percent in 1500 to about 25 percent in 1600. Female literacy similarly increases, from less than 1 percent to about 10 percent.

More than four hundred thousand people in England can read by the end of Elizabeth's reign.

England does not enjoy a free press. Henry VIII introduces censorship in the 1530s. In 1557 Queen Mary brings in the system whereby every publication in England must be registered with the Stationers' Company in London. This is confirmed by Elizabeth in 1559. At the same time it is decreed that all new books must be vetted by six members of the Privy Council. We have already seen how severe the recriminations could be in the case of John Stubbs and his publisher, both of whom have their right hands cut off for publishing a book contrary to the queen's dignity. Censorship severely delays publication too: Philip Stubbes remarks that sometimes authors have to wait months or even years before getting permission for a written work to be registered and published.[9] Plays are also checked before they can be performed, by the queen's Master of the Revels.

In 1586 a Star Chamber decree forbids the operation of printing presses outside London, except one each for the universities of Cambridge and Oxford. Despite these obstacles, the number of publications continues to grow rapidly. The number of books produced annually over Elizabeth's reign increases from 113 titles in 1558 (of which 94 are in English) to 456 in 1603 (of which 406 are in English).[10]

Book production per decade in England[11]

	1500s	1510s	1520s	1530s	1540s	1550s	1560s	1570s	1580s	1590s	1600s
Titles published	425	583	820	1063	1337	1605	1531	2079	2732	3017	4040
Proportion in English	55%	47%	47%	76%	88%	84%	85%	82%	80%	85%	88%

Education

So how do you set about getting a good education for your children in Elizabethan England? The first way is to employ a personal tutor to teach them in the home. In this way the renowned daughters of Sir Anthony Cooke learn their many languages. The same can be said for the unfortunate Lady Jane Grey, who is proficient in Greek, Latin, Hebrew, French, and Italian before her studies are cut short. However, wealth and social privilege do not automatically create scholars out of noble children. Mary, queen of Scots understands Latin but cannot speak it, and she has no knowledge of English except for the few words she picks up in captivity after 1567 (her first language being French).[12] As for young men, there are many whose educational achievements fall short of their fathers' hopes. Part of the problem lies in tutors' being so lowly in status compared with their noble charges that they rarely dare to rebuke them. In a great household, for example, the sons will sit at the high table on the dais while the tutor sits with the servants. If a noble youth doesn't want to sit and study, his tutor is going to have a hard time teaching him.

Tutors are only expected to perform a portion of a young person's education. Ladies will be expected to learn to dance, do needlework, and play an instrument, normally the lute or the virginals, as well as learn Latin and French or Italian. These things they are taught by other ladies and specialist music masters. Young men are expected to master a whole range of skills. Lord Herbert of Cherbury states that gentlemen should learn to dance, fence, ride warhorses, and swim. Some people are of two minds about the swimming, however: they argue that more people have drowned trying to learn how to swim than have been saved through practicing the art. Puritans, as you would expect, are firmly against dancing. As Philip Stubbes writes in a characteristically forthright passage:

> If you would have your son soft, womanish, unclean, smooth-mouthed, affected to bawdry, scurrility, filthy rhymes and unseemly talking; briefly if you would have him as it were transnatured into a woman or worse, and inclined to all kinds of whoredom and abomination, set him to dancing school and to learn music.

The other form of education is schooling. The process begins at a petty school, under the guidance of a local schoolmaster, who will teach your sons to read and write using a horn book—a page inscribed with the alphabet preserved under a sheet of transparent horn and encased in a wooden frame. Schoolmasters these days have to obtain licenses from the local bishop to practice in villages and towns. Some run small schools in their homes; others have taken over the teaching roles previously performed by chantry priests. Some clergymen and their wives see teaching as an act of charity, and give free lessons to boys. A primary education is thus not hard to obtain, if you are keen for your son to be taught. Schools that take girls are much rarer; clergymen might allow a girl to sit in on classes, but most girls who learn to read are taught in the home.

At the age of seven or eight, most farmers' sons will either start work on their fathers' farms or, if their fathers are poor, be apprenticed to other householders, to prepare for a career in service. Those who are lucky enough to go to school full-time will be sent to one of the many grammar schools that are to be found in towns all over the country.

Pupils can expect a studying day of at least ten hours, starting at 6 or 7 a.m. At Eton boys are woken at 5 a.m.; lessons begin at 6 a.m. and go on to 8 p.m. Teaching is generally in Latin and is a matter of learning by rote, the main textbook being William Lily's *Short Introduction of Grammar* (1540). A private school run by Claudius Hollyband in St. Paul's Churchyard teaches Latin until 11 a.m., then breaks for dinner, and teaches French in the afternoon.[13] At Stratford grammar school in the 1560s, the master, John Brownsword, uses the works of the great Christian humanist Erasmus as well as Ovid, Terence, Cicero (normally referred to as "Tully"), Horace, Sallust, and Virgil. He also advocates the teaching of Greek. This shows what a high standard of education is available at Stratford: Greek is taught at only a handful of schools in England. When Ben Jonson later writes that Shakespeare has "small Latin and less Greek," he might be trying to belittle his learning; but think how remarkable it is that a boy educated at a provincial grammar school can have even a smattering of Greek.[14]

Educating boys who would rather be out hunting, swimming, or riding tends to be a confrontational process. Some masters pride themselves on their strictness and attribute their educational achievements to their wielding of the rod. William Horman, sometime headmaster of Eton, has a number of lines in his *Vulgaria* that suggest boys can expect tough tuition, perhaps reflecting his own philosophy of education: "Some children be well-ruled for love, some for fear, some not without beating or correction"; "he made a sore complaint and showed openly his naked body all to be beaten"; or "some be so shrewd to their guiders that they needs be beaten." Needless to say, most people tend not to look back on school as the happiest days of their lives.

If you are on a scholarly path in Elizabethan times, you will go up to Oxford or Cambridge at about the age of fourteen. Elizabethans are proud of their two fine old establishments. Unfortunately there is not enough demand to warrant a third proper university in England. Oxford and Cambridge between them have only about three thousand students. The syllabus is still based on the medieval trivium (logic, rhetoric, and philosophy). After acquiring sufficient skill in these subjects, young men advance to the liberal sciences or quadrivium: arithmetic, geometry, music, and astronomy. Elizabethans call these subjects the "trivials" and "quadrivials" (hence our use of the word "trivial" for something of minor importance). Only after this program of study, which normally takes four years, will you receive your bachelor of arts degree. After three or four more years of study in one of the liberal arts, you may become a master of arts. Most people stop at that point. If you decide to do a third degree, you can choose between a doctorate in civil law or medicine, or continue to study divinity. The last is the hardest option: you must study for a minimum of seven years after receiving your master of arts degree; the actual doctorate then takes another three years. The whole process of becoming a doctor of divinity thus lasts at least eighteen years—so think carefully before embarking on this career path. Given the high mortality in towns, there is a 40 percent chance you will die before you graduate.

Knowledge of the Wider World

Elizabeth's kingdom is not an island, given its border with Scotland. In fact, the whole island of Great Britain becomes a political island—in the sense of being isolated from Europe—only in January 1558, when England's last Continental possession, Calais, falls to the French. Even then Elizabeth still rules over much of Ireland. And there remains a strong desire for England to be part of a greater political unity, with overseas territories, as it has been for centuries. The government conducts lengthy negotiations to try and restore Calais to English hands, and although they are doomed, the idea never goes away. Instead it shifts to America. If England cannot have its Calais in the Old World, then it will build its bridgehead in the New.[15]

What really drives Englishmen to open up the New World, however, is not a political plan or a burning curiosity to discover new places. It is money. In 1562, 1564, and 1567 John Hawkins makes voyages to Guinea in sub-Saharan Africa to capture black slaves to sell for profit in the New World. Although he removes only a few hundred—very few compared with the ten to twelve thousand sold annually by Portuguese traders in

Lisbon—he proves that voyages to Africa can be lucrative. It is a dangerous business. On his 1567 voyage, Hawkins takes two hundred prisoners on the Cape Verde Islands, but when he sails across the Atlantic to sell his slaves he is attacked by a Spanish fleet. His entire crew of two hundred mariners is forced to flee in two boats, and, unable to transport so many men back to England, he leaves a hundred of them behind at a port in the Gulf of Mexico where they are later killed by the Spanish. Hawkins himself finally makes it back to Cornwall in January 1569. In 1588 he receives a knighthood to add to the crest that the queen granted him in 1565, which incorporates the image of a chained black slave.

Sailing with Hawkins on that ill-fated 1567 voyage is a young man from Devon called Francis Drake. The trip leaves him with a vision of the wealth to be seized and a thirst for revenge on the Spaniards who have killed so many of his fellow mariners. In 1572 he manages to capture the annual Spanish convoy bringing bullion back from the New World. Eight years later he achieves an even greater feat when he completes a circumnavigation and, in so doing, becomes the first man to captain a ship all the way around the world (see Chapter Seven). He returns to England a hero. Quite how much money he brings back to Plymouth only Drake himself knows, but the Spanish believe it to be 1.5 million pesos—over £600,000, or twice the English government's annual revenue. Drake surrenders a large portion of this to the queen and in exchange receives a knighthood. Unsurprisingly, his success and fame prompt other men to follow his example. The second English captain to sail round the world, Thomas Cavendish, sets out in 1586; when he returns in 1588 blue damask sails decorate his ships and gold chains the necks of his men.

The success of men like Hawkins, Drake, and Cavendish facilitates the expansion of England's overseas trade. But the idea of an empire—overseas dominions—does not come from an explorer but originates with a historian. In November 1577 Dr. John Dee is studying the history of the Celtic people of Britain. Learning that the Welsh prince Madoc sailed to America in the twelfth century and that King Arthur conquered not only parts of France and Germany but also the North Pole (according to the old romances), Dee believes that Elizabeth should reclaim these lost territories because she is the heir to both the Welsh princes and King Arthur. On November 22, 1577, he rides to see the queen at Windsor.[16] The intellectual seeds of empire are planted.

In June 1578 Humphrey Gilbert receives official letters from Elizabeth that give him the right, for six years, to search out and settle remote lands that are not already in the hands of a Christian monarch, and to hold them from the queen as his own lordship. Elizabeth's government has gone beyond sanctioning armed trading and piracy and begun a policy of conquest and settlement. Gilbert claims Newfoundland for the queen (and himself) on August 5, 1583: it is Elizabeth's first territorial acquisition. Gilbert dies on the return voyage, but his half-brother, Walter Raleigh, is inspired to take up where he left off, sending out expeditions to Virginia, where Roanoke is founded in 1585. It does not thrive: English sailors return the following year to find the inhabitants starving, and by 1590 the settlement is abandoned. Raleigh sends another expedition in 1587 to establish a farming colony, but that too is unsuccessful. Nevertheless the English persevere. The first permanent settlement in America is established at Jamestown in 1607.

Geographic knowledge does not just remain with the captains and navigators who sail with Hawkins, Drake, and Cavendish. Crew members write accounts of their voyages. The remarkable Thomas Harriot, who learns Algonquian from two native Americans in England before traveling to Roanoke, publishes his *Briefe and true report of the new found land of Virginia* in 1588. Other writers collect eyewitness accounts. By far the most influential of these is Richard Hakluyt, who publishes *Divers Voyages Touching the Discoverie of America* in 1582 and the first edition of his greatest work, *The Principal Navigations, Voyages, Traffiques and Discoveries of the English Nation* in 1589. And it is not just English travel accounts that are published; many writers, including Hakluyt himself, search out works by foreign authors about their discoveries. The first of these, giving details of the Spanish discoveries in America, is Richard Eden's *Decades of the New World,* published in 1555.

As for knowledge in the other direction, Englishmen have been traveling across Northern Europe to Asia since the Middle Ages. There were English agents in the Grand Duchy of Muscovy (modern Russia) in the fourteenth century, and the English maintain close contact with the kingdoms of Denmark and Sweden through the trade in Baltic timber and fish. In the second half of the sixteenth century, such ventures are placed on a more formal footing with the establishment of large companies to finance them. The Muscovy Company is established in 1555; many London merchants regard trade with the grand duchy as much more profitable than venturing into the New World, as it does not entail fighting with Spaniards. Another important group of international traders, the Merchant Adventurers of London, is given a new charter in 1564. Martin Frobisher establishes his Cathay Company in 1577 and tries three times to sail to China through the Northwest Passage—an impossible task in the sixteenth century. In 1579 the Eastland Company is established, with a depot at Elbing in Poland, and the following year sees the foundation of the Levant Company. The Barbary Company trading with Morocco is set up in 1585.

At the same time, more and more private merchants are finding their way around the world. For sheer endurance and determination in subzero temperatures, you have to take your hat off to John Davis, whose career takes him from the freezing seas of the Falkland Islands (and a diet consisting of only penguin) to Baffin Bay, west of Greenland. Hardly less inspiring is the journey of Ralph Fitch, who spends nine years traveling through Asia, returning to England in 1591. Partly as a result of Fitch's experiences, the English East India Company is established in 1600. The company's first expedition, under James Lancaster, sails from Torbay to Indonesia, establishing an English trading post in Java. The most remarkable of all Eastern adventurers, however, is Will Adams from Gillingham in Kent. Having previously sailed with Drake and searched for a Northeast Passage to China by sailing north of Siberia, he serves with the Barbary Company. Changing employer yet again in 1598, he becomes the pilot for a fleet of five Dutch ships sailing to Japan, landing there in 1600. It takes eleven years for a letter by Adams to reach England but nevertheless, by the end of the reign, Queen Elizabeth's subjects have traveled the whole globe and met the shogun Tokugawa Ieyasu; they can tell stories of the splendors of civilizations on every continent—not to speak of disease-ridden tropics and frozen wastes.

All this is the stuff of legend—but what does the housewife in the marketplace know of faraway lands? Most people know about different types of imported foodstuffs—oranges, pomegranates, and sugar—and where they come from, even if they cannot afford them. They are familiar with the most famous exotic beasts, such as lions, camels, tigers, and elephants, and can picture them from stories they have been told. But unless they themselves travel, their knowledge is superficial. William Horman informs his young charges that "a camel will bear more burden of packs than three horses" and "will go an hundred mile in a day"; yet he also notes that "there is such hatred between the dragons and the elephant that one will kill the other," and that "the ostrich is greatest of all birds and eats and digests iron." While you might find a cup fashioned out of a coconut in a goldsmith's shop in London and even come across a porcelain bowl imported from China, you will find great ignorance of the customs and religion of the regions where these things come from.

Only the nobility and gentry travel overseas purely for the sake of their education. The grand tour through Germany to Italy is beginning to become popular as a good way for a young gentleman to finish his education. The inspiration for it derives partly from the increased teaching of the classics, partly an awareness of the Renaissance—just think how many references there are in Shakespeare to Italians compared with French, Spaniards, or Germans—and partly from new publications in English about the regions of Italy. It is also the result of many English Protestants seeking asylum in Protestant Germany and in the tolerant cities of Padua and Venice during the reign of Queen Mary. When these émigrés return to England in Elizabeth's reign, they talk glowingly about the wonders of Italy. Richard Smith, journeying in the company of Sir Edward Unton in 1563, writes about all the places they visit. Here he describes a crocodile they see in Venice:

a certain horrible beast which was taken in Ethiopia nine months before we saw him. This beast was supposed to be a crocodile. He was by estimate about fourteen foot long, his scales so hard and thick that no pike was able to pierce him to do him a great harm. His hind legs were longer than his fore legs, his nails great and long, his tail cutting like a saw, his head long, his mouth very wide [and] his teeth very great. He was taken with great iron hooks and a sheep's head and a great chain of iron.[17]

Smith is less impressed with the local people, writing that the citizens of Padua "differ much in apparel from the Venetians although little in pride and deceitfulness," and he regularly castigates the Italians as "sluttish" and "crafty beggars." In 1597 Sir Thomas Chaloner writes to the earl of Essex that "a rabble of English roam now in Italy."[18] Everyone wants to see Rome; but people also want to learn the different manners and customs of foreign countries, try the different clothes, taste the strange food, and see the pretty women. Commenting on the beauty of the local women is the one thing that English diarists traveling abroad share with foreign travelers in England.

Attitudes to Foreigners

The word "foreigner" does not just mean a denizen of an overseas country: it means someone who does not come from the same town or city as you. People make a distinction between English "foreigners" and people from overseas, whom they call "aliens." If you go to the theater you will see the latter presented in archetypal ways according to their nation: all Italians are shown as deceivers, all Frenchmen are fops, and all Dutchmen boors. Turks are always bloody and Moors lascivious and devilish.[19] The polymath Andrew Boorde writes about the countries of Europe in a similar manner, describing each nation in rhyme:

> I am a poor man born in Norway
> Hawks and fish of me merchants do buy all day
> And I was born in Iceland, as brute as a beast,
> When I eat candle's ends I am at a feast.
> Tallow and raw stockfish I do love to eat—
> In my country it is right good meat.

And so on for each nation. According to Boorde, the Cornish are the worst cooks and the worst brewers in the world, the Welsh are all poor and given to thieving, and the Irish are just poor. The Flemish are all drunkards and eat butter. The Dutch make good cloth but are too partial to English beer. Brabanters are praised except for their similar propensity to drink too much. Germans are idle and will not change their style of costume. Danes too are lazy, and Poles eat honey all the time.

Attitudes to the French are complicated. England and France have been at war, intermittently, for centuries. The war comes to an end in 1564, after which attitudes are less bellicose; but an undercurrent of hostility remains. Until 1585, when the Spanish war breaks out, the French are the only real Continental threat to English security. On the other hand, if an Englishman has been abroad, he has almost certainly traveled through France; if he speaks just one foreign language, it is almost certainly French. Boorde is noticeably positive about the French, commenting on their inventiveness, especially in clothing. So there can be familiarity and respect as well as distrust toward people abroad.

English attitudes as perceived by the foreigners themselves tend to reflect hostility, ignorance, and suspicion. The Venetian Michiel Soriano comes out with his "hostile to foreigners" comment (mentioned above) even though the Republic of Venice is relatively tolerant of English people at the time. Alessandro Magno, also of Venice, comments on the suspicious way everyone looks at him when he goes to hear a Catholic Mass at the house of an ambassador in 1562.[20]

These comments come from wealthy travelers who are just visiting England. If their experiences are so negative, what are things like for the thousands of immigrants who permanently reside in the kingdom? From the very start of the reign, Protestants come to London seeking safety from Catholic persecution in Holland, Spain, and France. In 1563 the government becomes increasingly concerned and creates a census of foreigners in the capital: the total stands at 4,543. The numbers swell dramatically when the Dutch Calvinists flee from the duke of Alva in 1567; the 1568 census reveals 9,302 foreigners in London, of whom 7,163 are Dutch and 1,674 French. Another large influx of Huguenots (French Protestants) arrives in 1572, after the St. Bartholomew's Day Massacre.

The presence of so many foreigners worries Londoners. Many fear that the foreign merchants will take away their trade. They also bitterly resent the fact that the newcomers do not have to obey the same customs as English citizens.[21] The government fears (rightly) that there are spies among the immigrants and that the various factions among them are bringing in both radical Protestant and Catholic propaganda.[22] Cultural differences are accentuated by the immigrants' worshipping in French, Italian, and Dutch Calvinist churches; for a short while, there is even a Spanish Calvinist church in London.[23] Such isolation irritates many people, who remark on the foreigners' lack of community spirit. Sir Walter Raleigh declares in 1593 that charity is wasted on immigrants, who do not support the queen, and who take the profits that should rightly go to Englishmen.[24] John Stow echoes these sentiments, stating that thirty years ago, when there were just three Dutch people living in the parish of St. Botolph, it used to raise £27 every year to help the poor. But now, with thirty households of Dutch people in the parish, barely £11 can be gathered, "for the stranger will not contribute to such charges as other citizens do."[25] For all these reasons, the privy council adopts the policy of moving immigrants out to provincial towns—but they are hardly any more welcome there. In Halstead in Essex, a small Dutch community incurs the hatred of the local populace, which accuses them of practicing offensive trades, making water filthy, and causing nuisances. They are forced to leave their homes and return to Colchester.[26]

Attitudes to foreigners are not entirely negative. French and Spanish dress is deemed sophisticated and alluring, and foreign styles are adopted by everyone trying to create a good impression.[27] Dutch starching is enthusiastically taken up in the 1560s. Immigrant Italians are praised for their musical abilities and their instrument-making skills. Quite a large number become naturalized citizens. And some individuals show that immigrants can become accepted in society. No one speaks ill of Sir Horatio Palavicino. He gives up his Italian citizenship and becomes English in 1586 (receiving letters patent to that effect). Moreover, he advises the queen on the economy and has a fortune reputed to be in the region of £100,000 by the time of his death in 1600. That much money commands universal respect.

Racism

Black people, Native Americans, and Ottoman Turks are seen by Elizabethans as fundamentally different. Such people are not Christians, and so it is not possible to appeal to common virtues and morals, which makes them doubly foreign. The result is a cruel racism. This is not a peculiarly English trait; racist attitudes are endemic throughout sixteenth-century Europe. But while Turks are simply dismissed as heathens, and Gypsies rejected as vagabonds and thieves, the sub-Saharan African exemplifies all that the Elizabethan Englishman finds strange and incomprehensible.

Africans are called "Moors," "Blackamoors," "Ethiopians," "Nigers" or "Negros." Andrew Boorde divides them into "white moors and black moors" and states that the latter are taken as slaves "to do all manner of service but they be set most commonly to vile things." André Thevet, author of *The New Found Worlde* (1568), explains that those of the north of Africa are "brown colored, whom we call white Moors, others are clean black: the most parte go all naked." Thevet adds that the heat of their climate makes black women promiscuous and the men "poor, ignorant and brutish." Robert Gainsh's account of an English voyage to Guinea in 1554 (which brings back half a dozen black slaves to England) reports that the inhabitants of Central Africa live in "horrible wildernesses and mountains" among "wild and monstrous beasts and serpents," adding that "women are common for they contract no matrimony neither have respect to chastity." Writing in 1559, William Cunningham agrees that black people are "savage, monstrous and rude." In 1577 an edition of Richard Eden's *History of Travayle in the West and East Indies* describes the land of "the black Moors called Ethiopians or Negros, all which are watered with the river Negro, called in old time Niger. In the said regions are no cities but only certain low cottages made of boughs of trees plastered with chalk and covered with straw." He explains that the inhabitants are, apart from a few Muslims, "pure gentiles and idolators, without profession of any religion or other knowledge of God."[28]

To be fair to Elizabethans, their views are affected by preconceived notions of the Garden of Eden and the subsequent Fall from Grace. It is possible to discern some respect for the black man: he is living in a natural world, unchanged since Creation. When Elizabeth knights Sir Francis Drake, on April 4, 1581, on the deck of the *Golden Hind,* she gives him a present of a locket; on the inside is a miniature portrait of herself by Nicholas Hilliard and, on the outside, an image of a black man engraved in sardonyx, set in gold, and surrounded by pearls, rubies, and diamonds.[29] The memento combines the queen's image with that of a black man. But although you might occasionally notice such indications of respect for the "noble savage," there is no escaping the fact that the vast majority of interracial exchanges are fundamentally exploitative and un-Christian.

As the slave trade becomes more established and more lucrative, so the racism becomes worse. In 1578 George Best argues that black skin has nothing to do with the heat of the sun (on the evidence that a black African man and a white Englishwoman will produce a black child). He concludes that black people are damned because of illicit fornication by one of Noah's sons in the Ark. By 1584 black skin is being linked with witchcraft. In this year Reginald Scot publishes his *Discoverie of Witchcraft,* in which he describes an ugly devil as having "horns on his head, fire in his mouth, a tail, eyes like a bison, fangs like a dog, claws like a bear, *a skin like a Niger* and a voice roaring like a lion." Soon the godless, naked, sexually promiscuous inhabitants of Central Africa are associated with Satan himself, who is often portrayed as black in English religious pictures.

These views are to be noted at all levels of society. The playwrights Christopher Marlowe, George Peele, Francis Beaumont, and John Fletcher all describe royal personages being drawn in their chariots by black men. James VI of Scotland—Elizabeth's successor as ruler of England—makes such a scene reality, and has black slaves pull him along in a coach. In Shakespeare's *Titus Andronicus* (1593), Aaron the Moor is loved by Tamora, the queen of the Goths, who has a child by him; but Aaron is a man party to "murders, rapes and massacres, acts of black night, abominable deeds." He himself murders an innocent nurse to cover up his adultery with Tamora. He is not portrayed as ignorant; indeed, there is a fierce intelligence in him. Shakespeare gives him the line: "Look how the black slave smiles upon the father, as who should say: 'Old lad, I am thine own.'" But the character is still not a kind one. Not until Shakespeare writes *Othello*, in 1604, does he produce a sympathetic portrait of a black character.

The slave trade does not result in huge numbers of Africans coming to England. In fact, the queen discourages the slavers from bringing them here, on the grounds that there are already too many unemployed people in England. In 1596 she even gives a license to a Lübeck merchant to transport them out of the country. But a fashion for black servants has begun to take root. The queen herself has some in the royal household in 1574–75; she also employs black musicians and dancers.[30] Sir William Pole, Sir John Hawkins, Sir Walter Raleigh, and Sir Francis Drake all keep black servants. Apart from gentlemen's houses, you will come across black people most frequently in ports. They are invariably described in ways that make it clear they are still owned. In Plymouth, for example, in 1583 there is "Bastien, a blackamoor of Mr. William Hawkins," and ten years later we learn of "Christian, Richard Sheere's blackamoor." As the name suggests, the crucial thing for any black person living in England is to be baptized: it is the essential first step toward becoming acceptable in a society that associates black skin with the devil.[31]

Scientific Knowledge

The sixteenth century has left us with a number of household names in the world of science. In astronomy we have Copernicus, author of *De Revolutionibus Orbium Celestium* (1543), in which he suggests that the Earth orbits the sun. In anatomy we have Vesalius's *De Humani Corporis Fabrica*

(1543), the first detailed look at the workings of the human body. And in medicine there is the work of Paracelsus, whose use of chemical substances to treat ailments has a profound effect on medical science. The silver-nosed Tycho Brahe—who lost his nose in a duel—catalogs the stars, and at the end of the century Galileo not only demonstrates the correctness of Copernicus's theory but makes a whole series of discoveries: from the moons of Jupiter to the existence of sunspots, from the constancy of the speed at which objects fall to the regularity of the swinging of a pendulum. You could say that all these men are explorers, in a manner of speaking, and that Columbus is the inspiration to them all, for he has demonstrated unequivocally that the ancient Greeks and Romans did not know everything. In fact, Copernicus's discoveries in astronomy have earned him the epithet "the Columbus of the heavens." But all these men are Continental: Copernicus is Polish, Vesalius Flemish, Paracelsus German, Brahe Danish, and Galileo Italian. Is there no English genius to rival these famous pioneers of science?

England is home to a number of groundbreaking scientists—or practitioners of "natural philosophy," to use the correct Elizabethan terminology. Natural philosophy is an inquiry into the truth of the world, and thus there is no conceptual difference between a geographer and a scientist. Someone using mathematics to establish the width of the Atlantic is as much a "natural philosopher" as an astronomer. It is not surprising that English "scientific" discoveries go hand in hand with English imperial ambitions. As explorers set out to find new countries overseas, natural philosophers are in ever-increasing demand to answer questions of navigation, astronomy, mathematics, and physics. Discoveries of new lands bring knowledge of new animals, new plants, and new medicines; in turn, they inspire the classification of all the known plants and animals to assist further inquiries. The scientific and geographical exploration of the Earth and the stars can thus be construed as one great multifaceted experiment: a loop of discovery and inquiry that results in exponentially increased levels of scientific activity.

Dr. John Dee and his pupil Thomas Digges are both inspired by Copernicus's *De Revolutionibus Orbium Celestium* and write approvingly of his theory. Soon, however, these astronomers start to ask even more fundamental questions about the nature of the universe. A new comet in the sky in 1572 reveals to Digges that, contrary to Aristotle's teaching, the stars are not fixed in their places; the heavens are not crystalline in their structure;

and the moving celestial objects—the moon, Mercury, Venus, the sun, Mars, Jupiter, and Saturn—do not all revolve around the Earth.[32] In 1583 Digges revises his father's almanac, which recites all the pre-Copernican beliefs and the Aristotelian concept of the heavens, and in an addendum explains why Copernicus's theory of the planets orbiting the sun is correct. He even shows how Aristotle came to be so wrong.[33]

Three other men are obvious candidates for the most influential English natural philosopher of Elizabeth's reign. The statesman Francis Bacon deserves mention not for any particular discovery but because he formulates the modern scientific approach—the "Baconian method"—in his great work, *Novum Organum*. Although it will not be published until 1620, Bacon is very much a man of Elizabeth's reign; born in 1561, he is the son of Sir Nicholas Bacon and nephew of Sir William Cecil. Bacon argues that, through a process of experimenting and identifying the criteria for a phenomenon, you can develop a hypothesis which can then be tested. He lays the foundation for a form of research that is intellectually far superior to simply looking for answers in the books of writers from the ancient world. No doubt that sounds obvious to you—but while it is true that many natural philosophers in Elizabeth's reign are already applying this method, they are being dismissed by contemporaries who will not shift their faith in the old authorities. Thomas Blundeville, for example, publishes a book in 1594 in which he ridicules Copernicus for his theory that the Earth orbits the sun, stating that: "Ptolemy, Aristotle, and all other old writers affirm the Earth to be in the midst, and to remain unmoveable and to be in the very center of the world, proving the same . . . the Holy Scripture affirming the foundations of the Earth to be laid so sure that it never should move at any time."[34] Anyone who has listened to an aging professor spouting rubbish and telling you that *you* must believe it because *he* read it in a book will surely look at Bacon with gratitude and respect.

The second great English natural philosopher is Thomas Harriot—the same Harriot who teaches himself Algonquian and sails to America in 1584. Having charted the Roanoke area and written his book on Virginia, he devotes his time to mathematics. He works out a means of correcting the apparent distortions of Mercator's projection of the world in two dimensions. He discovers the sine law of refraction, establishes how to describe the parabola of a cannonball in flight, and makes the first ever astronomical observations using a telescope. Not only does he apply the instrument to the moon's surface four months before Galileo, he makes observations about Jupiter's satellites and sunspots before the great Italian. And astronomy is just his hobby: his main achievement is in the field of algebra.

Probably the greatest Elizabethan natural philosopher, however, is William Gilbert. A trained physician, he is highly successful in his medical practice and obtains a coat of arms in 1577. Being acquainted with the explorers Francis Drake and Thomas Cavendish, he becomes interested in nautical affairs, especially the mathematics of navigation. He publishes his great work *De Magnete* in 1600. In this book he argues that the Earth is one great lodestone or magnet. He explains how the nautical compass works and puts forward suggestions as to how mariners might calculate longitude as well as latitude. He demonstrates that magnetism is an immaterial force, capable of operating through solid bodies and empty space. He is one of the first to formulate the idea that space is a vacuum and that the Earth revolves along the axis of its magnetic poles. Galileo sits up and takes note. But that is not all. Gilbert is also the father of electricity, on account of his experiments with new electrostatic substances and his observations of the electrostatic properties of matter.[35]

It is fitting that, when it finally appears, Bacon's *Novum Organum* has a picture of a ship as its frontispiece, sailing off in search of new lands. Science as exploration enlarges the understanding of the flora and fauna of the world. The famous botanist John Gerard produces *The herball, or the Generall historie of plantes* in 1597. This is a truly impressive work, containing references to every plant imaginable, including exotica such as the "Indian nut tree." Coconuts have been known for many years—cups have been made out of them since the late Middle Ages—but Gerard's book contains an image of the actual tree as well as the fruit, and a description of the leaves and the white flesh of the nut as well as the taste of the milk.[36] His work is methodologically much more thorough than that of earlier botanists too. He notes, for example, that although it is commonly supposed that the mandrake takes the shape of a man's legs and will shriek and cause the death of the man that uproots it, this is

> false and most untrue. For I myself and my servants also have dug up, planted, and re-planted very many: & yet never could either perceive shape of man or woman, but sometimes one straight root, sometimes

two, and often six or seven branches coming from the main great root.[37]

The educated elite in Elizabethan society now has the intellectual means to question received knowledge and to direct new research. It is not surprising that one in ten books published during the reign is in a field of science.[38]

Superstition and Witchcraft

Mathematical brilliance and minds attuned to scientific experimentation are perhaps to be expected among the educated elite, but what about the more humble elements of society? When writers tell you that you can cause a man to feel great pain by burning his excrement, that you should not lend fire to a neighbor or else your horses will die, or that if a woman loses her hose in the street it means her husband is unfaithful, you have to suspect that your worldview may not be compatible with those of the locals.[39]

Today we commonly take for granted that there is a fundamental conflict between scientific knowledge and religious beliefs. It is also widely assumed that, as science expands its reach, so superstition and religion diminish.[40] These assumptions are wrong. Just as the typical sixteenth-century man cannot separate the physical from the metaphysical (as we have seen in the previous chapter), so he cannot separate scientific knowledge from his faith. In fact, many discoveries are rooted in religion. One sixteenth-century medical work carries a pertinent quotation from the Bible on its title page: "God hath created medicines of the earth and he that is wise will not condemn them."[41] Ordinary people express similar views. Maria Thynne comments to her husband, "Though God's power can work miracles, yet we cannot build upon it that because He can, He will, for then He would not say He made herbs for the use of man."[42] Some believe that God has created remedies for all the diseases in the world in the form of plants and mankind has a spiritual duty to discover them through expanding its botanical knowledge. It follows therefore that any scientific discoveries which help men navigate the world and bring back exotic remedies also have their divine purpose. Religion is the father of science.

Given this, it is hardly surprising that natural philosophy extends far beyond what we would consider the boundaries of science. Numerology, alchemy, and astrology are just three of the pseudo-sciences that are regarded as quite acceptable subjects for natural philosophers. Numerology has a long history; in the words of John Dee: "All things (which from the very first being of things, have been framed and made) do appear to be formed by the reason of numbers."[43] Alchemy is the old chemistry that inspired Paracelsus and which still has many practitioners. In 1564 the queen makes a contract with an alchemist called Cornelius Alvetanus to manufacture 50,000 marks of pure gold each year. Unfortunately for both parties, he fails and is locked in the Tower for his deception.[44] As for astrology, while some people deplore attempts to discern the future from looking at the stars, it is a valid branch of scientific investigation for many others. The physician Simon Forman consults his astrological charts not only to know the best time to draw blood or to diagnose a sickness but also to predict his clients' future. In 1601 seventy-two women visit him seeking astrological advice: they ask him about their marriage prospects, whether certain men love them, when and if their seafaring husbands will return home, whether they should set out on a journey, and whether they should buy property. Clergymen too rely on the stars: a Mr. Broughton comes to Simon seeking information on whether he will be made dean of Chester Cathedral.[45] Even the government has been known to ask for astrological advice. Dr. John Dee is summoned to cast a horoscope to divine the most auspicious date for Elizabeth's coronation in 1559.[46]

Men explore superstitious phenomena in the belief that they are investigating the real world. The very sense that *anything is possible* is what allows experimentation to be so open-minded. If you can't distinguish between scientific truth and superstitious belief, it is not irrational to investigate any phenomenon as if it might be a scientific truth. In 1582 Dr. Dee embarks on a series of experiments with another alchemist, Edward Kelley; together they seek knowledge of angels through séances. In April 1587 an angel called Madimi orders the two men to hold everything in common, even to the extent of sharing their wives with each other. They seek clarification "whether the sense is of carnal use (contrary to the seventh Commandment) or of Spiritual love." "Carnal use," replies the angel. Who are they to stand in the way of science? The alchemists and their wives duly comply.

As you can see, ignorance shades into superstition and credulity, and these in turn shade into faith and knowledge, just as they do today. Dreams are interesting: no one can deny that they happen, but *why* do they happen, and what do they mean? Many people believe that dreams can be interpreted systematically to establish the future, just as the biblical Joseph explained the pharaoh's dreams. In 1576 Thomas Hill publishes his *The Most Pleasant Art of the Interpretation of Dreams*. If you open his book at random, you find the statement "If a woman dreameth that her lover cometh to present her a swine's head as a friendly gift, declareth that she shall after hate her lover and forsake him, for the hog is ungrateful to Venus's works." On the facing page there is something even more bizarre: if a man "dreameth that he hath three privy members standing together" it means he was an apprenticed servant and is now a free man and will have three names where once he had but one. But if he dreams that three ears of corn are growing out of his breast, and he has them plucked away, he will have two sons who "through an evil calamity and mishap shall be slain and thieves also beset his house."[47] Odd, you may think, and hardly scientific. But dream interpretation intrigues all generations—you only have to think of Freudian psychoanalysis to realize Thomas Hill is not alone in trying to interpret dreams meaningfully.

Ghosts are another interesting case. In the modern world, many people still believe in ghosts. In the sixteenth century, the denial of Purgatory by Protestants implies that the souls of the deceased go straight to Heaven or Hell and so they cannot return to Earth. The Puritan William Perkins is therefore astounded that good Protestant folk can be so "ignorant" as to believe that the dead might reappear. However, as Shakespeare's plays *Hamlet* and *Macbeth* both show, the belief that the ghosts of the dead might appear between midnight and cockcrow is as current in Protestant England as it was in the Catholic Middle Ages. In 1599 Thomas Platter remarks on a building near Tyburn so haunted that no one can live in it.[48] Yet there are many superstitions which are not shared by all; indeed, there are some skeptics. Although William Horman's *Vulgaria* includes such superstitious lines as "Old witches do make a great matter of paring of a man's fingernails," you are also told that "the readers of dreams often times expound them more to please than to say truth," and that "the world can never be delivered clearly of superstitious opinions." Obviously, Horman himself is a skeptic. Another line reads:

> Some make search and divination by water, some by basins, some by axes, some by glasses, some by the nail of the finger, some by dead carrion, some by conjuring of a soul, and such other and all be accursed or peevish; yet lewd folk take great heed and credence of such things.

There you have it. Although sixteenth-century knowledge incorporates much that we call superstition, there are Elizabethan skeptics who disbelieve many of the old wives' tales and folklore of the time. Given that most people don't rightly know whether the Earth goes around the sun or the sun goes around the Earth, it is hardly surprising that people have doubts about the meanings of dreams and the existence of ghosts.

Witchcraft

In 1552, when Elizabeth is still a young woman, Bishop Latimer writes: "A great many of us, when we be in trouble or sickness, or lose anything, we run hither and thither to witches or sorcerers, whom we call wise men." Eighteen years after her death we read in Robert Burton's famous *Anatomy of Melancholy*, "Sorcerers are too common; cunning men, wizards and white witches, as they call them, in every village, which, if they be sought unto, will help almost all infirmities of body and mind."[49] Across the reign, therefore, you will find a widespread belief in the power of witchcraft. In some places it is the fourth most common form of crime, after sexual offenses, nonattendance at church, and violent assault.[50] You might think of it as a superstition, but in Elizabethan England witches not only exist, they are *officially recognized in law* as having the power to hurt and kill people with their cunning. If you are accused of bringing about someone's death through witchcraft, you might end up being sentenced to hang for the crime—even if you have no idea of how to cast a spell.

Note: you risk being hanged, not burned. The English do not burn people for witchcraft; that sort of thing goes on only in Scotland and Continental Europe. In England witchcraft is not regarded as a religion or a heresy: in theory you can be a good Christian and a witch. Witches at this time do not yet congregate as a body, nor do they celebrate the sabbat together— that all comes later, in the next century.[51] Nor are witches yet presumed to make a compact with the devil; that too is a later development. There is even a time in Elizabeth's reign when, technically speaking, witchcraft is not against the law. In 1542 an act of Henry VIII makes witchcraft a hanging offense, but it is repealed on the king's death in 1547; thereafter, there is no anti-witchcraft law until the Witchcraft Act of 1563. This is far more lenient than Henry VIII's legislation. It does not sanction the execution of all practitioners of the dark arts, nor does it condemn witches to death for the lesser magic arts of finding lost things, destroying cattle and goods, or causing men to fall in love. The 1563 act makes it a felony only (1) to invoke evil spirits for any purpose whatsoever; and (2) to cause the death of someone by witchcraft. That is all. If an attempt to kill someone through witchcraft is proved but unsuccessful—if the victim is only maimed, for example, or if only animals are killed—then the punishment is merely a year in prison, albeit with quarterly appearances in the pillory.[52] Even when someone is found guilty of murder by witchcraft, the authorities are very cautious about rushing to hang the culprit. In 1565 Matilda Parke and Alice Meade, both of Exeter, are convicted of practicing magic upon their fellow citizens but the magistrates do all they can to avoid hanging them.[53]

Nevertheless, be careful if you are tempted to dabble in witchcraft. If your neighbor claims you went to her house and said threatening words to her, and then her son or daughter grows sick and dies, you might be arrested, tried, and hanged for witchcraft. Witnesses will be examined as to whether you may have dealt with any familiars, especially toads or cats. Your body will be searched for signs of unnatural marks: by these you are supposed to feed blood to your familiars to reward them. If one is found, it will be pricked to see whether it hurts; if someone does this to you in court, scream your head off, as it will be presumed otherwise that it is a mark of the devil. If you are accused of sorcery, witnesses will be asked to testify that you spoke with named infernal spirits, such as Marbas (who can cure all diseases), Furcas (who will give you cunning), Asmodai (who can help you become invisible), or Allocer (who will procure you the love of any woman).[54] It is difficult to defend yourself against such accusations: often it will be just your word against your enemy's.

This brings us to one last point about witchcraft: it is heavily biased against women. The 1563 act itself is not sexist but, despite this, 90 percent of those accused of witchcraft in England are women.[55] You may suspect that this is a consequence of women being so thoroughly disempowered by society; for many women, their only chance to get back at those who have wronged them is by way of spells and curses. Alternatively you may suspect that accusations of witchcraft are entirely made up and just another form of female oppression. Either way, as you ride along the leafy lanes of England, and notice an isolated thatched cottage set back from the road, bear in mind that it may very well contain a witch. And if you say that she does not have the power to kill or harm you, the other villagers will think *you* are the one who is deluded.

A Sense of History

Elizabethan people have a heightened awareness of their place in history, unlike their medieval forebears. If you look at medieval paintings of biblical scenes, the people from the ancient world wear medieval dress, wield medieval weapons, and sail medieval ships. The rulers may have changed, but to the medieval mind, life is the same now as it was fifteen hundred years ago: harvests fail and plagues come and go, kings are toppled and kingdoms invaded. In marked contrast, intelligent Elizabethan people realize that they are fundamentally different from their distant forebears. "A long-sleeved gown was despised of the Romans," notes William Horman. A carved wooden chimneypiece at Holdenby House in Northamptonshire depicts centurions in *Roman* armor, boots, and short tunics—very different from any dress in the sixteenth century.

What has brought about this awareness of historical change? Francis Bacon gives a succinct answer in *Novum Organum:* "Printing, gunpowder and the compass: these three have changed the whole face and state of things throughout the world." But a sense of technological advancement is only part of the story. Anyone in England can see that the old way of life has gone. The great abbeys are in ruins; farmers now pile their grain in monastic granges; and merchants stock their goods in the empty halls of the friaries. Aristocratic families are busy renovating their old castles, building spacious domestic quarters within the old walls, complete with large expanses of glazing, ornate gardens, and long galleries. In 1574, in a semi-derelict chapel in Wigmore Castle in Herefordshire, Dr. John Dee finds heaps of old documents dumped on the floor, where they have been lying since the last member of the lordly family died in 1425.[56] All over the country educated gentlemen are making similar discoveries in old chambers dripping with lost time.

This sense of a world that is irretrievably lost encourages some men to record as much as they can of the past. The biggest impetus comes from John Leland, who travels the length and breadth of England and Wales between 1535 and 1543, describing the old castles, palaces, churches, and towns he visits. He consults old documents and searches the remains of monastic libraries for literary evidence that sheds light on the antiquity of these places. The publication of his work *The laboryouse journey and serche of Johan Leylande for Englandes antiquitee* (1549) inspires other historians.

William Lambarde produces his *Perambulation of Kent* in 1576; William Harrison's *Description of England* appears the following year; and William Camden's *Britannia*—arranged county by county—is published in 1586. Suddenly—from nowhere it seems—every region has acquired a new "survey" of its past. The same goes for the nation as a whole, with the publication of Richard Grafton's *Chronicle at Large* and Raphael Holinshed's *Chronicles* in 1568 and 1577 respectively. The latter is one of the major sources used by William Shakespeare for his history plays.

As a result of this sudden and dramatic upsurge of interest in history, the Society of Antiquaries is formed in 1572, meeting at the heralds' office in Derby House, London. Members read papers to the society, and share and discuss their research. Among their number are William Camden, Richard Carew, Sampson Erdeswicke, William Lambarde, and John Stow, together with several historians, lawyers, heralds, and archivists, such as Arthur Agarde, Thomas Talbot, and Robert Cotton, who collects the greatest library of English historical manuscripts ever assembled.[57] But such is the power of history that very quickly this society becomes controversial. In English law, past precedent can be taken as a legal principle, and historical documents concerning the succession to the throne are highly sensitive. When Robert Cotton lays his hands on Edward VI's "device" for the succession—in which the king recognizes Lady Jane Grey as heir to the throne—he is asked to surrender it to the government so it can be destroyed.[58] That is just one example: he has many more sensitive documents. Later, when the queen is petitioned to incorporate the society and make premises available, she demurs. She thinks history is dangerous, as her imprisonment of John Hayward for writing about Henry IV demonstrates. And she is not alone. In the next reign the antiquaries are forced to disband, and a few years after that, Robert Cotton's library is closed by royal decree.

Society's conception of itself develops over the course of Elizabeth's reign—and its character changes accordingly. At the end it is still violent and charitable, corrupt and courageous, racist and proud. But it has seen that it has broken away from its medieval roots and that there is no going back. And with that sense of being different from the past comes a vision that things will be different in the future. Thomas Norton, a playwright, historian, and MP, starts to use history to predict the years to come.[59] The poets working at the end of the reign also understand the uniqueness of their position in time, referring to "the age" in which they live as distinct from other ages. That self-consciousness is one of the most striking features of the Elizabethan character, made more so to the time traveler by its absence in earlier generations. It is another of the reasons why you will probably find you have more in common with Elizabethan people than with their medieval forebears. They have discovered the essence of modernity, with all its novelty, excitement, and unpredictability. And who can blame them for being excited? After all, who knows what they will discover next?

CHAPTER FIVE

Basic Essentials

In a strange country, even minor everyday concerns can cause difficulties. Which coins do you use to buy something to eat? How do you greet people? How do you behave at table? How do you tell the time? You won't find the answers to these questions in traditional history books, so this chapter provides some essential information on these little differences.

Languages

From Shakespeare's plays and poems, you are at least passingly familiar with the language: you know it is not quite the same as our modern speech. The patterns and constructions are different. There are signs and signifiers, in the forms of puns and allusions, which may well pass over your head. However, most of the difficulties are simply a matter of vocabulary. The English language, which developed rapidly in the two centuries before Elizabeth's reign, has more or less reached its modern form and now is changing mainly through the adoption of new words from Latin, Greek, and foreign languages. There are many of these—Shakespeare's vocabulary of twenty thousand words is about twice that available to a writer at the start of the reign—and 90 percent of them will present you with no problem.[1] Unfortunately there is no such thing as an English dictionary to help you with the remaining 10 percent. The earliest—the *Table Alphabetical* by Robert Cawdrey—is in preparation but does not appear until 1604. Even then, it is not a dictionary as such but a list of difficult words from Latin and Greek that might confuse people.

Expletives should present you with few problems, as the tone of voice gives away the meaning. You may not be able to define "blithering" (it means "senselessly talkative"), but you know that if someone calls you "a blithering idiot" he is not paying you a compliment. Likewise, if someone shouts "Sirrah!" at you, you will be shaken out of the misguided modern idea that this is a synonym for "Sir" (a mark of respect); rather it is a derogatory form of address used to talk down to boys, servants, and men lower than the speaker in the social hierarchy. When most educated people make an exclamation, they say something like "Zounds!" or (to give it its full form) "God's wounds." You may also hear people exclaim "God's blood!" and "God's death," both of which are used by the queen herself. In fact, Elizabeth is even known to utter the word "Jesus!" as an expletive.[2] As you may realize, this is highly inappropriate if you are in the company of Puritans. You will already be familiar with exclamations such as "O God" and "Good God," which you hear in many an Elizabethan home.[3] To these you need to add "Fie!" as a common exclamation of amazement, outrage, or disgust; and the word "Faith!" is used as an exclamation when agreeing with someone emphatically.

With regard to more normal speech, there are two problems. The first is that you will come across words that you simply don't know. If someone says "swive" (fornicate), "cup-shotten" (drunk), "foison" (profusion), "hol-pen" (helped), "beldam" (old woman), or "jakes" (toilet), you either know the word or you don't, and if you don't you'll have to ask. The second prob-lem is a more difficult one: many words that the Elizabethans use and which we still use in the modern world have changed their meaning over the in-tervening centuries. Think of the whole English language as a vast river into which rivulets of foreign words and people's witticisms and new expe-riences flow constantly, the water turning over and altering all the while. Its continual flow and alteration make it a living language—it is a river, not a stagnant pool of archaic words—and any markers placed in this flow are bound to be swept aside. Take the word "nice," for example. In Elizabeth's time it has no connotations of fluffiness—quite the opposite. It means "ex-act" or "accurate," and is quite a cold word: the phrase "they are so nice in measuring their bread" means they are so precise in weighing it, not that they are generous. The word "cute" changes similarly: it means "sharp" and there's nothing kittenish about it. You would be wrong to presume the word "mean" has the same meaning as today. It can refer to something little or humble: a man "of mean estate" has little in the way of financial capital; and if he is "of mean parentage," this does not imply that his father and mother did not love him but that they did not have much cash. "The meanest woman in town" is not an insult but a description of poverty, deserving of pity rather than condemnation. The word "several" in particular is bound to trip you up: to an Elizabethan it means "separate" (not "a few"), so "they went their several ways" means they went different ways, not to different places together. If a man is said to be "romantic" this means he is "heroic" or like someone in a fable—not that he's given his true love red roses. "Mess" is not just a chaotic situation but more commonly the word used to describe a sitting at a dinner table: if you and another person "share the same mess" it means you're both eating from the same plates. "Occupy" has many meanings, most of which are variations on the word "use"—for instance, "He occupied no silver vessel or plate." A merchant at a fair can be an "occupier,"[4] and if a man "occupies" a woman it means he has sex with her. "House of easement" is another word for "privy" or "latrine," and so is "house of office"—it has nothing to do with a place of work. Space forbids a long list of words to which you will need to adjust your vocabulary, but in case you come across them, here are a few more:

"avoidance" is taking away;
"ecstasy" is madness;
a "cheap" is a market;
"bootless" is unsuccessful;
"puke" is a bluish-black color;
"scarlet" is a high-quality woolen cloth;
"jerks" are blows (as from a cudgel);

"lawn" is a high-quality linen;
"to revolve" is to consider or ponder;
"counterfeit" means "likeness" not "fake");
"budget" is a bag;
"slops" are items of clothing;
"defecated" means "freed from dregs and other impurities" (as in the straining of ale);
"hold" can mean bet ("I hold ye a groat").

Misunderstanding these words presumes that you can hear them correctly in the first place. The range of local accents is far greater in the sixteenth century than it is in the modern world, with its relatively homogenized tones after decades of long-distance migration and communications. Sir Walter Raleigh never loses his broad Devon accent, despite being educated and spending much of his time at court or at sea. English-speaking Cornishmen have an equally "broad and rude" accent, according to Carew, complicating their speech with certain local words, among them "scrip" (escape), "bezibd" (fortunate), "dule" (comfort), "thew" (threaten), and "skew" (shun). Move farther up the country and you will find different accents and local expressions. And if you visit London you will find all these regional accents coexisting. As you will see from listening to Henry Machyn (originally from northeast Leicestershire), or from reading his phonetic "cronacle," a man might speak with a strong regional accent all his life, even though he moved to the capital as a boy and rarely (if ever) goes home.[5]

These are just the difficulties you will have with English speakers. There are many Welsh speakers still in Wales, despite Henry VIII's legislation and Edward VI's Act of Uniformity, which stipulated that English has to be used in all official walks of life. There is little secular Welsh literature. However, the tireless scholar William Salesbury tries to resuscitate the language through a Welsh translation of the Prayer Book in 1551, and along with Richard Davies, bishop of St. David's, he petitions Parliament to publish a Welsh translation of the Bible. You might think that Elizabeth's government would pour scorn on such a proposal, but it realizes that the native language may be an important instrument in converting the Welsh to Protestantism. When William Morgan's Welsh Bible is finally printed in 1588, it is as if the language has finally received divine approval. Moreover, the Welsh Bible has much the same effect on the language as its English equivalent has on the English tongue: it standardizes many phrases and expressions and, in a manner of speaking, acts as a channel for the wide river of the language. It encourages people to learn to read too. Salesbury, Davies, and Morgan save the Welsh language, giving it both spiritual and cultural meaning at precisely the time that the English government is considering eradicating it altogether.

The Cornish language is still holding on—but only just. Shortly before the start of the reign, Andrew Boorde comments: "In Cornwall is two speeches; the one is naughty English and the other Cornish speech. And there be many men and women the which cannot speak one word of English, but all Cornish."[6] The Cornish rebels of 1549, protesting against the introduction of the new English Prayer Book, declare, "We the Cornishmen (whereof certain of us understand no English) utterly refuse this new English."[7] But it seems the language collapses like the Prayer Book Rebellion. No Cornish translations of the Bible and the Prayer Book appear; in fact, nothing at all is published in Cornish and the language quickly withers away. In addition, Cornish gentlemen and scholars are keen to demonstrate their sophistication by distancing themselves from spoken Cornish. By the end of the reign you will have to travel westward of Truro to hear it spoken regularly.[8] Even there the language is fast dying, as Carew reports:

> English speech doth still encroach upon it, and hath driven the same into the uttermost skirts of the shire. Most of the inhabitants can [speak] no word of Cornish but very few are ignorant of English: and yet some so affect their own as to a stranger they will not speak it; for, if meeting them by chance, you inquire the way or any such matter, your answer shall be *mees navidua cowzs sawzneck* (I can speak no Saxonage).[9]

To a traveler, this is not very helpful. You might want to respond in like manner, with a suitable riposte in Cornish: perhaps a sarcastic *da durdal-athawhy* ("well, I thank you") or the pointed *molla tuenda laaz* ("ten thousand mischiefs in thy guts").[10] These phrases appear alongside the above passage in Carew's *Survey of Cornwall*, where he also points out the closeness of the Cornish for "sister" (*whoore*) and for prostitute (*whorra*). One wonders if his dislike of the Cornish language might be rooted in some embarrassing confusion between those two words.

The other languages still spoken in the realm, Latin and French, have fairly specific uses nowadays. Elizabethan courts still record everything in Latin, and some parish registers are kept in Latin too, so to some extent the language is still used throughout the country. Boys learn Latin at grammar school; you may recall Claudius Hollyband's private school, where Latin is taught in the morning and French in the afternoon. However, it is unusual to find anyone speaking Latin outside the rarefied circles of the universities of Oxford and Cambridge, the Inns of Court in London, some senior members of the clergy, and the odd occasion, such as conversations with foreign ambassadors or addresses to the queen. While it will stand you in good stead if you can speak Latin, as most well-educated people will understand you, it will not be a hindrance if you do not speak the language.

Many aristocrats and members of the gentry still use French in daily discourse. Hollyband himself publishes popular tuition books in French and Italian and even one in four languages: Italian, French, Latin, and English.[11] Interestingly, many educated Englishmen feel obliged to learn one of these tongues. In London and the other southern towns and cities there are a great many French and Italian immigrants, and for many the easiest way to earn a living in England is to teach their native tongue. When the Italian humanist Giordano Bruno visits England in 1584 he does not bother to learn more than a handful of words in English. As he puts it (writing of himself in the third person): "All gentlemen of any rank with whom he holds conversations can speak Latin, French, Spanish or Italian. They are aware that the English language is only used in this island and would consider themselves uncivilized if they knew no other tongue than their own."[12] Therefore, if you can't understand a regional accent on your journey, you could take a leaf out of Bruno's book and try to make use of your French or Italian.

Writing

When it comes to written communication you need to bear in mind that there are several forms of script commonly used. Least common but by no means unimportant are the scripts of government. Letters patent, charters, and other formal documents of public record are written in "court hand," a descendant of the medieval scripts used within Chancery. These documents will look "Gothic" to you: the script seems like an array of up-and-down lines, or minims, which all look the same. Yet as long as you understand the language in which the document is written (mostly Latin but sometimes English) these scripts are easy to read, for they are so carefully written. The same cannot be said for most people's handwriting. If you care to glance over the shoulder of an Elizabethan clerk as he notes down the proceedings of a quarter session hearing, you will be baffled. You will see that he is hastily writing a series of notes in abbreviated Latin, as required by law, even though he probably does not speak the language. The result is frequently an almost unintelligible mess of flourishes that look as if someone has squashed a thousand small, brown-legged spiders between the pages of the book.

It is not just the haste which makes a court clerk's writing so different from "court hand"; the entire script is different. Like most people, clerks write in "secretary hand" and the shapes of the letters are constantly changing. Old men born in the last decade of the fifteenth century still write in the 1550s with a long "r" that reaches well below the line, and an "h" that looks more like an old-fashioned "z," again reaching below the line. They still use the old letter "thorn," pronounced "th" and originally written "þ," but now more regularly appearing like a "y" (hence the frequent appearance of "ye" for "the"). Younger men educated in the 1530s or later will use a short "r." Most people write "v" and "u" interchangeably, although "v" is normally used at the start and "u" in the middle of the word—e.g., "vsually" (usually). About half of the letters of the secretary hand alphabet have no relation to the form of lettering with which you are familiar. Many symbols are squiggles above and below the line which have been taken from abbreviated medieval Latin script. Two forms of the letter "p," for example, stand for "per" (or "par") and "pro"; a line above a letter means an "m" has been omitted; a long curling flourish below the line at the end of a word represents a terminal "s."

Curiously, although it is in universal use in the sixteenth century, secretary hand is never printed. Printed books make use of italic and black-letter type. The former is not all slanting one way but called "italic" because it is developed in Italy. It is the script with which you are most familiar—because all modern typefaces descend from it—and is used for most general-interest books by the end of the reign. Black-letter is a printed version of the court hand of official documents. It is normally used for Bibles, formal texts, and some history and literary books. Horn books, used to teach people to read, are also printed in black-letter script. For this reason, the italic that you are used to will not be the easiest type for everyone to read. Some people who learned with a horn book never learn to read any of the other forms of writing. This is why you have some books printed in both italic and formal black-letter—such as Isabella Whitney's poetical works: the title pages and dedications are in the more educated italic, and the actual poems are in black-letter type, to make them easier for people with a limited education, especially women, to read.

As for numbers, Arabic figures are increasingly used for dates, which can be very long in Roman numerals—it is far easier to engrave "1588" on a coin die or a date stone than "MDLXXXVIII"—but accounting is still frequently done in Roman numerals. Some well-educated people simply can't "think" in Arabic numbers: Sir William Cecil translates all the figures supplied to him in Arabic back into Roman numerals when forming government policy.[13]

When you want to write something, first you need to decide what you are going to write on. This depends on how long the document is supposed to last. A charter or official document, a deed to some land, or a court roll will always be written on good-quality vellum or parchment made from sheepskins. After treatment that removes all the hair, these skins need to be degreased by adding "pounce" (powdered pumice or cuttlefish bone) into the skin, smoothed with an animal's tooth, and "sized" by coating with gelatin from the hooves of horses. If what you intend to write is more ephemeral, like a letter which can be discarded after being read once, or a series of accounts that you would not expect to last more than a year, you will write on paper. This can be cheap to purchase, although low-quality paper does not bear writing on both sides, as the ink is absorbed and shows through; it is made for peddlers to wrap their goods in and for toilet paper. A high-quality product such as "paper imperial" is used for lavish books, and some writers prefer its smooth qualities for handwriting too. Shopping lists or school exercises will not normally be written on paper but on "tables": these are wax-coated leaves of ivory, boxwood, and cypress which can be written on with a metal point, then scraped and reused.[14]

Metal pens are called "pontayles." They are made of iron, silver, or brass, and have one great virtue: they last a long time. However, they are also scratchy, so most people use a quill. Elizabeth prefers to use swan feathers; the most popular alternatives are a goose quill and a reed. You'll need to keep your penknife handy to trim it every so often, a spare piece of paper to test each newly cut nib, and probably a good few spare quills if you intend writing a book. You will also need an inkhorn. In towns you will be able to buy ready-made ink from an apothecary or a scrivener's shop, but most people in the country make their own. To do this you will need a quart of wine, five ounces of oak galls, three ounces of copperas, and two ounces of gum arabic. To make it last, add bay salt. To make it really black, add ground lampblack. If the ink is too thick, water it down with vinegar.[15]

Identity and Forms of Address

If you are visiting the sixteenth century, you are not going to be greeting many close relatives, so formal modes of address are important. You can refer to a common man—called, say, Smith—as "Goodman Smith" or "my goodman"; don't use "sirrah" unless you are yourself particularly superior and want to remind him of his lowliness. The goodman's wife you might call "Goodwife Smith" or "my goodwoman." You may hear her neighbors call her "Goody Smith," but this is only for those who know her well. Likewise, you shouldn't call her "madam" or "Mrs." or anything else reflecting a status she does not enjoy. "Widow Smith" is self-explanatory. When it comes to more socially elevated persons, forms of address get a little more complicated. A gentleman who is neither a lord nor a knight should be called "Mister." If he is knighted, he should always be addressed in speech by his Christian name: "Sir Francis." The word "esquire" is a much lower acknowledgment of official status but is principally used for men who have the right to bear a coat of arms (i.e., they are descended in the male line from a knight), and, in towns, for those who serve as magistrates. Do not say "Squire Brown," however, just "Mr. Brown." The female equivalent of "Mr." is "Mistress"—abbreviated to "Mtrs" or "Mrs."—hence you will find young girls and unmarried ladies described as "Mrs." (the term "Miss" for unmarried ladies will not come into use until the next century). When speaking to a "Mistress Johnson," rather than about her, you should generally call her "madam." Note that "madam" is only used when directly addressing a woman who is socially equal or superior to you. "My lady" and "your ladyship" are less specific but are generally reserved only for the nobility and the upper levels of the gentry. Physicians are not called "Doctor" unless they have a doctorate in medicine from a university: most gentlemen physicians, like gentlemen surgeons, are simply addressed as "Mister." Otherwise men referred to as "Dr." are so called because they have a doctorate in law or theology. You may still call clergymen "Father," and in the first half of the reign it is still customary to address the rector or vicar in the same way as you would a knight: "Sir Richard," "Sir Peter," and so on.[16]

As for the names themselves, more than half the men you meet will be called John, William, or Thomas. Half the women will be Mary, Elizabeth, Agnes, Joan, or Margaret. Most of the common Christian names are ones with which you are already familiar, but don't be surprised if you meet women called Urith, Charity, Patience, Purity, and Lettice; women born at Whitsun may well be called Pentecost. Some women are given names later associated with men, such as Julian, Timothy, and Richord. It is very rare indeed to find anyone with a middle name. While surnames are ubiquitous, a man's family name can be exchangeable with his occupation or abode, so that a tanner called John Beard might also be called John Tanner. This is one reason why there are so many people with an alias or two—written as

"John Tanner alias Neville alias Westcott." Another reason for an alias is to record the fact that a family member was sired out of wedlock. If an unmarried woman called Jones is made pregnant by a gentleman called Raleigh, her offspring may well be baptized as "John Jones alias Raleigh," especially if the gentleman acknowledges the child.

Time

Walking through the fields of a country estate you may well hear the bell of the manor-house chapel ring the hours for the workers. For many people, this is the only formal regulation of time that they know. In towns, the time is set by the church bells' ringing; if there is more than one church, one sets the time for the others. Hence you will sometimes find people in towns referring to "hours of the bell" instead of "hours of the clock." But this informality masks an important change: in the Elizabethan age time has become standardized. The medieval system of dividing the daylight and night time into twelve equal sections—so that an hour of daylight in summer is twice as long as in winter—is a thing of the past. People now count a day as we do: twelve hours each of sixty minutes, from midnight and from noon. Townsmen listen out for the bells that indicate the hour when the markets open or close, when the curfew is rung for all travelers to be indoors, or when the town gates are shut. Those in rural parishes listen for the ringing of the church bell when they need to attend a service or a session of the manorial court. Those clocks that have faces normally have only one hand, pointing to the hour; if you need to count minutes, you will use an hourglass, not a clock. Few people do so, however, except mariners, alchemists, astrologers, natural philosophers, and the clergy. Why the clergy, you ask? A good clergyman will expect to preach for two or even three hours at a time.

Announced by bells, time is therefore a very public thing in Elizabeth's reign. Only the gentry have "small clocks for a chamber to wake a man out of his sleep." A "clock with a dial" is likely to cost you £5 in the 1580s.[17] Even fewer people have watches like Elizabeth's diamond-encrusted one, worn on the end of a silver chain. When away from home, most people will either estimate the time in the old style—by the passage of the sun across the sky—or use a ring dial. This is a sundial in the form of a brass ring which you can wear on your finger. When you want to tell the time, you adjust it to the correct date (some of them have sliding bands to do this) and check the sunlight penetrating a hole in the top of the ring against the scale engraved inside it. The most elaborate time-telling rings also have a calendar, a table of Christian feasts, and the latitudes of major European cities so they can be used abroad. If you want one of these sophisticated timepieces, inquire at Humphrey Cole's shop in London, where the best examples are made.[18]

"A-mornings I rise ordinarily at seven o'clock," writes Robert Laneham in 1575. "Then ready, I go into chapel. Soon after eight, I get me commonly into my lord's chamber. . . . There at the cupboard, after I have eaten the manchet [an allowance of bread] . . . I drink me up a good bowl of ale."[19] His start to the day is typical. Claudius Hollyband expects his pupils to be with him at school at about eight; his dialogue books have a household servant berating her young master for still being in bed at seven. Hugh Rhodes urges his young charges to be up "at six o'clock, without delay." For craftsmen and laborers, the working day starts before 5 a.m. from mid-March until mid-September, as laid out in a statute of Henry VIII; they are expected not to take more than half an hour for breakfast (at about 7 a.m.) and an hour and a half for dinner, and to go on working until between 7 and 8 p.m. From mid-September to mid-March, laborers are expected to be working from dawn until dusk.[20] If it were not for Sundays and religious feast days—about twenty-seven holy days or "holidays" survive the Reformation—there would be little respite from toil.

Most Elizabethans tell the date in two ways: the year of the reign and the year since Christ's birth, Anno Domini. The former is calculated from November 17, 1558, so that "January 1, 1560" is written as 1 January in the second year of the reign, or "2 Reginae Elizabethae." The latter is measured not from New Year's Day but from Lady Day, March 25 each year, so "January 1, 1560" is actually in 1561 by modern calculations. Awkwardly, the change of the year on March 25 is not universally accepted. In France, the various dioceses use different dates: some use March 25 but others Christmas or Easter. To put an end to this confusion, in 1564 the king of France issues the Edict of Roussillon declaring that henceforth the year will always begin on January 1. Venice, the Holy Roman Empire, Spain, Prussia, Denmark, and Sweden have already shifted to this system by 1560; the Low Countries follow suit in the 1570s and 1580s; and Scotland also does so in 1600. This is most confusing for those living in Berwick, on the English–

Scottish border: between January 1 and March 25 each year, the Scottish date is one year greater than the English one.

An even greater complication for overseas travelers arises in 1582, when the whole of Catholic Europe shifts from the Julian to the Gregorian calendar. Astronomers have long understood that the Julian calendar of 365.25 days is about 10.75 minutes too long: by using it, one gains a day every 134 years. Reckoning from Christ's birth, this means that by the late sixteenth century all the religious feasts are ten days out. When the Gregorian calendar is introduced in France, Spain, and Italy, Thursday, October 4, 1582, is followed by Friday, October 15. The English system is thus ten days adrift from Europe, as well as starting the year on a different day. Also remember that certain dates are still measured by religious festivals, so you might find someone telling you the date as "the eve of the feast of the Purification of the Virgin." Given the disparities in calendars, this falls on different days in England and Catholic Europe. Things get really complicated when the feast in question is a movable one, like Whitsun or Easter. Henry Machyn marks his birthday as falling on the Wednesday after Whitsun, so he celebrates it on a different date each year. Of course, it would be a totally different day again if he were to go abroad. It is hardly surprising that by the time he is in his fifties he has lost track of how old he is, miscalculating his own age in his "cronacle."[21]

Units of Measurement

From early times, different parts of the country have had different measurements of distance, area, volume, liquid, and weight. From the thirteenth century on, there are attempts to regularize such basic units as the inch and the foot; but these are met with resistance. You may think it extraordinary that a monarch can stop the majority of the nation believing in Purgatory and transubstantiation and yet cannot persuade people to use a standard system of weights and measures—but there you are. The good news is that some progress is being made. A statute of 1496 establishes an English standard of eight gallons of wheat to a bushel; every gallon is to contain eight pounds of wheat; every pound, twelve ounces of troy weight; every ounce, twenty sterlings; and every sterling, "thirty-two corns of wheat from the middle of the ear of the wheat." This becomes the standard in most places except Devon and Cornwall. In the latter county, there are different measures according to whether you are a stranger or an inhabitant, and whether you are buying from the waterside or at a land market. At least cloth measures have become standardized—forty-five inches to the ell, twenty nails to the ell, so each nail of cloth is two and a quarter inches.

Some measurements are easier to regularize than others. Units that are used by travelers as well as locals tend to be standardized before Elizabeth's reign. Take the mile: all sorts of customary miles used to be employed up and down the country, but over the last hundred years or so the advantages of a standard mile have come to be recognized. The English mile of 1,760 yards becomes ubiquitous and is enforced by a royal proclamation in 1592. However, there is no unanimity on the unit of measurement for land under tillage. The statute acre was established way back in the thirteenth century as a measure of four perches by forty perches. All well and good—as long as your standard perch is accepted as five and a half yards (sixteen and a half feet). In Hampshire, the customary perch is five yards long; in Devon, six yards; in Cumberland, seven yards; and in Lancashire, it is eight and a half.[22] In this way, your customary acre turns out to be anything from 4,000 to 11,560 square yards—somewhat larger than the statute acre of 4,840 yards. Perhaps you will not be surprised to hear that the most extreme variation is to be found in Cornwall. A Cornish acre is related not to tillage but to feudal service: it is a quarter of a knight's fee, and comprises nine farthinglands; with each farthingland being about thirty statute acres, the whole "acre" measures about 270 statute acres.[23]

Shopping

The word "shop" means "workshop" as well as a place to buy things. In small towns and villages, it mostly relates to a workplace. In large cities, you will find the word being used for any permanent retail premises which are not part of the marketplace, just as in the modern world. Thus for locks you go to a locksmith's "shop," for shoes to a cobbler's "shop," and so on. In London, if you go shopping in the newly built Royal Exchange, you will find all the units being described as "shops," whether they are run by fabric merchants or goldsmiths.[24] Stepping outside, you might go to a cookshop for something to eat. Buying food in most towns, however, is something you will do at a market.

Every town has at least one market, open at least one day per week, and serving the immediate needs of the local community. Some towns have several markets in several places, each one selling different commodities, such as poultry, milk, and cheese. Unless you are a completely self-sufficient farmer, you will go into town on market day to buy eggs, butter, cheese, meat, or fish; you will also come for the gossip, the news, and to meet friends. You might also buy cloth; small items of metalwork such as candle-holders, nails, knives, and other tools; and leather items such as purses, pouches, bags, and belts. Livestock is also traded here: farmers bring their cows, sheep, and pigs on the hoof to sell to the slaughtermen and butchers, as well as chickens in cages and dead coneys. Cooked meat, pasties, and pies—the equivalent of modern "fast food"—are available to those who have come in from the country to do their shopping, as well as copious amounts of ale. Any announcements will be made by the town crier in the marketplace: royal proclamations, for example, or the decisions of the mayor and corporation of the town. Normally the market closes before dusk, to avoid pilfering from stalls when the light grows dim.

In addition to the market stalls, you will hear people crying their wares in the streets of large towns. Thomas Platter counts thirty-seven different commodities being cried in the streets of London in 1599.[25] Cherries, plums, and other soft fruit are often sold by women walking along with baskets; "oranges and lemons" is a cry you will frequently hear. Some vegetables are sold similarly—strings of onions, for example. Fish and oysters are sometimes sold from baskets and panniers too, and so are herbs, garlic, lettuce, and radishes. Basically, any goods that cannot be kept are hawked about to be sold quickly. The same goes for some services: fagots for lighting fires, a flame (to save the trouble of lighting a fire with a tinderbox), or a chimney sweep's services. When shopping, bear in mind the necessity of haggling. Paying the asking price is a sure way to be defrauded.

Some towns continue to hold a fair. This differs from a market in being an annual event, sometimes lasting several days. According to the almanacs published every year, there are 822 fairs still operating in England in Elizabeth's reign.[26] The principal purpose of these events is to supply whole-sale goods to retailers in towns and to allow goods to be bought in bulk by international merchants. Rare items supplied by an apothecary, for instance, might be purchased from a wholesaler, and a shopkeeper might buy high-quality cloth such as silk and lace. However, the heyday of the great fair, when all sorts of rarities could be purchased, has long since gone.

A high degree of regulation is required at any market or fair. Towns have much to lose if they acquire a reputation for attracting thieves, or if customers are defrauded by unscrupulous traders. Some prices are regulated by law, including those of bread, ale, and fuel: if you are charged too much for these, you can report the offender to a Justice of the Peace.[27] Most towns appoint officers (bedels or bailiffs) to oversee trade. They may set prices for certain items; in Exeter there is a 40 shillings fine for selling rabbits at more than 10 pence a brace.[28] They have official weighing and measuring houses to make sure quantities of grain and liquid are correct, ale-tasters to ensure that the ale is good, and constables to keep law and order. They do all they can to prevent forestalling (the purchase of goods or livestock before they come to market), regrating (the resale of goods previously bought at a lower price in the same market or another within four miles), and engrossment (the purchase of the entire stock of something to sell it at a higher price)—all these things are forbidden by law. This means that those who attempt to rip you off can be taken before the authorities and charged with criminal offenses, not just with breaking the local bylaws. Fines for forestalling and regrating are significant—at least 10 shillings, more often 40 shillings, and sometimes as much as £10.

Money, Work, and Wages

Long-term inflation increases in the sixteenth century. A greater population means that more people are chasing too little food, forcing prices up. At the same time, with a greater number of people available to work, employers reduce wages. Lower wages and increasing demand mean that when there is a shortage, food becomes unaffordable for many. In the 1550s, prices are approximately 50 percent higher than they were ten years earlier.[29]

One of the ways the government tries to rectify this is through improving the metal value of the coinage. Debased coins of Edward VI's reign are marked with symbols (a portcullis and a greyhound's head) denoting their lower values, and new high-standard silver coins are minted. The other method is to control wages: restricting what people earn limits how much they can pay for commodities, thereby reducing inflation. The strategy is successful. The debased coinage is swiftly eliminated. Prices in the 1560s are just 5.7 percent higher than in the 1550s, and the next two decades see ten-year inflation rates of 7.6 percent and 6.6 percent. While the price of grain and other foodstuffs fluctuates wildly according to availability, a basket of commodities increases in price by less than 1 percent per year over the whole reign.[30]

The following coins are minted in Elizabeth's reign:

Gold coins		Silver coins	
Sovereign	£1 10 shillings	Shilling	12 pence
Pound	20 shillings	Sixpence	6 pence
Ryal	15 shillings	Groat	4 pence
Half-pound	10 shillings	Threepence	3 pence
Angel	10 shillings	Half-groat	2 pence
Crown	5 shillings	Threehalfpence	1½ pence
Half-angel	5 shillings	Penny	1 penny
Half-crown	2 shillings 6 pence	Threefarthings	¾ penny
Quarter-angel	2 shillings 6 pence	Halfpenny	½ penny

You may ask why there are gold coins of duplicate value. The reason is that the pound sterling is only one of two units of account; the other is the mark (13 shillings 4 pence), which is two-thirds of a pound. The angel was originally worth half a mark (6 shillings 8 pence), and only acquires its value of 10 shillings in 1551, as the mark declines in importance. From 1601 on, the half-angel and quarter-angel are no longer minted and the crown and half-crown are minted as large silver coins. However, the older coins do not drop out of the money supply overnight. Thus, for a short period, there are three separate coins of 5 shilling value in circulation (a gold crown, a silver crown, and a gold half-angel) and likewise three 2 shilling 6 pence ones (two gold, one silver). Although it is proclaimed in 1600 that copper halfpennies and farthings are shortly to be minted, these do not actually appear, despite a chronic need for them in market stalls up and down the country.[31]

The above coins are all hammered—that is to say, they are made by placing a disk of the appropriate metal on an engraved die, placing the reverse die above it, and hammering it hard. As a result the coins wear easily and quickly. They are also regularly clipped—silver is cut from the edges—even though this is high treason and punishable by death.[32] But then, in 1561, a master moneyer from France called Eloye Mestrelle arrives in England, bringing with him a horse-powered screw press that permits massive pressure to be brought on the coin, creating a far more distinct image—almost as good as a modern coin.[33] He mints thousands of superb sixpences and a small number of other coins; but the machinery is very slow, and the mint employees, interested in a quick and efficient working method, never take to his system. After ten years' service, Mestrelle is dismissed. When in poverty he turns to counterfeiting coins, he is caught and hanged in 1578.

You may wonder what the above sums are worth in modern currency. Although some historians will try to give you an equivalent, it is misleading to pretend there is a standard exchange rate across the centuries. Different things acquire different monetary values at different times. In Worcestershire in the 1590s a pair of linen sheets costs 8 shillings—but what is the equivalent in the modern world? A pair of linen sheets today costs about £100: the increment from the 1590s to 2012 is 250 times the price.[34] A day laborer in the 1590s normally earns 4 pence per day and the value of his work has increased six thousand times to about £100. As for food, a chicken will cost you 4 pence (except in the famine years of 1594–97, when you might pay double that), a pint of cream 3 pence, one lemon 3 pence, and a pound of cherries 10 pence. The chicken (free range) has gone up in value roughly 240 times, but the lemon only about twenty times and the cherries sixty times. So has the purchasing power of £1 increased by a factor of 20, 250, or 6,000 since the 1590s? One cannot compare prices with a society that sets very different values on food and labor from our own times.

What if you need to borrow money? You cannot simply walk into a bank—there aren't any on the high street. However, various forms of credit are available. Many shopkeepers will allow you to run up a bill, if they know who you are and where you live; your debt will be recorded in a "shopbook." Another form of credit used frequently is that of borrowing from a local gentleman upon bond. You will undertake to repay a certain sum of money at a certain date and at a certain interest rate, as specified in a legal document. You are "bound" to repay that sum and the deed remains with the creditor until you have done so. An act of 1571, which legalizes the payment of interest for long-term credit (previously charging interest counted as usury), limits by law the amount that can be charged to 10 percent per annum. Bonds are now becoming increasingly popular. However, if you are a creditor, reclaiming the money can sometimes be difficult. Many testators stipulate that legacies should be paid only if money can be recovered from the deceased man's creditors, and when men die you often find their executors drawing up lists of "desperate debts"—sums which they have given up hope of being repaid.[35]

It was mentioned above that the government controls wages. In marked contrast to our modern legislation, which stipulates a *minimum* wage, the Labourers' Act of 1563 states that magistrates are annually to establish and enforce a local *maximum* for each occupation. In Colchester, for example, it is deemed that a "bailiff of husbandry"—a superintending farmer employed by a landowner—should receive no more than £2 13 shillings 4 pence annually, with a 10-shilling allowance for cloth (to make clothes). A paid farmhand should receive no more than £1 13 shillings 4 pence per year, with 6 shillings 8 pence for cloth. Day rates for laborers are set at a maximum of 3 pence per day with food and drink, or 7 pence without in the winter months. At harvest time they can increase to 8 pence per day with food and drink and 16 pence without. Masons, carpenters, and other skilled laborers may receive up to 4 pence per day with food and drink or 10 pence without.[36] In Exeter, laborers and apprentices in the building trades may earn up to 6 pence per day, or 8 pence if they are journeymen who have completed their apprenticeships, and 10 pence per day if they are masters of their craft.[37]

You might find the idea of a maximum wage a depressing prospect—working without a chance of improving your salary in reward for experience and skill—but there is no alternative. The unemployed can be put in the stocks until the authorities find them work to do. Girls over the age of twelve and women under the age of forty can be forced to do menial work for whomsoever the justices appoint, receiving appropriate wages. Boys of twelve and over, and men under the age of sixty, may be forced to work in agriculture on the same basis. Many crafts have a minimum period of appointment: you will not get paid unless you work for your employer for a full year. Moreover, it is unlawful to leave a position without giving three months' notice.

Working conditions can be tough. Even in a booming industry, like the wool trade, the hours are long, the work hard, the food questionable or simply nonexistent. Mass production is just starting, with a handful of factories in existence. These have two hundred looms operated by two hundred men, accompanied by two hundred women carding wool, and another two hundred spinning cloth. At least such factories are relatively safe. Consider what it is like in an Elizabethan coal mine, another booming industry in the north of the country. For a start the pay is not great: you will earn a maximum of 6 pence per day. Boys employed to pull the barrows along the underground shafts and to load the crane to lift the coal to the surface might earn as little as 1 penny per day for twelve hours underground in dark, coal-dust-laden conditions, likely to lead to a host of lung diseases. Nearly half the time, the mines cannot be worked because of flooding, escaping gas ("damp"), or overproduction—and if you don't work, you don't get paid. Overproduction means there is too much coal on the surface not yet sold and transported away for it to be worthwhile extracting more. Flooding puts you at risk of drowning. In addition, as the miners have to urinate and defecate in the tunnels, diseases spread through the water in which they are standing, and parasites burrow into their ankles and feet. Then there is the "damp"—and remember, all the lighting is done with tallow candles. Imagine you start to pull down a wall of coal and suddenly—*bang!* The explosion may not kill you outright: you may find yourself in the pitch-black tunnel with a broken leg and the water level rising. Every day's work puts your life at risk—the dangers are unquantifiable—and you will have to accept that accidents happen and men die. When a sough or drainage tunnel is dug, to empty water from the bottom of a shaft, some poor miner must crawl up it and break though the rock into the water-filled shaft. This frequently results in the death of the miner in question as the water rushes through and smashes him back down the sough. Head injuries and broken limbs are common, leaving men helpless as they drown in the darkness. And the reward for those that do this, if they survive? A bounty of just £2—that is how much it takes to tempt a miner to risk his life.[38]

It is much safer to go into service. This is very common, not least because there is a huge demand for cheap labor in the home. However, there is meaning in the phrase "England is a servant's prison." Children as young as six can be forcibly apprenticed as servants in a yeoman's household, receiving no wages, only board and lodging. Adult menservants will be lucky to earn as much as £2 per year and women just over half that. A good rate for female help is 8 pence per week (£1 14 shillings 8 pence per year), which is what Maria, a maidservant in Compton, Berkshire, earns in 1597; at the same time, the male laborers in the same household are earning more than three times as much: 2 shillings 4 pence per week.[39] Two marks (£1 6 shillings 8 pence) is the salary paid to each of the seven maidservants working at Thorndon Hall, Essex, in 1593; they are paid every three months.[40] Sometimes servants are paid even less frequently: live-in servants can go a whole year without salary. In 1583, Joan Jennings makes a claim for payment of her wages at the rate of £1 6 shillings 8 pence, which have not been paid for two years.[41] Although servants might be spoken to as social equals by their employer and his family, for the sake of Christian brotherhood or simple companionship, normally they are seen as inferiors, ordered around by their masters and his family. Young women also often have to put up with the unwanted sexual attention of their masters; it seems to be accepted that a master of a household will normally have sex with his female servants. In 1599 the mayor's court in Norwich declares that eighteen-year-old Katherine Vardine should be discharged from her service because her master has syphilis and therefore she is likely to contract the disease too.[42] To be a young woman in service is thus a double predicament. To refuse your master is likely to result in dismissal; but to give in is to risk disease and pregnancy, as well as dismissal when the pregnancy is discovered. Finally, should you kill your master, then the crime is one of petty treason. Men are simply hanged, as they would be for any murder. Women are burned at the stake.

Manners and Politeness

Numerous books on how to behave are published in the sixteenth century. One such volume is *The Boke of Nurture or Schoole of Good Manners,* compiled by Hugh Rhodes and published in 1577. Aimed at "men servants and children," it delivers advice on how to behave in a gentleman's house. As smaller houses ape the manners of their social superiors, Rhodes's advice should stand you in good stead wherever you go:

General

- Take off your cap when spoken to by a social superior
- In the company of a superior, speak only when you are spoken to
- Don't look away from someone when speaking to him
- Don't tell secrets to strangers
- Don't correct the faults in others that you commit yourself

- Rebuke men only when alone with them
- It is better to beat a proud man than to rebuke him
- Don't boast
- Don't meddle in other men's affairs
- Don't laugh at your own jokes
- Knock at the door of a house before entering
- Be courteous to strangers, but don't trust people you don't know

At table

- Wash your hands before you eat
- If you are sharing a dish with someone else, don't crumble your bread into it
- If you eat with a social superior, let him start on the food first
- Don't belch in another man's face
- Don't slurp your soup
- When you have finished your soup, wipe the bowl clean and set it down ready for use again
- Eat and drink quietly
- Wipe your mouth after you have drunk from a cup
- Don't dip your meat in the salt cellar
- Don't gnaw bones with your teeth
- Don't throw bones under the table
- Eat only small morsels of meat
- Don't cram food into your mouth
- Don't blow on your food in case you have bad breath
- Don't pare your nails or play with the tablecloth during the meal
- Don't scratch your head at the dinner table or put your finger in your mouth, or break wind
- Don't blow your nose on a napkin but on your handkerchief
- Keep your knife bright
- Don't stretch your arms at the table or lean across it
- Don't spit across the table
- Don't blow crumbs or spit on the floor near you
- Don't pick your teeth with a knife but use a small stick
- Don't share food with someone else if you have putrefied teeth

- When you get up from the table, say to your companions, "Much good do it ye" and bow to your master
- If you have to spit or blow your nose, don't leave it lying on the ground but tread it out of sight

What Hugh Rhodes doesn't tell you is how to greet people. This is a huge omission, for there is no surer way of getting off on the wrong foot than to begin a relationship with an inappropriate salutation. If you know someone well, just using his or her name is sufficient greeting—as you probably know from Shakespeare's plays. For others, and those who are simply acquaintances, the usual greetings include "God save you, sir/madam," and "Sir, God give you a good and long life." On greeting someone in the morning you might say, "Good morrow, mister/mistress . . ." or "God give you good morrow." Late in the day you might prefer "God give you good evening" or "God give you good night," and at the end of the night, "Good rest." On taking your leave of someone you might add, "God save and prosper you, sir."[43]

As you can see, manners remain more or less consistent across time. There are only slight differences. Nevertheless some might surprise you. For instance, it is customary to take your hat off when someone urinates or defecates in your company. Normally men may keep their hats on at all times except in church; but you may be amused to see a lord's servants all take their caps off if their master's horse starts to urinate in the street.[44] When inviting a man out to a dinner or a reception, you need also to invite his wife—"for in England it is not customary to invite a man without his wife," writes Thomas Platter, who is clearly bemused by this English quirk. Platter is also surprised by the ways people greet each other. Gentlemen, he says, "greet each other with a bared head and a bow. . . . The women, however, are greeted with a kiss, as in France." Samuel Kiechel, visiting England in 1585, notes that if a man is welcomed at the door by a woman, even if she is the wife or daughter of the master of the house, "he has the right to take her by the arm to kiss her, which is the custom of the country, and if anyone does not do so it is regarded . . . as . . . ill breeding on his part." Alessandro Magno also comments on kissing women as a way of greeting: "If a stranger enters a house and does not first of all kiss the mistress on the lips, they think him badly brought up."[45] Shakespeare's *Othello* refers to the same custom. On greeting Emilia, Cassio says to her husband, "Let it not gall your patience, good Iago, that I extend my manners; 'tis my breeding that gives me this bold show of courtesy," as he kisses her.

Now you see why Magno writes of Londoners in 1562, "They kiss a lot." You might have mixed feelings about this. On the one hand, it may be a delightful moment passed on the doorstep. On the other, you have to wonder if kissing strangers on the lips is a wise thing to do in a disease-ridden city—especially when in the following year no fewer than 17,404 people die of plague.

CHAPTER SIX

What to Wear

The word "fashionable" is synonymous with being up-to-date. Dressing fashionably says something about you: that you know what is going on. It is the same in Elizabethan England—in fact, even more so. Fashions change just as fast as in the modern world but the changes are more significant than on the catwalks of modern cities. In a society dominated by strict hierarchies, everyone is expected to dress according to his or her rank; the way you look is a statement of how much respect you deserve as a person. Only if you dress like a gentleman will you be accorded that status. Unless you dress like a lady, you will not be treated like one. Nor can you get by just wearing the smart clothes of ten years ago (at least, not without modifying them); ladies' clothes that were fashionable a decade ago have been passed down to the maidservants. Courtiers wear new fashions for only a short while: as soon as these become fashionable outside court circles, they begin to look for something different. As the writer and traveler Fynes Moryson puts it, "Whosoever wears the old, men look upon him as a picture in an arras [tapestry]."[1] In the sixteenth century, what you wear reveals what you are.

Dressing appropriately is not as straightforward as simply being smart or elegant. If a man is wearing a heavy gold chain around his neck, then clearly he is someone of importance—but what do the colors of his clothes mean? And what should you make of the designs of his wife's dress? If a lady's sleeve is patterned with a snake and a heart, what does that mean? Is the pelican significant? If she is revealing a large amount of cleavage, what does that say about her?

It is probably a good idea to begin with aspects of sexual and social propriety. Nowadays you will find only small codpieces. Large ones, stuffed with wool and looking like an erect male member, are out of date. They used to be popular in the reign of the six-times-married Henry VIII but they are not paraded about at the court of the Virgin Queen. Garments with overblown shoulders that reflect Henry's style to accentuate his manliness have also disappeared. It would be most out of place for a man to flaunt his powerful upper body in the face of the queen. Simply by being a woman, Elizabeth alters men's fashion. It is as if a pin has pricked those massive, dominating male shoulders and they have deflated, shrinking to a level where men can be men and not muscular ogres.

As regards female propriety, ladies *never* reveal their bare arms or legs in public. A washerwoman might bare her legs when standing in a tub of lye, trampling clothes; but such bare-legged women are at the very bottom of society. Showing a great deal of cleavage, however, is perfectly acceptable as long as you are not married. It does not matter how old you are; at the age of sixty-four the queen herself still puts her bosom on display. Paul Hentzner, a German lawyer, sees her in 1598 and remarks on "her bosom uncovered, as all the English ladies have it, until they marry."[2] The French ambassador, André Hurault, sees her the previous year and cannot help but look at her breasts. He meets her on three occasions and each time he describes her clothes, paying particular attention to her bosom. On the second occasion he notes that she is wearing a gown that reveals her skin as far as her navel, displaying not just the cleavage but the whole breast. The third time he notices that her skin is very wrinkled around the upper part of her breast but lower down it is very white.[3] It is probably safe to assume that, as long as you are not showing your bare arms or ankles, you will not run into any trouble—although too much breast will clearly attract the close attention of the French ambassador.

What you may and may not wear if you are lower in the social pecking order is not entirely a matter of choice. Just as in the medieval period, laws dictate which materials cannot be worn by people of lower ranks. Elizabeth issues a proclamation in 1559 that the sumptuary laws of 1533 and 1554 are still to be obeyed. The regulations of 1533 declare that you are not allowed to wear the following materials unless you are a peer of the realm: cloth of gold or silver; tinsel (silk mixed with gold or silver thread); satin mixed with gold or silver thread; or sable (fur). You have to be a lord, the child of an earl, a marquess, or a Knight of the Garter in order to wear the following: woolen cloth made abroad, red or blue velvet, black furs of genet and lynx. Only if you are a lord, a lord's son, a knight, or have an income of £200 per year, may you wear velvet gowns, velvet coats, leopard furs, embroidered clothes, and cloth pricked with gold, silver, or silk. Last, unless you have an income of £100 per year, you are not allowed to wear taffeta, satin, damask, outer garments containing silk, velvet garments (except jackets and doublets), or fur except from animals that live wild in England.[4] The law of 1554 forbids you from wearing silk in any accessories you might carry unless you have an income of £20 per year.

Do people obey this sumptuary legislation? In a word, no. Such proclamations are almost as ineffective as King Canute's staged attempt to hold back the sea. Transgressions can be reported to manorial courts but they rarely are; and in rural areas the fines are likely to be small.[5] In towns, words of reproof might be spoken but not much more: there are simply too many transgressors. If someone is caught and fined, the chances are he can pay quite happily and carry on as before. The same can be said for the Wool Cap Act of 1571, which states that all working people over the age of seven should wear a cap of wool every Sunday and holy day, with a fine of 3 shillings 4 pence for each day that they do not. Again, you might find yourself indicted, but on the whole you can expect little more than an admonishment and a small fine.

Types of cloth used in Elizabethan clothing[6]

Silks: Silk, velvet, satin, damask, taffeta, grosgrain, sarcenet
Linens: Lawn, cambric, holland, lockram, canvas, buckram
Woolens: Scarlet, broadcloth, scammel, kersey, russet, frizado, frieze, kendal, cotton, flannel, worsted, serge, bay, says
Mixtures: Cloths of gold, cloth of silver, tinsel, camlet (a lightweight mixture of silk and linen), cyprus (a near-transparent linen-silk mix), mockado (velvet made of wool), fustian (a linen or worsted warp with a cotton or wool weft), and linsey-woolsey (a linen-wool mix).

In the above list, the highest-quality fabric is named first, then the lower and coarser qualities of cloth, in order of fineness. Lawn is gossamer-fine and used for ruffs, ruffles (cuffs), collars, and partlets (similar to neckerchiefs). Cambric is very white and used for the best shirts, smocks, and collars. Holland is also white: the sort of linen that townsmen and women use for their shirts, smocks, starched ruffs, and aprons. Lockram is used for the same purposes by workingmen and women, and linsey-woolsey is used by poorer people for their gowns and petticoats. Cloth is class, and those who are socially aspiring need only invest in a finer fabric and take it to their tailor. Note that, despite the name, the only proper cotton in these fabrics is the thread used in fustian: the "cotton" noted above is a lightweight wool. Only at the end of Elizabeth's reign does pure cotton cloth start to be imported from the East, in the form of calico.[7]

When it comes to color, things get a little more difficult. Elizabeth grows up with a reputation for very modest dress, described by contemporaries as "sad" (meaning dark-colored). Puritan writers applaud her for her lack of ostentation in the early part of her reign, when she often wears black and white. White means "purity," and black symbolizes "constancy," and the two colors together represent "eternal virginity."[8] But there is more to this simplicity than caution in the face of public opinion and the symbolism of a virgin queen. England has relatively few natural dyes of great strength. Purple has to be obtained from Mediterranean whelks—thirty thousand of them to make an ounce of dye. Bright red is the next hardest dye to obtain and is thus the color that betokens aristocratic wealth and the power of the Church of Rome. There are four sources. An orange-red can be made from boiling brazilwood, which used to be traded in powdered form from Asia but now is mainly imported from the New World by the Portuguese (who name the country of their source, Brazil, after it). A brighter red, used to dye the broadcloth called scarlet, comes from kermes: a parasitic insect that lives on evergreen oaks in the Mediterranean and which, when pregnant, is killed with vinegar, dried in the sun, and opened to extract its wormlike larvae. When rolled into little balls called "grains" and soaked in water, these produce a bright red dye called "grain"—hence the words "ingrained" and, in connection with the worms, "vermilion." The third bright red is cochineal, insects indigenous to the Spanish dominion of Latin America. In England the only available red is madder, and its quality varies considerably, depending on the soil. To make an English "purple" (more of a violet, really), you have to mix madder with the one indigenous natural blue dye, woad. From the scarcity of strong, bright colors, you will appreciate that it suits Elizabeth very well to declare that black and white are her favorites. It belittles the riches of the Spanish and accentuates the symbolic purity and constancy of her own costume. From your point of view, it is not a good idea to turn up at court for the first time in a cloak dyed in cochineal.[9]

Avoidance of all things foreign does not extend to design. The English shamelessly take whatever they require from wherever they find it. Courtiers traveling abroad bring back new designs and materials for themselves and for their wives, mothers, and sisters. They learn more about the new fashions in Holland, Italy, and Germany from entertaining foreign gentlemen and ladies at home. The queen receives portraits of Continental royalty as gifts, showing the latest styles at foreign courts. Information about the new fashions overseas is also circulated by dressed dolls sent from France (which can be handed to the daughter of the household to play with after the style has been copied); in 1559–60 dolls to the value of £178 3 shillings 4 pence are imported through the port of London.[10]

The result of this fascination with the new is an eclectic style: people mix Spanish sleeves with French gowns and Dutch cloaks. The dramatist Thomas Dekker comments that

> The Englishman's dress is like a traitor's body that has been hanged, drawn and quartered, and is set up in various places: his cod-piece is in Denmark, the collar of his doublet and the belly in France, the wing and narrow sleeve in Italy, the short waist hangs over a butcher's stall in Utrecht, his huge slops speak Spanishly . . . and thus we that mock every nation for keeping of one fashion yet steal patches from every one of them to piece out our pride.[11]

The queen herself deliberately and enthusiastically encourages this magpielike approach. In fact, she may rightly claim to be one of the greatest patrons of fashion in history. In the inventory of all her clothes and personal jewels in the royal residences in 1600 we find she has 102 French gowns, 67 round gowns, 100 loose gowns, 126 kirtles, 136 foreparts, 125 petticoats, 96 cloaks, 85 doublets, and 99 "robes" (ensembles for specific occasions, such as her coronation or Parliament). Additionally she keeps 2 robes, 26 French gowns, 14 round gowns, 27 loose gowns, 23 kirtles, 58 foreparts, 27 petticoats, 41 cloaks, and 38 doublets at the Office of the Wardrobe at Blackfriars. It is the variety of these clothes that makes her such a fashion icon. Although she employs only two tailors during her whole reign—Walter Fyshe until 1582 and William Jones thereafter—she has gowns specially brought from France for her tailor to copy; she has four Spanish gowns made for her between 1571 and 1577. She has the earl of Leicester write to his Italian contacts in Antwerp asking for newly made bodies to be obtained for her in Italy and Spain. She obtains Venetian gowns and has others made for her "in the Italian fashion." Many of her partlets, smocks, and gowns come from Flanders. In 1569 she has Walter Fyshe replace the lining of her "Dutch gown of black velvet with Spanish sleeves" with white taffeta. She even has a Polish gown of black velvet.[12] For a woman who never in her life travels abroad, it is as if she is touring the world in her wardrobe.

Needless to say, the Puritans do not like this fanciful adoption of foreign style. John Aylmer writes of Elizabeth in 1559: "I am sure that her maidenly apparel, which she used in King Edward's time, made the nobleman's daughters and wives ashamed to be dressed and painted like peacocks."[13] But as the queen's dress becomes more lavish in the 1570s, so too does that of her courtiers. In 1577 William Harrison laments what he calls "the fantastical folly of our nation":

> I can tell better how to inveigh against this enormity than describe any certainty of our attire, such is our mutability, that today there is none to the Spanish guise, tomorrow the French toys are most fine and delectable, ere long no such apparel as that which is after the high Almain [German] fashion, by and by the Turkish manner is generally best liked of, otherwise Morisco gowns, Barbarian fleeces, the mandilion worn to Colleyweston ward [i.e., askew], and the short French breeches make a comely vesture that, except it were a dog in a doublet, you shall not see any so disguised as are my countrymen of England. And as these fashions are diverse so likewise it is a world to see the costliness and the curiosity, the excess and the vanity, the pomp and the bravery, the change and the variety, and finally the fickleness and the folly that is in all degrees, insomuch that nothing is more constant in England than inconstancy of attire. Oh, how much cost is bestowed nowadays upon our bodies and how little upon our souls!

Philip Stubbes is even more scathing in his *Anatomy of Abuses* (1583). He declares, "By wearing apparel more gorgeous, sumptuous and precious than our state, calling or condition of life requireth, we are puffed up into pride and induced to think of ourselves more than we ought, being but vile earth and miserable sinners." He continues in this manner for 144 pages, railing against ruffs, hats, hairstyles, "the strangest doublets," and "costly nether stockings," sparing neither man nor woman but seemingly taking delight in declaring that "their dirty dregs [should be] ripped up and cast into their diamond faces."[14] The strength of his invective is truly splendid. At one point, in describing his fellow Englishmen, he announces, "Neither the Libertines, nor the Epicures, nor yet the vilest Atheists that ever lived exceeded this people in pride."[15]

If you find such bitter castigations simply an inverted form of pride, then you will have some sympathy for the queen in the days of her most splendid raiment. In his advanced old age the above-mentioned John Aylmer (by now bishop of London) dares to criticize the queen for her extravagant dress. Elizabeth replies: "If the bishop holds more discourse on such matters, she will fit him for Heaven—but he should walk thither without a staff and leave his mantle behind." As Sir John Harington observes, if the bishop had first inquired as to the extent of her majesty's wardrobe, he would have chosen to preach on another topic.[16]

Women's Clothing

In a dialogue book of about 1600 by Peter Erondell you can read the words of a well-to-do woman, called Lady Ri-Melaine, to her waiting gentlewoman as she prepares to get dressed in the morning:

> Go fetch my clothes: bring my petticoat bodies, I mean my damask quilt bodies with whalebones. What lace do you give me here? This is too short, the tags are broken: I cannot lace myself with it, take it away, I will have that of green silk. When shall I have my undercoat? Give me my petticoat of wrought crimson velvet with silver fringe. Why do you not give me my nightgown for I take cold. Where be my stockings? Give me some clean socks; I will have no worsted hosen, show me my carnation silk stockings. Where laid you last night my garters? Take away these slippers, give me my velvet pantofles. Send for the shoemaker that he may have again these turn-over shoes, for they be too high. Put on my white pumps; set them up, I will have none of them: give me rather my Spanish leather shoes, for I will walk today.... Tie the strings with a strong double knot for fear they untie themselves.[17]

There are several words here that might cause you to scratch your head. Bodies? Pantofles? Turn-over shoes? It seems best to deal with these items of clothing one by one, starting with the first garment you will put on after you get out of the bath.

Smocks. The shift or chemise is normally called a smock in Elizabethan England. It is the basic undergarment that has been worn by women for centuries. It slips over the head and reaches down to the knees or beyond, sometimes with a square-cut neckline, sometimes with a round one. Early in the reign you see smocks with high necks that peep out over the collar of the overgarments, from which the fashion for the ruff develops. Smocks are usually made of linen, the quality varying according to your status. The highest quality normally used is cambric, followed by holland; ordinary people use lockram.[18] Those who cannot afford pure linen use linsey-woolsey. A high-quality smock is normally embroidered around the collar and perhaps along the sleeves with designs such as oak leaves and acorns.

There is an old tradition that a new husband cannot be held liable for his bride's debts if she wears nothing but her smock at her wedding. You would have thought that a bride might refuse to get married in church in her underwear, with all her family, friends, and peeping toms watching. But it happens. Some young women do have very heavy debts.[19]

Stockings and hose. At the start of Elizabeth's reign, Lady Ri-Melaine would not be calling for silk stockings: all ladies of whatever estate have to make do with stitched linen or woolen hose. But in 1561 the queen's silkwoman, Alice Montague, hands Elizabeth the fruits of her labors: for the last ten years, Alice has been trying to work out how to knit silk stockings. When the queen puts them on, she declares: "I like silk stockings so well because they are pleasant, fine and delicate, that henceforth I will wear no more cloth stockings."[20] Unfortunately for her majesty, Mrs. Montague cannot knit silk that quickly. In 1562 it is a yeoman of the guard who presents the queen with two pairs of black silk stockings, and he does the same again in 1563: presumably he manages to find a foreign supplier. Mrs. Montague triumphs again in 1564, making two pairs of black silk stockings. The following year, having got the hang of it, she knits nine pairs. Very soon, everyone wants them. In 1599 William Lee invents a machine for knitting stockings and other silk garments. Yet less wealthy women, who cannot afford knitted silk, have to put up with wrinkled woolen at their knees for many more years.[21]

You will note that women do not wear drawers. A simple length of washable linen performs the necessary function on a monthly basis for both queen and poor girl.[22] However, Elizabeth's funeral effigy does sport a pair of fustian drawers and there are references to "six pairs of double linen hose of fine holland cloth" made for her in 1587.[23] But do these relate to royal pairs of drawers or linen hosen with a seam up the back of the leg? Given that respectable ladies never wear skirts shorter than their ankles, perhaps you will forgive a degree of uncertainty on the matter.

Socks. These are made of linen or wool, but they tend to be worn only by the well-off. Most people cannot afford them—nor can they afford to wash them.

Waistcoats. The waistcoat goes over the head, is tailored to the waist, and may be sleeveless or have sleeves attached. They are garments for the wealthy, made of high-quality linen, sometimes padded for warmth and support, and often embroidered. If you do not need to leave your private chambers during the day you may well wear just a waistcoat over your smock and nightgown, perhaps with a gown draped over the top.[24]

Bodies. "A pair of bodies" is the sort of garment that Lady Ri-Melaine is referring to when she calls for "my petticoat bodies" and "my damask quilt bodies with whalebones." They wrap around you and form the right and left sides of a bodice, normally being laced up at the front. They may be short and done up tightly, like a corset, or they may be longer and have a petticoat attached to form an underdress. If serving the purpose of a corset, they are often called a "corse," and if laced up at the back, a "vasquine" or a "basquine" (hence the modern word "basque"). Bodies may be stiffened with wood, whalebone, or clusters of reed and quilted with a stiffer cloth, such as buckram. In extreme cases, horn might be used for strength. The queen's bodies are made of velvet, silk, satin, and even perfumed leather.[25]

Farthingale. This is a fabric-covered framework, incorporating up to fifty yards of whalebone, which supports a petticoat or gown. As the fashion shifts toward wider and wider skirts, up to four feet across at the hips, light but strong farthingales are required. Male writers joke about them having to be left in the street, as they are too wide for the front doors of houses.

There are two main forms of farthingale: Spanish and French. The Spanish farthingale is already a feature of court life at the start of the reign and spreads quickly through the lower ranks of society in the 1560s.

It is shaped like a cone, with wider hoops of whalebone at the bottom and narrower ones at the top. The French farthingale arrives in the 1570s: a cartwheel around the waist and shaped like a drum, with vertical sides. But the style for gowns open at the front, which are less elegant with a French farthingale, means that the Spanish design does not disappear altogether.

Petticoats. Every self-respecting woman wears a petticoat, whether she be a queen or a countrywoman. It is said in 1585 that Englishwomen dress awkwardly because they wear three petticoats, one over the other.[26] One suspects the foreign gentleman responsible for that remark has not looked beneath many Englishwomen's skirts. William Kempe, Shakespeare's companion, dances from London to Norwich in 1599 and manages to trip up a couple of pretty country girls along the way: he notes that both of them are wearing only one petticoat. Some petticoats are made of heavy woolen cloth for warmth (flannel or kersey); others are of lighter cloths, such as satin or taffeta (if you can afford them). Inventories show that 87 percent of petticoats among ordinary women are red, dyed with madder; the remainder are mostly black, white, or blue.[27]

Foreparts. There are two sorts of forepart: one that covers the front of the petticoat, and one that covers the stomach, often called a "stomacher." Both are ostentatious pieces that cover the undergarments where a doublet or gown is left open for effect. If you are wearing a round gown, the skirts of which are open at the front, creating a triangular gap from waist to floor, then you will wear a forepart over your petticoat. If you are wearing a kirtle, doublet, or jacket that is cut low or open at the front, you should wear a stomacher. The queen usually has hers made of white satin and covered in jewels.

Kirtles. As noted above, you can have a pair of bodies attached to a petticoat as a single garment. A variation on this is to wear a kirtle. Rich women wear kirtles with a gown to cover the laces at the back. In such cases, the embroidery of the kirtle's front is seen through the front openings of the gown. For less well-off women, "kirtle" is another word for an ordinary dress.

Gowns. The gown is the outermost garment, covering the body from shoulder to ankle. You might wear it over a kirtle, in which case it will be open over the breast and over the skirts, allowing the front of the kirtle to be seen. Alternatively you might wear it over a pair of bodies and a forepart-covered petticoat. You may come across "loose gowns," which are like long jackets that hang from the shoulders down to the ground and are loose around the waist, often without sleeves. You may also encounter "train gowns," with trains that are carried by a maidservant. A "French gown" is similar to a "train gown." A "round gown" is one with a round, wide hem, which creates a wide circle around the wearer's ankles; it is usually open at the front, allowing the kirtle to be seen.

Gowns normally have sleeves attached. The Spanish style is for each sleeve to be cut with a single long slash from shoulder to wrist, allowing the material to fall open, revealing the sleeve of the kirtle. This is a colorful display, for you will see the outer color of the gown itself, then the contrasting color of its lining, and then the contrasting color of the kirtle sleeve. Sometimes the kirtle sleeve will be slashed or "pinked" (have patterns of small holes cut in it) to reveal the sleeve of the smock. The French style is for the lower part of the sleeve to be cut close to the arm but the upper part to be much larger, so at the shoulders it is about eight to ten inches across and stands proud, like a pair of vertical "wings."

Doublets and jerkins. The doublet is an outer garment that fastens down the middle and extends low and ends in a point. When worn without sleeves, it is termed a jerkin. Both garments may have "wings" (raised shoulder pieces). You might wear a doublet with a matching petticoat, or an unbuttoned jerkin instead of a loose gown; you might wear it partly undone at the front, to show off either your cleavage or a forepart beneath. This is a fashion that women start to adopt soon after 1570, and it provokes the scorn of many Puritans. "What are they? Women? Masking in men's weeds?" exclaims the poet George Gascoigne in 1574.[28] Philip Stubbes is predictably outraged:

> The women also have their doublets and jerkins, as men have here, buttoned up the breast, and made with wings, welts and pinions on the shoulder points as men's apparel is, for all the world, and though this be a kind of attire appropriate only to men, yet they blush not to wear it, as if they could as well change their sex.... It is written in the 22 of Deuteronomy that what man so ever weareth women's apparel is accursed and what woman weareth a man's apparel is accursed also.... These women may not improperly be called *hermaphroditi*, that is monster of both kinds, half women, half men.[29]

Ruffs and ruffles. In the middle of the sixteenth century both men and women start showing the collars of their smocks and shirts over the top of their outer garments. This little detail becomes most fashionable, and people start accentuating the line of the shirt with a cord or hem, stiffening it. In the early 1560s they start adding small collars or "bands" to the top of the shirt, and by 1562 the most fashionable women are wearing wavy linen "ruff bands" around their necks. These are made separately from the shirt or smock, to help laundering. Normally they wholly encircle the neck, creating the impression of a head on a plate (as Ben Jonson famously points out).

The fashion for ruffs spreads throughout the whole of Europe: everyone who wishes to look smart wears one from about 1565. At first it is a modest item of dress, a long length of linen set into pleats, each pleat forming a figure-of-eight shape; but it becomes more flamboyant, especially after the method of starching the ruff is invented in the Low Countries. In 1564 a Flemish refugee, Mistress Dinghen van der Plasse, sets herself up as a linen starcher in London, catering for her fellow refugees.[30] Soon everyone wants starched ruffs with crisp folds. At the height of the craze, in the 1580s and 1590s, ruffs are made of up to six yards of starched material, with up to six hundred pleats in them, extending eight inches or more from the neck. The edge may be trimmed with lace or "cutwork" (a form of decorative lawn). In the 1590s it might also be dyed blue to make the wearer's face look fashionably pale.[31] Very large ruffs are supported on a board, which remains unseen, as the cutwork or lace edges project out beyond it. Nothing excites the indignation of Philip Stubbes quite as much as a large ruff of the finest linen:

> The women use great ruffs and neckerchiefs of holland, lawn, cambric, and such cloth as the greatest thread shall not be so big as the least hair that is; and lest they should fall down they are smeared and starched in the Devil's liquor, I mean starch; after that, dried with great diligence, streaked, patted and rubbed very nicely, and applied to their goodly necks and withal underpropped with supportasses . . . the stately arches of pride.[32]

Sometimes "ruffles"—matching ruffs around the wrists—are also worn. Ruffs are worn by prosperous country folk: a yeoman's wife going into town on market day is likely to wear one; and if her children ride with her they too will wear ruffs. Only working folk with no social pretensions never wear a ruff.

Partlets. A partlet is a neckerchief or, to be more precise, a small piece of decorated high-quality cloth (satin, lawn, cyprus, or network) covering the upper part of the breast. In the first part of Elizabeth's reign partlets are designed to resemble the top of the smock where a doublet or pair of bodies is square-cut at the top.

Mantle. A decorative garment that covers the shoulders. It may just be draped there or alternatively be tailored to match a round gown or a French gown, and may even have a train.

Veils. At the aristocratic end of the social spectrum the veil is not used to cover the face but for the opposite purpose, to show it off by framing the head and surrounding it with jewels. It is therefore pinned to the headdress and gown. Some extravagant veils worn by noblewomen are supported by wires and provide a billowing gauzy backdrop to the lady's face, projecting out even farther than the wide extent of Spanish sleeves and farthingale.[33] In more humble contexts a woman going about town might wrap a piece of fine linen around her face to protect it from the sun.

Shoes and boots. Elizabethan women have a number of different items of footwear to choose from: slippers, pantofles, shoes, pumps, mules, chopines, clogs, boots, and buskins. Lady Ri-Melaine tells her maidservant that she will not wear slippers but velvet pantofles, then changes her mind and asks for pumps, and finally opts for Spanish leather shoes. Slippers you know about: they are made of soft velvet, have no heel or fastening, and are for indoor use only. Expensive ones are lined with satin and taffeta in the upper part, and scarlet covers the inside of the sole. Pantofles are also "slippers"—in the sense that you slip your foot into them. The word is more versatile, however, and can refer to indoor slippers as well as outdoor slip-on shoes. Outdoor pantofles range greatly in form and material, some being made of leather and some of velvet, some with pinking (decorative holes) that make them more pliable. Pumps are made of leather and fit the foot closely, with a thin leather sole and no fastening. "Mules," or "chopines," have a wooden sole two or three inches high, and are effectively leather- or velvet-topped clogs, designed to encase your shoe or foot and support it above the mud of the street.[34] These are somewhat unstable; Lady Ri-Melaine is probably referring to these when she says her "turn-over shoes" are too high. Don't confuse these with "turn-shoes," which are leather shoes stitched inside out and then soaked to make them pliable and turned the right way round.[35]

Normal shoes for well-to-do women are made either of velvet or soft leather and have a sole of leather-covered cork, done up with laces or a buckle. If made of leather, they may be pinked. Less wealthy women will have shoes with soft leather uppers and hard leather soles. Shoe horns are commonly used to help put on a tight-fitting leather shoe. The leather itself might be of various kinds and colors: Spanish leather or calves' leather is soft and the most desirable. Green and red leather are both mentioned by Philip Stubbes, while white leather is used for the shoes and boots of the wealthy (it distinguishes them from working people, whose boots get dirty).

One of this reign's lasting fashion innovations is the high heel. Until the mid-sixteenth century shoes are entirely flat-soled, but from about 1540 the cork sole to the shoe starts to acquire a greater thickness toward the heel. That difference between sole and heel continues to increase; as a result, the soles of most high-quality shoes in Elizabeth's reign are a distinct wedge-shape, being higher at the back. In the 1580s shoemakers start experimenting with wooden heels and arches to ladies' shoes. In 1595, at the age of sixty-two, the queen orders her first pair of "high heels" (as she calls them) and as soon as she gives the innovation her endorsement, it becomes de rigueur for ladies up and down the country.[36] Elizabeth's outdoor boots or "buskins," made of soft brown leather, also acquire wooden heels by 1599. The "well-heeled" never look back.

Outdoor wear. People spend a great deal of time out of doors, not only for the sake of sport and amusement as in the modern world, but for necessary tasks, such as working, traveling, and shopping. Women usually wear a "safeguard" when out of the house: a skirt covering their household dress. A sleeveless cloak or a Dutch cloak (with sleeves) is used to cover the top part. The queen has many matching cloaks and safeguards made for her, so we learn of "one cloak and a safeguard of purple and yellow cloth of silver, like leaves striped downright, with a lace of carnation, silk, Venetian gold and flat damask silver lined with white satin."[37] Later in the reign you might choose a juppe instead: a French descendant of the medieval jupon; in its sixteenth-century form it is a padded traveling jacket. Elizabeth has forty-three matching juppes and safeguards, such as "one juppe and safeguard of peach color, gold camlet, with a raised work of Venetian gold [and] silver down, before and all over the sleeves."[38] Alternatively, you might wear a riding gown lined with fur.

Riding hoods of wool or velvet are usual when traveling, as are gloves, scarves, and mufflers (which cover the face and protect the wearer from the rising dust). Masks are also worn, especially in summer, in place of a gauze veil to protect the wearer against the sun and the dust of the road. In 1575 van Meteren remarks on the new fashion in England for women outside the home to wear "vizards" and "silk masks" (probably referring to the silk coverings).[39] Traveling masks are similar to Venetian masks: when worn with a velvet riding hood, they can be quite haunting. Perhaps Stubbes does not go too far (for once) when he remarks that

> When they ride abroad they have visors made of velvet . . . with which they cover all their faces, having holes made in them against their eyes; whereout they look so that if a man that knew not their guise before should chance to meet one of them he would think he met a monster or a devil, for face he can see none but two broad holes against her eyes, with glasses in them.[40]

The above is a basic palette of garments and styles. You can mix them together in many different ways. Fashion being what it is, as soon as something is accepted as normal, people want to do something different. Having said that, it is worth bearing in mind that not everyone has access to mantles and veils, gowns and kirtles. A poor working-class girl might own nothing but a smock and a cassock. Townswomen who cannot afford a farthingale will wear a bum-roll instead: a heavily padded bustle or bolster that encircles the waist and gives some projection to the gown. When walking any distance—to go to market for instance—most women will not use mules on their shoes but will wear boots: mules would be impractical. On such journeys most people make do with a hat and muffler or scarf rather than a riding hood or mask. Once in town, most women will remove their scarves and mufflers and walk barefaced along the streets, carrying their baskets. It is worth noting also that working women's skirts are slightly shorter than those of gentlewomen: when traipsing up and down muddy streets or farmyards you do not want your gown to be under your feet.

How much does it cost to clothe the wife of a moderately wealthy husbandman? In 1579 Alice Bates of Appleby has goods to the total value of £3 7 shillings 8 pence: almost half her wealth is in what she wears.[41] When Avis Gardner of Cropredy, Oxfordshire, dies in 1580, all she possesses is her clothing and the chest in which she keeps it all, the whole lot being worth 14 shillings 9 pence, including the chest "with lock and hinges."[42] For most women, clothing themselves in even relatively plain attire is an expensive business: a whole suit of clothes for a female servant in Berkshire in the 1590s costs 1 shilling 10 pence. Having a pair of shoes made for you may cost as much as 18d. Three pairs of hose, two petticoats, and mending a doublet will set you back 3 shillings 4 pence in 1597.[43] If your husband is a laborer earning just 2 shillings per week and spending at least half of that on food for the family, even buying someone else's old cast-off gown at 2 shillings 6 pence is a huge expense.

Women's Hair and Headwear

Early in the morning, while she is still in her nightgown, Lady Ri-Melaine orders her waiting gentlewoman, Jolye, to attend to her hair:

Lady Ri-Melaine: Jolye, come dress my head, set the table further from the fire, it is too near. Put my chair in its place. Why do you not set my great looking glass on the table? It is too high, set the support lower. Undo my night attire. Why do you not call the page to warm the rubbers? Let him be called: here, sirrah! Warm that—and take heed you burn it not. I pray you Jolye, rub well my head, for it is very full of dandruff. Are not my combs in the case? Where is my ivory comb? Comb me with the boxwood comb; give me first my combing cloth otherwise you will fill me full of hairs, the hairs will fall upon my clothes. Comb backward—O God! You comb too hard, you scratch me, you pull out my hairs. Can you not untangle them softly with your hands before you put the comb to it?

Jolye: Will it please you to rise up a little Madame? For your hairs are so long that they trail on the ground.

Lady Ri-Melaine: My daughter is like me in that; hath she not fair hairs? What say you of it?

Jolye: Truly Madame she has the fairest, the longest flaxen-color hairs that one can see. There needeth no curling of them for they are curled of themselves. . . .

Lady Ri-Melaine: I like her the better for it. . . . Page, take the comb-brushes and make clean my combs, take heed you do not make them clean with those that I use to my head. Take a quill to take away the filth from them, and then put them in the case. Go to, make an end of dressing my head.

Jolye: What doth it please you to wear today Madame? Will it please you to wear your hairs only or else to have your French hood?[44]

A number of things in this ritual might surprise you: not least the practice of artificially curling the hair. The "rubbers" being warmed by the fire are linen cloths for rubbing the hair clean. Almost everyone dresses the hair using combs, not brushes. Hairbrushes are expensive and used mainly for applying medicinal substances to the hair; they will not be commonly used for another two centuries.[45] But the modern preference for hair dyed blond is nothing new: "Maidens wear silk cauls with which they keep in order their hair made yellow with lye," writes William Horman. The wealthy might regularly change the color of their hair to suit their clothes. An alternative is to wear a wig: the queen has dozens in the 1590s and uses them to color-coordinate her hair with her dresses as well as to cover up her gray locks. All these things come in for sharp criticism from Philip Stubbes:

If curling and laying out their own natural hair were all (which is impious . . .) it were the less matter; but they are not simply content with their own hair but buy other hair, either of horses, mares, or any other strange beasts, dyeing it of what color they list themselves. And if there be any poor woman (as now and then we see God doth bless them with beauty as well as the rich) that hath fair hair, these nice dames will not rest till they have bought it. Or if any children have fair hair they will entice them into a secret place and for a penny or two they will cut off their hair, as I heard that one did in the city of London of late, who meeting a little child with very fair hair, inveigled her into a house, promised her a penny, and so cut off her hair. And this they wear . . . as though it were their own natural hair. . . . If any have hair of her own natural growing which is not fair enough then they will dye it in divers colors.[46]

The French hood that Lady Ri-Melaine's gentlewoman refers to is a close-fitting velvet one that has a rounded top and goes over a linen coif (often called a "biggin"). It will normally have a finely wrought border and the coif too will be embroidered. Less wealthy women wear a plain coif, if they are not wearing a hat, or fold a kerchief into a coif. The style of wearing tall hats with a crown also starts in the 1560s: "English burgher women usually wear high hats covered with velvet or silk for headgear," writes Thomas Platter in 1599.[47] Married women cover their hair, in line with the teachings of St. Paul; if they do not, they are considered dangerously wanton and ill-disciplined.[48] Girls and unmarried women tend not to wear hats or other sorts of headdress unless traveling.

Women's Accessories

At the start of her reign, when asked about gifts, Elizabeth casually remarks that she would like nothing more than a fan. This is probably meant as a mark of modesty but it results in her being given dozens of elaborate fans over the subsequent years. Some of these are extraordinarily decorative, such as "one fan of white feathers with a handle of gold having two snakes winding about it garnished with a ball of diamonds in the end and a crown on each side within a pair of wings garnished with diamonds."[49] Gloves are given as gifts to women as well, although they might also be bought for practical purposes. The University of Cambridge pays £3 for a pair of perfumed gloves garnished with embroidery and goldsmith's work to give to the queen in 1578.[50] Provincial glovers like John Shakespeare make less expensive items, costing as little as 4 pence: the leather used by the Stratford glovers comes from the skins of sheep, lambs, bucks, does, deer, calves, horses, and even dogs.[51] Linen handkerchiefs are relatively affordable: plain linen are the cheapest; lawn, cambric, and silk are more expensive, with embroidered and lace-trimmed examples being more expensive still. These are all twelve to fifteen inches square. The smaller variety of four or five inches are usually presents given by women to men—as love tokens rather than subtle hints on their personal hygiene.

The queen's personal jewelry is a national treasure. Mrs. Blanche Parry lists 628 jewels when she makes an inventory in 1587 for the benefit of her successor as lady of the queen's bedchamber. In the seventeenth century, when King James sells off the collection, there is an outcry. For present purposes, however, it is important to understand that the queen's use of jewelry and its symbolism firmly sets the standards for all other women in the country. Consider Elizabeth's snake and pelican jewels: in Geffrey Whitney's *A Choice of Emblems and Other Devices* (1586) you will read that snakes are symbols of wisdom and the pelican, which in folklore pecks at her own breast to revive her young with her own blood, stands for self-sacrifice. The queen is particularly keen on the latter, having given up her chance of marriage for her queenly duty.

Supposing you have sufficient money, you may choose long "carcanets" or necklaces of pearls to adorn your body. Extravagant hairstyles frequently incorporate jewels: these may be fixed with hooks to your curls or, if you are wearing a wig, with pins. Wealthy women will not only have jewelry attached to their clothes and their velvet hats and caps but will wear one special pendant jewel of symbolic relevance over the breast. "One pendant jewel," of course, may incorporate many pieces of gold and precious stones, such as the queen's "jewel of gold like a pelican, garnished with diamonds of sundry sorts and bigness under her feet, three rubies and a triangle diamond with three small short chains and a knob garnished with sparks of diamonds and rubies," and the fantastic gold, enamel, ebony, diamond, and pearl ship pendant presented to her by Francis Drake.[52]

Remember that it is not just the design that has symbolic value: the stones themselves carry subtle meanings. In the words of a goldsmith given voice in a phrasebook:

The diamond is esteemed the chiefest of stones and called the stone of love, forasmuch as it hath virtue to reconcile and renew (yea, rather increase) love in them that are married, being in discord, by a hidden virtue that nature (or, to speak more properly, God) hath given it, to draw good affection to those that carry it; but I would never wish a pusillanimous man to carry it for it manifesteth timidity of the heart. It hath power also to resist enchantments. The virtue of the emerald hath likewise force as the diamond against enchantments: it quencheth lasciviousness, increaseth riches, and beautifieth the speech. The agate stirreth up storms, giveth the interpretation of dreams, and maketh the person to be agreeable. The sapphire is a royal stone. . . . It chaseth away melancholy and is very profitable for the sight. . . . The amethyst is good against drunkenness, taketh away evil thoughts, and giveth good understanding.[53]

Most countrywomen do not wear jewelry. In 1597 the prosperous Berkshire husbandman Thomas Dyer and his wife have just two gold rings and one silver ring between them, even though their goods and chattels are worth £145.[54] Married women do not wear a wedding ring of gold unless they are moderately wealthy (their marital status is shown by the way they dress and cover their hair). Gold rings are sometimes given to friends and relatives on the death of a person, so some people of humble means do wear gold rings, but in memory of the dead, not as a show of status. Pendant earrings are also known; Philip Stubbes fulminates against those who "are not ashamed to make holes in their ears whereat they hang rings and other jewels of gold and precious stones."[55] Small bands of gold are affordable to the provincial yeoman's or merchant's wife, but again we are talking about the minority of moderately wealthy women. Most women do not have pierced ears.[56]

Makeup and Perfume

Mirrors or looking glasses are available, both in square varieties that stand on a table and round versions for hanging on the wall. As you can imagine, the Puritans do not approve of either. "The devil could never have found a more pestilent evil than this," declares Stubbes, adding: "These looking glasses be called the devil's bellows, wherewith he bloweth the blast of pride into our hearts, and those that look in them may be said to look in the devil's arse while he infuseth the venomous wind of pride into their souls."[57] It has to be added that mirrors and looking glasses aren't cheap; you are unlikely to see one outside the houses of wealthy merchants and gentlemen.

"The women of England," Stubbes observes, "color their faces with certain oils, liquors, unguents and waters made to that end. . . . Their souls are thereby deformed and they brought deeper into the displeasure and indignation of the Almighty."[58] You will gather from this that women in Puritan families do not use makeup. Others do: it has long been the fashion to make your face white with lead-based ceruse. "They white their face, neck and paps with ceruse, their lips with red and their cheeks with purple," explains Horman.[59] This has the advantage of covering up any scars you might have left over from some disfiguring disease like smallpox. Sir Hugh Plat offers a different recipe in 1602, and although it will not give you lead poisoning, it has a certain unattractive quality:

> Wash barrows' grease [the lard of castrated pigs] often times in May-dew that hath been clarified in the sun till it be exceeding white, then take marshmallow roots scraping off the outsides, then make thin slices of them and mix them; set them to macerate in a seething bath and scum it well till it be thoroughly clarified and will come to be rope [viscous].[60]

If rubbing that lot into your face leaves you smelling less than fragrant, Elizabethan London has the answer. Some very strong perfumes are available in the capital, mainly ambergris (a secretion of the sperm whale), musk (a secretion of the musk deer), and civet (a secretion of the civet cat). These can be purchased in small multicolored glass bottles. These bottles can be jewels in their own right, edged with gold and garnished with rubies and emeralds; some even have screw tops.[61] A cheap alternative is a linen pouch stuffed with lavender. In between the two you have pomanders. Made of metal or boxwood, intricately carved and carried on a silken cord from the waist, these are filled with aromatic spices, such as cloves, nutmeg, and cumin (at the higher end of the market), or petals and herbs (at the lower).[62] Sir Hugh Plat's exotic recipe is one you might like to try:

> Take an ounce of the finest garden mold, cleaned and steeped seven days in change of rosewater: then take the best ladanum [a gum resin], benzoin, both storaxes, ambergris, civet and musk: incorporate them together and work them into what form you please. Then if your breath be not too valiant, it will make you smell as sweet as any lady's dog.[63]

Men's Clothing

In infancy, boys are dressed in skirts, the same as girls. At the age of about five or six, they are "breeched"—given breeches to wear instead—and dressed like young men. The clothes a lad now wears are mentioned in the following discussion between a schoolboy and a household maid as he gets ready for school (having got up late, of course, as schoolboys do in all centuries):

> *Margaret (the servant):* Ho, Francis! Rise and get you to school! You shall be beaten for it is past seven. Make yourself ready quickly, say your prayers, then you shall have your breakfast.
>
> *Francis:* Margaret, give me my hosen, dispatch, I pray you. Where is my doublet? Bring my garters and my shoes; give me that shoeing horn.
>
> *Margaret:* Take first a clean shirt, for yours is foul.
>
> *Francis:* Make haste then, for I do tarry too long.
>
> *Margaret:* It is moist yet. Tarry a little that I may dry it by the fire.
>
> *Francis:* I cannot tarry so long—go your way, I will have none of it.
>
> *Margaret:* Your mother will chide me if you go to school without your clean shirt.
>
> *Francis:* I had rather thou should be shent [blamed] than I should either be chid or beaten. Where have you laid my girdle and my inkhorn? Where is my jerkin of Spanish leather? Where be my socks of linen? Where is my cap, my mittens, my slippers, my handkerchief, my points, my satchel, my penknife and my books? Where is all my gear? I have nothing ready. I will tell my father: I will cause you to be beaten.[64]

Shirts. Note that the schoolboy Francis is already wearing a shirt when he starts to get dressed—he simply puts his clothes over the same shirt he slept in, even though Margaret tries to persuade him to put on a clean one. He obviously does not have such a large supply of these that several clean ones are ready to be worn. This says something not only about his status but also about his personal hygiene: most well-to-do people clean their bodies through constant washing of the linen that rubs on their skin. Cambric and holland come up fresh and white after a good scrub; lockram and linsey-woolsey are cheaper fabrics and can withstand a harder cleaning process. Most shirts are long, thigh-length, with slits up the sides so the tails can be tucked between the legs (instead of wearing drawers, which are more expensive).[65] Although linen is by far the most common cloth for a man's shirt, there are some made of silk. The 1533 sumptuary law states clearly that commoners should not wear them, but some Essex gentlemen are known to wear silk shirts.[66] Most, however, are not pure silk but linen embroidered with silk thread.

Hosen, breeches, and slops. A "pair of hose" or "hosen" can mean practically any garment a man might wear below his waist: socks, stockings, netherstocks, breeches, braies, trunk hose, pluderhose, slops, and even "trousers" (as worn by sailors). At the start of the reign, most hosen are all of one piece, covering the whole leg, like a pair of tights. Separate breeches and stockings arrive in the 1570s,[67] and by the 1580s a single-piece stocking is thought of in London as something fit for a country bumpkin. When visiting London in this period, you should wear breeches (otherwise known as trunk hose or slops) from the waist down, possibly with canions (stockings or "upperstocks") down to below the knee. On your lower leg you should wear netherstocks, which are like stockings up to the knee and over, covering the bottom of the canions and fastened around the bottom of the thigh with a garter. The netherstocks may be made of expensive material, such as satin, in which case they will not enclose the foot; instead an easily washable linen sock will be used. Expensive netherstocks are sometimes decorated with "quirks," or embroidered designs around the ankle. Less showy varieties are knitted.[68]

Various forms of breeches are available. At the bottom end of the social spectrum you have plain leather or serge breeches, reaching down to the knee. At the top end you have French or round hosen, gallyhosen (or galligaskins), and Venetians made of costly but hard-wearing fabrics, such as velvet, satin, and damask. French hosen tend to be short and rounded, ending mid-thigh. Sometimes these are stuffed with "bombast" or wool to make them firm. Galligaskins are wider and more voluminous, tied with garters below the knee. Venetians are longer and baggy, tied beneath the knee and covering the tops of the netherstocks. All of these varieties of hosen might incorporate elements of "pluderhosen," a German style in which the breeches have slits in the sides and incorporate "panes" of other material, juxtaposing the beauty of different colors and fabrics.[69]

Drawers. You may find the word "hosen" being used to refer to drawers—people are not too particular when it comes to discussing men's undergarments. Boys don't normally wear them but, as mentioned above, tuck their shirttails between their legs. Some men at the start of the reign continue the old custom of wearing linen braies, which are like close-fitting linen drawers. However, for those who can afford them, silk-embroidered linen drawers are the underclothes of choice for the sixteenth-century man of fashion. These are loose and extend halfway down the thigh, hanging in pleated folds from a linen cord at the waist.[70]

Waistcoat. Like women's waistcoats, these are undergarments tailored to the waist, designed to be worn over a shirt but beneath a coat or doublet. Also like women's waistcoats, they are put on over the head. Sometimes they are called "petticoats," especially if they hang lower than the waist;[71] you might also hear them called "vests" (not to be confused with the modern undergarment of the same name, even though they are worn principally for warmth). Waistcoats are often padded; those worn beneath a coat may have small pockets. For the wealthy they can be extraordinarily lavish, tailored from silk, velvet, or cambric, with sleeves embroidered with cloth of silver—especially stylish when worn beneath a casually open doublet or jacket.[72]

Doublets. The doublet is a lined garment that opens at the front. Normally it has sleeves and is buttoned up like a jacket. Alternatively it may be laced with leather "points." Some hang long; others are short and stop at the waist, sometimes holding up the breeches. Others still are tailored as a suit of apparel in the same material as the breeches. You might choose a light linen doublet in summer and a padded worsted one in winter; you will also come across leather ones. Prosperous men will wear a doublet of velvet; the less well-off are looking at worsted and serge.[73] With the decline of the codpiece, the stuffed peascod doublet slowly takes over as the outward projection of virility: it speaks of both manly courage and the satisfaction of being well fed. As for the fashionable Londoners in 1580, who better to describe their doublets but the arch-critic Stubbes:

> Their doublets are no less monstrous than the rest, for now the fashion
> is to have them hang down to the middle of their thighs or at least to
> their privy members, being so hard quilted, stuffed, bombasted and
> sewed as they can neither work nor yet well play in them, through the
> excessive heat and stiffness thereof; and therefore are forced to wear
> them loose about them for the most part, otherwise they could very
> hardly either stoop or bow themselves to the ground, so stiff and sturdy
> they stand about them. Now what handsomeness can be in these dou-
> blets which stand on their bellies as big or much bigger than a man's
> codpiece (so that their bellies are thicker than all their bodies beside)

let wise men judge. For my part . . . I see no good end whereto they serve except it be to show the disposition of the wearer: how he is inclined . . . to gluttony, gormandice, riot, drunkenness and excess.[74]

(You have to admit that Stubbes has to be the most entertaining writer of the period whom you would not want actually to meet in person.)

Ruffs. The ruff is a peculiarly unisexual garment. There is a male style of wearing a ruff—open at the front, with bands or ties dangling loose. This is especially popular with big-bearded men. But as the fashion extends to the wide ruffs of the 1580s, the majority of men wear ruffs similar to those worn by women, closed all round the neck, forming a large "cartwheel" shape. The finest are made of cambric, holland, and lawn. Stubbes, of course, mocks them all as unnecessary fripperies: "If it happen that a shower of rain catch them before they can get harbor, then their great ruffs strike sail and down they fall like dishcloths fluttering in the wind."[75]

Jerkins. By Elizabeth's reign, the jerkin has become a garment worn by all sorts of people. A worker in the fields may wear a leather jerkin over his shirt. Sailors often wear them too, fastened with eyelets and hooks or leather buttons.[76] The most fashionable aristocrat may also wear a jerkin, albeit one of velvet with silver buttons and stuffed shoulder wings.

Gowns. Ankle-length, fur-trimmed, loose-sleeved, and normally dark-colored, they are often worn by dignified men of a certain age. They are also a mark of men with a profession: academics, lawyers, physicians, and clergymen can be recognized by their gowns.

Cloaks. Hanging from the shoulders, they might have a collar of fur and be as long as a gown. Alternatively they might be collarless and short, more like a mantle. The German style of cloak is more like a jacket with sleeves hanging loose. The mandilion is another version of this; when one is worn as a cloak, at an angle, and with the sleeves hanging empty, it is described as being worn "Colley-Westonward" (as mentioned by Harrison earlier in this chapter). For the courtier, cloaks are essential: the earl of Essex has twenty-eight of them.[77]

Hats. At the start of the reign, the knitted or cloth cap is the ubiquitous item of headgear. In the 1560s felt hats with crowns become fashionable, and people in towns start to pay more attention to what they wear on their heads. Different colored hatbands are used, some of them with embroidery or jewels. Dyed feathers are also worn in the hatband: London merchants import feathers worth £1,863 for this purpose in 1559–60. The brim is sometimes curled up along the sides and attached to the hat. Most of all, the crown starts to rise—and rise. By the 1580s hats with a fifteen-inch-high crown are not unknown. Philip Stubbes rubs his hands with glee and declares:

> As the fashions be rare and strange, so is the stuff whereof their hats be made divers also: for some are of silk, some of velvet, some of taffeta, some of sarcenet, some of wool, and (which is more curious), some of a certain kind of fine hair. These they call beaver hats, of 20s, 30s or 40s a piece, fetched from beyond the seas, from whence a great sort of other vanities come besides. For he is of no account or estimation among them if he have not a velvet or taffeta hat, and that must be pinked and cunningly carved of the best fashion.[78]

Although many men disobey the 1571 act enforcing the wearing of wool caps on Sundays, the fact that such legislation is passed gives you an idea of how common the cap is among ordinary folk. Most of these are dyed black—or as black as the wearer can afford: true black is expensive. Although high-crowned hats start to be worn from the 1560s, you will still find gentlemen wearing caps in the latter part of the reign.

Shoes and boots. The Elizabethan worker's shoes and boots are made of leather, with thick soles. The same goes for his social superior. The difference lies in the quality of the leather, the size, and the decoration (such as pinking and coloring). The best leather is Spanish, called cordwain in England; those who work with it are called cordwainers. Workingmen tend to wear short boots of hard leather—ankle boots and calf-high start-ups—whereas gentlemen wear high boots of soft leather, such as buskins (knee-length) and gamaches (high boots). Galoshes are overshoes, worn for protecting your pumps and cork-soled shoes when out of doors. Otherwise, men's shoes are similar to women's. The production price of a pair of ordinary shoes varies from 10 pence per pair to 1 shilling 1¼ pence; the sale price (after the retailer's markup) is accordingly more than this, between 1 shilling and 18 pence.[79]

How much can you expect to spend on clothes? Let's say you are a butcher or baker, and you enter a London tailors' shop in 1597. There you will find all the tailors sitting around cross-legged on their benches. You ask the head man for a cloak, a coat, a little jerkin, a pair of hosen, and a Spanish cape to be made for you. The cost might be as little as 2 shillings 6 pence, plus food and drink for the workers.[80] However, you should note that the made-to-measure nature of the garments does not by itself guarantee quality; bad tailoring is more often to be found in the sixteenth century than in the modern world, where a tailored piece of clothing is, by definition, a high-quality item. If you are looking for real quality from a London tailor, the suit made for an ambassador to the court in 1595 will give you a better indication of cost:

6¾ yards of velvet for breeches at 15 shillings a yard	£5 3 shillings 6 pence
Four yards of fustian	4 shillings
½ ell of double taffeta	5 shillings
3½ yards of cloth for a cloak	£2 2 shillings 3 pence
1 yard of lining	2 shillings 9 pence
Gold braid for the cloak, gold lace	£1 10 shillings 9 pence
2½ yards of silk	2 shillings 6 pence
Lining	9 shillings 3 pence
Silk hose	£1 10 shillings
Three dozen buttons for a doublet	10 shillings
For making the cloak	6 shillings
For making the doublet and breeches	6 shillings 8 pence
Total	£12 12 shillings 8 pence

If that does not quite satisfy you, do not worry; in fashionable Elizabethan England, the sky's the limit, especially if you are a gentleman trying to make an impression at court. According to Philip Stubbes, some men have been known to pay £10 just on one shirt.[81]

Men's Hair and Beards

Enter a barber's shop in London, or have a barber come to your house, and you will have such a range of hairstyles presented to you that you will be quite bewildered. Would you like a Dutch cut or a French one? A Spanish one or an Italian? New? Old-style? Gentlemanly? Common? Would the esteemed gentleman/goodman like to look "terrible to his enemies or amiable to his friends, grim and stern in countenance or pleasant and demure"? When it comes to the actual haircut, you will have your head rubbed down with linen cloths ("rubbers") and combed several times with ivory combs of increasing fineness. Only then does the cut begin. Note that most men carry their own two-sided comb: one side is of widely spaced teeth for disentangling hair; the other has narrow teeth, for combing out the nits that may be living in it. Wealthy men have combs of ivory; less wealthy men carry combs of carved wood.[82]

With beards, there is also considerable scope for personal invention. William Harrison exhorts his readers to consider the shape of their faces when discussing their beards with their barbers. Dignified courtiers such as Sir Christopher Hatton, Sir Walter Raleigh, and Sir William Cecil go for the full mustache and beard, simply trimming them to look neat. A young gentleman with curly hair might rather have a small mustache and otherwise be clean shaven. Robert Dudley, earl of Leicester, opts for the bushy beard look in later life. George Clifford, earl of Cumberland, who has very distinctive long curling brown hair, has a pointed beard and wide mustache when he sits for his portrait as the queen's champion in 1592. His predecessor in that role, Sir Henry Lee, whose hair is short and curling, chooses a thin mustache and a small, tapering goateelike beard when he is painted in 1568, shaving not only his cheeks but his sideburns. This is not dissimilar to the style adopted by Shakespeare, Richard Burbage, Edmund Spenser, and other writers and actors at the end of the reign, all of whom have short, trimmed, pointed beards and mustaches. In contrast, Sir Philip Sidney, the dashing young poet, is completely clean-shaven in the 1580s. So is the physician Andrew Boorde: he hates beards because when he had one he was sick in it, and it took a very long time to remove the smell. Note that to be clean-shaven, you should try to go to the barber once a week; after two weeks, the clean-shaven look is wearing thin. The regulations of the Inns of Court in London deem a student officially to have a beard if he has not shaved for three weeks.

Men's Acccessories

There are three items that all men carry, or should be expected to have about their person. The first is a comb, already mentioned. The next is a sharp knife, for eating and other day-to-day tasks. The third is a purse for coins: normally a small leather or cloth bag on the end of a leather cord attached to the belt. Beyond these three, there is an unpredictable variety.

Wealthy men wear jewelry. For a royal favorite this might mean a jeweled gold chain with a pendant jewel containing the queen's image. Alternatively it might mean a ring. Rings are not always worn on the finger: when it is given as a gift, you might wear it on a band around your arm or on a chain around the neck. This fondness for jewelry doesn't yet extend to earrings, however. Although a famous seventeenth-century portrait of Shakespeare shows him sporting a simple earring in his left ear, it is highly unlikely you will see any men with pierced ears in Elizabeth's reign.

Another important accessory is weaponry. The aristocrat may well wear a breastplate or gorget (collar armor) when having a portrait painted—and may even wear a full suit of armor if taking part in a celebratory joust—but apart from these he will rarely don armor. For him—and for you, if you move in such circles—it is the sword that matters. Swords are status symbols: in London no one can carry one unless he is a knight. You can buy them easily enough: a thirty-four-ounce silver-handled rapier fit for a lord will cost you £11 in the 1580s; or, at the bottom end of the market, you can pick up a secondhand sword and dagger for 3 shillings 4 pence.[83] William Harrison comments that "seldom shall you see any of my countrymen about 18 or 20 years old to go without a dagger at least at his back or by his side." Of course, having such weapons close to hand inclines people to use them. In this respect, a little fashion accessory is a dangerous thing.

Not all swords are merely status symbols. Outside towns, even men of modest means will own weapons of some sort, in line with the legislation for the militia (the amateur force for the defense of the realm). Men with goods worth between £10 and £20 have to provide a bow, a sheaf of arrows, a steel helmet, and a bill or halberd when the militia is called out. Those with goods worth between £20 and £40 have to provide two bows with arrows, two steel helmets, one halberd, and one steel "almain rivet" (light armor for a foot soldier, consisting of a breastplate and back plate with thigh guards). So it goes on, with higher allocations of armor to be provided by those with greater wealth and income from land. Men who do not have sufficient wherewithal to supply arms and armor very often have to use them on behalf of their social superiors, donning the almain rivets and carrying the bills that their manorial lords keep for the purpose. This is why you will find so many coats of armor and weapons hung up in manor houses. Militia men are regularly inspected for the state of the armor they carry; and selected men undergo regular training too—they are called "the trained bands"—so if you are selected to serve in the militia this is what you may well end up wearing.[84]

Other accessories relate to people's work and occupations. Physicians and surgeons often have to ride out of town to see their patients, so on top of their long, fur-trimmed gowns they wear gabardines (overcoats) and caps. Gentlemen wear spurs when riding, partly as a sign of status and partly for urging their horses on. Miners wear practical garb similar to that of normal laborers (a thigh-length coat or doublet and belt, knee-length breeches, and boots) but with the addition of a protective, padded round cap and a candleholder between their teeth. Up on the downs, the shepherds have their smocks, hats, and crooks. Mariners wear trousers or slops, and loose upper garments over their shirts. The butler in a gentleman's house can frequently be seen in an apron, as are many workingmen and women, from butchers and smiths (in leather aprons) to brewers, bakers, fishmongers, and cooks (in aprons made of canvas and serge).

Nightwear

Most men wear a nightshirt and cap in bed. Francis, the previously mentioned late-in-rising schoolboy, sleeps in his day shirt at night, and probably most boys of his age do likewise, changing their shirt in the morning if they have a clean spare. Even if you reserve a separate shirt to wear in bed it will be essentially the same garment as a day shirt. If there is any difference it will be that the night shirt has a collar, rather than the ties to attach a ruff. The nightcap normally takes the form of an easily washed linen cap, saving the pillowcase from the grease of the hair. A few gentlemen have adopted the ladies' fashion of wearing a nightgown—a loose, comfortable, lined gown, which can be worn over the nightshirt—but these are not actually for sleeping in but for keeping warm when getting dressed or having your hair rubbed.[85]

Women and girls also wear nightrails very similar to or the same as their smocks. Lace-trimmed perfumed cambric is favored among those who can afford it, together with a linen coif or cap.

Women's nightgowns can be of the most lavish material, designed to receive visitors as well as keep the wearer warm between leaving the bed and getting dressed. Even the queen wears them to meet people. Hers are made of silk, taffeta, and velvet, lined with sarcenet and trimmed with gold and silver lace[86]—the nearest modern equivalent would be a dressing gown, but on a lavish scale far beyond most people's idea of nightclothes. In 1578 she allows a young man to catch her in her nightgown at Whitehall and declares herself to be "much ashamed thereof."[87] In fact, it is striking how often she is caught in her nightgown. In December 1597 she allows the French ambassador (the breast-fixated one) and his companions to see her in her nightgown and exclaims: "What will these gentlemen say to see me so attired? I am much disturbed that they should see me in this state." The ambassador notes that it is past one o'clock in the afternoon.[88]

Cleaning Clothes

The finest clothes are of little significance if they are dirty. In fact, ostentatious but dirty clothes may well have the opposite effect from that which you intend. This presents a real challenge to those who have to make fine clothes presentable. As William Horman points out, "If woolen clothes be taken no heed of and shaken and brushed, they will be moth meat and all to eat." Nor are moths the only enemy: mice, damp, mildew, and dust also cause problems. The solution to the mouse problem is easy: get a cat. The others are trickier.

There is no washing process for cloth of gold, silk, satin, taffeta, and suchlike garments. If there is a small stain, it can perhaps be sponged off. Otherwise delicate and expensive clothes are cleaned by having the lining removed by a tailor, who will pass it to a laundress to wash separately, before sewing it back into the garment. The showy outer part will be brushed or rubbed with a linen cloth. "Old men brushed their study clothes with cow tails as we do hair brushes," explains Horman. The brushes in question are shaped like modern shaving brushes: they consist of dyed pigs' bristles protruding from a bone handle.[89] Once brushed, the clothes are perfumed with powdered orris root, damask rose powder, civet, or ambergris, and then wrapped carefully in linen bags before being returned to their coffers. Furs are treated with fuller's earth, beaten, trimmed, and similarly perfumed. To combat damp and mildew, clothes that have not been worn for a while are regularly aired. Large quantities of coal are transported to the Tower and other royal palaces to air the queen's expensive clothes: they are hung out on long cords across the heated room.[90]

When it comes to the actual washing of woolens and linens, you need a tub, hot water, a scrubbing board (for the coarser cloths), and soap. And a woman. Men do not wash things in Elizabethan England: it is exclusively women's work and is hard labor—hard on your hands and legs as well as your skin. Washing is usually done in a kitchen, where it is at least easy to boil the water.[91] As for the soap, many recipe books contain instructions for making it at home: "Take one strike [two bushels] of ashes and a quart of lime . . . mingle both these together. Then you must fill a pan of water and seethe them well. So done, you must take four pounds of beast's tallow [fat] and put it into the lye, and seethe them together until it be hard."[92] If you would rather buy soap, three sorts are commonly available. Black soap is the cheapest: a liquid soap made in London from potash and train oil (extracted from whale blubber), costing about ½ pence per pound. Better is gray soap, a viscous liquid speckled with white, made in Bristol from potash and tallow (a liquid version of the above recipe), costing 1 penny or 1¼ pence per pound. Both these varieties smell disgusting and are caustic, so Mediterranean soap, made from potash and olive oil, is far superior. The best imported variety is Castile soap: a hard white cake from Spain, costing somewhat more (3 pence or 3½ pence per pound). In 1559–60 £9,725 worth of soap is imported into London, with another £4,665 worth of potash for making soap.[93] Going to a washerwoman and asking for a good-quality shirt to be laundered carefully will cost you about 1 penny. Washing a servant's linen for a year costs about 16 pence. Note that the finer and whiter the linen, the more expensive the soap. You cannot use black or gray soap on cambric without turning it gray.

When the clothes are clean they can be dried in the sun, if the weather is clement. In the fields outside London you will find washerwomen carrying their heavy baskets full of clean washing to dry on the grass or on hedges. In winter, clothes can be dried by the kitchen fire. Ironing as we know it has not yet been invented: flattening linen is done with warmed large stones or, in some wealthy households, the use of a screw press.

Given all this attention to appearance and detail, it is fitting to give Philip Stubbes the last word, in one of his finest tirades against English clothes; so passionate is his invective that you get a real sense of how much people enjoyed their splendid apparel in Elizabethan England:

> I think verily that Satan, Prince of Darkness, is let loose in that land—
> else it could never so far exceed as it doth for the like pride. . . . Thrice
> accursed be these years which bringeth forth such unsavory fruits; and
> unhappy are that people whom Satan hath so bewitched and capti-
> vated in pride.[94]

CHAPTER SEVEN

Traveling

Road Transport

The use of the word "road" as a noun is an Elizabethan invention, occasionally to be heard from the 1560s onward.[1] The terms "highway," "path," "lane," "street," and "way" are more normally used. Nevertheless, whatever you call them, roads themselves are among the oldest parts of the man-made landscape. Many of the routes in use date from Roman times. Even in a city, whose houses are rebuilt over and over again, the twists and turns of ancient paths lie like ghosts between the changing structures. And transport along these roads is similarly unchanging. Standing at a town gate on market day you'll still see hundreds of people approaching—driving cattle or sheep, leading carts laden with sacks and crates, or walking with baskets on their arms or on their heads (holding it in place with a wreath of hay).[2] Men are carrying dossars (huge baskets) on their backs or leading slow packhorses laden with panniers. Nothing much changes, you think . . . until you hear the rumble of wheels behind you, the crack of the whip, and the speeding coachman's cry of warning.

Coaches

In many ways the increased use of the four-wheeled coach or "car" goes hand in hand with the rise of the gentry and new wealth in the towns and cities. There have been passenger coaches since at least the thirteenth century, but until now they have been exclusively for royalty and aristocrats. Very soon after Elizabeth's coronation, however, the number of coaches on the roads dramatically increases. This is mainly due to the return of Protestant émigrés from the Continent, where coaches have been popular among the wealthy for a number of years; in 1560 five hundred coaches are in use in the city of Antwerp alone.[3] William Boonen, arriving from the Netherlands in 1564, so impresses the queen with his coach-driving skills that she appoints him her personal coachman.[4] It is a good example of how the Protestant revolution affects all walks of life.

In the royal household coaches are referred to as "close cars" ("close" meaning "enclosed," as opposed to open to the elements). Most Londoners refer to them as "caroches"—a corruption of the Italian *carrozze*, which are stately carriages for the very wealthy. Initially the task of making the royal close cars falls to the royal wheelwright; but in 1569 it goes to a designated "coachmaker," William Rippon, who has been producing coaches for the aristocracy for several years.[5] The queen has four made for her between 1578 and 1586; they all have timber bases with iron frames forming the superstructure, sides of leather, and linings of linen and brightly painted cerecloth. They have locking doors, for her majesty's security. When the queen goes on a royal progress, she may have between three and four hundred carts and wagons with her, using up to twenty-four hundred horses; but her own presence consists of her personal coach, a spare one (if the first should break down), and what we might call the "royal convenience" coach, containing a close stool (portable toilet) in case the queen or any of her ladies in waiting is caught short when traveling.[6]

Another reason for the sudden popularity of coaches is the lowering of the cost of production. In the Middle Ages a coach was an elaborate construction that would have set you back several hundred pounds. In Elizabeth's reign most people feel they don't need carved and gilt woodwork or embroidered silk hangings; it is enough simply to be traveling on four wheels. In 1573 a new coach can be obtained for just £34 14 shillings, plus 2 shillings 6 pence for painting your coat of arms on the side.[7] A secondhand one might cost as little as £8: the earl of Essex has one valued at this price, and the earl of Bedford has two old coaches valued together at £10 in 1585.[8] This does not include a team of four or six horses (at £10 or more per pair). Do not underestimate the cost of the horses' feed, especially if you are staying in town. When the purchaser of a brand-new coach, Mistress Kytson, arrives in London in 1574, she spends £2 11 shillings 9 pence on her food and that of all her menservants. Their horses, however, consume £2 18 shillings 4 pence of feed in the same time.[9]

It is predominantly women who create the new demand for coaches. This is partly because the English consider it a somewhat effeminate way for a gentleman to travel.[10] Although Lady Cecil travels by coach, her husband, Sir William, usually rides, and he continues to do so even when he is getting on in years.[11] Similarly Dr. John Dee in 1595 hires a coach to send his wife and children from Mortlake to Coventry while he follows on horseback.[12] Foreign men visiting England have fewer qualms about traveling by coach. Some German and Swiss tourists find English saddles uncomfortable, so they hire coaches. Coaches are available for hire in London, at a rate of 16 shillings per day plus food for the coachman and feed for the horses. Bear in mind, if you stop at an inn and your driver hears that the road ahead is very boggy, he may refuse to take his coach that way. Coaches are very easily damaged on the rough roads, and repairs are cripplingly expensive for the coachman.

This expansion of wheeled traffic causes a hostile reaction in some quarters, especially in London, where fulminations against speeding coaches are just as vehement as those against motorcars three centuries later. Inevitably there are accidents. In 1562 twelve-year-old Bridget Serten is killed when a cart crushes her against the wall of Aldgate.[13] In his *Survey of London,* John Stow writes:

> The number of cars, drays, carts and coaches more than hath been accustomed, the streets and lanes being straightened, must needs be dangerous, as daily experience proveth. The coachman rides behind the horse tails, lasheth them and looketh not behind him; the drayman sitteth and sleepeth on his dray and letteth his horse lead him home. I know that by the good laws and customs of this city shod carts [carts with iron tires on their wheels] are forbidden to enter the same, except upon reasonable causes . . . also that the forehorse of every carriage should be led by hand—but these good orders are not observed. . . . Now of late years the use of coaches brought out of Germany is taken up and made so common as there is neither distinction of time nor difference of persons observed; for the world runs on wheels with many whose parents were glad to go on foot.[14]

John Taylor, a waterman on the Thames and a poet in his spare time, echoes this complaint; but his main concern is the loss of business. "This is the rattling, rowling, rumbling age, and the world runs on wheels," he writes. "The hackneymen who were wont to have furnished travelers in all places with fitting and serviceable horses for any journey (by the multitude of coaches) are undone by the dozen."

For such reasons a bill is presented to Parliament in 1601 proposing the limitation of the use of coaches. It is read twice and then rejected.[15]

The State of the Roads

The driver who refuses to drive his cart along a certain road is not just being precious. Roman and medieval roads were intended for people and animals on foot, not for coaches with iron-tired wheels. According to William Harrison, "In the clay or cledgy soil [the roads] are very deep and troublesome in the winter half." In towns too, the vast majority of roads are not paved. Gravel is put down at the worst-affected junctions to soak up the mud, but otherwise carts must pass over deep ruts of dry mud or soft wet soil. Any extant stones of Roman paved roads near the surface are likely to be more of a hindrance than a help for a coachman. Landowners and tenants of land bordering on the highways are meant to maintain the ditches which drain the roads but they do not always do so. Once soaked by a blocked drain, the road quickly turns into a quagmire.

Driving a coach or cart through a town is just as hazardous. Many people have nowhere to stack firewood other than in the street, sometimes under the eaves of their houses but sometimes partly blocking the way. Many towns have bylaws forbidding this; nevertheless it is a perennial problem. Crates, branches, trunks of trees, broken wagons awaiting repairs, split timber, barrels, troughs are all likely to be found in the streets. People dig in the roads for sand or clay to daub their wattle buildings and leave great holes. Sawpits, often more than six feet deep, are no less dangerous, especially where dug directly beside the road so that large trunks can be easily offloaded. People are fined for digging wells in or just beside the highway; in 1573 a servant girl of Rettendon falls into a roadside well and drowns.[16]

Some modern historians claim that nothing is done to improve the state of communications in Elizabeth's reign.[17] But that is not true. Several Acts of Parliament to remedy the poor state of the roads are passed, the most important of which just predates Elizabeth's accession. The Act of 1555 establishes the process whereby the churchwardens in every parish appoint two surveyors of the highways at Easter. These surveyors announce four days in the year on which all parishioners will repair the roads. Every farmer must send a cart with two of his men and every cottager has to give his own labor, or else be fined heavily. This legislation is greatly extended in scope by a second act in 1563, which purposefully envisages a reform of communications in England. It restricts the size of gravel and sand pits, enforces the digging and scouring of ditches and drains beside the main roads, allows surveyors to take small stones freely from quarries to mend the roads, increases the number of days to be devoted to road works to six in each year, and raises the fines that have to be paid by defaulters. In 1576 a third act amplifies and extends the existing legislation; in addition, acts are passed on the repair of particular stretches of road, such as the highways in Sussex, Surrey, and Kent, in 1585 and 1597.[18] If you travel in the summer you can see the law being obeyed—at least in part. In 1581 in Great Easton, Essex, two dozen farmers and cottagers send their carts or offer their labor to help with highway maintenance; twenty-seven others pay fines of 10 shillings for not providing a cart or 12 pence a day for not working, and these fines are spent on further work on the highways.[19] William Harrison confirms that, in general, the wealthy prefer to pay the fines, so that on average only two of the six days are worked by everyone.[20]

The fundamental problem with the whole approach is that the people who are expected to do all the work do not significantly benefit from it. Most of them travel on foot or on horseback: they have little need or inclination to rebuild the roads for the benefit of wealthy coach passengers— rich women and "effeminate" men—or royal messengers. The majority of country folk simply walk round the quagmires in winter and step over the hardened ruts in summer; they can live with these obstacles. Not until the burden is placed on the road user does it become economically feasible to maintain the highways properly—and that will not happen for another century.

Bridges

Chapter One began with the observation that "different societies see landscapes differently." It won't take you long to realize that different societies *think* of the landscape differently too. Whereas most modern people think of England in terms of a road network, most Elizabethans think in terms of a network of rivers. This, in fact, remains a common way of thinking about the country well into the next century.[21]

There are many different types of bridge. London Bridge has already been described, as has Hugh Clopton's fourteen-arch bridge at Stratford-on-Avon. You will see other impressive medieval bridges elsewhere: the eleven-arch stone bridge over the Medway at Rochester, the eighteen-arch stone bridge over the Exe at Exeter, or the bridge over the Thames at Wallingford, which has twenty-two arches. Most are more modest, however, and often made of timber. There are even timber bridges over the Thames at Caversham and Sonning. Note that just because a bridge is built of stone does not mean that it is better than a wooden one. Some old stone bridges are very narrow—four to five feet is not unusual in rural areas. Improving the highways seems pointless if vehicles cannot traverse the rivers.

Not all bridges are in good repair. You will take one look at some of them and fear that you are taking your life in your hands. In winter the heavy water flow disturbs the piers, even if they are made of stone, and this in turn weakens the superstructure; wooden bridges often tumble into the fury of a river in full spate. The Bridges Act of 1530 empowers magistrates to determine those responsible for the upkeep of a bridge and to levy a charge if they fail in their duty. But this does not always solve the problem. Bridges cross rivers which normally mark the ancient boundaries between two landholdings; and where there are two landowners, frequently neither one wants to take responsibility for a dilapidated bridge. Do the people want to pay for the bridge instead? No. So you have a case like that at Ingatestone in 1567: The bridge is ruinous and the magistrates determine that it is the responsibility of the landowners to repair it. Lord of the land on one side is Sir William Petre. Can the magistrates force Sir William to pay? They try—and try again the next year, and again the next. They are still trying to get the bridge repaired five years after it was first reported to be in a bad state.[22] Nor is the queen any better at repairing rotten bridges. Although she is happy to endorse parliamentary bills for bridges and roads to be mended at other people's cost, she does little to repair the broken bridges on her own manors.[23] Here too there seems to be a mismatch of liability and benefit. Only where an important bridge clearly benefits the local community are you likely to find it well cared for at municipal expense. When the floods of 1588 break both ends of the bridge at Stratford-upon-Avon, for example, the town authorities quickly see to its repair.[24]

Horses

You will need a horse if you intend to travel along the roads of England. It is all very well saying that you don't mind walking and would quite like the exercise—many people do walk the length and breadth of the country—but you will soon see the reason in having a mount. It has less to do with energy expenditure than status and keeping clean. Gentlemen and ladies do not walk along the highways: they either ride or are carried in a coach. The only other option is a litter. This is a compartment or carriage supported on two long poles. In towns it might be carried by servants: some women use them for shopping in preference to a coach, being easier to maneuver in the streets of a city. Traveling any distance, however, will require you to have a horse harness for the litter. Although old-fashioned in comparison with coaches, they are still in use among the aristocracy.

Various types of horse are available. A palfrey is a good-quality riding horse, ideal for long distances. A courser is high and fast, excellent for hunting. English carthorses are famous for their strength: William Harrison claims that five or six of them will draw three thousandweight on a long journey, or four hundredweight if alone. Sumpter horses or packhorses are not for riding but for carrying bundles of goods. Harrison adds that horses bred for riding in England tend to be gelded; this makes them calmer in temperament than stallions and suitable for female riders. (Remember that gentlewomen are expected to ride sidesaddle, and that includes the wives of self-respecting yeomen too.) He also notes that many "outlandish horses" have started to be imported, including Spanish jennets and Neapolitan coursers. Thomas Blundeville lists eleven types in *The fower chiefyst offices belonging to horsemanshippe* (1566)—namely Turkish, Barbary, Sardinian/Corsican, Neapolitan courser, Spanish jennet, Hungarian, High Almain (German), Irish hobby, Flemish, Friesland, and Swiss. They all have their distinct qualities. A Turkish horse will stop at nothing, bravely leaping over every obstacle. Barbary horses can gallop on the flat for ages. Flanders horses are huge and can draw massive weights, like modern shire horses. Spanish jennets are swift and prized by noblemen. "The Irish hobby," Blundeville writes, "is a pretty fine horse, having a good head and a body indifferently well proportioned, saving that many of them be slender and pin-buttocked. They be tender mouthed, nimble, light, pleasant and apt to be taught, and for the most part they be amblers and therefore very mete for the saddle." His favorite, however, is the Neapolitan courser:

> A trim horse being both comely and strongly made, and of so much goodness, of so gentle a nature and of so high a courage as any horse is ... In my opinion their gentle nature and docility, their comely shape, their strength, their courage, their sure footmanship, their well-reining, their lofty pace, their clean trotting, their strong galloping and their swift running well considered ... they excel numbers of other races.

When it comes to buying your own steed, you would be well advised to go straight to the most famous breeder in the country, Sir Nicholas Arnold. Alternatively, you might head to a horse fair, such as those at Ripon, Stourbridge, and Smithfield (London). Qualities valued by contemporaries tend to include color, shape of limbs, and whether they have an easy ambling pace. Color is not as obvious as you might think: it carries with it a mass of superstitions. Blundeville states that a white forefoot on the far side is a good sign, as is a white rear foot on the near side; but the opposite of these are indicators of an evil disposition. Any white rising high up the leg is also a bad sign. Prices vary hugely: expect to pay well in excess of £3 at a fair for a good riding horse—more for a really fine beast—but you might be able to pick up an adequate older horse for much less. Ask around in a village: someone will have a horse for sale privately, in the same way that people sell secondhand cars privately in the modern world. The average secondhand price is between £1 and £2 (the price increasing slowly over the course of the reign).[25] However, you can find old horses going for 5 shillings or less in the 1580s, and an untrained yearling colt can be picked up for 6 shillings 8 pence.[26]

An alternative to buying a horse is to hire one. You can do this at many inns, where they are lent out to trustworthy clients. Or you might hire a post-horse. Early in the sixteenth century three post routes from London are established. One goes north to Berwick, on the Scottish border. Another goes to Dover—by way of Dartford, Rochester, Sittingbourne, and

Canterbury—and a third to Plymouth. Each "post" is a series of stations, approximately twenty miles apart, where you can hire horses at the standard rate of 3 pence per mile (2½ pence if you are on government business), dropping off the horse at another post house or station, and paying an extra 6 pence for the "post-boy" to return it. In each place at least two horses have to be kept by law constantly ready day and night, fully harnessed, with two bags for any state packets that need to be carried. If you are traveling, you can "ride with the post" on the other horse, the official messenger bringing it back. In some places more horses are kept at the town's expense (Leicester, for instance, keeps four).[27] Sir Thomas Randolph is appointed chief postmaster in 1571 and briefly introduces a fourth post, to Beaumaris in Wales and across to Ireland; but this falters after five months and is not revived until 1598.[28] Anyone can make use of the post in Elizabeth's reign but private packets have to go as "bye-letters"—they can be taken only with the state packets, not separately. If you want to send a package privately, use a carrier: someone who regularly rides between towns transporting goods.

How fast will you be able to travel? This depends on several factors: the season, the weather, the cost of changing horses on a long-distance ride, and how long you can stay in the saddle. On dry roads in midsummer, presuming you have a strong backside and thighs, you should be able to keep going for the post's minimum speed of seven miles per hour. People riding their own horses in a hurry to get to London from Exeter are able to do the 170-mile journey in three days. Riding back with the post to Dover in late October 1599, Thomas Platter manages to do the forty-four miles from Gravesend in five hours, nine miles an hour, which he calls "great speed."[29] In summer you should be able to cover a hundred miles in a day—if your thighs can withstand the strain. In winter, however, with the roads muddy and only eight hours of light, and with no change of horses, you will be very lucky to do much more than two or three miles an hour—twenty rain-soaked, miserable miles in a day. The most impressive record is that set by Sir Robert Carey, who is given the task of riding from London to Scotland to announce to King James VI of Scotland that Queen Elizabeth is dead. He sets out between nine and ten o'clock on the morning of March 25, 1603, and reaches Doncaster that night, having covered 162 miles in one day. The following day he rides another 136 miles to his own house at Widdrington. Due to a bad fall on the afternoon of the third day, which leaves him with a bleeding head, he has to ride more slowly; but still he manages to complete the last 99 miles to Edinburgh by nightfall. He rides the whole journey of 397 miles in three days, covering the first 347 miles in two days and three hours.[30]

Finding Your Way

You cannot carry a road map with you. Christopher Saxton's stunning set of maps is printed in 1579, but it is bulky and costly. Even though it is the most advanced set of English county maps yet made, and will provide the basis for all other maps for more than a century, it is still not detailed enough to guide you. More practical guides take the form of printed tables that give distances between towns and the directions in which you need to travel. Some are arranged in a circular form, with London at the center and all other cities and towns radiating out in a sequence of circles, with the distance from the preceding town given in brackets. Other versions are printed in French for the benefit of foreign visitors, such as *La Guide des Chemins d'Angleterre* (Paris, 1579).

The other solution to finding your way, of course, is to ask directions:

Traveler: I pray you set me a little in my right way out of the village.
Plowman: Keep still to the right hand until you come to the corner of a wood, then turn at the left hand.
Traveler: Have we no thieves in the forest?
Plowman: No sir, for the provost-marshal hung the other day half a dozen at the gallows, which you see before you at the top of that hill.
Traveler: Truly I fear lest we be here robbed. We shall spur a little harder for it waxeth night.[31]

If traveling at night, it will be the moon you need to guide you, as Alessandro Magno finds out on a return journey from Richmond in 1562:

Seeing that we were faring badly and not knowing what we ought to do—whether to go on or turn back—we were very frightened. Then one of my companions spoke up. He said that London lay to the east, and as the moon rises in the east we should follow it so as not to get lost. . . . We could hear on all sides many owls hooting and my companion, who was greatly afraid, begged me to hurry saying that these were robbers who were calling to one another. . . . Finally we came to a village where my companion wanted to remain. He reminded me that the way was unsafe, dark and extremely muddy and that we had to pass through places where, only a few days before, people had been murdered. . . . Since we did not wish to stray from the way but had to admit that we did not know it, we hired a man as our guide and, having armed him sufficiently, we placed him on horseback. When we got back to the path which my companion had said was unsafe, he still wished to turn back. He argued also that it was dangerous to approach London at that hour for, although there were soldiers around at that time who had been ordered by the queen to help the Huguenots, one should not believe that the road would be safe.[32]

We normally associate highwaymen with the eighteenth century but there are just as many in Elizabethan England—if not more. Vagrancy has greatly inflated the numbers of desperate thieves who will lurk behind trees and bushes to take travelers by surprise. Notorious places for thieves are Gad's Hill near Rochester, Shooter's Hill by Blackheath, Salisbury Plain, and Newmarket Heath.[33] These are just the most famous. Between 1567 and 1602 suspected criminals are tried for the theft of more than £1,000 of money and jewels stolen on the highways in Essex—and that figure represents only the sixty cases that come to court.[34] If you travel anywhere near Cambridge watch out for Gamaliel Ratsey, a gentleman soldier who has become a notorious highwayman, complete with a mask and wicked sense of humor. He has been known to make a Cambridge scholar give an oration while being robbed, and has himself lectured a company of actors on their art after relieving them of their valuables.

Robberies often follow a pattern. After a night carousing in an inn with your fellow travelers, you head off to bed. But the inn's servants know that you have money to spend and which way you are heading. They watch to see how many are in your party when you set out in the morning, and a messenger leaves the inn in a hurry. Your party is making its way beneath overhanging trees and around muddy stretches of road in jolly conversation when you suddenly find yourselves confronted by men bearing swords, cudgels, and possibly a caliver or an arquebus (long-barreled guns). You turn, only to find the path behind cut off. What do you do? You realize that you can either live without your cash and other valuables or fight to keep them. The highwaymen will normally take all your money and jewels, any expensive items of clothing, and your horses, and leave you tied up away from the highway but in such a manner that you can work yourself free after an hour or so. As you start to walk on to the next inn or town in nothing but your underclothes, you can take some small comfort from the fact that you are not the first and won't be the last to experience this humiliation.

And then it will start to rain.

River Transport

Small rivers are obstacles and, for the traveler, a nuisance. Large rivers, however, enhance your travel options. Where a river is significantly deep, you will normally find a ferry. In some places, such as along the River Witham between Lincoln and Boston, there are no bridges but five established ferry routes. These will either transport you across the river or, one after another, take you down the twenty-four-mile stretch of water to Boston.[35] Similarly the Long Ferry travels up the river from Gravesend to London. This picks up the passengers riding with the post from Dover and takes them up to the city. Catch it just after breakfast and it should deliver you into the city about 2 p.m., or sooner if the tide is in your favor.[36]

In London, the River Thames is so crucial to transport that you will soon come to think of it as the city's main highway. There are many alleys and lanes leading to stairs down to the water where you can pick up a wherry. This is a water-borne taxi system: each wherry normally has one waterman who will row his passengers directly to their destination, whether upstream, downstream, or on the far bank. You will never have difficulty finding one: there are more than two thousand on the river.[37] In the mornings you will see them all tied up to the jetties and stairways, bobbing about on the tide. Each has an upholstered seat at the back wide enough for two people to sit side by side.[38] Over this seat is a canopy, which can be raised or lowered according to the weather.

Crossing the river—for instance, to go from the city to the playhouses on the south bank—will cost you a penny each way. Traveling upstream or downstream is more expensive: the fare from Temple to Westminster is 2 pence, and from Blackfriars to Westminster 3 pence. The fare also changes with the tide: a trip to Greenwich from the city costs 8 pence with the tide but 12 pence if the tide is against you.[39]

If there are many of you traveling together, you may consider hiring a barge or a tilt boat. Passenger barges are rowed by a team of oarsmen; many noblemen have their own, simply hiring watermen when they need them. A tilt boat is a barge with a canopy running its whole length and it has neither oarsmen nor a sail; rather, it is pulled along by oarsmen in a separate steerage boat. It will cost you 10 shillings to travel in one all the way from London to Windsor and back. The queen has an impressive glass-sided boat for such journeys, kept in a dock on the Thames and attracting many curious sightseers.

Traveling by water is not without its dangers. In London and Rochester, where the great bridges are built on starlings, there is the problem of the tide. When the tide goes out the Thames turns into rapids under London Bridge, rushing out with considerable force. This makes it impossible to row or sail upstream under the bridge and highly dangerous to attempt to go downstream: an exploit called "shooting the bridge." In 1599 some Catholic fugitives are caught by the river at night:

> They rowed back toward the bridge but by now the tide had turned and was flowing strongly. It forced their little boat against the piles driven into the bed of the river, to break the force of the water. It stuck, and it was impossible to move it forwards or backward. Meanwhile the water was rising and striking the boat with such force that with every wave it looked as if it would capsize and the occupants be thrown into the river. They could only pray to God and shout for help.[40]

If you fear ending up in this situation, then make sure you have a life preserver with you. These are made from pigs' bladders and inflated by blowing into them.[41] If going anywhere near London Bridge, it might be a good idea to have one or two blown up in advance.

Seafaring

We have seen at the beginning of the book that the appearance of an English town in 1558 is not hugely changed from the late Middle Ages. The same cannot be said for the docks in England. Most seagoing vessels need to be rebuilt every twenty-five or thirty years, but in the sixteenth century designs are developing so rapidly that ships built before the mid-1550s are regarded as too old-fashioned to be rebuilt and simply broken up. Only one royal ship facing the Armada fleet in July 1588, the two-hundred-ton *Bull*, is more than forty years old; the average age of the thirty-four English vessels in the English navy is just fifteen years.

Types of Ships

By modern standards, most seagoing ships are small. Only the big royal warships are over four hundred tons burden.[42] The largest of these is the *Triumph*, built in 1561. Her keel is a hundred feet long, she is forty feet in the beam, and she has a tonnage of 955 tons. In 1599, she carries a complement of five hundred men and forty-four guns, including four cannon (firing sixty-pound shot), three demi-cannon (firing thirty-pound shot), seventeen culverins (long-barreled, eighteen-pound shot), eight demi-culverins (nine-pound), six sakers (six-pound), and six falconets (approximately one-pound).[43] Unfortunately, great ships like her are too slow and difficult to maneuver easily. Sir John Hawkins therefore pioneers the "race-built" galleon, so called because the castles are lowered or "razed." Traditional warships have a high forecastle at the prow and an even higher sterncastle, from which archers can shoot down on their enemy. However, the effective use of cannon has resulted in battles now being fought at a distance, so castles are more of a hindrance than an advantage. Race-built galleons have just an open area at the front of the vessel and a covered deck and the captain's cabin at the stern. Cutting down the weight of the superstructure makes the ships lighter and thus faster, more maneuverable, and more stable. The earliest race-built galleon is the 368-ton *Foresight*, seventy-eight feet long and twenty-eight feet wide, launched at Deptford in 1570. It is soon followed by others, including the 460-ton *Dreadnought*, the 360-ton *Swiftsure* (1573), and the 500-ton *Revenge* (1577).

It is these ships that constitute the famous "wooden walls of England." Have a look at the fleet that chases the Spanish Armada up the Channel in July 1588. As mentioned above, thirty-four of them are from the royal navy; the rest—no fewer than 163 of them—are privately owned vessels. The royal ships are not all as large as the *Triumph* or the race-built galleons—among them are small pinnaces, such as the 60-ton *Moon*, built in 1586—but the privately owned vessels are not all small either. Some are quite impressive: for instance, the *Galleon Leicester* and the *Merchant Royal* are both 400 tons; the *Edward Bonaventure* and *Roebuck*, 300 tons. Thirty-five other merchantmen have a burden of 140 tons or more, another hundred are over 100 tons, and another 656 over 40 tons.[44] This is no accident: the government encourages the building of large ships in order to be able to co-opt them for defense, paying a bounty of 5 shillings per ton. Thomas Wilson reports in 1600 that the navy has thirty-six warships and fourteen pinnaces, but this

> is not the twentieth part of the strength of England. . . . When there was a fleet of 240 ships of war sent into Spain and four other fleets of merchants sent to the Levant, to Russia, Barbary and Bordeaux, all at one time abroad, yet you should never see the Thames between London Bridge and Blackwall (four English miles in length) without two or three hundred ships or vessels, besides the infinite number of men of war that were then and ever roving abroad to the Indies and Spanish dominions to get purchase, as they call it, whereby a number grow rich.[45]

The vast majority of seagoing ships are not glamorous galleons but humble fishing vessels and traders. You do see many carvels, barques, and other merchantmen of forty to a hundred tons in English ports but they will be hugely outnumbered by smaller boats. On the lower reaches of the Thames there are sailing hoys, which ply the trade along the north coast of Kent and the south coast of Essex, and tide-barges going up to Billingsgate on the flood tide and returning to their Essex or Kent port on the ebb.[46] If you look at the wharves of the main ports you will find substantial ketches (strongly built two-masted coasting vessels with three triangular sails, used mainly for long-distance fishing), mongers (trading vessels not dissimilar to ketches), dredgers and crayers or half-ketches (smaller fishing boats), and lighters (flat-bottomed boats for river work as well as short sea journeys, like modern barges). Smaller than these are the cock boats (boats attached to ships, used for fishing) and skiffs (clinker-built rowing boats, sometimes with a single small mast).[47] At times these boats can play an important role: Sir Francis Drake receives news of the arrival of the Armada from a ketch off the coast of Devon.[48]

Seamanship

Your greatest hardship when traveling on small boats like these is likely to be inclement weather and a little nausea. Small boats tend not to go very far from land, so if the weather turns stormy you can simply head back into port. If you are contemplating a long voyage, however, things are more complicated. The very act of handling an oceangoing vessel is both demanding and dangerous. Setting and stowing the sails requires crew members to go aloft and suspend themselves along each yard—and the heights are dizzying: the *Ark Royal* has a mainmast over one hundred feet tall. Imagine being out in the Atlantic in a merchantman as a storm is building up and the rain comes down hard; the captain may order the sails to be furled, to protect them or to prevent the ship being blown off course. As the vessel pitches and tosses like a cork on the waves, you might be the one to have to climb forty or fifty feet up the mast and then clamber out along the yard, pull in the sailcloth as you balance on the pitching timber, thrusting to and fro with the violent motion of the ship. If you fall from that height and land on the deck you will break a limb at the least. Fall from the topsail or topgallant onto the gunwales and that will be the end of you. Fall into the sea and you will almost certainly drown. Now imagine having to stow the sails in a gale in fading light, at nightfall.

Even steering a boat can be dangerous. In heavy seas it might take six or seven men to control the tiller of a very large vessel, and they have to do this below deck, without being able to see the sea and the sky. You will not find a ship's wheel anywhere—it has not been invented yet. Instead most Elizabethan ships are steered by the sails and the whipstaff: a long steering pole which pivots at a point below deck, controlling the rudder. This allows the helmsman to remain on deck where he can see the direction in which he is heading, but the pivot can increase the difficulty of holding the rudder steady in high seas: a sudden surge can tear it from his hands and even break the whipstaff.

Then there are the problems of navigation. The time-honored skills of a maritime pilot are of little use when it comes to crossing an ocean. A pilot knows the ports and the headlands, the currents and the phases of the moon and their tides; but he will rarely sail out of sight of land. He does not use a chart but a compass, a plumb line, and his experience. When it comes to long-distance travel, these tools are not good enough, especially at night.

Sixteenth-century navigators do not always get it right, as James Hooper, captain of the *Desire*, will testify. On a voyage to the Azores he changes course against the advice of his shipmates and sails straight past the islands—continuing for five days before admitting he has "no better knowledge than the mainmast" where the Azores lie.[49] However, most navigators learn how to deal with the complicated mathematics. They take as their starting point a simple direction across a chart, dead reckoning the distance and setting out that way. The key lies in constantly recalibrating their position in relation to their destination by establishing the latitude. Using a quadrant, a mariner's astrolabe, or a cross-staff, they can calculate this by measuring the height of the Pole Star above the horizon in the northern hemisphere; in the southern hemisphere they use the Southern Cross. Obviously these measurements can be made only at dawn or dusk, when navigators can see both the stars and the horizon, so they use the height of the sun at midday as a supplementary measure and determine latitude according to tables worked out by the Portuguese in the fifteenth century. As for speed, the basic method of a log and a series of knots on a rope has recently been invented, so you can establish distances in miles and leagues, as opposed to old-fashioned "keenings" (multiples of the visible distance of the horizon from land). Deep-water soundings can be taken with a lead weight and a hundred-fathom rope to measure the depth of the sea floor: if it is more than six hundred feet, you are off the Continental Shelf. Practical charts also exist: they are called "cards" or "plats" and are attached to sticks and stored in elm tubes.[50] Most Elizabethan ships carry several compasses, in case one breaks or the needle needs remagnetizing with a lodestone. If you use a traverse board to keep check of the changes of tack and update it with each half-hourly watch (measured with an hourglass), you should be able to plot your way across the ocean.[51]

One thing you can take comfort from is how quickly the science of seamanship advances in England in this period. There are very few treatises on navigation in English before 1574, so those that do exist are mostly translations; in 1561 Richard Eden publishes *The Arte of Navigation Translated out of Spanysh into English,* thereby making available Martin Cortés's important work for the first time. But in 1574 it is joined on the bookshelves by William Bourne's *A Regiment for the Sea: containing very necessary matters for all sorts of sea-men and travelers,* the first English-composed practical treatise on navigation. Alongside the old techniques of pilotage it includes tables on calculating tides and latitude by means of the stars, and soon becomes the essential mariners' aid. Bourne observes that just twenty years ago "masters of ships hath derided and mocked them that have occupied their cards and plats and also the observation of the altitude of the Pole saying that they care not for sheepskin for they could keep a better account upon a board." But now navigation has become a mathematical art. By the end of the reign a dozen books have further advanced the science of navigation. In *Certain Errors in Navigation* (1599) Edward Wright shows how to adopt Mercator's projection to plot an exact course across the oceans; and John Davis—the same man who sails from the Falkland Islands to Baffin Island—demonstrates in his *Seaman's Secrets* (1594) the use of the backstaff for more accurately measuring the height of the Pole Star, sun, and Southern Cross. This makes use of the work of the brilliant natural philosopher Thomas Harriot, which will not be significantly bettered until the eighteenth century.[52] Within forty years the English develop from being borrowers of the art of navigation to becoming pioneering experts.

Life at Sea

In some respects life at sea is like life on land. Men eat, drink, sleep, and perform their routine functions according to the hours of the clock—but the ways in which they go about it aboard ship, living in an overcrowded world of wood, wind, and water, differ greatly. Space is at a premium, even on a large ship. You might notice the low ceilings below deck—five feet eight inches is not unusual on the main deck, less on the orlop deck below— but as the crew are mostly between five feet five inches and five feet nine inches tall, only a small minority find this a significant problem.[53] However, head height is the least of your worries. The *Ark Royal* is a large ship, but even she has little more than two thousand square feet of space on each of her three decks, and more than half of that is used for storage and stowage of provisions, ammunition, fresh water, and spare sails. Then there are the fifty-five guns, which require about five hundred square feet of space. This means that, when it comes to sleeping, the crew of 420 men have less than six square feet each—and this includes the upper deck, much of which is open to the elements. There simply is not enough room for everyone to lie down at once. Hammocks have not yet been introduced and people lie where they can—and curse anyone who gets up in the night and stumbles across his shipmates as he makes his way for the heads. Still, a third of the crew will be on duty on deck, wishing the night away, with the boat heaving, waves splashing over the side, and the rain falling. At sea, it is fair to say, you will not get much sleep.

It follows from this that people eat differently aboard ship too. Keeping food is difficult. Meat can be salted and stored in barrels but it goes off; similarly, it is hard to keep enough ground flour dry and free from rats to bake enough bread. The standard ration for men at sea in 1565 is a generous 4½ pence per day in port or 5 pence at sea, which provides a gallon of beer and a pound of biscuit or bread, half a pound of cheese, and four ounces of butter per day, and half a pound of meat four days a week and stockfish or four herrings the other three days.[54] Dried peas and oats may be used in stewing up the meat but very little fresh food is available. You may walk into the captain's cabin and see the table laden with grapes, prunes, plums, apples, and pears, together with pewter plates and spoons, goblets, and wine flagons, but this is purely for him and any of his fellow officers dining with him; most mariners will not have fresh fruit. Indeed, if their allowance of meat goes rancid or the weevils eat into the ship's biscuit, they will go hungry. Each man has in his chest a turned bowl, a lidded wooden flask, and a wooden spoon, and he eats squatting where he can, either in the dim light below deck or up in the fresh air, amid the barrels, cannon, and hundreds of other men. But what he actually consumes will be as much a matter of luck as the type of food laid in store at the start of the voyage.

This struggle for food is a key feature of life at sea. If the meat goes rancid it may well bring the crew down with sickness and leave them unable to man the ship properly. Outbreaks of dysentery are often blamed on corrupted meat. On one of his voyages, Francis Drake tries out a suggestion of Sir Hugh Plat's and feeds his crew on pasta, as it is easy to keep and full of nutrition. But this still does not provide the vitamins sailors needs on a long trip. Vitamin D is not a problem as the body makes it naturally in sunlight and men spend most of their time in the beating sun; but the lack of vitamin C is a serious issue. Many more sailors die of scurvy than drown.

Life aboard ship, as you can see, is pretty desperate. Many sailors have lost teeth. Most suffer from tooth decay and gum disease. Their breath stinks, overpowering even the stench of their bodies. Apart from the officers, they do not wash or shave; the surgeon aboard a large ship has more pressing things to do than shaving men. Their foul clothing harbors dung beetles and fleas.[55] Their hair is often riddled with the larvae of insects, such as the puparia of the seaweed fly. Many seamen use wooden combs but these provide only limited relief. The men all have to share the same toilet facilities: the "heads," a place at the front of the vessel, where you urinate and defecate through a floor of slotted planks. It stinks and it is rife with diseases. Only the captain and his senior officers have their own chamber pots. Any dogs, cats, and rats on board will not be so careful where they defecate, and the atmosphere below decks on a long journey is a noxious mix of urine, sweat, vomit, and animal excrement that will severely test your love of the sea. Just as your eyes have to adjust to the darkness when going below, so too your nose will have to get used to the smell.

You may be perturbed to see how young the mariners are who live in these conditions: 82 percent of all the men aboard are below the age of thirty and include boys as young as ten or eleven. As you can imagine, their chances of reaching adulthood are slim.[56] Discipline is essential to keep such large groups of young men under control. Expect to hear the shrill blast of the boatswain's call regularly. Time is reckoned in strict half-hourly turns of the hourglass or sand clock; a watch is eight turns. This four-hour period regulates everything from when men may eat to when they are on duty, when they must pray, when they have to swab the deck and heads, and when the ship should change tack. Sailors work from dawn until eight o'clock in the evening. Cleaning the ship, attending to its rigging, setting or stowing the sails, mending the ropes, fishing, calculating positions, caulking the vessel to preserve its seaworthiness—there is very little scope for idleness. From eight until midnight the men are allowed to relax, unless their ship is in danger from the elements or the enemy. They may play cards or tables (a form of backgammon) and music: fiddles and pipes are popular at sea.[57] In a well-run ship a strict disciplinary code is enforced. Punishments range from a 1-penny fine for swearing or blasphemy to ducking in the sea for minor offenses such as petty theft or sleeping on duty, flogging for disobedience, and loss of limb or hanging for striking an officer, murder and mutiny.

With regard to safety, if the owners do not rebuild a vessel, she will grow progressively less seaworthy. If the captain is negligent and does not enforce the caulking of the hull, it will leak. If the sails are not kept in order and are allowed to tear, the ship may find itself at the mercy of pirates. If the navigator does not take regular soundings, there is a danger the ship will run aground. There are very few lighthouses. If you get caught in a heavy gale, the advisable course of action is to furl your sails, run before the wind, and pray.[58]

The other great threats to the safety of a ship are piracy and war. On May 19, 1585, after years of English raids on Spanish settlements in Latin America and the seizing of many Spanish cargo ships, Philip of Spain orders the detention of all English ships in his ports. A number of English corn ships happen to be in Bilbao: the merchants who own them lose everything and the sailors are thrown into prison, where many of them die. Just being an honest merchant is a dangerous business. For this reason every seagoing ship is armed. Even a small pinnace will have half a dozen guns. If you do take part in the plundering of Spanish vessels, the rule is to observe the quantities due to the authorities. Attacks against the Spanish do not count as piracy if you pay half of all your loot to the queen and a tenth to the admiral of England. The remaining 40 percent may be shared by the captain and crew.[59] However, if you seize the cargo of a foreign country and keep it for yourself, you are regarded as a pirate and the government will try to hunt you down. After 1585 the Spanish similarly prey on English shipping, hoping to capture and ransom passengers to and from the Continent as well as looting English merchant ships.

The Spaniards are not your only enemies at sea. The Barbary pirates—the original "barbarians"—are beginning to make an impact during the queen's reign. These crews from North Africa principally operate in the Mediterranean and off the Spanish coast; they are not yet openly sailing in British waters, so only ships that sail long distances are under threat, such as vessels of the newly established Barbary Company. But a few unfortunate Englishmen are among the tens of thousands of Europeans taken captive and forced into slavery. In about 1585 a ship belonging to Sir Thomas Leighton is captured by Barbary pirates and its English crew taken as slaves. One of them, Giles Napper, serves as a galley slave in Barbary for two and a half years until he is able to escape.[60] The Barbary pirates become a serious threat in 1601 when a Dutchman called Simon Danseker leads them through the Strait of Gibraltar to prey on European vessels in the Atlantic. Very soon afterward, an Englishman, Jack Ward, turns to piracy and leads the Muslim corsairs into the English shipping lanes, to seize boats from within sight of the English shore. No one in a coastal town is safe. You come across women who do not know whether they are widows or not—all they know is that their husbands went to sea and never came back. Such women are in a terrible plight, for they cannot presume their husbands are dead until seven years have passed; only then can they remarry. In the meantime they have to fend for themselves. If their sons are also serving aboard captured ships, then their plight is doubly awful, for the pirates will eagerly take boys to sell in the slave markets of Morocco, Algiers, Tripoli, and Tunis.

When you contemplate all the dangers from pirates and shipwreck, all the hardship and diseases and the terrible conditions aboard, you may decide that traveling by ship is not for you. But it makes the achievements of the Englishmen who do sail round the world in this reign all the more remarkable. Consider what Drake has to put up with on his great circumnavigation. He sets sail in November 1577 with five ships and about two hundred men. His own ship, the 150-ton *Pelican,* is the largest, with eighteen guns. The other four are John Wynter's eighty-ton *Elizabeth,* with eleven guns; the fifty-ton *Marigold;* the thirty-ton *Swan;* and the fifteen-ton *Benedict.* The last three have just twelve guns between them. After attacking and looting six Spanish and Portuguese vessels, the *Benedict* is exchanged for a captured forty-ton ship, which is renamed the *Christopher.* A sixth ship is added when a Portuguese merchant vessel is seized, and renamed the *Mary.* Drake appoints Thomas Doughty of the *Swan* captain of this new vessel but it is soon after this that he accuses Doughty of plotting against him. Things now go from bad to worse. After stripping the *Swan* of her crew and burning her, after executing Doughty and stripping all the other captains of their ranks and appointing them as his own subordinates, Drake continues through the Strait of Magellan. When a violent storm blows up, the *Marigold* sinks with its twenty-man crew, and the other ships are dispersed in the freezing Southern Pacific. Having lost sixty men to cold, hunger, and disease, Drake is forced to abandon the *Mary.* At this point John Wynter in the *Elizabeth* absconds back to England with his survivors. With the *Pelican* the only one of his original five ships left—now renamed the *Golden Hind*—Drake sails up the coast of Chile. Only thirty of the seventy men left aboard are able to fight, but while most people would

be glad still to be alive, Drake goes on the rampage, attacking Spanish vessels and looting every ship he takes. One prize is accidentally lost when a
drunk sailor drops a lamp in the hold and sets light to the vessel, but he
continues, capturing ships laden with valuable cargoes. By this time Drake
is showing signs of mental instability. Worried lest his Portuguese pilot be-
tray him, he tricks the man into going ashore and abandons him. After
sacking the ship's chaplain he conducts his own religious services. When
the *Golden Hind* runs aground on some rocks in the middle of the Pacific,
his chaplain declares that the disaster is God's judgment for Drake's execution of Doughty. Drake forces the chaplain to wear an insulting label and
threatens to hang him if he should remove it for the duration of the voyage.
A black woman captured in America is put ashore in Indonesia (after Drake
and his men have got her pregnant); but her presence during the Pacific
crossing hardly relieves the tension, only adding to the jealousies and suspi-
cions of the crew. The *Golden Hind* finally arrives back in Plymouth on
September 26, 1580, almost three years after setting out, becoming only the
second ship to sail round the world, and the first to be captained all the way
by the same man.[61]

If the above does not put you off maritime exploration, consider the case
of Peter Carder. This chap sails in the *Elizabeth* under the command of
John Wynter. He is thus caught in the storm sailing through the Strait of
Magellan and heads back to England with Wynter. When Carder and several other men are set ashore in a small boat on the coast of Brazil to look
for fresh water, they are attacked by Portuguese sailors who fatally wound
five Englishmen and take the others prisoner. After spending some time in
jail Carder is put in the custody of a Portuguese merchant, who makes him
work on his plantation alongside black slaves for several years until Carder
escapes to Pernambuco and embarks on a Portuguese ship heading back to
Europe. Captured by Englishmen on the return journey and almost
wrecked off Ireland, he finally arrives home in November 1586—nine years
after setting out.[62]

Carder subsequently spins out his story. He claims that when sheltering
on an island devoid of fresh water for two months, he was forced to drink
his own urine; and that he lived with a tribe of moon-worshipping polygamous cannibals for a number of years. These polygamous cannibals
really do exist—but Carder himself does not meet them; he simply borrows
these elements of his story from others. Nevertheless, he is honest in one

respect: his story is testimony to the many sufferings you may encounter at sea even if you do return home. Over half of those who set out with Drake do not. When the *Golden Hind* finally puts into Plymouth in 1580, there are just fifty-six men on board, and fewer than forty men return with Wynter in the *Elizabeth*. Statistically speaking, sailing round the world in the sixteenth century is considerably more dangerous than going into space in the twentieth.

CHAPTER EIGHT

Where to Stay

Where you lay your head in Elizabethan England is—like everything else—very much a matter of status. Poor men will not be offered accommodation in a nobleman's house, and most noblemen would not deign even to set foot inside a cottage. Travelers can't expect cheap accommodation at a monastery anymore: hospitality is no longer a matter of charity. No doubt the idea still exists in some remote places but too many people are now on the road for this generosity to be widespread. If you have no money, you will rest wherever you can—in a barn, a woodshed, a cave, under the eaves of a house, or simply in the fields. However, provided you have the means to pay and there is room, you will be able to stay at an inn. Charity might have lost its purchasing power but that of silver is stronger than ever.

Inns

The greater inns are one of the pleasures of traveling in Elizabethan England. You can hardly mistake the lavishly painted sign, hanging outside a fine London establishment. Leading your horse beneath the wide entrance arch into the yard, which may well be cobbled or paved, you will see two or three stories of galleries on either side of you. These provide access to the chambers. A boy will unsaddle your horse and take it through to the stables at the rear of the property, and an ostler will take your bags and lead you to the innkeeper so you may be "appointed a chamber."

Entering a chamber in a good-quality establishment, you will find at least one bedstead, normally with posts and curtains round it, slung with ropes on which a straw mat is placed, and with a couple of featherbeds on top ("featherbed" actually refers to the mattress). Foreign travelers frequently comment on the cleanliness of English inns. Expect clean linen sheets "wherein no man hath lodged since they came from the laundress," as William Harrison sweetly puts it, as well as blankets, coverlets, and quilts. The feather-filled pillows should similarly have clean linen pillowcases. In many rooms there will also be a truckle bed for servants or children. You will find extra bedding in a chest, and there may be a second chest for your own belongings. Other items you are likely to find in your chamber include a table covered with a linen tablecloth and two or three stools or chairs. If the walls are not wainscoted (paneled with wood), then they will generally be hung with painted cloths: these look like tapestries but are much cheaper and give a similar warmth to the room. In a city inn, the chamber windows look out over an inner courtyard and the rooms are quite dark on the first floor because of the overhanging gallery above. At dusk you will be given a candle and candleholder to see your way to bed. It is not unusual also to find dried fragrant flowers on a tin plate in the room to sweeten the air.

The largest London inns have fifty or more chambers and can accommodate two hundred visitors, as well as their horses. Rooms are often shared by the members of a traveling party, with single occupancy costing more. You may choose to eat in the hall or in private, in your chamber. In the hall you will no doubt be accosted by the bands of musicians who inevitably press their services on guests in the hope of earning some coins. Prosperous Londoners wishing to throw a feast for their friends and family use the hall of an inn for this purpose, so you may encounter a rowdy party, forcing you to resort to your chamber. Plays are often acted in the yards of big inns at two o'clock in the afternoon, with the gallery making an excellent viewing platform.

The innkeeper is legally responsible for the safety of his guests, and will do all he can to prevent theft or violence on his premises. Your room door will probably be lockable and you will have charge of the key (the innkeeper has a skeleton key that undoes all the doors). At dusk the main gate is locked and nonresidents are asked to leave. Theft at an inn is therefore highly unlikely—but that comes with a caveat. Do you recall the ostler who took the bags from your horse when you arrived? For the price of a drink he may tell someone who you are, what is in your bags, and where you are heading. . . . If you remember the lesson from the last chapter, you will tell him nothing. That goes for your charming fellow guests too, some of whom are wearing fine clothes—which may come courtesy of other travelers like yourself.

What about inns in provincial towns? Many are as fine and well appointed as their London equivalents. On the whole, however, they are much smaller. Let us say you ride into Farnham in 1563, looking for a bed for the night. There you will come across a traditional inn run by Joan Hawle, a widow. Passing beneath the gatehouse arch and entering the hall, you will find it dimly lit, open to the rafters, and with a central stone hearth. Smoke from the glowing fire rises to escape through a hole in the roof. Above the fire a couple of pots are hanging from iron frames. On the rush-covered floor lies a pair of bellows next to a fire shovel and a pair of tongs. Three large tapestry-like painted cloths hang on the walls. There are two tables with benches on either side; the benches are covered with mats and cushions, and there are a couple of stools. There are no barrels of wine or beer stored in here: they are kept in the buttery next door and pots or flasks are carried through to customers in the hall as and when required.

This is all pretty rudimentary compared with the great establishments in London. But it is more than adequate for most travelers. Joan has four letting rooms, besides her own accommodation. A door in the hall leads through to a large parlor where you will find two oak-framed beds with carved testers at their heads and feather mattresses, bolsters, blankets, and quilts. Also in here are an oak cupboard, a trestle table, a bench with a rush-work mat on it, four stools, and a chair. There are two carpets: these are for covering the tables and cupboards; they are not used on the floor. Go upstairs to the chamber directly above and you will find a similar room with a trestle table, benches, and a settle as well as two beds—one great wooden bed and a truckle bed. In the chamber above the gate there are two bedsteads; and over the buttery there is another chamber with three further beds. None of these rooms is glazed: the windows are covered with wooden shutters. But nevertheless they are large enough for you and a friend to sleep relatively comfortably. Joan's own private parlor doubles up as a storeroom and if you lift the lids of the five wooden chests in there you will find folded sheets of canvas (ten pairs), lockram (four pairs), a holland sheet, as well as six tablecloths of canvas. Firewood can be found in the barn on the other side of the yard, along with oats and hay for the guests' horses. If it comes to the worst, there is even a spare bed above the stable.[1]

Returning to Farnham forty years later you will find that inns have improved. Stop by at the one run by George Whittingham. He has eight chambers for guests, containing a total of eighteen beds. Let's say he offers you the "Chapel Chamber" for the night: therein you will find the walls covered with painted hangings, and on one side a standing bedstead with a truckle bed. There are also two cupboards against the wall, both covered with woven carpets, and a table with a cushion-covered bench and two cushion-covered chairs. There are firedogs in the fireplace. Best of all, the room is glazed. You can expect lockram sheets, and he even has some of holland. If you find yourself in the "New Chamber" next door, your four-poster bed-stead will have curtains and a valance too. Call for the servant and you can ask for beer, white wine, claret, or sack, and be served in silver bowls, not just pewter. Given the stock of ten chamber pots, you will even have the luxury of not having to leave your room at night if you feel the urge.[2]

Stately Homes

Some of the finest stately homes ever built in England are constructed in Elizabeth's reign—Burghley, Wollaton Hall, Hardwick Hall, Montacute, and Longleat among them. William Harrison declares, "If ever curious building did flourish in England, it is in these our years, wherein our work-men excel." But you might be surprised to find that almost all the nobility and a large percentage of the gentry are still living in the medieval houses and castles that their ancestors built. If you are the guest of an earl with an income of £3,000 a year, don't expect to be accommodated in a luxurious suite of rooms in a stately home designed by one of the great architects of the age. It is more likely that you will find yourself in a dark chamber in a thirteenth-century turret built to defend some strategic site but now main-tained as a matter of family pride.

Old money is rarely concentrated in one man's hands; the chances are that a third of your host's income is set aside for his mother, the dowager countess. Therefore many noble families simply cannot afford the cost of replacing an old castle with a new house. To compete with Sir Francis Wil-loughby, builder of Wollaton Hall, they will need to spend about £5,000. To build something like Hardwick Hall will cost almost as much.[3] Pride does not allow them to build on a more modest scale. Besides, all that castellated antiquity is still meaningful: a castle speaks of long-standing high status and connections and ancestral loyalties stretching back centuries.

This also goes for the royal family. The royal residences of Windsor Castle, Eltham Palace, Greenwich Palace, the Tower of London, Westmin-ster, Woodstock, and Hatfield are all medieval. Nonsuch Palace, built by Henry VIII in 1538, has been sold off to the earl of Arundel, but it is re-turned to the queen's ownership in 1591. The other "modern" palaces in the royal estate are Richmond Palace (built by Henry VII in the 1490s) and Henry VIII's remodeled palaces at Whitehall and Hampton Court. Elizabeth keeps Hampton Court as a sort of shrine to her father, full of his possessions. She is more sanguine about the others: of the twenty palaces she inherits, she gives away seven. New Hall, in Essex, is in a poor state of repair, so she passes it to the earl of Sussex informing him that she will come to visit, thereby encouraging him to repair the place and build a new suite of stately rooms. She gives Kenilworth Castle to her favorite Robert Dudley, who similarly beautifies it in order to receive the queen in state. As for the more remote castles up and down the country, many are sold off; Wigmore Castle in Herefordshire, for example, goes to the Harley family for £2,600 in 1601. The queen spends an average of £4,000 per year on the palaces she retains, mainly remodeling and redecorating chambers and adding gardens.[4] Like the nobility, the monarchy is well behind the vanguard of architectural innovation—strapped for cash and incarcerated by its own heritage.

Who, then, does build in Elizabethan England? In short, the "new men"—men who have not inherited great wealth but who have made fortunes through royal service, their own ingenuity, or business acumen. Sir William Cecil builds Burghley (Lincolnshire) and Theobalds (Hertfordshire) as well as Cecil House on the Strand in London. His annual expenditure on building regularly runs to over £2,000.[5] Other newly rich civil servants include Sir Christopher Hatton, who builds Holdenby House (Northamptonshire); Sir Francis Walsingham, who builds Barn Elms (Surrey); and Sir John Thynne, who builds Longleat (Wiltshire). Perhaps the most daring architectural feat of the reign—Wollaton Hall (Nottinghamshire), with its astonishing prospect room above the great hall—is built by a member of the local gentry, Sir Francis Willoughby, who is able to exploit the coal mines on his manors but almost bankrupts himself in his pursuit of architectural magnificence.[6] You do find some exceptions to the rule that it is newly rich commoners who build the great Elizabethan houses. Lord Cobham adds wings to Cobham Hall (Kent) and a few lords plan new houses (Lord Buckhurst, for example). And of course we must remember the patroness responsible for perhaps the most aesthetically perfect house of the age, Hardwick Hall. Bess of Hardwick is the dowager countess of Shrewsbury and therefore fails to qualify as a "new man" on both accounts. However, she was born into a relatively unimportant section of the gentry and has made her money by outliving four rich husbands. When she sets about building Hardwick in 1590, this grand old noblewoman of sixty-three is in many ways "new money" too.

All this effectively means that, perhaps for the only time before the twentieth century, if you want to stay in a stately home you will not stay with the nobility. A new social order has arrived—and these self-made men are keen to embrace a new architecture to emphasize their status. The principles of this architecture arrive in England in a variety of ways: English tourists pick up ideas on the Grand Tour; skilled French and Italian workmen come to England looking for work; and, most important, illustrated publications by continental architects, such as Vredemen de Vries, Vitruvius, Sebastiano Serlio, and Andrea Palladio are imported.[7] In addition, there is the landmark publication of John Shute's *The First and Chief Grounds of Architecture* (1563). In the 1550s the duke of Northumberland sends Shute to Italy to study the country's buildings and on his return he produces the earliest published English treatise on the subject. The result is a completely new style. Whereas the highest priority of a medieval nobleman was to defend his kin and his land, and his castle was accordingly a fortified shell of thick walls and small windows within which he might withstand a siege, the Elizabethan courtier's highest priority is to demonstrate his connections. A grand Elizabethan courtier's or lawyer's residence thus differs from its medieval equivalent in its most fundamental respect: it is designed to show off rather than shut out.

What is it about the new architecture that will excite you most? Externally it will be the classical proportions of the building as a whole and the elements within its façade, especially the use of features such as sculptural figures, cupolas, recesses, and porticoes, and the orders of columns and capitals: Tuscan, Ionic, Doric, Corinthian, and Composite. Internally it will undoubtedly be the light that astonishes you. In old houses without glass the windows have to be small; consequently the rooms are dark. Indoor light is therefore synonymous with wealth, and sunlight streams in the huge glazed windows of these new houses. The old line that Hardwick Hall is "more glass than wall" could be applied to almost any newly built house in Elizabethan England. Holdenby Hall has twice as much glass as Hardwick.

Sir Francis Willoughby's great house, Wollaton Hall, is built on a hill overlooking its park. It is a revolutionary building in many respects, not least because it has no courtyard: it looks outward, not inward. You enter along a corridor that leads through the building into the screens passage and then—voilà!—suddenly, just as your eyes have adjusted to the dim corridor, you find yourself in a high hall of splendor and light, with huge windows and the walls wainscoted. Two great fireplaces stand on either side and between them two long oak tables stretch the length of the room, where all the servants dine. Mounted on the walls are halberds and poleaxes—parts of the armor that Sir Francis is required to provide by law for the militia.[8] Look up and you will see a splendid roof of painted beams. These are not actually beams, for they do not hold the roof up; they are suspended from the floor of the prospect room high above. It is an astonishing design for 1588, a triumph from the pen of the greatest architect of the age, Robert Smythson.

Sir Francis does not usually dine in the hall but in the dining parlor, which is off to one side, overlooking the garden. If invited to share a meal with the family here you will eat at a linen-covered table in front of a large stone fireplace, on chairs and benches covered with green cushions. The walls are paneled but otherwise quite bare; there are just two maps, of Nottinghamshire and Lincolnshire, and no paintings. The vogue for collecting art is only just beginning in the sixteenth century, and most owners of stately homes have all their pictures displayed in one space, normally the long gallery. Here the family walk together as a leisurely form of indoor exercise when the weather is inclement. Guests are frequently invited to join them, to view the likenesses of the queen and great men of the day; the display of such portraits implies your host is well connected to the sitters. In some great houses figures from history are placed in the long gallery. Portraits of past kings and busts of Roman emperors provoke discussion of their characters as the guests walk to and fro, comparing Caesar and Augustus, Charlemagne and Alexander the Great.[9]

The hall is still an important space for the household but it is no longer the focal point for the family; the great chamber has surpassed it. This room, which is normally reached by a staircase from the upper end of the hall, is the nearest thing the Elizabethans have to the modern living room. The windows are large, allowing in plenty of light for reading. The ceiling is made of elaborately molded plaster, the walls are paneled or hung with a tapestry, and the floor is covered with squares of woven rush matting. Some great chambers have elaborate paintings above the wainscot. Here you will find the best furniture: court cupboards, buffets, and tables covered with Persian carpets, occasionally even a table made of inlaid marble or a portable chamber clock. If there is no separate dining parlor, the family will eat here, attended by servants and with musicians playing through the meal. This is also where they will relax and perhaps play a tune on the virginals. Dancing takes place here, and plays might be performed to a small audience if there are companies of players in the vicinity. The great chamber is also where you will play chess, dice, and cards, and drink and talk late into the night.

The number of people in a rich man's household varies enormously. Aristocratic families normally have between one and two hundred servants and gentleman companions; the earl of Derby has 115, for example.[10] The cost of maintaining these old-style establishments is another reason why the old nobility cannot afford to build splendid new palaces. The new stately homes tend to have smaller, pared-down households. Sir Thomas Tresham, builder of Rushton (Northamptonshire), has fifty-two servants; Bess of Hardwick fifty; Lord Paget only twenty-nine.[11] At Wollaton, Sir Francis Willoughby has thirty-six, including a steward, an usher of the hall, grooms of the hall, a butler, an under-butler, yeomen of the chambers, a clerk, a cook, a carter, a slaughterman, grooms of the stables, and pages. All of these are men: the only women in a large Elizabethan household are gentlewomen serving the lady of the house or her daughters. Other women are employed from outside the household for tasks like needlework and laundry, but they do not eat in hall or form part of the official household. Only the royal household has a significant number of women but even in that establishment there are only the four gentlewomen of the bedchamber, the seven gentlewomen of the privy chamber, and a few maids of honor and chamberers.

Sir Francis's thirty-six servants might seem like a small number to be rattling around in a large hall like Wollaton. Sometimes, however, it is full to bursting. One occasion is November 11, 1588, when Sir Francis entertains the earl and countess of Rutland and several local gentlemen and their retinues; no fewer than 120 men and women fill the hall for a feast.[12] If you think that sounds onerous, have some sympathy for those blessed with a visit from the queen. When she arrives at a country house the owner is expected to provide accommodation for twenty-four courtiers and their households, her principal secretary, a number of government officials, and all their servants—several hundred of them. When Elizabeth arrives at Theobalds in 1583 she takes Sir William's hall as her great chamber, his parlor as her presence chamber, and his great chamber as her privy chamber. Sir William ends up having to eat in a gallery and his servants have to sleep on straw mattresses in the attic of a storeroom. Nevertheless, the visit is a great success. Over the years the queen visits him thirteen times.[13]

Presuming you arrive at a country house when the queen is not in the neighborhood, you will have your own bedchamber. Expect to find woven rush matting on the floor and brightly colored tapestries on all the walls, these being cut away around the door and windows to admit light. You should find curtains and curtain rails in the bedchambers.[14] Elizabethan bed frames can be large, so the bed will dominate the room. The Great Bed of Ware, mentioned by Shakespeare, is eleven feet square, but this is unique: six feet by seven is more usual. Beds can be just as impressive for their carving and fabric as for their dimensions. Stay the night at Fulford in Devon and you might sleep in a four-poster bed with a carved frame of semi-naked Native Americans, these being all the fashion in 1585. Some beds have elaborately carved testers commemorating a marriage. Some are lavishly hung with taffeta curtains; others have silk-embroidered cloth-of-gold curtains. The featherbed mattresses are piled on top of one another, with a down-stuffed one on top; beds in stately homes are therefore very soft. Pillowcases and sheets are normally holland, and the pillowcase might have a coat of arms embroidered on it.[15] Chests of drawers are very rare—they are mainly used for storing documents at this period—so if there is storage for your clothes it will probably be a three-paneled chest with an elaborately carved front.[16] If covered with a Turkish or Persian carpet and cushions, this may double up as a seat. Adjacent you may have a withdrawing room, where your servant will be expected to sleep.[17]

With regard to personal grooming in the morning, you may find a mirror or "looking glass" in your chamber. Alternatively, you could ask your host if you may borrow a handheld mirror: these are common in good houses. A second table or high cupboard will have a silver or brass ewer and basin, with linen towels for washing your face and hands. As for the loo, you may find a latten or pewter chamber pot in your room, or a close stool, and maybe a glass urinal (if you wish your physician to inspect your urine). As Horman puts it, "See that I lack not by my bedside a chair of easement with a vessel under and a urinal by." You will have the option of wiping your "nether end" with blanket, "cotton" (fine wool), linen, or, in some places, paper bought especially for the purpose.[18]

Every great house should have a pièce de résistance, some specific marvel that everyone who sees it will talk about long after. At Wollaton it is the prospect room: a huge, light room built on top of the hall, looking down on the towers of the rest of the building and across the surrounding park. Nor is it intended just to be used on a fine day: Sir Francis is interested in astronomy and so invites his guests up to the upper roof to view the stars. At other places the gatehouse is the most imposing spectacle: at Tixall in Staffordshire Sir Walter Aston adds to his father's recent timber-framed manor house an elegant three-story stone gatehouse (where, incidentally, I am writing this chapter), with Doric, Ionic, and Corinthian columns on each face, extensive large windows, and a roof walk. At Longford Castle, the triangular nature of the whole design provides the talking point; at Rushton, the triangular lodge in the grounds similarly provokes admiration. Other places have unusual banqueting houses in the grounds or on their roofs, designed to amuse and impress.

These new great houses all tend to have one other particular feature that their medieval predecessors lack: a formal garden. Whereas the medieval garden used to be a place where noblewomen could go to read, pick flowers, or otherwise just escape the hustle and bustle of the household, an Elizabethan garden is a place for both sexes, an area in which Renaissance and aesthetic ideas about architecture, nature, and order come together. Henry VIII's gardens at Hampton Court, Nonsuch Palace, and Whitehall provide the original patterns for the English pleasure garden. Glass windows are another reason that pleasure gardens have caught on so quickly: while you would hardly glance out of the small drafty windows of an old castle, you might regularly sit in the wide glass-filled windows of a new house and admire the view. Much use is made of heraldic symbols, sundials, and sculpture around these gardens but it is the use of the square that predominates. It can be found in every great garden, whether marked out in stone, water, or a box hedge. Within each square you will find a design in the shape of an elaborate knot (hence "knot gardens"). "Open knots" are patterns of rosemary, thyme, hyssop, and other herbs, the spaces between the plants being filled with sand or brick dust or different colored earths; in "closed knots" these spaces are filled with different colored flowers.[19] The borders of these squares are formed by shrubs and hedges, including hawthorn, bush firs, ivy, roses, juniper, holly, elm, and box. In some places, feats of topiary are worked in rosemary, yew, or box. In the privy garden at Whitehall you may see shapes of men and women, centaurs, sirens, and serving maids with baskets, created by interweaving dry twigs with the growing shrubs.[20]

Pleasure gardens are quickly taken up by the owners of stately homes who hope—or fear—that Elizabeth will visit them. At Kenilworth, Robert Dudley lays out eight knot gardens in a rectangle within the outer wall, adding a fountain at the center and a terrace alongside the keep from which the garden might best be viewed. John, Lord Lumley, redesigns the gardens of Nonsuch Palace in the 1580s with square knots, topiary, obelisks, marble basins, and sculptural fountains. You will see a pelican spouting water into a wide stone dish and admire a marble Venus whose nipples gush forth jets of water. At Wollaton, Sir Francis Willoughby and his architect Robert Smythson take the Elizabethan obsession with squares to new heights, treating the whole house as the central square of a plan of nine, with eight square gardens arranged around the house, several of which are divided again into smaller knot gardens.[21]

Perhaps the most interesting set of gardens is at Theobalds. In addition to his many duties and other interests, Sir William Cecil is a passionate gardener and garden designer. A German visitor to Theobalds, marveling at the hall of the house and its design of six trees on each side, is astounded when the steward opens the windows overlooking the gardens, and birds fly into the hall, perch themselves in the artificial trees, and begin to sing.[22] Sir William's formal garden is actually divided into a privy garden and a great garden. The privy garden is a large square enclosed by a wall. Inside this runs a gravel path with a topiary hedge cut into shapes and interspersed with cherry trees on the inner side. Flights of steps run down to a grass walk where there is another small hedge, and then a third inner square. At the heart of this you will find the knot garden, with tulips, lilies, and peonies planted in the borders of the ascents. The great garden alongside it extends to over seven acres, containing nine square knot gardens in one great square. Each of these knot gardens measures seventy feet by seventy feet, with a path twenty-two feet wide between each one. In the middle of the central knot is a white marble fountain. In other knots are sculptures and obelisks, and even a small mound set within a maze dedicated to Venus. Elsewhere there is a summerhouse with busts of the first twelve Roman emperors.[23]

You will, of course, be very lucky to be invited to stay in a stately residence like Wollaton or Theobalds. Sir Francis Willoughby's instructions to his usher on the matter of casual visitors are very clear: he should welcome into the hall all those who have a genuine reason to call upon the owner and give them food and drink; but anyone of an idle or immoral disposition is to be removed immediately. Even if you are considered sufficiently respectable to tarry, you will not necessarily be invited up to see the state rooms or the enviable prospect room. But if you do get to stay in one of the new stately houses, with their elegant classical proportions, high ceilings, acres of glass, bright tapestries, and huge square gardens, it will be an experience to remember.

Rural Houses

To the modern eye, some of the smaller manor houses of Elizabethan England are just as aesthetically pleasing as the stately homes. Hundreds are under construction. William Harrison writes in 1577 that "Every man almost is a builder and he that hath bought any small parcel of ground, be it never so little, will not be quiet till he has pulled down the old house (if any were there standing) and set up a new after his own devising." Today, when you need better accommodation, you move house; in Elizabethan England, you rebuild. Huge numbers of medieval hall houses are being turned into well-proportioned residences of two or three stories—over a thousand in Devon alone.[24] Across the country, many of the dissolved monasteries are being refashioned to provide extensive living accommodation, such as Newstead Abbey for the Byrons in Nottinghamshire and Buckland Abbey for the Grenvilles in Devon.

The furnishings of these gentlemen's residences are, in varying degrees, comparable with those of the stately homes. The beds may be less skillfully carved and hung with less costly curtains; the chests may be less lavishly painted; and you will not find an inlaid marble table or a gilt chamber clock; but you will see certain items of luxury. You might find status symbols like a mirror, a set of virginals, and a portrait or two of members of the family. Your chamber may well have curtains on rails that you can draw across the windows. However, as you go down the scale of family prestige and household size—from large houses with twenty or more servants to those of gentlemen and yeomen with just one or two—the furnishings become more utilitarian. So do the rooms. It is not just that the sheets of a bed in a yeoman's house are of a lower quality and the bed itself is smaller (in order to fit into a smaller chamber with a lower ceiling); the use of the space is altogether more practical.

Consider the house of Mrs. Katherine Doyle of Merton, Oxfordshire, the widow of a gentleman, in 1585. The value of her movable goods is the substantial sum of £591, including £300 owed to her as a result of three financial agreements. Despite this wealth, and despite the size of her house, she has very few actual living rooms. You enter through a parlor with a table, chairs, stools, and benches in the middle, a cupboard on one side, and painted hangings on the walls. The next room is a high old-fashioned hall, open to the rafters, where there is another table; this doubles up as a kitchen. After that you are through to the dairy, where there is a cheese press, vats, churns, cream pots, and wooden pails; and then the buttery, where you will find eleven barrels on shelves along one wall and a table in the middle, as well as bottles of leather and wicker-wrapped glass. The remaining three downstairs rooms are similarly practical: there is a larder containing a mortar for spices, a bread grater, a ladle, a mustard mill, a large chafer for heating water, buckets, dripping pans, and skimmers. There is a malt chamber where you will find sacks of malt, barrels of salt, hops, sieves, and oatmeal; and there is a cheese chamber, containing eighty cheeses on a rack, plus tubs, barrels of verjuice, a soap box, pots of fat, and suchlike. The three upstairs chambers are used for sleeping, and here there are touches of refinement: in the great chamber you will see an impressive four-poster bed with three feather mattresses, a white needlework valance, nine pillows, and a truckle bed beneath. Mistress Doyle also has jewelry worth £37 and such luxuries as a looking glass (3 shillings 4 pence), a writing desk (6 shillings 8 pence), silk curtains (16 shillings), and a lute (£1 10 shillings). Nevertheless, six of the ten rooms in the house are used for storage or food processing, in addition to the storehouse outside in the yard.[25]

The Yeoman's House

Over Elizabeth's reign the standard of yeomen's houses improves significantly. Brick fireplaces are usual in new houses from about 1570 and glass windows are introduced soon after. The average price of a new house increases accordingly, from £26 in the 1560s and 1570s to £35 in the 1580s and £42 in the 1590s.[26] William Harrison remarks on the improvements in yeomen's living standards, stating that old men dwelling in Radwinter, Essex, have noted three things that have hugely changed in their lifetimes. One is "the multitude of chimneys lately erected," the others are bedding—the shift from rough straw pallets to featherbeds and pillows—and the third the change of vessels from treen (wooden) platters to pewter, and wooden spoons into silver or tin. Examples of such changes can be found across the country. Robert Furse, a Devon yeoman, inherits his father's modest estate in 1572, with its old hall house. He divides the hall by inserting a floor, builds a handsome stone porch at the front and a grand granite newel staircase at the rear, and glazes all the windows.[27] In this way the transformation of yeomen's houses reflects the rebuilding of the town houses that we saw in Stratford at the start of this book.

It has to be said that Robert Furse is in the vanguard of change. A close inspection of yeomen's houses in Oxfordshire and Surrey reveals that the majority are still living in traditional drafty hall houses. Similarly, not every yeoman has made the transition to featherbeds by 1577, as Harrison suggests. Come to William and Isabel Walter's house in the early 1580s, he being a yeoman of Mitcham, Surrey. The house is thatched, timber-framed, and whitewashed, at the end of a dusty lane, with three timber-framed outbuildings grouped around a yard. The front door is oak, secured with a latch and a lock. You enter an unlit flagstone-floored corridor in which there is just a bolting hutch (a chest used for sifting flour) and a ladder going up to the next floor. In the hall there is a small unglazed window in each of the two external walls: there are no curtains and at night they are closed by shutters. The roof is double-height, open to the rafters, and the floor is covered in rushes. There is a hearth in the middle of the room, on raised flat stones. A wooden cradle and two spinning wheels stand nearby and an oak cupboard leans against the wall. On the other side of the hall there is a trestle table, a bench, two stools, and two small chairs. You will find no paneling in here, no painted hanging cloth; there is nothing decorative to cover the bare whitewashed walls.

Return to the entrance passage by the way you entered and lift the latch to the door to the parlor; within you will see two bedsteads. These have bases of wooden boards and flock-filled mattresses on top. The ceiling in this room is about seven feet in height. This is the only room with any decoration, having three painted cloths on the walls. In the dim light of the small unshuttered window you will see one cupboard and six chests. A door on the far side of the room leads to a storage room where there are shelves stacked with wooden platters, pewter dishes, a basin, a pewter flagon, salt cellars, a pewter spoon, candlesticks, and wooden tubs. Return to the entrance corridor. The other door there leads to a servant's bed-chamber: a small, dim room containing an old bed and some dumped metal, a plowshare, and three scythes. Ascend the ladder in the entrance passageway and go up through the trapdoor, and you will see that the chamber above the parlor is almost empty: there is nothing in here but a saddle and a basket of hemp. If you go back down and walk through the hall, and out of the door on the far side, this will take you to the buttery where you will see two large and two small barrels in the gloom, a churn, and a couple of leather bottles. There is a ladder here too: in the loft room above is a bedstead, a bow and six arrows, a pair of cards (for carding wool), and three pieces of woolen cloth. The kitchen, containing brass pots, a caul-dron, and other iron cooking utensils as well as brewing vats, is in a sepa-rate small building built a few yards away to avoid setting fire to the house.[28]

As you walk through William Walter's house, you cannot help but feel that he and his wife live spartan lives. He is not a poor man: as well as rent-ing this farm in Mitcham he owns a nineteen-acre farm in Kent. His chat-tels alone amount to £96. But the items inside the house only amount to £13; the remainder is farm stuff. He seems remarkably reluctant to exchange agricultural wealth and security for indoor luxury—but he is by no means alone. Look at Jefferie Smith's house in Sutton, Surrey, in 1597. He is a mar-ried yeoman with several children, some of whom have already grown up, and twice as well off as William Walter (his goods being valued at £204). But like that of Goodman Walter, most of his wealth lies in the barns and the fields around his house:

poultry (8 shillings)
three horses (£6 10 shillings)
six pigs (£2 13 shillings 4 pence)
eight cows (£16)
three bullocks (£4)
150 sheep (£37 10 shillings)
twenty lambs (£3)
nineteen acres of wheat (£27 10 shillings)

four acres of rye (£5)
thirty-two acres of barley (£32)
fourteen acres of oats (£10)
ten acres of tares (£5)
four acres of peas (£2 13 shillings 4 pence)
1½ acres of beans (£1 5 shillings)

All that comes to £153 9 shillings 8 pence. If you add the value of the lease of his farm (£10) and wool, malt, and other stored farm produce (more than £30), you can see that he too has little wealth in his domestic furnishings. His house has no glass. A newly added chamber above the hall is given over entirely to storing wool, corn, malt, and linen. His only luxuries are the featherbeds he has in his hall and inner chamber.[29]

You probably realize that the idea of a pleasure garden is incompatible with yeomen's priorities: they seek comfort in their self-sufficiency, not in luxuries. Outside Jefferie Smith's house is a range of outbuildings: a bolting house (for sifting flour), a kitchen with a storage loft above it, a milk house, two cart houses, a storehouse, a barn, and a gatehouse with a well in it. The privy is at the bottom of the plot, far away from the house, and you will have to go there each time you feel the call of nature; there are no chamber pots or close stools. The garden here is a place for herbs, vegetables, fruit and nut trees, the storage of lumber, and occasionally beekeeping; if you see any flowers, they are self-seeded or planted for use in medicines. It is a far cry from the sculpted gardens at Theobalds and Hampton Court. But William Walter's and Jefferie Smith's houses both have something in common with the stately homes described above: they are the homes of "the haves." There are many more people to be classed among the "have-nots," who are starving on the roads or sleeping in servants' rooms and rising at dawn to light the kitchen fire.

Workers' Houses

Writing in the 1580s, Carew describes old husbandmen's cottages in Cornwall as having

walls of earth [cob], low thatched roofs, few partitions, no planchings [ceilings] or glass windows and scarcely any chimneys other than a hole in the wall to let out the smoke; their bed, straw and a blanket; as for sheets, so much linen cloth had not stepped over the narrow channel between them and [England]. To conclude, a mazer and a drinking cup and a pan or two comprised all their substance: but now most of these fashions are universally banished, and the Cornish husbandman conformeth himself with a better supplied civility to the Eastern pattern.[30]

Has the lot of the husbandman really improved, as Carew suggests? Are William Harrison's three lifestyle improvements—chimneys, bedding, and pewter—true for husbandmen and laborers too?

The richest husbandmen have certainly seen improvements to their lifestyle since the reign of Henry VIII. For example, Ralph Newbury, husbandman of Cropredy, Oxfordshire, has chattels worth £166 when he dies in 1578. His house is nothing special; it consists of just a chamber, a parlor, a hall, a buttery, and a kitchen—no chimneys or window glass for him. But he has several featherbeds, a carpet of "red and black" upon his table, pillows, cushions, twenty tin spoons, three drinking cups and a drinking glass, a mortar and pestle of brass, pewter platters, pewter basins, brass candlesticks, and a chamber pot.[31] However, he represents the wealthy end of the workers' spectrum. Many husbandmen at the end of the reign are still living in houses of one or two rooms without glass or chimneys, even if they do have a few items of pewter. Thomas Lipscomb, husbandman of Cranleigh, Surrey, lives in a one-room cottage in the 1580s with his wife and son. In that one hall they sleep and cook, store their clothes and food (there are flitches of bacon hanging from the rafters), and keep all their cooking and baking equipment.[32]

An act of 1589 stipulates that all new cottages must be provided with four acres of land. In some respects this is quite generous: a lot of people hold no more than that from the lord of their manor.[33] But this very generosity means that fewer cottages are built: landlords do not want to give away so much land to every laborer. Even where four acres are set aside, you cannot feed a family on the produce of that area alone, especially as a portion of the land must be left fallow each year. Hence the majority of cottagers have to supplement their farming by labor. William Gullyvor of Cropredy is a day laborer in 1568; the value of his estate is £3 16 shillings. Most of this is represented by the £3 of livestock he owns—two cows and four sheep. Enter his two-room cottage and you will find in the hall nothing but a table, a bench, a frying pan, two wooden pails, three small platters, three saucers, a kettle, and a small pot of brass. In the other room, there is just the bedstead, four chests, his sheets, and a loom. You will therefore take many contemporary statements of improved living conditions with a pinch of salt. While it is true that people with money to spare invest in the luxuries identified by William Harrison, the only one that is universal is the spread of pewter. If you want to sleep on a featherbed and linen sheets in rural England, you will choose to stay in the house of a prosperous yeoman—although you may find that he has not invested in glass and curtains. But then, these are uncertain times. If you visit England in the famine years of 1594–97, you will be glad that your host has stored extra grain and cheeses in his spare bedchamber, and not put all his money into glass.

Town Houses

There is just as great a range of wealth and architectural novelty in the towns. In fact, the range is even greater because here you will find a concentration of extremely wealthy people in a small space, all trying to show off their social status and importance. There is thus greater competition for pre-eminence, and more ostentation. Look at the carving on the shops and houses in any substantial market town: the tall frontages, large glass windows, painted plasterwork figures, coats of arms, carved and painted joinery, and brightly colored signs all show that the merchant classes are using their houses and shops to draw attention to themselves and their businesses. Meanwhile, at the bottom end of the social spectrum, you have a greater number of poor workers living practically on top of one another in slum accommodation, competing for the very basics of life.

The largest and most prestigious houses in any town are those arranged around a courtyard and entered by a gatehouse. The majority are timber-framed and two or three stories high; the timbers are cut to size in a sawpit elsewhere and erected into a frame onsite, filled in with either wickerwork and clay or brick, and then plastered and wainscoted. In provincial towns you may have substantial houses built around two courtyards, such as Thomas Taylor's house in the small town of Witney (Oxfordshire), which contains twenty-four separate rooms around two quadrangles. Mr. Taylor is wealthy—he has movable goods to the value of £409 at the time of his death in 1583—and so it is unsurprising to find that his hall, both parlors, and all the main chambers are glazed. The hall is paneled all the way round, with tapestry hanging down above the wainscot. Two of the five glazed windows in the hall have iron casements (window frames that open), and so do several others in the chambers. These have colored curtains, hung by hooks from iron rods. There is a turned chair in the hall, a settle, and a round table; this last piece of furniture and two rectangular tables are covered with carpets. Elsewhere in the house other items will catch your eye: pewter fruit dishes, a mousetrap, toasting irons, books, candle snuffers, folding tables, a Venetian carpet cloth, cushions covered in tapestry, cushions of needlework, and a looking glass. In the outer courtyard there are two sows and three pigs; in the inner one you will find twenty chickens, three hens, three pullets, one cock, a goose, and "one turkey cock and two turkey hens." Turkeys are first introduced to England in the 1520s and are rare specimens until Elizabeth's reign, when their value as a roasting bird is widely recognized and their popularity suddenly increases.[34]

Let's move down the social scale and say that you're going to call on a blacksmith living in Oxford, by the name of Thomas Heath, in the 1580s. His house is situated in the parish of St. Michael's, inside the North Gate. It consists of a shop with a cellar beneath, a hall and buttery on the ground floor, a staircase with two small rooms above it, then a "middle chamber" and a "little chamber" on the first floor, a "higher chamber" above the kitchen, and a garden. Although his house is within the walls of Oxford, he keeps two cows, a horse, a sow, and five pigs in his garden. In the shop, there are the tools of his trade.[35] The whole value of his movable goods is just £38. Nevertheless, his hall is equipped with glass in an iron casement. There is a chimney too, with iron firedogs. He has plenty of pewter in his buttery, and five candlesticks. He even has four old flowerpots for growing potherbs. Upstairs, the beds in the middle chamber are old and have flock mattresses, but there are featherbeds in the little chamber, and this too has glass in the windows. In his high chamber, where Thomas Heath himself sleeps, there are featherbeds, linen sheets and towels, cushions, glazed windows, a "brush and a glass," and a book. In short, this blacksmith enjoys a standard of living higher than that of many yeomen living in the country— for the simple reason that he does not keep 80 percent of his wealth in his fields and barns. His animals and hay are worth £5 and the tools of his trade another £7 11 shillings 10 pence; he can afford to spend a far greater proportion of his money on pewter, featherbeds, and glazing.[36]

In many houses most of the foregoing things are absent. If your relations in town are poor, then there may be no spare bed and no clean linen when you call on them. You will sleep in canvas sheets without a pillow on a straw mattress, and cook over a fireplace in the one room your host occupies. In a house of five or six rooms, each one occupied by a separate family, you will come face-to-face with the significance of overcrowding. Just think what it must be like staying in a house like Shipdams in Norwich (which we visited in Chapter Two), with ten chambers occupied by poor or destitute people. A straw mattress, a sheet, a blanket, and a wooden bowl or drinking vessel are probably all they have. Noise will be another issue: you can never get enough sleep in a house tenanted by the destitute, with some people staying up late and arguing, babies crying, prostitutes' customers coming and going at all hours and in all states of drunkenness, and still others getting up before five o'clock to look for work. But the main problem you will encounter in such a lodging is the lack of water.

Most people in the country have a choice of water sources. The preferred supply is rainwater: "We have none other water but that that falleth upon the house and runneth into a great trough by dropping down," writes William Horman. Second best is springwater, which is considered to be much purer than well water, the third option; most yeomen and husbandmen have a well in or near their house.[37] In the countryside people do not normally take water from rivers except for brewing and washing—but in the city, river water is the best one can hope for. The wealthy have private conduits bringing water from the river into their houses but the supply is often little more than a trickle, being conveyed in very thin pipes which do little more than drip water after the tap is turned on full. The small dimensions of the pipes (normally described as "quills" of water) mean they are often blocked by a stone or an eel. Unfortunately, if the latter is causing the blockage you will have to wait until the fish decomposes for the supply to recommence.[38]

Large towns have water-bearers who haul water to people's houses in large three-gallon containers, wide at the bottom and narrow at the top, bound with iron hoops. Normally one delivery will cost you a penny: this is not cheap, especially considering you don't know where the water has actually come from. Large towns also have systems of bringing water into the center through public conduits. Unfortunately, these are often old and in decay, and the lead of the pipes is sometimes stolen because of its high value. Still, the most common way of obtaining water in a city is to fill a bucket at one of these conduits. In Exeter there is an underground water supply system which has been in use since the Middle Ages, but here the old pipes running through these tunnels need constant attendance as the elm pipes rot and the joints of the lead ones weaken. Plymouth is even worse off, despite being at the confluence of two rivers and the sea. In 1585 a new act is passed allowing Sir Francis Drake to build a leat to bring water seventeen miles from the River Meavy on Dartmoor to the town. Just as enterprising are the machines pumping water from beneath London Bridge: Peter Morrice contracts with the lord mayor to supply water to people's houses by using a waterwheel-powered system which is running by the end of 1582. A rival, Bevis Bulmer, sets up a similar pump shortly afterward. Again, only the wealthy need apply. And of course it is Thames water—tidal and salty, suitable only for washing things. Even if you pay for this system you will still need to obtain fresh water from the conduits.

The result of all this is a hierarchy of water provision. If you rent a room at the top of a five-story dwelling in London, obtaining water is a long and tiresome business. You have to go out with a pair of buckets on a yoke over your shoulders, walk to the conduit, queue up, fill the buckets, walk back home, and carry the water up to your lodging, slopping it on the wooden stairs. Washing your face and hands is therefore much more easily done at the conduit. You may even find some people scouring cooking pans there, while others nearby shuffle impatiently with their empty buckets.

Standing there at the conduit, waiting your turn, you can see that there are considerable discomforts to living in a city unless you have your own house and servants. In the country you could have slept in a chamber full of sheaves of corn and maturing cheeses, with a ewer of fresh water by the window and a cockerel crowing in the yard. However, you would be a long way from the excitement of the markets, the taverns, the dancing, and the music—a long way from where everything is happening. Most of the London playwrights rent chambers from householders and return home only to sleep: they live between the taverns and the theaters. Robert Greene rents a bedchamber from a cordwainer in Dowgate, Ben Jonson rents a room from a comb-maker near the Elephant and Castle, Thomas Nashe lodges with a printer in Hosier Lane, and Shakespeare stays in a house in Silver

Street, where he rents a chamber from a hairdresser.[39] You cannot imagine any of these men happily giving up his city room and friends for a quiet life as a hardworking farmer. And while they are not typical, they are representative of the majority in one respect: the quality of their lives does not primarily depend on easy access to water or having glass windows. These things might strike you as being crucial factors in deciding where to stay but, after you have spent an evening in the Mermaid with Jonson and Shakespeare, enjoying the repartee, oysters, and double beer, you frankly won't give a damn that there is no running water in your chamber. In fact, you might be amazed at the discomforts you can tolerate.

CHAPTER NINE

What to Eat and Drink

Food is valuable in Elizabethan England, far more so than in the modern world. A flock of 180 sheep is worth more than the average detached house.[1] The difficulties of transportation mean that the food supply depends heavily on what grows locally and how much surplus is available. It also depends on the season. Harvest is obviously a time of much grain and fruit. Animals are traditionally slaughtered on Martinmas (November 11) if the owner cannot afford to feed them through the winter.[2] Even the availability of fresh fish depends on the season. There is no use in trying to buy fresh turbot in December if you are more than twenty miles from the coast: only in summer is sea fish carried to markets that far inland.

These cycles are not quite as straightforward as they appear. Rich landowners do not normally sell their grain immediately after the harvest is in, when prices are low; instead they store it until the numerous small-scale producers have sold all theirs and prices go up again. Pig farmers keep their flitches of bacon back in storage until they can get a better price for them later in the winter. Such tactics are made even more profitable by the unhappy fact that harvests can fail, causing local—and sometimes national— food shortages. Large towns are less vulnerable, being part of an international market that sees preserved foods traded long-distance; but much of the countryside is dependent on fresh food. After a poor harvest, prices for all commodities—not just grain—rise dramatically and the poor are unable to make ends meet. When two or three harvests fail in succession across the whole country, as they do in the years 1594–97, people starve to death; during this famine one hundred people die in Stratford-upon-Avon alone.[3] But you still have producers holding back corn supplies, even though hoarding is forbidden by law. In Stratford in 1597 seventy-five townsmen are found guilty of hoarding corn, including William Shakespeare, who is hanging on to ten quarters of malt. Worse than this, "engrossers" buy up all the local supply of an important commodity, such as eggs or butter, in order to drive up the price. In the 1590s certain unscrupulous businessmen buy up to twenty thousand pounds of butter—and this is disastrous because it is an important part of people's diet.[4] Combined with hoarding, this has dramatic consequences for the poor. In some places the famine of 1594–97 proves as deadly as the plague of 1563.

It is easy to write the line "people starve to death"; it is much harder to deal with the harsh reality. But you need to understand this point, if only to see how little choice you might have in what you eat. The itinerant poor might literally die in the street. The following examples show how famine hits the Cumberland parish of Greystoke. Here "a poor fellow destitute of succor" is found in the highway and is carried to the constable's house, where he dies. A miller's daughter dies in her bed, weakened from lack of food. A beggar boy from the Scottish Borders is found writhing in agony in the road and dies soon afterward "in great misery." Another "poor, hunger-starved beggar boy" is found in the street and carried into a house, where he dies. A widow is discovered dead in a barn. A four-year-old local boy dies "for want of food and means," as does his mother. A total of sixty-two people die in Greystoke in just one year—during which time the parish sees no marriages and only three children conceived. You hear the story of a man leaving his home and walking hundreds of miles in search of work or food and returning after a couple of months with sufficient money only to find that his wife and children have all since died.[5] Now you can see why so many people living in Kent in the 1590s walked there, as we have seen in Chapter Two.

If you are hungry, you might feel inclined to turn to poaching. But be careful: this is risky. Taking livestock is theft, and theft is a felony which carries the death sentence. Killing wild animals that live on another man's land is also against the law; even taking a single fish from a river can result in a fine of a shilling or more.[6] It is unlikely that you will be hanged for taking a wild animal such as a rabbit; but, even so, you will get a fine amounting to three times the value of the animal as well as three months in prison, and you will have to enter into a bond to guarantee your good behavior in the future; a second offense will be treated more harshly. If a gamekeeper attacks you and you defend yourself, you can be charged with assault. You may find yourself on the gallows if you injure him.

If you want to know which years are a good time to visit and which years to avoid, the following is a guide to the extremes. The years of greatest plenty—i.e., those in which the price of grain is 20 percent or more below the average—are 1564, 1566, 1569–71, 1583–84, 1587–88, 1592–93, and 1602, the very best being 1592 and 1593, when grain prices are just 56 percent and 65 percent of the average. So much grain is produced in 1592 that Francis Bacon proudly declares that England can now afford to feed other nations as well as her own people.[7] It is an unfortunate remark, for it is very soon followed by a great dearth. The harvest of 1594 is poor, that of 1595 is worse, and the following year worse still: wheat hits 170 percent of its normal price, oats reach a level of 191 percent, and rye has to be imported from Denmark.[8] Other bad years—when the price of grain is 20 percent or more above the rolling average—are 1573, 1586, and 1600. The year 1590 is almost as bad, made worse by the high cost of livestock. Prices for animal products hit new heights and never really diminish.[9]

In such circumstances, storage of food is most important. The principal rule is to have separate places for different types of commodity: dry things can be kept in a pantry with bread and dry linen; wet things are normally stored in the buttery. Wine and meat must be kept apart, and cellars should be avoided on account of their dampness. Meat should be seethed in summer to keep it fresh, then kept in a cool cellar, soaked in vinegar with juniper seeds and salt.[10] Most yeomen will have vats and presses for making cheeses—a valuable source of protein in the long winter season. Similarly, most livestock owners have troughs for salting meat or allowing it to steep in brine. William Horman has some further advice for keeping meat. "The place that the meat should be kept in store should be very cold and dry and out of the way of the sun, lest such places wax filthy and foisty," he writes, adding that "the vessels that serve to keep meat in store should be of earth or glass and not great but rather many and little, clean or well pitched."

Keeping fruit throughout the year requires special effort. Soft fruit—gooseberries, cherries, damsons, plums, and quinces—can be preserved in a jam. However, most methods call for a lot of sugar, which is expensive. A recipe for preserving quinces begins: "Take 4lb of quinces and 4lb of sugar, a quart of fair [rose] water and let it boil once up and have four whites of new laid eggs and one of the shells, and beat them very well for the space of half an hour."[11] Oranges and lemons are imported in large quantities—£1,756 worth of them enter the port of London in 1559—and cookbooks include methods of preserving these in the form of marmalade; but again the processes require a lot of sugar. In London you can buy ready-made marmalade imported from the Continent, as well as dates and figs; but these are for the tables of the wealthy. For the vast majority of yeomen in the country, it is vitally important to store hard fruit through the whole year. To do this, select faultless apples and pears without a bruise or other mark, and leave a length of stalk on them. Place them carefully in your fruit house or "hoard house" on clean dry straw, make sure they are not touching each other, and turn them very carefully every month to avoid their collecting moisture. And, most important, keep the door to the fruit house shut, "lest children make havoc there."[12]

Harvest time and fruit-picking impose one form of seasonality. Another is entirely artificial. The medieval Church used to restrict the eating of meat on Wednesdays, Fridays, and Saturdays, as well as in Advent and Lent and on the vigils of certain saints' feast days. In 1549 Edward VI reestablishes Fridays and Saturdays as nonmeat days, as well as Lent and other religious feasts. In 1563 Elizabeth's government imposes fasting on Wednesdays too, including a prohibition on slaughtering animals. There is an important difference compared to pre-Reformation times, however: avoidance of meat is no longer a religious observance but secular law. The purpose of fasting on Wednesdays is specifically to encourage the eating of fish, to support the fishing industry. People therefore respond differently. Some households uphold the old religious fasts during Advent and Lent, as if they are still observing the religious law; others ignore Advent but observe the Lenten fast. Still others ignore Wednesdays and just fast on Fridays and Saturdays.[13] But be careful if you adopt a partial regime: heavy fines are levied for eating meat on nonmeat days. The standard fine is £3 or three months imprisonment, but in 1561 a London butcher slaughtering three oxen in Lent is fined £20.[14] Fines can be levied on the head of a household for every single member who breaks the fast, so if you have lots of servants, make sure they all obey the law.

If you are really determined to eat meat all week, it is possible to buy a license to do so. It will cost you £1 6 shillings 8 pence if you are a lord or a lady, 13 shillings 4 pence if you are a knight or his wife, and 6s 8d if you are anyone else. Even these licenses do not allow you to eat beef or veal between Michaelmas and May 1.[15] There is some respite at the end of the reign: the law against eating meat on Wednesdays is repealed in 1585. At the same time, there is a general slackening of fish-eating and an increase in the consumption of meat. By the 1590s most wealthy households have dropped the strict Lenten fast and replaced it with a reduced-meat diet. In 1593 the government bows to the inevitable and reduces the punitive £3 fine to £1. Now many households begin to eat meat in Lent and on Fridays and Saturdays, if the head of the household wishes to do so, even though it is still technically against the law.

Elizabethan people also consider their health when choosing what to eat. "I eat rye bread not for niggardliness but for a point of physic," declares William Horman. This is unsurprising: we do much the same in the modern world. But our ideas about healthy food are very different from Elizabethan ones. For example, while we make use of sage in our cooking on account of its taste, Elizabethans use it because it is thought to sharpen the brain. Sir Thomas Elyot is worth listening to on this subject. Although he is a layman and not a physician, his book, *The Castel of Health,* proves hugely influential—it goes into its sixteenth edition in 1595. He declares that mutton is the most wholesome meat you can eat and that fish is not so good because it thins the blood. He also thinks that spices and vegetables are bad for you. He admits that fresh fruit was once a staple of Mankind in the Garden of Eden but suggests that our bodies have changed since those days; now "all fruits are noyful to man and do engender ill humors."[16] His contemporary the physician Andrew Boorde is also skeptical about the value of fresh fruit. He recounts how he once went on a pilgrimage to Santiago de Compostela and urged his fellow pilgrims not to drink the local water or eat the fruit. They ignored him—and as a result they all died. You can hardly blame him for concluding that a diet consisting exclusively of meat and beer is better for you than one that includes fruit and water.[17]

Perhaps the most misguided English attitude is that toward the tomato. This is discovered in the New World and soon cultivated and eaten in Spain and Italy. Yet in England the smell of the plant is thought to be "rank and stinking" and tomatoes are therefore avoided. John Gerard, who grows them, declares in his *Herball* (1597), "They yield very little nourishment to the body." Hence they are cultivated only for their red beauty, and after being shown off they are thrown away or fed to pigs.[18]

Mealtimes

When do you eat in Elizabethan England? You will be glad to know that a great revolution in English diet has taken place: breakfast has arrived! In medieval times almost no one ate breakfast, and many Elizabethan medical writers still maintain that it is bad for you, being necessary for only workers and travelers. But now most people eat breakfast: the rich, the not-so-rich—even schoolboys.[19] "To rise early is not the best chance but to breakfast is the surest thing," declares Claudius Hollyband.[20]

What you eat for breakfast varies a little. Robert Laneham, a gentleman servant, has just a manchet—a small round loaf made with the finest white flour. Less important servants receive a cheat bread—a white loaf of lower quality. The third quality is brown bread, which still contains all the bran. Schoolboys eat brown bread with a little butter and some fruit. Bread and butter is said to be the countryman's breakfast; while bread, butter, and sage is the breakfast of choice for a number of gentlemen (especially those anxious to sharpen their brains).[21] You might also drink small beer with your buttered bread and sage, or watered-down wine. Breakfast at Wollaton Hall consists of bread, ale, and a sweet omelet (eggs, butter, sugar, and currants).[22] Few people eat meat at breakfast. The earl and countess of Northumberland are served each morning with "a loaf of bread cut into trenchers, a couple of manchets, two pints of beer, two pints of wine, two pieces of salt fish, six baked herring, and four white [pickled] herring or a dish of sprats." On meat days the fish is replaced with a chine of boiled beef or mutton.[23] You can't help but notice the quantities of alcohol: a pint of beer *and* a pint of wine each morning should set you up for the day quite nicely.

The time for your next meal depends on who and where you are. Noblemen, gentlemen, and scholars eat dinner at 11 a.m., in the old medieval tradition. This is the main meal of the day. They follow this with a supper, a much smaller meal at about 5 p.m. Londoners and merchants eat about an hour later, having their dinner at 12 noon and supper at about 6 p.m. Sir William Holles is thought to be most peculiar, waiting until 1 p.m. for his dinner at Houghton in Nottinghamshire.[24]

Obviously special occasions alter these routines. It is customary for all the wedding guests to be invited to breakfast before the ceremony, so many have had a good tipple before they go to church; they then rush to the inn afterward to partake of the beef and mustard, frumenty (wheat and spices boiled in milk), and mince pies traditionally served at the wedding feast. Similarly after a funeral, it is customary to hold a "drinking." Be prepared to imbibe large quantities of wine or beer—and write off the rest of the day—if someone invites you to such a sorrow-drowning occasion.

Food in a Wealthy Household

Food is like clothing in that it is an opportunity for the wealthy to show off, reminding everyone of their social status. Long before you even taste a morsel in a large house you will observe the clean diamond-patterned linen tablecloths and the similar high-quality napkins folded into elaborate shapes. In some houses you will see silverware to the value of £1,000 or more—plates, saucers, dishes, bowls, flagons, knives, spoons, salts, even egg cups. You will find that great attention is paid to the order of precedence: seating plans are not designed for people to enjoy their neighbors' company but in accordance with social hierarchy. If you are a gentleman (or your husband is), the pair of you may well be seated in the great chamber with the head of the household. If you are lower in the pecking order, you will eat in the hall.

Cooks in wealthy households are for the most part "musical-headed Frenchmen," or so William Harrison declares. As for the food they prepare, you will be astonished by the variety and quantity of meat. On every meat day the kitchens prepare dishes of beef, veal, mutton, lamb, pork, chicken, goose, rabbit, and pigeon. And those are just the basic meats. All sorts of rare birds that you have probably never considered eating may appear before you—stewed, poached, boiled, baked, and roasted. If a rich man is trying to impress you he may serve teal, snipe, and curlew. He will give you venison because of its prestige value: it cannot normally be bought or sold, only hunted by the wealthy. If it is a fish day you may be served sturgeon, porpoise, or seal. One recipe begins: "Take your porpoise or seal and parboil it, seasoning it with pepper and salt, and bake it."[25] Another form of ostentation lies in the number of servants bringing food to the table: fifteen servants wait on the Willoughby family at Wollaton. In an earl's house you can expect to see even more process in, all carrying silver plates.

Before we look at the full range of food on the menu, it is important to give a caveat: you should not assume that *every* meal is a gut-busting indulgence. Some rich men eat frugally: Mr. Percival Willoughby (Sir Francis's son-in-law) has been known to sit down with a couple of servants and consume just a quarter of mutton (a quarter of the sheep, that is, at 16 pence), a piece of beef (8 pence), and bread and butter (12 pence) in a light supper.[26] However, most meals are much more extravagant. A formal dinner at Wollaton will start in the late morning and go on for at least two hours.

If Sir Francis invites you to dinner, remember to wash your hands before the meal: the old style is for a ewerer to pour water for you but these days it is more common for a basin to be provided for all to dip their hands in. Having washed your hands, dry them on the towel provided and take your place. If there is a clergyman present he will say grace; if not, another man will be appointed. It need not be an extensive thanksgiving; most men have a short rhyme prepared for such a duty, such as:

> O Lord which givest thy creatures for our food
> Herbs, beasts, birds, fish and other gifts of thine,
> Bless these thy gifts, that they may do us good,
> And we may live to praise thy name divine.
> And when the time has come this life to end
> Vouchsafe our souls to Heaven may ascend.[27]

You will have a silver or pewter plate laid out on the table in front of you, together with a cup, spoon, and loaf of bread. In front of the master of the household will be the salt—an elaborate silver or gold vessel—and a pepper box. Use your own knife unless one has been provided from a household set. Do not expect to see a fork: eating with a knife and fork is an Italian custom generally regarded in England as foppish. Young men who want to advertise the fact that they have been on the Grand Tour occasionally insist on using a fork, much to the annoyance of their hosts. Court ladies also sometimes eat with one.

In a rich household, the carver will cut the meats and place them on pewter or silver dishes which the servants will then carry to your table and place in front of you, together with the appropriate sauces. Sir Francis Willoughby strictly observes Fridays and Saturdays as nonmeat days; therefore, if you happen to visit on one of these, expect four or five of the following dishes to appear, one after another in the following order, along with a dish of butter. Remember not to eat too much: this is just the first course.

1. A sallat [salad] with boiled eggs
2. A pottage of sand eels and lampreys
3. Red [smoked] herring covered with sugar
4. White [pickled] herring, ling, or whiting with mustard sauce
5. Minced salt salmon in a sauce of mustard, vinegar, and sugar

6. Pickled conger eel, shad, or mackerel
7. Plaice or thornback ray with vinegar, or wine and salt, or mustard
8. Cod, bass, mullet, or perch
9. Eels, trout, or roach upon sops [bread soaked in the liquor in which the fish was cooked]
10. Pike in pike sauce
11. Tench in jelly
12. A custard tart.[28]

You might note that you start with a vegetarian dish: a salad. The wealthy have long disdained to look at anything green as a food in itself: as we have seen, vegetables are thought to be "noyful to man." But attitudes are slowly changing. The still-life paintings of the sixteenth century demonstrate a new inquisitiveness about the natural world—and that includes food. Fruit and vegetables are now frequently depicted in artwork and sculpture. New vegetables such as the edible carrot and tubers from the New World are reverently treated, almost as if they have come straight from the Garden of Eden. Many householders now have a salad on a fast day, following the lead of the trend-setting Italians. If your host is among them, expect to be presented with a concoction of leafy greens and herbs—coleworts, lettuce, sage, garlic, rampions, chervil, onions, leeks, borage, mint, fennel, watercress, rosemary, cucumber, and parsley—washed and drenched in olive oil with vinegar, salt, and sugar.[29]

There will be an interlude before the second course. When the carvers reappear, bearing their silver platters, expect another four or five dishes selected from the following list, served in this order:

1. Flounders in pike sauce
2. Salmon, conger eel, brill, turbot, or halibut in a vinegar sauce
3. Bream or carp upon sops
4. Fried sole
5. Roast lampreys or porpoise in galantine sauce
6. Sturgeon, crayfish, crab, or shrimps in a vinegar sauce
7. Baked lamprey
8. Cheese tart
9. Figs, apples, raisins, and pears
10. Blanched almonds

Most people would rather call on Sir Francis on a meat day, especially on a Sunday which, in most great houses, is a day for luxuriating in the food available. This is the likely palette of first courses served on a Sunday, from which four or five will be prepared for you (turn up after November 1 if you want to eat the swan):

1. Brawn in mustard
2. Capons stewed in white broth
3. A leg of venison in beef broth
4. A chine of beef and a breast of mutton boiled
5. Mutton pies
6. Three green [young] geese in a dish of sorrel sauce
7. A stubble goose [a goose left to feed itself on stubble in the fields] with mustard and vinegar
8. A swan in sauce chaudron
9. A pig roast
10. A double rib of roast beef, with pepper-and-vinegar sauce
11. A loin or breast of veal with orange sauce
12. Half a lamb or a kid
13. Two capons roasted, either in wine-and-salt sauce or a sauce of ale and salt (but not the latter if it be served with the sops)
14. Two pasties of fallow deer in a dish
15. A custard tart

And for the second course, expect four to five dishes from the following list:

1. Jelly
2. Peacock in wine and salt
3. Two coneys or half a dozen rabbits in a mustard-and-sugar sauce
4. Six chickens upon sorrel sops
5. Six pigeons
6. Mallard, teal, gulls, stork or heronsew [young heron] in a mustard and vinegar sauce
7. Crane, curlew, bittern, or bustard in a galantine sauce
8. Pheasant, or six rails [corncrakes], cooked in salt water with sliced onions
9. Six woodcocks cooked in mustard and sugar

10. Six partridges
11. A dozen quail
12. A dish of larks
13. A pasty of red deer
14. Tart, gingerbread, fritters

The usual practice is to pick a little at each dish. Lift the meat onto your plate with your knife, cut away the bones, gristle, and any other parts you don't want, and dip the morsel into the sauces provided in the saucers. The bones and unwanted parts you may put into a "voider"—you will find one on the table. Then move on to the next dish. Do not worry about waste; you are not expected to eat everything. Any leftovers will be reused the next day, eaten by the servants, or handed out to paupers at the kitchen door.

The principal difference between the daily fare described above and a feast is the level of ostentation. At a feast, *all* the above dishes in each course will be served, not just a selection. The best silverware will be on show. There will be dancing and playing of musical instruments—shawms, trumpets, and sackbuts—as the host and his principal guests make their way to the great chamber to dine. The meal itself may be accompanied by violins and softer instruments. The hall will be decorated and all the servants will crowd in to enjoy the wide array of food. A man like Sir Francis Willoughby will sometimes slaughter an ox to celebrate a feast at his house, so that everyone may have as much meat as he desires, including the servants.[30] At Christmas the wealthy are expected to entertain the less fortunate members of society. Rich men with extensive estates treat their tenants to a feast on at least one of the twelve days set aside for the celebrations. This might entail the serving of beef, mutton, goose, pork, capon, coney, chicken, and such exotics as woodcock, turkey, and swan, as well as the ever-popular venison pasties. Extra bread and beer will be laid on for all those who come to the house unbidden; it is not done to turn away the poor at this time of year.

At a truly great feast, dozens of dishes are laid out at each course. When Robert Dudley entertains the queen at Kenilworth in 1575, she is served by two hundred gentlemen carrying over a thousand dishes of silver and glass.[31] Two years later Elizabeth decides to call on Lord North at Kirtling; she stays from suppertime on Sunday September 1 to after dinner on Tuesday September 3, and this is the food that Lord North has to provide for the two-day visit:

> *Bread:* 1,200 manchet loaves, 3,600 loaves of cheat bread, and 276 extra loaves
>
> *Meat:* 11½ cows, 17½ veal calves, 67 sheep, 7 lambs, 34 pigs, 96 coneys, 8 stags made into 48 pasties, 16 bucks made into 128 pasties, and 8 gammons of bacon
>
> *Birds:* 32 geese, 363 capons, 6 turkeys, 32 swans, 273 ducks, 1 crane, 38 heronsews, 110 bitterns, 12 shovelers, 1,194 chickens, 2,604 pigeons, 106 pewits, 68 godwits, 18 gulls, 99 dotterels, 8 snipe, 29 knots, 28 plovers, 5 stints, 18 redshanks, 2 yerwhelps, 22 partridges, 1 pheasant, 344 quail, and 2 curlews
>
> *Fish:* 3 kegs of sturgeon, 96 crayfish, 8 turbot, a cartload and 2 horse loads of oysters, 1 barrel of anchovies, 2 pike, 2 carp, 4 tench, 12 perch, and 300 red [smoked] herring
>
> *Other:* 2,201 cows' tongues, feet, and udders, 18 pounds lard, 430 pounds butter, 2,522 eggs, 6 Dutch cheeses, 10 marchpanes [marzipans], £16 4s worth of sugar, and £29 1s 9d worth of salad, roots, and herbs

When you add Lord North's gifts to her majesty's officers and his expenses in decorating the rooms, putting up a temporary banqueting house, building several temporary kitchens, and hiring extra pewterware and cooks from London, you will see that a royal feast is prohibitively expensive and disruptive. The whole visit, during which he entertains more than two thousand people, costs him £642 4 shillings 2 pence (not including a present of a jewel worth £120 for the queen). For those two days his house becomes a town about the same size as Stratford. This is quite a contrast for Elizabeth, who, when at one of her own palaces, usually dines alone.[32]

After a feast there comes the "banquet." This is a particularly English form of conspicuous consumption: a sweet course that has its own drama. There will be music as people mingle and pick at sweetmeats, preserved fruit, and acres of sugar and marzipan confections that are designed in the shapes of animals, trees, fruit, flowers, or household items such as cups, glasses, and plates. The marzipan is colored with saffron and egg yolk, azurite blue and gold leaf. If green is required, spinach is used; if white, milk curds.[33] Curiously, a rich man's banquet is probably the only place you will be offered a potato: William Harrison refers to "the potato and such venerous roots as are brought out of Spain, Portugal and the Indies to furnish up our banquets." All these things are laid out on tables or placed in baskets, arranged to please the eye. Banquets may be held out of doors or in a banqueting house in the grounds of a mansion. Some go on late into the night; others are held over the course of an afternoon. It is hardly surprising that the term "banquet" later becomes synonymous with a long, ostentatious feast.

Food in a Middling Household

As you pass down the social ladder, the character of dining changes. A wealthy Guildford merchant, like the vintner Symon Tally, has a great chamber and enough linen tablecloths and napkins to emulate the rich. He has "platters, dishes, chargers, saucers . . . all of pewter" and eight silver bowls, three silver salt cellars, and eighteen silver spoons.[34] However, the food at his table is produced on a much smaller scale than at Wollaton. He does not have a huge household to maintain, only his family and a few servants.Nor does he have tenants to feed at Christmas. If entertaining a few gentlemen he might provide many of the same meats that you will find at Sir Francis Willoughby's table: lamb, pheasant, quail, lark, chicken, rabbit, leveret, woodcock, snipe, pigeon, and heron—although it is unlikely that he will have exotics such as young stork or bittern, and he will provide venison only if he has been given some by a wealthy friend.[35] On the other hand, if he and his wife just dine by themselves, they will be served a first course of ham-and-pea pottage and perhaps powdered (salted) beef with mustard, followed by a second course of one or two roast meats, bread and butter, a custard tart, and fruit. Of course, the standard of all this fare depends on the skills of the cook—there is an old English proverb: "God sends us meat and the devil cooks." Looking at the contemporary recipes for poached freshwater fish and boiled chicken, you might agree.

With the exceptions of some exotica, there is no great difference between the diets of the middling sort and the rich. In 1562 Alessandro Magno sits down each day to a dinner in his London inn that consists of a choice of two or three types of roast meat or meat pies, savories, fruit tarts, and cheese.[36] In June 1560 Henry Machyn attends the feast at which his friend the herald William Harvey is elected warden of the Skinners' Company, and he notes that the banquet afterward consists of spiced bread, cherries, strawberries, pippins, marmalade, suckets, comfits, and Portuguese oranges.[37] Cooking with spices and sugar is another feature that middle-class households share with the rich.[38] But on the whole, the less wealthy the household, the more you'll find that practicality takes precedence over ostentation and taste. Meals are served to the family in the hall. Food is provided by the householder's wife, not a male cook, and meat is carved by the head of the household, not a servant.

What does the average housewife in town cook for her family? This is a question best answered by looking at the recipe books aimed at the literate townswoman of the day, such as John Partridge's *The Treasurie of Commodious Conceites and Hidden Secrets*, first published in 1573. This popular little volume is priced at just 4 pence; the eighth edition appears in 1596, and an enlargement is produced in 1600.[39] It contains instructions for some high-status dishes, such as marchpane wrapped in gold leaf for a banquet; but most of the recipes are for meals that every housewife might be expected to make. This is what Partridge says about baking a chicken:

> Truss your chickens, cut the feet off, put them in a coffin [a case of pastry], then for every chicken put in a handful of gooseberries and a quantity of butter . . . then take a good quantity of sugar and cinnamon, with sufficient salt, put them into the pie, let it bake one hour and a half. When it is baked, take the yolk of an egg and half a goblet of verjuice with sufficient sugar sodden together, and serve it.

Fish days in a middling household depend hugely on geographical location as well as wealth. In winter you will need to stay by the coast to get the most popular seawater fish, such as conger, turbot, mullet, and gurnard; or in a city to be able to buy freshwater fish like pike, roach, and tench. Most people only occasionally eat these fish; the most common varieties consumed are smoked and pickled herrings, and dried and salted cod. The latter are caught in the waters off Iceland or Newfoundland and can be transported long distances in their preserved state; they are therefore available all year round. Oysters can be transported live and are eaten in huge quantities by the rich and middling sort alike, both whole and chopped up in oyster pies. Eels are popular among all classes, especially shredded and baked with aples in a pie.

When it comes to dairy products, you will find a mixture of attitudes. Butter is eaten at almost every opportunity; milk is largely avoided. Cheese is available in several forms: green (new) cheese, hard cheese (such as ched-dar), soft cheese, cheese with herbs, and particular regional cheeses. All of these are becoming more popular, as cheese is seen increasingly as fit for the dinner tables of the wealthy. Cheshire cheeses are brought south for the privy council's dinners in 1590. Dutch cheeses to the value of £2,482 are imported in 1559–60. Parmesan too is imported, from Italy, and commonly grated with sage and sugar. Curiously, the English never adopt the custom of making "cheese with worms" in the German fashion. Andrew Boorde is not the only Englishman who balks at the practice of deliberately breeding maggots in a cheese—and then eating them together.[40]

The moderately well-off have always tended to eat more vegetables than their social superiors, so, as the very wealthy start to eat a little more fruit and vegetables, yeomen and merchants have no qualms about following suit. Cookery books include recipes for puddings baked in a turnip, stuffed carrots, and cucumbers stuffed with pigs' livers. In case you don't believe me, here is the recipe:

> Take your cucumber and cut out all the meat that is within it. Then take the liver of a lamb or a pig, and grapes or gooseberries, and grated bread, pepper, salt, cloves and mace and a little suet, and the yolks of three eggs, and mingle them all together and put in the cucumber, and let your broth boil. . . . The broth must be made of mutton broth, vinegar and butter, strained bread and salt.[41]

Artichokes, which were unheard of in England at the start of Henry VIII's reign, are now common. Pumpkins too have recently been introduced from France, as have melons.[42] Cauliflowers are another novelty, introduced from Italy in a dinner given to the privy council in November 1590.[43] In East Anglia and the southeast, immigrants from Holland and Flanders introduce their market gardens from the 1570s, thereby bringing in new vegetables such as the edible carrot, chervil, and lamb's lettuce. They also import great quantities of vegetables from Flanders to London, where they are sold near the gates of St. Paul's Cathedral: 12,600 cabbages, sixty-five barrels of onions, and 10,400 ropes of onions in the month of November 1596 alone.[44] Cabbages, parsnips, carrots, and turnips are cultivated around London— the largest cabbages weighing up to twenty-eight pounds—and all of these are boiled and eaten with butter.[45] The old fears of fruit-eating are similarly weakening. The pioneering gardening writer Thomas Tusser lists twenty-seven varieties of fruit trees to be cultivated. William Harrison declares that the gardens of old were just a dunghill compared with those of his own time. Somewhat surprisingly, however, you will hardly ever find mushrooms on the table. Even though many different edible types grow in the woods and fields up and down the country—and John Gerard notes in his *Herball* that there are common mushrooms "to be eaten"—people are simply too cautious of the poisonous varieties. "Mushrumps" are well known to Shakespeare and his contemporaries but they never regard these as food: they consider them more suitable for elves to sit under.[46]

Food in a Poor Household

For the poor, the question of "what to eat" is somewhat disingenuous: they eat whatever they possibly can. "A few herbs well chopped together will make a mess of good pottage to a hungry man," writes William Horman patronizingly, ignoring the low nutritional value of herbs by themselves. The hard fact is that a laborer's daily wage will barely pay for the food he requires. The diet fed to sailors in the navy in 1565, mentioned in Chapter Seven, amounts to a substantial fifty-eight hundred calories per day— almost double the requirement of three thousand calories for a moderately active man; but that diet costs 4½ pence per day.[47] A laborer in Elizabeth's reign earning 4 pence per day cannot afford more than fifty-one hundred calories—not enough to feed his family as well as himself, let alone pay for clothes and other requirements. His children will suffer from malnutrition unless the family manages to produce more calories from their garden than they require to work the soil. Small wonder so many laborers' sons are ready to join the navy.

Bread underpins the diet of the poor. In the country, most households will bake their own; in towns, you will go to a baker to buy it. Its importance is becoming even greater now that the wealthy have started eating cheese, which used to be the other mainstay of the poor. The quality of the bread depends on harvest conditions. In a year when wheat is plentiful and cheap, the urban poor may well be able to afford white bread, at least occasionally. However, most of the time they and their country cousins will eat bread made from rye, barley, or maslin (a mixture of wheat and rye). When times are tough, you make bread with whatever you can. William Harrison notes that in times of dearth the poor have to make bread from peas, beans, oats, and acorns. People do not do this without resistance; they feel ashamed to eat foods that are normally eaten by animals, and it is a sad day when a father has to say grace over a loaf of acorn bread; but when his corn is lying sodden and dead in the fields, what else can he do?

Not all the poor are starving, of course. Consider Joan Mychel, a widow living in a two-room cottage in Chertsey in 1559. She is not destitute: she has chattels worth £17, including a dozen old pewter platters, dishes, and saucers with which to entertain her guests, although most of her tableware is wooden, including her spoons.[48] Her food consists largely of pottage. It might be cooked with a modicum of bacon or the leftovers of a chicken: these are boiled in a cauldron over the fire, and garlic, oats, cabbages, radishes, pumpkins, coleworts, peas, beans, or lentils added from her garden. On a nonmeat day, salt cod replaces the bacon—if she can afford it. In autumn and winter, root vegetables such as turnips, parsnips, and carrots are added to the pot, which are now eaten by "the common people, all the time of Autumn and chiefly upon the fish days."[49] In summer, she throws in herbs such as hyssop, thyme, and parsley.[50] If no meat is available, she will use the bones of a chicken carcass. Spices are quite beyond her reach but she will make her own verjuice and vinegar and use salt sparingly. When entertaining, Joan will take a pumpkin, remove the pith and seeds, fill it with apples, and bake it. Butter is freshened over and over again, to stop it going rancid. Apples, pears, blackberries, and cherries are gathered when plentiful and preserved as long as possible. When food is precious, you will find a large measure of thrift in every poor household.

What to Drink

During Elizabeth's reign drinking glasses begin to replace wooden and pewter cups on the tables of the wealthy. Like glass windows, drinking glasses are a status symbol. English-made vessels, with a characteristic greenish tinge (due to the use of fern leaves in the manufacturing process), are the cheapest, at about 2 pence each. Venetian glasses from Murano, being the best quality, cost at least five times as much.[51] Glasses worth £663 are imported in 1559–60; this rises to £1,622 in 1565.[52] But the transformation to glassware is not as quick as you might expect. In part this is because of the queen granting a monopoly on the business in 1575 to an Italian glassmaker in London, Giacomo Verzelini.[53] There is nothing wrong with Verzelini's craftsmanship—far from it: his work is superb—but his monopoly means it is now illegal to import Venetian glass, and there is only so much one glassmaker can produce. In fact, glass drinking vessels are as rare as silver ones in the provincial towns. Most people, even well-off vintners like Simon Tally of Guildford, drink wine from pewter goblets.[54] You will very rarely see a glass in a husbandman's house. Beer and ale are drunk out of wooden mazers, stoneware flagons, earthenware mugs, or pewter pots, pottles, or tankards. Gold cups are extremely rare, although the queen has forty-three of them, inherited from her father.[55]

One thing you will probably not drink in Elizabethan England is water. All sorts of diseases are conveyed by water and most people understand that it is harmful—hence all the references to "fair water" and "rosewater" in the recipes we encountered above. If you are lucky enough to be staying in the country and have rainwater collected in a cistern, you might consider using it to water down your wine but even so, most people won't touch it. If they have no beer or wine they will opt for mead or metheglin. Mead is honey fermented in water, metheglin a similar concoction with herbs. Cider and perry are both commonly drunk in the country; they are popular among the poor not just because they are cheap but because they do not, like beer, consume grain, which can instead be baked into bread. While milk is the other staple drink of the poor, yeomen don't drink it and give away the whey they have left over after making cream and butter, which is considered suitable for only women and children. If you do happen to notice a yeoman with a flagon of milk (or olive oil), he is consuming it as a prophylactic prior to a heavy bout of wine drinking.

Wine

Wine is a luxury, one of the clearest delineations between a gentleman's style of living and that of everyone else. Fynes Moryson declares that "Clowns and vulgar men drink only beer or ale but gentlemen carouse only in wine."[56] Wine grapes have not grown in England for the last two hundred years, so it has to be imported. Most of the kingdom's wine—more than £68,000 worth in 1559–60, equating to about sixty-eight thousand hogsheads—arrives in the port of London, and a fair deal of it is consumed in the same city.[57] When it arrives, heavy customs duties are levied by the port officials. Also, any wine that is to be drunk in a country house or an inland town has to be transported over long distances, and so the cost mounts up.

Just as a gentleman's dinner normally consists of several sorts of meat, so too it involves different wines. Thomas Platter attends a lavish reception given by the lord mayor in October 1599 and remarks that he is offered "the best beer and all manner of heavy and light wines to follow, as for instance, Greek, Spanish, Languedoc, French and German."[58] When Lord North entertains Queen Elizabeth and her entourage in 1577, he orders 378 gallons of claret, sixty-three gallons of white wine, twenty gallons of sack, and six gallons of hippocras. Claret is a clear, light red wine from Gascony. The white wine is most probably from La Rochelle in France or "Rhenish" (from the Rhineland). Sack is a very popular dry amber wine from Spain, which the English drink sweetened with sugar. Hippocras is a peculiarly English drink: wine spiced with cinnamon and ginger and, again, sweetened with sugar. It is normally drunk at a banquet or a celebratory occasion, such as a wedding or a baptism. Henry Machyn notes many occasions in his diary when London festivities end with the serving of hippocras.

The above wines are not the only types drunk in England. You will also come across malmsey (a sweet wine from Crete), muscatel (a sweet wine from France), and bastard (a red wine from Burgundy). William Harrison writes that fifty-six wine-producing regions are represented in the London market and adds that there are thirty named sorts of wine from Italy, Greece, Spain, and the Canaries, including such exotics as catepument, raspis, osy, Capri, and Rumney. "Green wine"—the "green" referring to the youth of the wine, not its color—is thought to be especially healthy. People therefore don't store wine to improve it; most wines are drunk within a year or two of being imported.

If you are seeking something stronger than wine, it is possible to find distilled *brandewijn* or brandy, made by Flemish immigrants. Several medical self-help books have recipes for *aqua vitae*, which is distilled from wines and herbs. The purpose of including the herbs is to capture their "essence," in an alchemical sense, so their life-giving properties are transferred to the drinker. In fact, this is the whole purpose of the drink, so you will find distilled liquor not in a tavern but in an apothecary's shop. It is not until the next century that people regularly imbibe strong alcohol for fun, rather than purely medicinal reasons.

Beer and Ale

Beer and ale are regarded as more or less synonymous in the modern world but they are very different things in Elizabethan times. Beer is made from malt barley, water, and hops and keeps well—and the longer you keep it before it goes stale, the better it will be. Ale is not made with hops and has to be drunk quickly, within three days at the most; and is much less popular as a result. However, it can be made quickly to a great strength, using a high ratio of malt to water, and so it still is brewed. It is also regularly used by cooks in their sauces.

The quantities drunk will no doubt surprise you. When entertaining the queen in 1577, Lord North orders 3,996 gallons of beer and 384 gallons of ale. The daily allowance for a man—whether he be a servant or a nobleman—in many large houses is a gallon of beer, and this is not a notional amount: people really do drink that much on a regular basis. And some of it is strong stuff. The best beer is called March beer, because that is when it is brewed, and if you drink a gallon of that in a day you will not be good for much else. In some places you find it called "double beer," because double the amount of malt is used, which means it can be as intoxicating as wine.[59] Small beer for the servants is made with less malt in relation to the quantity of water; it is therefore not as strong, nor does it keep more than a month.

As with wine, beer is stored in barrels and decanted into leather jacks or earthenware bottles as required. Bottled beer can be purchased in stoneware bottles bearing the face of a rotund bearded man. However, if you buy one, drink it quickly, for the yeast in the beer will continue to ferment, the pressure will build up and the bottle will eventually explode. If you want to taste a good range, you can find them at any country fair. They have poetic names like their modern equivalents. William Harrison lists Huffcap, The Mad Dog, Father Whoreson, Angels' Food, Dragon's Milk, Go-by-the-Wall, Stride Wide, and Lift-Leg. While these have the power to turn those who drink them into "ale-knights who . . . will not dare to stir from their stools but sit pinking with their narrow eyes, as half-sleeping, until the fume of their adversary be digested," beer and ale are not without their healthy connotations.[60] Some beers are brewed with herbs, thereby containing the essence of something health-giving. Others are made into restorative possets, through the addition of spices and milk. Alternatively you might want to add an egg yolk and sugar or honey, thereby making caudled ale, which is often recommended for the sick.

Not everyone approves of English ale and beer. Mediterranean visitors in particular cannot understand the Englishman's love of it. Alessandro Magno writes in his journal that English beer is "healthy but sickening to taste. It is cloudy like horse's urine and has husks on top."[61] Andrew Boorde is even more disparaging about Cornish ale: "It will make you spew. . . . It is like wash that pigs have wrestled in."[62]

CHAPTER TEN

Hygiene, Illness, and Medicine

There is no concept of "health and safety" in Elizabethan England, so you will inevitably feel vulnerable when you arrive. Nauseating smells and sights will assail your senses; contemporary standards of cleanliness will worry you. People die every day from unknown ailments, the young as often as the old. Infectious diseases periodically kill thousands within a few weeks. Even when plague is not in town, it lurks as an anxiety in the back of people's minds and, when it does strike, their worry turns to terror. On top of the illnesses, the chances of being attacked and hurt are much higher than in the modern world, and workplace injuries are far more common. Whatever you do in Elizabethan England, you will have need of medical advice or surgery at some stage. But before suggesting what you should do to stay well, and what to do if you fall ill, it is necessary to lay out why Elizabethans *think* they get sick. This will help you understand the medical strategies they adopt, some of which you might consider more fearsome than your ailment.

Elizabethans do not understand infection and contagion as we do. It is not that they are completely ignorant as to how illnesses spread—physicians believe they know perfectly well—it is rather that their understanding is very different from ours. The principal ideas underpinning most Elizabethan medical thinking come from Galen, who lived in the second century A.D. Physicians will cite him as an unquestionable authority when they explain to you that your health depends on a balance of the four humors: yellow bile or choler, black bile, phlegm, and blood. If there is too much choler in your body, you will grow choleric; too much blood and you will be sanguine; too much phlegm and you will be phlegmatic; and too much black bile makes you melancholic. It is from these imbalances that sickness arises.

How do these humors get out of balance? This is where the overlapping ideas of Elizabethan medicine might leave you a little confused. By far the most important cause is divine intervention. People believe that illnesses may be sent to punish them for a sin—or simply because God wants them to die and go to Heaven. Some hold that God, by sending them an illness, is giving them a chance to atone for some previous transgression through suffering, and so they are thankful for their affliction. Other causes of illness are old age, excitement, or contagion through close proximity to other ill people and decaying matter. Filthy areas such as stagnant pools and dead bodies create a miasma around them, and if the air or water of a miasma enters the body, it disrupts the humors. In *The boke for to Lerne a man to be wyse in the building of his howse for the helth of his soule and body* (c. 1540), Andrew Boorde lays out some key concerns:

> If the air be fresh, pure and clean about the mansion house it doth conserve the life of man, it doth comfort the brain and the powers natural, engendering and making good blood, in which consisteth the life of man. And contrarily evil and corrupt airs doth infect the blood and doth engender many corrupt humors and doth putrefy the brain and doth corrupt the heart, and therefore it doth breed many diseases and infirmities through which man's life is abbreviated and shortened. Many things doth infect, putrefy and corrupt the air: the first is the influence of sundry stars and standing water, stinking mists and carrion lying long about the ground; many people in a small room lying uncleanly and being filthy and sluttish.

You get the picture. If something smells bad, the air is putrefied; breathe in that air and you will fall ill.

People believe that the balance of the humors is also upset by eating too much or too little of something. As noted in the previous chapter, Thomas Elyot believes that fish and fresh fruit are bad for you, and that white bread is more nutritious than bread with the bran. William Horman maintains that drinking cold liquids after prolonged activity is very dangerous for the health. Richard Carew states that the "eating of fish, especially newly taken and of the livers, gives rise to leprosy."[1] Although you will know that brown bread is more nutritious than white, and that fish does not cause leprosy, you will probably agree with the general idea—that what you ingest affects your health. You probably already subscribe to the belief that carrion and stagnant water are likely to cause disease. What you are less likely to swallow is that the stars can cause an imbalance in your bodily humors. Or that such things as humors control your health. Or that illnesses can be triggered by witchcraft. Or that black marks can be caused by fairies pinching you in the cradle.[2] Or that God has sent you a disease simply so you can prove your virtues by suffering.

The theory of the humors is just the basic framework into which physicians fit a number of other ideas. Galen teaches that every living thing is composed of the four elements: fire, earth, air, and water. Each of these corresponds with one of the four humors. Fire, which is said to be hot and dry, corresponds with choler; water (cold and wet) with phlegm; earth (dry and cold) with black bile; and air (hot and wet) with blood. These properties are all associated with parts of the body, so the brain is cold and moist, the kidneys hot and moist, and so on. If an imbalance in the humors clashes with the properties of an organ, the patient will be ill. No distinction is made between mental and physical illness; the mind is seen as being similarly vulnerable to imbalances. Physicians recognize that the body is to a certain degree self-regulating, through the excretion of tears, urine, feces, and sweat, but they also believe that further purges, bleedings, and vomits must be applied to rid the body of the substances corrupting the organs.

Sanitation

Noisome smells and noxious fumes are common in Elizabethan England but that does not mean that people do not notice them. Nor is it simply that they tolerate them. This is a difficult subject, so it is worth looking at it in a little depth to understand it properly.

When you wander along a country lane you might smell the earth, especially if it has recently rained. If it is summer you might smell the pollen, and in late summer the cut hay. What you will not be so aware of is the clean air. It is such a ubiquitous and subtle smell that you notice only by its absence, when something particularly fetid, alluring, or sweet overpowers your olfactory senses. Your mind calibrates your sense of smell and, as with your sense of balance, you only notice the fresh air when it changes. If you walk into a small room in the corner of which there is a privy, a twelve-foot shaft full of several hundred gallons of decomposing excrement and urine that has been lying there, seeping into the clay for two or three years, you will notice that change immediately. Suddenly your olfactory senses are off balance. What differentiates you and the Elizabethan person who lives in this room is how prepared you are for this assault on your senses and the connotations of health, disease, and poverty you associate with the smell. Also, and most important, there may be a profound difference in how much shame you think the householder should feel about introducing someone else to this stinking environment.

As you will soon find, the idea that everyone cheerfully puts up with noxious fumes is a modern myth. Everywhere people comment on the nuisances of latrines. Yes, you will come across people urinating or defecating in fireplaces at night when they are staying in somebody else's house, but what else do you do when no chamber pot is provided? People remark on such difficult situations precisely because they are extraordinary. Andrew Boorde states categorically that pissing in chimneys is not to be tolerated: it contributes to the stinking airs that he, like most people, believes is the cause of illness.[3] Remembering a room he rented some years earlier, the physician Simon Forman writes that, "The evil stink of the privy did annoy me much and because many [patients] did resort unto me there I left it because it was little and too high up and because of the stink."[4] Forman is not only unhappy with the smell on his own account: he is obviously embarrassed to have patients visiting him in a place that is filled with corrupt air. This room is one of the upper chambers in a stone building, so the cesspit is a long way below. The smell he describes comes from the stone flue that drops to the cesspit: the urine and excrement that have caught on the stonework on the way down, and the vapors that are blown up the flue by the draft.

As a result, it is simply wrong to say that Elizabethan people are generally more tolerant of filth and smell than we are.[5] There is not one standard for Elizabethan England and a different one for us; rather there is a wide range of thresholds of tolerance and senses of shame, both then and now, and a wide range of solutions. Queen Elizabeth will not tolerate dyeing with woad or burning coal within five miles of her palaces.[6] Rich people, who are accustomed to removing the smells of the body and perfuming themselves on a daily basis, would not dream of asking you to sit in a chamber that stinks of urine and feces. The queen's godson, Sir John Harington, even builds a flushing water closet, with a stone bowl and a brass sluice, at his house, Kelston, near Bath. In his book *A New Discourse of a Stale Subject Called the Metamorphosis of Ajax* (1596), he explains that smoke and the stench of privies "are two of those pains of Hell . . . and therefore I have endeavored in my poor buildings to avoid those two inconveniences as much as I may."⁷ The queen also has a flushing loo built for herself at Richmond. In the great houses movable "chairs of easement" (commodes) are emptied and tucked away when not in use. Privies are situated some distance from living quarters, behind a closed door, with the chute being stopped with a lid or a cushion. Townsmen living in wealthy neighborhoods do not empty their chamber pots in the streets: to do so risks being reported to the civic authorities by their neighbors and fined. In his book on how to construct your house, Andrew Boorde recommends that his readers build their privies over flowing water to remove the filth in the same way a flushing toilet does. Sir William Petre's Ingatestone Hall in Essex has running water (controlled by taps) and drains in sealed underground pipes which take away the waste from the five privies in the house. Sir William even builds an inspection chamber for making sure the whole system continues to run properly. If people can afford to remove the smells of feces and urine from their living quarters, they do so.

Affordability is the key. In the country it is not expensive to have a clean-smelling house: build your house of easement at the end of the garden and just visit it when necessary. For the vast majority of people living in towns and cities this isn't possible. It costs £1 10 shillings 8 pence to build a water closet like Sir John Harington's—but you would need your own drain and a plentiful water supply, which almost no one has. Even a cesspit is expensive to maintain: in London it requires a team of twelve men to dig out sixteen tons of excrement in an average household latrine over the course of two nights, several large barrels to contain the ordure, carts to take it away, food for the workers, candles (as it has to be done by night), juniper to refresh the pit, brickwork to rebuild the funnels of the privy chute (which have to be broken by the emptying operation), and, last but not least, the cost of cleaning up the house after sixteen tons of excrement, slopping about in barrels, has been carried through it. The total cost of such an operation in 1575 is £2 4 shillings—the equivalent of 132 days' work for a laborer.⁸ You can see why the tenements of the poor have stinking cesspits, and why people in the city slums dump their filth into the gutter and allow their cesspits to overflow into the street. The authorities in large cities have no choice but to build public latrines. Exeter's city council orders new public facilities to be provided in 1568 and London has several communal jakes, the largest being sensibly situated above the Thames on London Bridge (al though this is also where the pumping engines that supply private water are situated).[9] Ironically, the smell of excrement is not something Elizabethans connect with backwardness or the rustic past but with progress and urbanization.[10]

Household Cleanliness

Rotting vegetable matter is merely unpleasant but rotten meat and fish can seriously undermine your health. Cleaning your plates and bowls is thus important. After a meal, you will wipe your knife clean on your napkin and put it back in its sheath. Spoons and any other cutlery provided at your meal will be taken out to the scullery or kitchen and washed along with the pewter plates and cooking dishes. "Wash all the greasy dishes and vessels in the lead cauldron or pan in hot water and set them clean upon the scullery board," William Horman instructs his pupils. No soap is used in washing pots and plates, just hot water. If pieces of fish or meat have stuck to the bottom of the frying pan, the recommended process is to soak it first in boiling water and then scour it. Scouring requires a handful of straw and some potash sprinkled in the bottom of the pan: scrub until it is clean, rinse, and set it to dry. Similar measures are taken for the serving jugs for drinks like beer and ale. The butler at Wollaton is specifically charged with keeping his leather jacks (large flasks) free from "furring and unsweet savor."[11]

As for the state of cleanliness elsewhere in the house, much depends on the availability of soap. Dirty sheets are likely to harbor insect life and vermin; bed bugs and fleas are ubiquitous. On the subject of fleas, Thomas Moffet writes, "Though they trouble us much, yet they neither stink as walllice doe, nor is it any disgrace to a man to be troubled with them, as it is to be lousy." Clearly not everyone is as determined to rid themselves of the pestilential little devils as you will be. But Moffet does not speak for the whole of society: many people go to great lengths to kill fleas, fumigating rooms and bedclothes, and pressing everything tightly in chests in the hope of suffocating them. Again we have a wide range of tolerances and opinions.

Those who associate smells with dangerous ailments cannot bear their bedchamber to smell of anything other than fresh air. Andrew Boorde echoes Galen in urging householders to make sure they have a draft blowing through the chambers of their houses to carry away the smell of people. You, of course, know that the mere smell of someone cannot infect you. In their reaction to human fumes you will find some Elizabethans more fastidious than you are, rushing to the nearest pomander lest they smell something that will corrupt their humors. It is somewhat ironic, therefore, that many modern people think of their Elizabethan ancestors as less concerned about dirt than they are. One of the reasons that fires are kept burning in the chambers of so many houses is to take away any dangerous smells lurking there and to air the room. Mind you, the smell of a bedchamber in the morning is nothing compared with that of a hall if the rushes have not been changed for a few weeks, with dogs urinating on the floor and rats running free. Sir John Davies describes the hall of a country house as "stinking with dogs and muted with hawks." It is not surprising, therefore, that Sir Francis Willoughby has banned dogs from entering the hall at Wollaton.

Bodily Cleanliness

Personal hygiene is perhaps the second most discussed and second worst documented aspect of the history of the human body (after sex, in both respects). For the starving poor, bodily filth is a major contributor to ill health. If you own only one woolen garment, which becomes dirty and riddled with lice and fleas, you will have the carriers of typhus and plague living on your skin all the time. An account of some beggars in Norwich states, "So cared they not for apparel, though the cold stuck so deep into them, that what with diseases and want of shifting [changing of clothes], their flesh was eaten with vermin, and corrupt diseases grew on them so fast and so grievously that they were past remedy."[12] These men appear to their fellow Elizabethans as walking sources of infection, and the general consensus is that you should do all you can to avoid coming into contact with them, their parasites, and their bodily fluids. As if you needed telling . . .

For most people, personal cleanliness is less a health-related issue than a social one. William Bullein states, "Plain people in the country, [such] as carters, threshers, ditchers, colliers and plowmen, seldom wash their hands, as appeareth by their filthiness, and very few times comb their heads, as is seen by flocks, nits, grease, feathers, straw and such like, which hang in their hairs."[13] Nothing in that list is a serious health threat; rather Bullein is disquieted because these country folk are not socially presentable. Thus cleanliness serves as a marker to distinguish between those that are cultured and sophisticated and those that are not. The rich expect their own kind to do something about their bodily smells, to be clean and decent, even fragrant. The socially respectable classes are similarly ashamed of smelling as if they have not washed for weeks. But as you go down the social scale, especially in an urban environment, people place a lower priority on disguising their bodily odors. In the Elizabethan mind filthy people are associated with corrupt vapors and ill health. They smell so bad that they have become walking miasmas, and people believe that their stinking breath or the foul air around them will cause other people to fall ill.

As you can see, Elizabethans clean themselves for both social and health-related reasons, very much like us. But, unlike us, the *ways* in which they clean themselves are constrained by social and health-related factors too. To understand this, you need to think about water. Sixteenth-century people believe that water can infect them through the pores of their skin and the crevices of their body, and so they display a marked reluctance to immerse themselves wholly in a bath unless they know the water is pure. In the previous century Londoners frequented the bathhouses at Southwark, where they were tended by Flemish women in steaming-hot tubs. The men among them were normally treated to more than a wash and a rubdown, so when syphilis arrived in England in 1500 it spread rapidly through the bathing community. In short, people who bathed fell ill. Henry VIII accordingly shut down all the bathhouses in Southwark. Although a small handful opened up again under Edward VI, people are more cautious nowadays. In Elizabeth's reign, having a bath is seen as risky and unnecessary: not only might you catch a disease, it costs a great deal of time, effort, and money to prepare one. If you are living in a town you will have to go to the conduit and carry home enough water, heat it above a fire, and pour it into a bathtub; in an age of trickling water supplies and firewood shortages, that is not something you can do very often.

So what should you do to clean yourself? Sir John Harington offers the following advice:

When you arise in the morning, avoid [i.e., empty yourself of] all superfluities as well by urine as by the belly. . . . Avoid also from the nostrils and the lungs all filthy matter as well by cleansing as by spittle and cleanse the face, head and whole body & love you to be clean and well-apparelled for from our cradles let us abhor uncleanness, which neither nature or reason can endure.[14]

Harington is a courtier and so this advice is to be trusted if you want to impress people of high status. However, he is unusual in suggesting that you should clean your *whole body* every morning. Francis, the schoolboy in Claudius Hollyband's book, is nowhere near as thorough:

Francis: Peter, bring me some water to wash my hands and my face. I will have no river water for it is troubled. Give me well or fountain water. Take the ewer and pour upon my hands: pour high.

Margaret: Can you not wash in the basin? Shall you always have a servant at your tail? You are too wanton!

Francis: Wilt thou that I wash my mouth and my face where I have washed my hands as they do in many houses in England? Give me a towel, maiden; now give me my breakfast, for I am ready. Make haste!

Note that he dresses first and washes himself afterward, and then he just cleans his hands, face, and mouth—the parts that show. Schoolboys have never been the most attentive students of bodily cleanliness but his morning routine is not dissimilar to Andrew Boorde's advice: "Comb your head often . . . and wash your hands and wrists, your face and eyes and your teeth with cold water."[15] William Vaughan prescribes a complete morning ritual along these lines:

1. When you are about to rise up, stretch yourself strongly. . . .
2. Rub and chafe your body with the palms of your hands, or with a coarse linen cloth: the breast, back and belly gently but the arms, thighs and legs roughly, until they seem ruddy and warm;
3. Evacuate yourself;
4. Put on your apparel, which in the summer time must be for the most part silk or buff, made of bucks' skin, for it resisteth venomous and contagious airs. . . .
5. Comb your head softly and easily with an ivory comb. . . .

6. Pick and rub your teeth. . . .

7. Wash your face, eyes, ears and hands with fountain water.

8. Say your morning prayers and desire God to bless you.[16]

But what about the rest of the body, you may wonder? What about the schoolboy's feet? What about his hair? Francis's bedchamber must smell like a miasma all on its own. This is where all that linen underclothing comes in useful: linen absorbs the moisture of the body and soaks up the sweat. People therefore "wash" in linen, rubbing the skin with linen towels and changing their shirts every day. In the modern world we are fixated on washing in soap and water but there are many other ways to remove dirt. The Romans used olive oil and a strigil. In the late sixteenth century, when water is scarce and liable to carry infection, it makes sense to clean your body with something else—like linen. Hence the importance of having access to a good laundress: a respectable family will want to have clean linen every day—towels as well as shirts, smocks, ruffs, hose, and socks.[17]

Linen is also used for cleaning hair. Lady Ri-Melaine asks for her rubbers (linen towels) to be warmed by the fire prior to having her hair rubbed clean with them. A more thorough hair washing can be done at a basin filled with hot water and lye. Of course, not everyone does this. "Some cherish their bushes of hair with much combing and washing in lye," writes William Horman, implying that others do not. Christopher Sly has his "foul head" balmed "in warm distilled waters" to convince him he is a lord in Shakespeare's *Taming of the Shrew.*

If you have a bathtub, servants, and enough firewood and reliable water, you might bathe as often as you like. However, as that list of conditions suggests, most people do not immerse themselves very often. In one of the most famous quotations of the period, the Venetian ambassador writes home with the news that Queen Elizabeth has a bath every month "whether she needs it or not."[18] People have sniggeringly presumed from this that the queen is unclean, while in fact it denotes nothing of the sort. Baths are normally taken for medicinal purposes, not for cleaning the body, so the Venetian ambassador is simply reporting that Elizabeth bathes regularly even if she is not ill. You can be confident that Elizabeth washes every day with linen towels, washes her face and hands each morning and night, and cleans her hands with water before and after every meal. She is known to be fussy about her health. She travels with her own portable bath and has bathing facilities in all her palaces, so it is likely that she actually has a bath more than once a month. At Whitehall her bathroom has water pouring from oyster shells; at Windsor she has a bathroom paneled with large mirrors.[19] Such luxury baths are fragranced with herbs in the water, and plentiful amounts of cloth are obtained to line the bathtub. Sponges are used to sit on and to wipe the body. If you are ever in the queen's presence, you will smell not her body but her perfume.

The less wealthy have a bath as and when the need justifies the risk and the expense. Babies are regularly bathed because small bathtubs are easy to prepare.[20] Londoners working in filthy trades, such as latrine cleaners, normally go for a swim in the Thames after they have finished their work. Laborers in the countryside often choose to do the same in local ponds and rivers. Thomas Staple, John Joplyn, and George Lee are martyrs to the cause of personal cleanliness, as all three men drown while washing themselves in ponds and rivers in Kent, Leicestershire, and Cambridgeshire, respectively, in the summer of 1558.[21] In 1571 the vice-chancellor of Cambridge University forbids students from going into pools and rivers "whether to swim or to wash." But prohibition is merely encouragement to some. Everard Digby, a fellow of St. John's College, Cambridge, publishes the first treatise on swimming, *De Arte Natandi*, in 1587. It is abridged and translated into English by Christopher Middleton in 1595, providing simple instructions for swimming safely, cheaply, and healthily.

Just as people believe they can infect themselves by allowing water to enter the pores of their skin, so too they believe they can cure themselves of certain afflictions in the same way. For this reason some people take a bath not to clean themselves but for medical reasons. William Bullein writes most approvingly on the subject in *The Government of Health* (1558):

There is also baths and sweating in hot houses for the pocks, scurvy, scabs, hemorrhoids [and] piles, which hot houses have the virtue of helping the said diseases. . . . The best bathing is in a great vessel or a little close place with the evaporation of divers sweet herbs well sodden in water, which have virtue to open the pores softly, letting out feeble and gross vapors which lieth between the skin and the flesh. This kind of bathing is good in the time of pestilence [plague] or quartan fever; at the end of the bath it is good to anoint the body with some sweet oil to mollify and make soft the sinews. And thus to conclude of bathing, it is very wholesome [as long as] it be not done upon an empty stomach.[22]

As Bullein notes, not all baths involve water. There is a long if not widespread tradition of dry and moist baths in England, which work by making the patient sweat. In 1600 an entrepreneur starts advertising a "new kind of artificial bathes lately invented." This contraption is a leather-covered box eighteen feet in circumference, which can be delivered to your house. With half an hour's preparation you can use it to wash yourself in the following four ways:

> First a dry airy heat warming the cold moist air and preparing the body for sweat by a clean fire in one side;
> Secondly, a moist vaporous heat, by a sweet boiling perfume;
> Thirdly a dry vaporous heat by a sweet boiling perfume;
> Fourthly, and lastly but chiefly, a moist heat by water, milk, oil or any other liquor, simple or compound, which cometh at pleasure from all parts powering downwards, flying upward, sprinkling round about with many trickling streams like strong showers of rain by a continual circular motion, and therefore penetrating and working more powerfully upon all parts of the body, except the head, which is only free for the benefit of fresh air; so covertly that neither the party bathed nor the attendants in the chamber can either see, hear or well perceive, how, whence, or by what direct means the warm water or liquor cometh and goeth with such a manifold distribution and speedy conveyance.[23]

It sounds a bit like being trapped in an oversized dishwasher. As for showering in hot milk or oil, I'll leave you to guess whether this is primarily for health or beauty.

Oral Hygiene

The bodily odor that Elizabethans tend to remark on most is the breath. You will recall Hugh Plat's statement that his pomander mixture will make you smell as sweet as any lady's dog "if your breath be not too valiant." You might also know the sonnet by Shakespeare, "My mistress's eyes are nothing like the sun . . ." in which he emphasizes the corporeal and earthy character of her body; he does not mention her bodily smell, only "the breath that from my mistress reeks." Indeed, Shakespeare often mentions smelly breath: "His breath stinks with eating toasted cheese," says Smith in *The Second Part of King Henry VI,* and in *King John* there is the "black contagious breath" of night. But such things are not to be marveled at, for cleaning the teeth and mouth is a difficult business in Elizabethan England. Most people are missing one or two teeth and suffer from severe dental caries.[24] Even the queen's teeth are yellow in the early part of her reign and they go completely black in her old age. Interestingly, a German observer states categorically that the reason for Elizabeth's bad teeth is the English propensity to eat too much sugar, so the main cause of tooth decay is known.[25]

What can you do to clean your teeth and freshen your breath? Try picking your teeth with a toothpick made of a piece of quill or wood: this will help prevent decay and stops the rotting food caught between your teeth from making your breath smell. Not brushing your teeth results in the build-up of plaque, so remove this with a "tooth cloth" (a length of wet linen).[26] Boorde recommends washing the teeth every day with water and rock alum. For freshening the breath, you could chew spices such as cumin seeds or aniseed. Or you could use a dentifrice (tooth powder) such as the following:

> First in the morning eat or swallow two or three cloves and keep between the gums and the cheeks two cloves, or else . . . take an ounce of savory, half an ounce of galingale, a quarter ounce of the wood of aloes, make powder of this and eat or drink a portion in the morning and a little after dinner, and as much to bedward.[27]

Some surgeons and apothecaries might offer you "tooth blanch" to whiten your teeth, made from powdered cuttlefish bone.[28] After rubbing your teeth with the powder, wash your mouth out with white wine and "spirit of vitriol" (sulfuric acid) and rub your teeth with a tooth cloth. An alternative is mouthwash. John Partridge's recipe is simply rosemary flowers boiled in water.[29]

If all else fails, and the toothache drives you mad, you have three courses of action. The first, most civilized one is to go to a tooth-drawer, who will take the offending tooth out using a special lever called a pelican. This has a hook, which the tooth-drawer places on the tongue side of the tooth, a bolster on the outer edge of the tooth, and a handle with which he levers it out.[30] Alternatively you could ask a surgeon to perform the task. The third option is to ask the local blacksmith, who will remove it with his pliers for a modest fee.

Illness

The Elizabethan understanding of why people get ill, outlined at the start of this chapter, will make it difficult for you to accept a physician's diagnosis of your ailment. If the nature of your problem is unclear, the physician will want to know the time you started to notice the symptoms. Some physicians will calculate the position of the stars at the moment that your humors went out of balance. Most will want to know what you have been eating, in order to see whether food might be the cause. All of them will want to have a good look at your urine. Sixteen pages of Andrew Boorde's *Breviary of Helthe* are devoted to interpreting the health of the body by the color, substance, and clarity of the patient's urine, so a urine that "is ruddy, like unto gold, doth signify a beginning of some sickness engendered in the liver and the stomach, and if it be thin in substance it doth signify abundance of phlegm, which will engender some kinds of fevers."[31] Do not be surprised, therefore, if in response to your request for medical help, a physician sends a glass urinal for you to fill. In fact, unless you are rich, most would prefer to see your urine than you in person. For the sake of their dignity, most physicians are reluctant to get too close to their sick patients.

There is an added complication in that it is not just sixteenth-century medical assumptions that will be wrong; your own interpretation of your symptoms may be equally wayward. Elizabethan people suffer from some afflictions that no longer exist in modern England. Plague is the obvious example but it is by no means the only one. Sweating sickness kills tens of thousands of people on its first appearance in 1485 and periodically thereafter. It is a terrifying disease because sufferers die within hours. It doesn't return after a particularly bad outbreak in 1556 but people do not know whether it has gone for good; they still fear it, and it continues to be part of the medical landscape for many years. Other diseases have not disappeared but have changed their character and may even have different symptoms: syphilis is a good example (discussed below). For this reason, the strangeness of the Elizabethan medical landscape is like the strangeness of the actual landscape: you will recognize the lines of distant hills, and perhaps the curve of a great river; but apart from the largest, most obvious features, very little will be familiar.

Perhaps the most difficult thing to come to terms with is the scale of death. Influenza, for example, is an affliction which you no doubt have come across. However, you have never encountered anything like Elizabethan flu. It arrives in December 1557 and lasts for eighteen months. In the ten-month period August 1558 to May 1559 the annual death rate almost trebles to 7.2 percent (normally it is 2.5 percent).[32] More than 150,000 people die from it—5 percent of the population. This is proportionally much worse than the great influenza pandemic of 1918–19 (0.53 percent mortality).[33] Another familiar disease is malaria, which Elizabethans refer to as ague or fever. You might associate this with more tropical countries of the modern world but in marshy areas in sixteenth-century England, such as the Lincolnshire and Cambridgeshire Fens, the Norfolk Broads, and Romney Marsh in Kent, it kills thousands. No one suspects that it has anything to do with mosquitoes; rather people believe it is the corrupted air arising from the low-lying dank marsh (hence the term *mal-aria*). As a result, you will have no chance of getting proper treatment for the disease. Infant mortality in and around Romney Marsh is exceptionally high, with 25–30 percent of children dying before their fourth birthday. Overall the death rate there is in excess of 5 percent, double the annual average, so it is like living in an area afflicted by a permanent influenza epidemic. You will find no physicians there.[34] Most local rectors and vicars live elsewhere, employing clerks to conduct the funerals, marriages, and baptisms on their behalf. As one writer reports of the parishes of Burmarsh and Dymchurch, which lie within Romney Marsh: "Both the air and the water make dreadful havoc on the health of inhabitants of this sickly and contagious country, a character sufficiently corroborated by their pallid countenances and short lives."[35]

Plague

Serious though influenza and malaria are, they are not the biggest killers of the age. That title belongs to the plague or "pestilence." No one knows precisely how many die over the course of the reign but the total is probably around 250,000.[36] In 1565 the people of Bristol count up the plague victims for that year and arrive at the figure of 2,070, almost 20 percent of the population. Ten years later, after another deadly outbreak, they record a further 2,000 fatalities. Norwich sees its worst outbreak in 1579–80, when 4,193 people die of plague, a quarter of the population, half of the victims being immigrants.[37] In 1564 plague kills two hundred people in Stratford-upon-Avon (13 percent).[38] Exeter experiences comparable outbreaks in 1570 (16 percent) and in 1590–91 (15 percent).[39] This last epidemic originates in Portugal and is brought to Devon by mariners. It is ironic that the great naval ships that deliver the English from the Spanish threat bring another danger in the form of plague.[40] In 1602 a new outbreak of plague sweeps along the south coast by way of Plymouth and Dartmouth; the following year it kills another 2,000 in Bristol and 1,800 in Norwich.[41]

Shocking though these figures are, they are dwarfed by those for London. The plague of 1563 is so severe that the city authorities start to compile Bills of Mortality, recording the numbers of people that die in each parish. This marks the beginning of official health statistics.

Deaths in London 1563–1603, from the Bills of Mortality [42]

Year	Plague deaths	Total dead
1563	17,404	20,372
1578	3,568	7,830
1582	3,075	6,930
1593	10,675	17,893
1603	32,257	40,040

The grim reality is that plague in the capital is as common as the stench of the cesspits and almost as unavoidable. You cannot predict where it will strike: People living next door to infected houses are left unaffected. Some people are not touched even when others in their own house have it.

What can you do to avoid the plague? The answer is: very little. Although there are no fewer than twenty-three medical treatises dedicated to it by 1600, including hundreds of recipes for medicines, none of them will help you. Nor will perfuming your room and airing it with fire save you—despite this being the official advice of the College of Physicians. But *you* have the advantage of knowing that a fleabite can convey the plague, and that the black rat that carries the plague flea does not like to move about very much, so leaving an affected area is a good strategy. Also, plague is most frequently transferred between people in towns, and it dies down in winter, when the rat population is less active. Therefore avoid towns in summer; stay out of the poorer parishes in particular, which are more severely affected than rich ones. It is possible that plague is occasionally passed from person to person in the breath, so be careful about gatherings of lots of people when the plague is in town (and kissing too many strangers). Remember also that plague can be transferred from person to person indirectly—for example, through a coat worn by a plague victim.[43] It is therefore wise to avoid secondhand clothing. Change your clothes and bedclothes regularly, and wash them thoroughly. The fact is that Thomas Moffet's observation—that it is no "disgrace" for a man to be troubled with fleas—probably explains why the plague spreads so quickly.

But what if it comes to the worst? What if you have painful black buboes in your groin and armpits, and experience the rapid pulse, the headaches, the terrific thirst, and delirium that are the tokens of the plague? There is little you can do. Physicians will prescribe the traditional medicines of dragon water, mithridatium, and theriac if they hear you are suffering but you will suspect that these are cynical attempts to relieve a dying person of his money. The physicians themselves will not normally come near you. Simon Forman, who does attend plague sufferers, is a rare exception: this is because he has himself survived the disease and believes he cannot catch it again. However, his remedy amounts to little more than avoiding eating onions and keeping warm. He has a recipe for getting rid of the plague sores that will afflict you afterward if you survive the disease; but that is a very big "if."[44] It seems the best advice is provided by Nicholas Bownd in his book *Medicines for the Plague*: "In these dangerous times God must be our only defense."[45]

The important date to bear in mind is 1578. In this year the privy council draws up a series of seventeen orders to limit the spread of plague. From now on, when an outbreak occurs, magistrates in each town meet every two or three weeks to review the progress of the disease, consulting the "searchers" who inspect the corpses for causes of death. The clothing and bedding of plague victims is henceforth to be burned and funerals are to take place at dusk, to discourage people from attending. Most important of all, any house where an infected person lives is to be boarded up for at least six weeks, with all the family and servants inside, whether they are sick or healthy. Watchmen are to stand guard to make sure no one leaves. You will weep to hear the cries from a woman who has been boarded up with her husband, children, and servants because one of them has been found to have the plague. People struggle to understand why the affliction has been sent upon them, why God would have cursed their family. In reality, the watchmen appointed by the JPs are not all coldhearted; some of them interpret their role as more of a facilitator to those locked up: sending messages and bringing medicines and other things that they cannot get while incarcerated.[46] But still such isolation is terrifying to experience and distressing to witness.

Incredible though it may seem, if you catch the plague, old and poor women will volunteer to be boarded up with you, to clean, cook, and look after you.[47] There is a good chance that they too will die, but they will be very well paid—as much as 6 shillings 8 pence or even 8 shillings per week.[48] Six weeks' isolation at 6 shillings 8 pence per week is £2: this is the poor woman's equivalent of the miner's reward for breaking through the sough into a flooded mine and risking death in return for £2. But when those boards are nailed over your door and windows, plunging you into that dim purgatory between death and recovery, you could be incarcerated in your home for several months. In the case of Thomas Smallbone, of Bucklebury in Berkshire, both he and his mother-in-law die, followed by his son and wife, after which the house is inhabited by just his two remaining children and the servants. You do not want to imagine the plight of the children, especially when they too start shivering with fever. The house remains boarded up for eight months; only the servants survive.[49]

Given these circumstances you can understand why some plague victims take extreme action. According to the register of Malpas, Cheshire,

Richard Dawson, being sick of the plague and perceiving he must die at that time, arose out of his bed and made his grave, and caused his nephew, John Dawson, to cast straw into the grave, which was not far from the house, and went and laid himself down in the said grave, and caused clothes to be laid upon [him], and so departed out of this world.[50]

Other Diseases

The range of diseases suffered in Elizabethan England is considerable, perhaps as great as that experienced in the modern world. Your own cautious approach to sanitation should save you from the "bloody flux" (dysentery), the "burning ague" (typhus), and typhoid fever. Your knowledge about vitamins C and D should protect you from scurvy and rickets. There are many occupational illnesses that you will know to avoid, such as mercury poisoning from manufacturing mirrors, and lung diseases from working in mines. But there will be some illnesses that you cannot avoid. Tuberculosis is common and incurable; it is passed from one sufferer to the next in the breath. If you suffer from some form of mental problem you will find that people talk about you as "frantic"—but they will have very little idea what to do. One option would be to send you to the Hospital of St. Mary of Bethlehem, otherwise known as Bedlam, just outside London, which looks after a small number of the insane for a fee. Another is to provide a keeper, lock you away in a room with your head shaved (to cool your brain), carefully monitor your diet, and occasionally bleed you by a vein in your head.

There is insufficient space to discuss every disease but two perhaps should be mentioned—the two "poxes," smallpox and the great pox.

The first treatise on smallpox, published by Simon Kellwaye in 1593, states that the cause is "alteration of the air, in drawing some putrefied and corrupt quality into it, which doth cause an ebullition of our blood." The disease is carried in the pus of pustules and the "dust" from drying scabs, so it is indeed wise to treat the air around sufferers as dangerously "corrupt." If you catch it you will experience high fever, muscle pain, severe headaches, vomiting, diarrhea, and a mass of virus-filled pustules erupting over your face and body. In Elizabeth's reign, however, it is generally considered a children's disease, like measles, with which it is frequently bracketed by physicians. Although it often kills children, it is rarely lethal for adults in Elizabethan England; the queen herself survives a serious attack in 1562. Only in the 1630s will it become a terrifying killer, fatal to adults and children alike, and feared as much as the plague. Even so, you do not want to catch it; it leaves a mass of disgusting pocks or marks on your face and body, so even surviving it can be horrific.

The other pox is the great pox, also known in England as the "French disease." This too is a disease which changes over the course of time. When it first came to Europe from the New World in the 1490s it would kill you in a few weeks. By 1558 it has evolved into the infection you know today as syphilis, which causes nasty sores on the private parts and other areas of the body but which people can live with for decades. It is transmitted mainly by sexual intercourse or, less frequently, in the womb, from infected mother to child. William Clowes, the surgeon who publishes a treatise on it in 1585, understands its origins perfectly well: "I wish all men generally, especially those that be infected, to loath, detest, hate and abhor that stinking sin that is the original cause of this infection."[51] As you can imagine, that is something of a vain hope in Elizabethan England. Attitudes toward women do not help: we have already heard of Katherine Vardine of Norwich, who is saved from her master's venereal disease by a court decision. The physician Simon Forman is another man who uses his position to secure sexual satisfaction, seducing a large number of women who come to him for medical and astrological advice. (Now you can see why he did not like his room to smell of the privy.) It does not matter to him whether they are married; he seems to relish writing down the names of the husbands he has cuckolded. His medical notes reveal that he sometimes has sex with several different female patients in one day. Small wonder that syphilis continues to plague society.

Sex also tends to lead to pregnancy. Obviously this is not a disease, but childbirth can easily result in complications and put the woman's life in danger. Normally the birthing chamber is a female-only space, where midwives attend the woman in labor; men are not welcome. Giving birth is also a social occasion: a close female friend will feel slighted if you do not invite her to witness the event. However, when things go wrong, physicians and surgeons may be called upon, but very often nothing can be done. Forceps are unknown. Cesarean sections are invariably fatal for the woman. Two percent of all confinements end up with a dead mother.[52] Giving birth to five children thus represents a risk of death of one in ten; yet many women give birth ten times or more. As for painkillers, it is highly unlikely that anything effective will be provided. With so much pain and death, you have to wonder whether any children would be born at all if society were not dominated by men.

Medical Care in the Home

What do you do when you fall ill? In Elizabethan times as now, you do not necessarily seek professional medical advice straightaway. If you know what is wrong with you, you will know what sort of help you need—whether that be your spouse or your mother, a specific medicine from an apothecary or a professional physician or surgeon. If things are really bad and you think you may die, you will ask not for a physician but for a clergyman, as the salvation of your soul will take priority. If, on the other hand, you do not know what is wrong with you, you will engage the most appropriate help stage by stage. You will start with the medical knowledge available in the home, which might be quite extensive. If that is inadequate you will seek help from the women in the community and those unofficial medical men who sell "cures"—ready-made medicines guaranteed to help any ailment or a specific condition. Only after all of those have failed will you send for a medical practitioner from the nearest town.

Medical help therefore involves several stages of amateur assistance. A housewife is expected not just to be a cook, mother, cleaner, seamstress, and (in the country) farmhand, she also needs to be an amateur physician. This is especially the case in medical backwaters like Romney Marsh, where there are no resident physicians. In such places women are expected to pool their knowledge and experience, and to share recipes for medicines that they have found to be efficacious. Printing has changed the medical landscape, for there are now many self-help books available which contain medical recipes. These go through many editions and are read by a succession of different owners. People borrow books and copy out the medical recipes, if they can write; so you don't even need to own one. This is another good reason for women in this period to teach themselves to read—so they can assemble a larger body of knowledge with which to care for the family.

The homely remedies you will find in a self-help book vary enormously in nature and scope. Most of those in Thomas Dawson's *The Good Huswife's Jewell* (1585) are general-purpose medicines, such as "a strong broth for a sick man" (powdered almonds, the brain of a chicken, and cream, seasoned with sugar).[53] A substantial minority of recipes in such books—between 10 and 20 percent—incorporate animal parts or excrements, in the spirit of medieval medicines. Dawson, for example, recommends a recipe for broken sinews that starts, "Take worms while they be nice.... Stamp [i.e., crush] them and lay it to the sore, and it will knit the sinew that be broken in two." His recipe to use on shortened sinews begins "Take the head of a black sheep, camomile, sorrel leaves, sage, of each a handful, and bray these herbs in a mortar. . . ." Should you not fancy black sheep's head in your medicine, here is an alternative ointment:

> Take eight swallows ready to fly out of the nest. Drive away the breeders when you take them out, and let them not touch the earth. Stamp them until the feathers cannot be perceived in a stone mortar. Put to it lavender cotton, of the strings of strawberries, the tops of mother [wild] thyme, the tops of rosemary, of each a handful. Take all their weight of May butter and a quart more. Then make it up in bales and put it into an earthenware pot for eight days close stopped, that no air take them. Take it out and, on as soft a fire as maybe, seethe it so that it do but simmer. Then strain it, and reserve it to your use.[54]

All in all, the hearty broths in Dawson's book sound far more health-giving than his medical recipes.

John Partridge's *The Widowe's Treasure* is aimed at older women who make a living from providing medical assistance. We have already heard of women looking after plague victims, but it is important to realize that they are not just opportunists desperate for money: they are experienced women who will travel to the next parish to attend a sick person if so required. They are not called nurses at this time—"nursing" means wet-nursing—but they tend the ill in much the same way as a nurse would: cleaning bedclothes, feeding the patient, and generally helping at the bedside. Normal payment for attending a seriously ill person is 4 pence per day and 4 to 6 pence per night.[55] The recipes with which Partridge provides these women include everything from therapeutic drinks to aid passing water, to ointments and extreme medicines for people suffering from fatal diseases. To help a person get to sleep he advises: "Take a spoonful of woman's milk, a spoonful of rosewater, and a spoonful of the juice of a lettuce, boil them in a dish. Then take some fine flax and make your plaster as broad as you will have it lie on your forehead, then moisten it with the same liquor and grate a little nutmeg over it."[56] For toothache he advises you to "take roots of henbane sodden in vinegar and rosewater, put the decoction in your mouth." A recipe for killing body lice involves quicksilver (mercury) in grease rubbed into a linen belt tied around the patient; another for the same purpose suggests anointing the lice-ridden sufferer with powdered frankincense mixed with boar's fat.

Things could be worse. In parts of the country you will come across superstitious practices, such as lowering an infant with whooping cough into a cesspit and holding him there in the corrupt air. Snakeskin is widely thought to be a remedy for a number of diseases, and, according to William Horman, so is the "unwashed wool that grows between the hind legs of a black sheep." I doubt you will find anyone who can explain the medical reasoning behind that last one. It makes the theory of the humors look reassuringly sophisticated.

Medical Practitioners

If you have tried all the available local help and are still suffering, your next resort will be to a professional medical practitioner. There are three categories which slightly overlap: a physician diagnoses and treats illnesses that occur within the body; a surgeon treats broken limbs and the surface of the body, including any wounds and ulcers; and an apothecary provides medicines and ointments for both inward and outward use. An apothecary is often connected to a physician, who will direct you to collect the medicines he prescribes from "his" apothecary. Strictly speaking, an apothecary is not qualified to diagnose your condition, but if the cause of your suffering is obvious he may well sell you something to ease the pain or cure it.

At the start of the reign you will find very few qualified medical men. Most physicians are unregulated and, unless you can afford the services of a university-trained doctor of medicine, you may be better off with a barber-surgeon. But Elizabeth's reign witnesses a great surge in the numbers of men qualifying as physicians and surgeons; by 1603 there are more than two thousand medical practitioners in the country.[57] In addition, the immense popularity of self-help books leads to a demand for specific medicines, and so more apothecaries open up shops. At the end of the reign there are about 190 physicians, surgeons, and apothecaries practicing in the diocese of Canterbury alone—one practitioner for every four hundred people, not including midwives and wet nurses. The same proportion can be found in London.[58] Although not every region in England has as many practitioners as the southeast, the ratio does not compare badly to modern medical provision: at the time of writing, the United Kingdom has one medical practitioner for every 250 people.[59]

Physicians and surgeons can be qualified in a variety of ways. The most highly qualified are those who have studied at a university and gone on to read for a medical degree, either a bachelor of medicine or a doctorate in medicine. There are only about a hundred such men in the country, because of the length and cost of the training, which is especially expensive for those who study at a foreign university, such as Leiden, Basel, Padua, Heidelberg, Bologna, and Montpellier. The most eminent of all are the Fellows of the College of Physicians in London. In 1572 there are eighteen of them, their number growing to thirty by 1589.[60] They supposedly oversee medical practice throughout the kingdom and take action against unlicensed physicians and surgeons. In reality, however, it is only Londoners who tend to fall foul of the college's monopoly-protecting court.

A license is a different sort of qualification, granted not after training but after acquiring sufficient practical experience. Practitioners can obtain one from the College of Physicians or a university but the great majority are licensed by a bishop. Surgeons may also be recognized officially by joining a city's company of barber-surgeons, membership in which is attained by serving an apprenticeship and passing an examination.[61] However, in the southeast, only just over half of all the physicians and surgeons are licensed, university-trained, or have served an apprenticeship. In the West Country and in the north, even fewer practitioners are qualified.[62] You will also notice that there are many part-time "physicians," men who combine their medical work with other occupations. William Clowes, a professional surgeon, is rather disparaging of such amateurs. In his book on syphilis he expresses astonishment at how medicine and surgery are abused by "painters . . . glaziers . . . tailors . . . weavers . . . joiners . . . cutlers . . . cooks . . . bakers . . . chandlers . . . tinkers, toothdrawers, pedlars, ostlers, carters, porters, horse-gelders, horse-leeches, idiots, apple-squires, broomsmen, bawds, witches, conjurers, soothsayers, sow-gelders, rogues, rat-catchers, renegades and proctors of spittle-houses, with such other like rotten and stinking weeds."[63]

In Elizabeth's reign every full-time apothecary or surgeon is based in a town, and so are most licensed physicians. This has led some modern historians to presume that you cannot get medical help in the country.[64] Don't believe them. Norwich has at least seventy medical practitioners (one for every two hundred people in the city), and Canterbury has about forty (one for every 125 citizens), so it is certainly much easier to obtain medical help in an emergency if you do live in a town; but surgeons and physicians travel out to see their patients in rural areas. In the case of Canterbury's physicians, about half their business lies outside the city.[65] In addition, sick people send friends or servants to the apothecaries in towns to pick up medicines, just as we do today. In rural counties in the north and the West Country, however, where practitioners are much scarcer, people travel much farther for medical help. They are also more inclined to make do with the medical knowledge in the community.[66]

Will any of these people actually be able to help you if you fall ill? Given the widely accepted ideas about the humors of the body, the positions of the stars, the eagerness with which a surgeon will bleed you, and the seriousness with which a physician will look at and sniff your urine, you may doubt it. However, you should not ignore the fact that the popularity of medicine is increasing with enthusiasm, not decreasing with cynicism. Faced with a serious illness, large numbers of people will pay substantial amounts of money for medical help. On average a physician in 1600 will receive 13 shillings from a wealthy client and 10 shillings from a less well-off one. An apothecary will charge 20 shillings and 8 shillings respectively, the less prosperous patients being prescribed cheaper medicines. These are large sums of money by most people's standards, and they show that people put faith in their physicians. Those that survive serious illnesses such as typhus and smallpox, and have the scars of their pustules treated successfully, will tell you that it is money well spent.[67] Whether you will agree is likely to depend on what you are prescribed. If you are suffering from gout and a physician prescribes colchicum, you are likely to be satisfied: the same remedy is still in use today. You are in good hands if he gives you aniseed for gastric wind or a cough; again, this remedy is still in use today—as are many herb-based medicines from the period. However, you will be less pleased if, at great cost, he tells you to take powdered Egyptian mummy (*mummia*): this is every bit as dubious as Horman's unwashed sheep wool. And as for Sir Hugh Plat's remedy of "the powdered skull of a man killed in war" as a cure for tertian fever—I would seek a second opinion. In fact, seek it from the Stratford physician John Hall for an emetic infusion and syrup of violets, which is what he uses to cure the poet Michael Drayton of the same disease.[68]

When it comes to surgery you can expect more accurate knowledge. As injuries are so common, surgeons have many opportunities to practice— removing arrowheads and bullets, stitching up cuts, replacing sections of skull, and mending organs damaged by sword wounds. They know that if they need to amputate a limb they can take advantage of the painkilling qualities of the body's endorphins if they are quick enough. If not, they have opiate-based painkillers and alcohol. Knowledge of anatomy is much better than it was thanks to the availability of Vesalius's *De Humani Corporis Fabrica* (1543) and the possibility of dissection; the Barber-Surgeons Act of 1540 makes provision for the surgeons of London to be given the corpses of four executed criminals every year for examination. Hence a surgeon will be able to staunch blood flow, mend broken bones, reset dislocated limbs, cauterize wounds, treat sores, and extricate objects as well as his modern counterpart. As for amputation, you will need a strong stomach to be a surgeon. In his *Certaine Workes of Chirurgerie*, Thomas Gale explains that gunshot wounds sometimes lead to gangrene and the mortification of the flesh, in which case you have to amputate the limb in order to save the patient's life. Having fed the patient to make him strong, and having tightly applied a "defensive" (tourniquet), the surgeon should proceed as follows:

When you have all things prepared, with bolsters and rollers [bandages], and other things thereto pertaining, you shall go to the patient and comfort him as I have said before, covering his eyes and setting him in some place convenient, having certain persons meet for the same purpose to hold his body and his arms [in case] he let not your operation, and other apt persons to hold the member that you will take away. You shall then quickly with a sharp incision knife cut the flesh round about to the bone, within half an inch of the defensive that was before laid on. And one thing you must take heed of: there lieth a nerve between the two bones of the leg beneath the knee which you must cut asunder with your incision knife, lest in sawing the bones . . . it might be so plucked and torn with the saw provoking great accidents such as sincope, spasms, dolour, yes, and death also, which I myself have often times seen. Then when you have made your incision perfect with a fine saw you shall cut asunder the bones speedily and with as little shaking of the member as you may, then lay upon the ends of the bones a little lint dipped in oil of roses and so wrung out again, the oil being first made warm.[69]

The great failing of Elizabethan surgeons is their inadequate knowledge of infection. They clean their instruments after using them but the idea of sterilizing them is a thing of the distant future, and so diseases are easily passed between patients. Blood poisoning is therefore common, and even the best surgery is often fatal. All in all, you might think that those who die suddenly or unexpectedly in their sleep, with no chance of receiving medical or surgical help, are the lucky ones.

CHAPTER ELEVEN

Law and Disorder

You might suspect that sixteenth-century England is something like the Wild West when it comes to law and order. Violence is endemic and you will not find a policeman if someone attacks you. But that is more or less where the similarities end, and the lack of policemen is in fact an entirely superficial impression. There is rather a lot of policing going on. It is conducted not by a national police force but by sheriffs, deputy lieutenants, constables, watchmen, bailiffs, bedels, reeves, churchwardens, and even good old yeomen. On top of all this, there are other forms of social control—from heralds policing the right to bear arms to ale-tasters and bread weighers who make sure that the beer sold in a town is fresh and the bread up to scratch. It is true that, when a crime is committed, forensic science doesn't come into play; if a murdered body is found and no one is prepared to give evidence, the murderer is likely to get away with it. Nevertheless, it will be the amount of policing that astonishes you, not the lack of it.

In the cities and large towns, especially London, the exercise of the law is very visible. There are watchmen patrolling the streets at night. You will hear the cries of those in the high-walled jails by the city gates, reaching out from behind the bars of their cells. You will witness prostitutes, pimps, beggars, and other moral offenders being carted through the streets of the city to and from Bridewell. You will see the gaunt faces of men and women on their way to Tyburn to be hanged for theft or murder. In the taverns you will see men with holes gouged in their ears for vagrancy. In Cheapside you might notice men and women locked in the pillories. You will see men being brought in by constables from the neighboring districts to be interrogated in London. And from time to time you will witness mob justice, such as in March 1561 when a thief steals a child's silver necklace in Tower Street and is pursued by onlookers. They catch him in Mark Lane and beat him to death. Regardless of whether there is an official police force, wherever there are people you will find law and its enforcement.[1]

The Heart of Justice

On July 17, 1579, a young man named Thomas Appletree is fooling about with some friends in a boat on the Thames near Greenwich. He has a loaded gun, which to the great amusement of the party he fires three or four times at random. Unknown to him, the glass-sided royal barge is slowly floating toward them. The queen is aboard, discussing with the French ambassador the possibility of her marrying the duke of Anjou, when one of Thomas Appletree's bullets strikes the helmsman six feet from her and leaves him lying on the deck, bleeding profusely. The queen tosses the injured man her scarf and tells him to be of good cheer: the bullet was surely meant for her and the fact that it struck him is good news, for the assassin has failed. Later, there is a thorough investigation, and Appletree is soon found. He confesses and is duly condemned to death for endangering the queen's life. A gallows is set up on the bank of the river so he may be hanged close to the scene of his crime. Before his execution, Appletree makes a speech to the assembled crowds. He is no traitor, he says, but admits that through his carelessness he has endangered the life of the sovereign and therefore deserves to die. When he has said good-bye to his friends, the hangman places the noose over his head. Just then, when he is on the very brink of death, a man in the crowd steps forward with a pardon from the queen. She knows Appletree is just a silly young man, but he had to be taught a lesson.[2]

This event illustrates a unique duality in English law: justice is enacted in the name of the monarch but it is not of the monarch's making. The common law of England—based on the presumption that it applies commonly to all subjects—is an ancient system that depends on the examination of past precedent. This is the fundamental difference between English law and the laws of Continental kingdoms, which depend on Roman law (which does not depend on past precedent but on the ruling of the monarch). Although Parliament passes legislation for the queen to approve, it is not essentially a lawmaking body; rather its purpose is to clarify and explain how the courts should interpret the common law in specific contexts. Where it finds the existing law inadequate, Parliament introduces new legislation; but that does not remove the requirement for the new law to respect past precedents. While this seems to suggest that the monarch has nothing to do with the administration of justice, quite the opposite is true.

She can willfully circumvent the laws codified by Parliament, throw past precedents to the wind—and grant a man like Thomas Appletree a pardon.

The privy council has a special role to play in the Tudor legal system. When it meets in a certain room in the Palace of Westminster it acts as a law court, formally described as "the lords of the council sitting in the Star Chamber." Commonly known just as "Star Chamber," it tries those who have failed to act on orders and proclamations sent out by the privy council. It also deals with serious breaches of the peace, duels, conspiracies, riots, libels, defamation of character, disputes over land ownership, and assaults on persons of rank. Only Star Chamber has the power to authorize the use of torture. You should worry if you are summoned to one of its sessions: privy councilors will try you on the basis of written depositions from witnesses—you yourself will not always be allowed to say anything. The public is permitted to watch this display of legal power but you, the accused, might be summoned only to hear the judgment. The councilors do not have to abide by the legal system when sentencing you: they can give you any punishment they think fit, from imprisonment in the Tower to whipping, branding, or the pillory. They can punish you by cutting off your ears, slitting your nose, or imposing a heavy fine. There is no jury: every single councilor present is a judge. You can see why Star Chamber is occasionally compared to a court-martial.[3]

The justification for this disregard for legal form is to stave off threats to the monarch and the state. Repeated assassination attempts mean that Elizabeth has little choice but to empower the privy council to take action. This leads to a growing network of spies, all reporting to Sir William Cecil and (after 1573) Francis Walsingham. It is a spy in the French embassy who reveals the Throgmorton Plot of 1583, the plan to encourage a Catholic uprising while Spanish forces invade England. In 1586 a trap carefully laid by spies working for Francis Walsingham delivers proof that the imprisoned Mary, queen of Scots is party to a plot to kill Elizabeth. An enthusiastic young Catholic gentleman by the name of Anthony Babington is behind the scheme. Coded letters are smuggled in and out of Chartley, where the Scots queen is imprisoned, hidden in waterproof wallets inside ale barrels. When Babington writes to Mary asking for her blessing on his plan to make her queen of England, she replies, giving him her approval. Walsingham's secretary intercepts the letters and manages to break the code. There can be no doubting Mary's treason; her trial and execution soon follow.

This unofficial "secret service" established by Sir William Cecil and Francis Walsingham deals with more than just attempts on Elizabeth's life. Walsingham's spies send him information from every part of England. He also maintains thirteen spies in France, ten in the Low Countries, five in Italy, five in Spain, nine in Germany, and even three in Turkey.[4] Cecil similarly has agents in the London prisons, listening out for any conversations that might prove useful. It is fair to say that, wherever you go, you can never be sure of escaping the long arm of Cecil and Walsingham.

The privy council controls England itself through liaison with the royal officers in each county. These are the sheriffs, lords lieutenant, and Justices of the Peace. The sheriff presides over the county court, takes action against riots, and oversees visits by the queen and royal judges during the assize sessions. The lord lieutenant is in charge of civil defense in each county. It is his responsibility to muster the militia, and to make sure its equipment is satisfactory and the men are suitably trained. He also has to ensure the coastal beacons are ready to be lit in case an enemy lands in force. As a rule of thumb, therefore, the sheriffs and JPs deal with homegrown disturbances and the lords lieutenant with foreign threats. In 1570, for example, when the Northern Rebellion is about to break out, the privy council writes to the JPs in the region, urging them to take precautions. Martial law is imposed, 129 prosperous men are arrested and held for trial, and five hundred poor men are summarily executed as a lesson to others.[5] In July 1586, with fears of an invasion from Spain, it is the lords lieutenant who receive orders to muster the militia in their counties, to be ready to light the beacons, and to repel the invaders.

The Criminal Underworld

It goes without saying that there are criminals among all classes. The highest nobleman in the land, the duke of Norfolk, is executed for treason. Many Catholic conspirators are members of the aristocracy and gentry. Gentlemen are taken before the courts for murder, and upstanding householders find themselves indicted for assault after they have given an overzealous tax-collector a bruised head. Some members of the gentry even turn to piracy and highway robbery. We have already met Gamaliel Ratsey, the most famous highwayman of the time. This son of a Lincolnshire gentleman is something of a Robin Hood figure in the East Midlands: cunning, witty, courageous, generous to the poor, and possessed of a sense of natural justice. Having robbed two wealthy wool merchants near Stamford, he knights them as "Sir Walter Woolsack and Sir Samuel Sheepskin."[6] However, the upper echelons of society do not typically take part in illegal activities. Most criminals are to be found among the lower classes, and it is their number and variety of tricks that you most want to guard against. Indeed, entering a city you need to be wary of the "coney-catchers"—people who will regard you as a coney from the country just waiting to be caught.

Various books are available which give details of the different types of criminal and their methods, the best known being Thomas Harman's *A Caveat or Warning for Common Cursitors* (1566). This gives lengthy descriptions of the lowlifes you will meet, many of whom you will recognize as vagabonds because of the large hole in their right ear, which is burned through with a hot iron in line with the law of 1572.[7]

An *Abram-man* or *Abraham-man* is a beggar who walks bare-armed and bare-legged and pretends to be mad, so called after the Abraham ward in Bedlam, where the insane are housed. Some will charm you with their madness and sing or dance. If they come to a farm they will demand food in strident tones, and frighten young women with their wanton looks, in order to be paid to go away.

A *ruffler* carries a weapon of some sort and will tell you that he is a discharged soldier. He begs for his relief. If you do not satisfy him, he will use his weapon on you. A typical scene is that a man comes riding up beside you on the road. He will greet you and converse with you pleasantly until you approach a wood. Then he will reach forward, take the reins of your mount, and, without explanation, lead you into the wood. The next thing you know he will have your purse, clothes, and horse.

An *upright man* is a ruffian and thief who travels the highways, carrying a staff, with authority over all the other criminals in "his" area. He also commands the doxies (women) of other thieves and uses them to pilfer from those he distracts in conversation at a fair, or to receive stolen goods from a house where he has temporarily taken service.

Doxy is the term for a woman who is the sexual partner of one or more thieves answering to an upright man. According to the *Caveat for Common Cursitors,* "These doxies be broken and spoiled of their maidenhead by the upright men, and then they have their name of doxies, and not before."

A *mort* is a homeless woman. If she is married she is called an *autem mort;* if not, she is a *walking mort.* When she has fallen in with a group of thieves and been "broken in" by the upright man, she becomes a doxy.

A *dell* is an innocent, unmarried girl or young woman who is on the road. According to Harman, "These go abroad young, either by the death of their parents and nobody to look unto them, or else by some sharp mistress that they do serve, so they run away. . . . Or she is naturally born one, and then she is a wild dell. These are broken very young. When they have been lain with by the upright man then they be doxies and no dells."

A *rogue* is not as authoritative or physically imposing as an upright man but similarly a man who makes his living on the highways, thieving at fairs, and breaking into the houses of the wealthy.

A *wild rogue* is a thief with no abode who does not answer to an upright man. Some beg, pretending to seek a long-lost kinsman or friend. Others intimidate their victims with their staff. If one begs a penny from you, he will take your readiness to give as a sign that you have disposable wealth in your purse. According to Harman, a wild rogue will often support several womenfolk who accompany him on his travels.

A *prigman* is a man who takes clothes while they are drying in fields or on hedges, or steals chickens and sells them at the nearest alehouse.

A *whip-jack* or *freshwater mariner* is a beggar who claims to be an out-of-work seafarer, and who may present a fake license to that effect. His chief trade is to rob booths at fairs or to pilfer from stalls.

A *frater* begs or steals from women as they go to and from markets.

A *queer-bird* has lately been released from prison; he is supposedly looking for work but steals what he can in the meantime.

A *palliard* or *clapperdudgeon* is a thief or beggar in a patched cloak and little else, who will plead poverty at any opportunity.

A *washman* is a palliard who lies down in the highway and feigns injury or illness seeking the help of a good Samaritan whom he will then try to rob.

An *Irish toyle* is a traveling salesman who overcharges for his substandard wares.

A *jarkman* is a forger—a "jark" being slang for a seal. He can read and write and forges documents such as licenses to beg, to pass between ports, and to act as a proctor in court.

A *kinchin co* is a runaway boy on the highways, who will eventually fall in with a crowd of ruffians and become one of them. Hence a runaway girl is a *kinchin mort.*

A *courtesy man* is a handsome, well-dressed man who pretends to be your friend when you arrive in a strange town. He will accept drinks and presents from you, but when you are not looking, will relieve you of your purse and any other valuables. Often to be found in the best inns.

A *prigger of prancers* is a horse thief. He will take a horse from a pasture or from a man who stops at an inn. Often priggers pretend to be locals when travelers stop in a village. If someone offers to walk your horse while you have a pot of beer, do not accept—you will never see your mount again.

A *hooker* or *angler* walks about the town during the day watching out for things that can be reached from an open window, especially linen and woolen clothes. He then returns at night with a staff with an iron hook and, having lifted the latch of the shutter with a knife, uses the hook to take the clothes. These are then passed to his doxy to sell at an alehouse.

A *counterfeit crank* is a man who pretends to suffer from the falling sickness (epilepsy), or who goes about filthy and naked in order to encourage people to pity him and to give him alms. He may put soap in his mouth to make it froth and appear all the more frantic.

A *dummerer* pretends to be unable to speak in order to beg from sympathetic people.

A *demander for glimmer* is an attractive and vivacious young woman, often the doxy of an upright man, who approaches her victims in an alehouse. She will use her charms to win their affection, and then seek some token made of silver or gold, suggesting that if they give her something valuable they might meet her at some distance from the town to have sex. Whether or not the woman is at the appointed trysting place, her would-be lovers will lose whatever valuables they bring—as well as their purses—when they arrive and meet the upright man.

As you can see, in the criminal fraternity, women are the sexual companions of the men, the lookouts, and the temptresses—and either abused or looked after, according to their luck. Prostitution goes hand in hand with criminality, both in its straightforward form—being paid for sex—and in an infinite variety of other ways, such as blackmailing a man who has been seduced or thieving from him while he is without his hosen. However, many women evade justice. The law is not clear as to whether a married woman can be held responsible for her actions.[8] For this reason many a doxy will marry a rogue or an upright man: if she is caught thieving with her husband and he is a known criminal, he will hang but she will not, claiming that she was simply obeying him. Some judges treat women more leniently because they are less criminally adept; they steal less frequently and when they are caught they often hold stolen goods of low value. As a result, 85 percent of all those indicted for theft are men.[9] Violent crimes are even more closely aligned with gender: almost all cases of assault and murder that come to court are instances of men fighting. A woman is not thought to be capable of beating a man, so unless she actually kills her male victim, or beats up another woman, she is unlikely to find herself in court on a charge of affray.

There is one exception to this: rioting is as much a female occupation as a male one.[10] This is because it is one of the few forms of protest open to women—and when you take action as a group you lessen the danger to yourself as an individual. In August 1577 a commotion breaks out at Brentwood, Essex, when thirty women take the law into their own hands. They seize Richard Brooke, schoolmaster of Brentwood grammar school, and beat him thoroughly for some misdemeanor—probably an injustice to one of their number. The women resist arrest and by the time the sheriff and the JPs arrive they are holed up in the church, armed with pitchforks, bills, a pikestaff, two hot spits, two kettles of boiling water, three bows, nine arrows, a hatchet, a hammer, and a large stone. When the JPs try to arrest them, several men refuse to assist and many of the women escape.[11] One suspects the men know where their best interests lie.

Secular Courts

In Elizabethan England, as today, there are many different courts. At Westminster you have four royal courts: the Court of the Exchequer, which deals with money owed to the monarch; the Court of Queen's Bench, which adjudicates on the monarch's other interests; the Court of Common Pleas, which deals with legal disputes between subjects; and the Court of Chancery, which is responsible for inheritances, trusts, marriage settlements, and property. Then there is Parliament, which judges certain cases of treason, and Star Chamber. Throughout the country local courts deal with a welter of criminal and civil cases. The most serious ones, felonies, are brought before the royal judges at the periodic assizes held in each county. The sessions held before JPs on a quarterly basis—the "quarter sessions"—deal with the next level of criminal activity, mostly misdemeanors (indictable crimes that do not carry the death penalty). The JPs also enforce regulations, collect rates due for the maintenance of highways and the poor law, and issue licenses (for example, to beg, to sell victuals, etc.). County courts, presided over by the sheriff, act as small-claims courts as well as overseeing elections to Parliament. Hundred courts exist in two forms: there are the ordinary courts, which deal with nuisances between two or more manors (such as flooding, effluent, pollution, broken bridges, and blocked highways); and the high constable's sessions, or "petty sessions," dealing with the punishment of vagabonds, apprenticeships, payment of excess wages, playing unlawful games, and sowing sedition. The mayors of incorporated towns also hold courts, dealing with everything from selling poor-quality merchandise to stealing. Finally, you have thousands of manorial courts, which have two functions. The "court baron" of a manor looks after the land and its usage by tenants and keeps the court roll that records who has tenure of what land. A "court leet" deals with the election of manorial officers, disputes between tenants, and misdemeanors (but not felonies) committed by them. In some manors the two functions are brought together in one court, with the bailiff presiding; but it is fair to say that the system is in rapid decline, with many courts leet no longer being held, and many courts baron meeting only very occasionally, as land is increasingly enclosed or let out on lease.

Punishments

If you are indicted on a felony, misdemeanor, or trespass, you need to know what sentence to expect. The following account for most of the punishments that these courts can deliver, in relation to the offenses committed.

Hanging. If you hide in a dark corner of Francis Hunt's stables in Colchester on Christmas Eve 1575 you will see a servant enter, position a bucket behind Mr. Hunt's mare, drop his hose, and bugger the animal. Unfortunately for the servant, Mr. Hunt himself is hiding in the shadows. He reports the servant to the JPs and, at the next jail delivery, sees him sentenced to be hanged.[12] You might find it perverse that the statutory punishment for having sex with a horse is death, while a woman selling an eleven-year-old girl to strangers for sex is merely paraded around the city in a cart—but such is Elizabethan life.[13] Capital punishment is applied in relation to capital offenses, and a horse, being a man's property, has more legal protection from sexual abuse than a poor girl.

Hanging is the most common punishment for manslaughter, infanticide, murder, rape, arson, causing death by witchcraft, grand larceny (theft of goods worth more than 12d), highway robbery, buggery (unnatural sexual acts, normally with an animal), and sodomy. If you are indicted for any of these, the constable of the hundred or manor where you are arrested will take you to the county jail where you will await the next assize session. This is when the royal judges from the Court of Queen's Bench and the Court of Common Pleas arrive to deliver justice. There are just six circuits covering the whole country, and each judge needs to go round all the counties in his circuit, so you might have to wait some months in jail before you have your day in court.

The sessions in London take place quarterly and, as Thomas Platter notes, "rarely does a law day in London in all the four sessions pass without some twenty to thirty persons, both men and women, being gibbeted."[14] It is hardly an exaggeration. At the sessions held at Newgate Prison on February 21, 1561, seventeen men and two women are found guilty of capital offenses and taken off to be hanged at Tyburn. At the next sitting of the court, three days later, eighteen men and two women are ordered to be hanged.[15] On this occasion the barber-surgeons of the city are allowed to select one of the fresh corpses for anatomical experimentation. Many notorious criminals look on their execution as a chance to show off, giving away souvenirs to the crowd who turn out to watch them die. In 1583 a famous pirate wears crimson taffeta breeches on the day of his execution; he tears them off and gives shreds of them to his friends as he walks to his death.[16] Most people are placed in a cart to be transported to the gallows. When the cart reaches the place of execution, they are made to stand. A leather hood is placed over the head of each condemned man and woman and a noose around each of their necks. The nooses hang in a line from a triangular frame supported on three sturdy posts. Then the cart is pulled away, leaving them all suspended, slowly being strangled by their own weight. They try to breathe and their bodies start to jerk in a sort of dance; it is then that their friends will step forward, take hold of the body, and pull it down suddenly to break the neck and hasten death. Where a violent offense such as murder was committed with malice aforethought, the gallows is set up as close to the scene of the crime as possible, even if it means that it has to be erected in the precincts of a church. On several occasions during the reign you will see gallows set up by the west door of St. Paul's Cathedral, after people have been found guilty of committing murder in the city's largest churchyard. For pirates there is a special place of execution: at the low-water mark at Wapping. There all the ships entering the port of London see the dead mariners suspended with their feet in the water: the bodies remain there until three tides have covered them. Henry Machyn records such a hanging on April 25, 1562, when five sailors are executed for robbery at sea.[17] One has the noose around his neck when a reprieve comes for him from the privy council. It seems Appletree is not the only one to escape death by the blessing of a moment.

As you can see, not everyone condemned to death actually hangs. Some escape due to their connections with people of influence. Others claim benefit of the clergy. This ancient law states that, if a man can read a passage from the Bible, he should be judged as a priest and handed over to his bishop for punishment; in such cases he will not hang but will be branded on the left hand with a hot iron (he will hang if caught a second time). Many grave crimes, such as rape, arson, highway robbery, and forcible entry, are beyond the scope of benefit of the clergy, having been specifically excluded by various kings down the ages; but the old law is still used regularly to escape the noose in cases of theft and manslaughter, despite increasing literacy. Ben Jonson reads "the neck verse" to escape execution after killing a fellow actor in a duel in 1598. Obviously women cannot plead benefit of the clergy, as they cannot be priests; however, women can "plead their belly." Pregnant women cannot be legally executed but must be allowed to give birth first. Hence many women in jail awaiting the judges try to get themselves with child, hoping to slip through the system afterward.

As a result of these loopholes, only 24 percent of those facing serious offenses in an assize court are hanged; 35 percent are acquitted, 27 percent claim benefit of the clergy, 6 percent successfully plead pregnancy, 5 percent are whipped, 1 percent are sentenced to remain in prison for a specific term, and the remaining 2 percent get away with a fine or die in prison awaiting trial.[18] You don't have to be cynical to see that benefit of the clergy probably acts as an incentive to learn to read. Of those who do hang, 75 percent have been convicted of some form of theft—stealing food, horses, money, or livestock—18 percent are found guilty of witchcraft, and 6 percent of murder. The others are rapists, buggerers, sodomites, arsonists, and house-breakers.

Drawing, hanging, and quartering. If a man is found guilty of treason he is sentenced to be "drawn" to the gallows on a hurdle or sled, hanged, and then cut down while still alive and eviscerated, with his guts and private parts thrown into a specially prepared fire; then he is cut into quarters. If this happens to you, the butcher employed for the task will cut you in half at the waist, dividing your body in two. Then your head will be severed from your body and your rib cage divided down the middle, so that half your chest and one arm form a quarter. Your pelvis is then cleaved in two, each part with a leg attached, forming the last two quarters. Each of these quarters is then displayed in a prominent place in a town where you are well known. Your head will probably find its way onto a spike on London Bridge.

This is the full traitor's death, as suffered by many Catholic sympathizers in Elizabeth's reign, including Dr. John Story, who is "drawn from the Tower of London to Tyburn, and there hanged, disemboweled and quartered, his head set on London Bridge and his quarters on the gates of the city."[19] The "drawing" on a sled to the gallows is a ritualized humiliation, and an important part of the cruel ceremony.[20] Robert Mantell, alias Bloys, is executed in this way in 1581 for pretending to be the still-living Edward VI. Six years later a smith living in Hatfield Peverel is sentenced to death for treason for simply expressing his belief that Edward VI might still be alive.[21]

Beheading. The nobility are not hanged for treason but beheaded. The duke of Norfolk is executed in this manner on Tower Hill (just to the north of the Tower of London) in 1572. The earl of Northumberland is beheaded at York in the same year, and the earl of Essex loses his head on Tower Green for high treason in 1601. Most famously of all, Mary, queen of Scots, is beheaded for her complicity in the Babington Plot at Fotheringay in 1587.

The above-mentioned aristocrats are not the only people to be judicially beheaded in Elizabeth's reign. The Halifax gibbet—a precursor of the guillotine—is used for all those found guilty of theft in the town of Halifax. Here the people do not wait for the assize judges. According to William Harrison, if you steal something worth 13½ pence or more in Halifax, you will be forthwith beheaded on the next market day (Tuesday, Thursday, or Saturday):

The engine wherewith the execution is done is a square block of wood of the length of 4½ feet, which does ride up and down in a slot ... between two pieces of timber that are framed and set upright, of five yards in height. In the nether end of the sliding block is an ax, keyed or fastened with an iron into the wood, which being drawn up to the top of the frame is there fastened by a wooden pin ... unto the middle of which pin also there is a long rope fastened that cometh down among the people, so when the offender hath made his confession and laid his head over the nethermost block every man there present doth either take hold of the rope (or putteth forth his arm so near to the same as he can get, in token that he is willing to see true justice executed), and, pulling out the pin in this manner, the head-block wherein the ax is fastened doth fall down with such a violence that, if the neck of the transgressor were as big as a bull, it should be cut asunder at a stroke and roll from the body by a huge distance.

Twenty-three men and two women are beheaded in this way over the course of Elizabeth's reign.

Burning at the stake. You have already come across instances of people being burned alive for heresy, such as the Anabaptists in Aldgate in 1575. In addition, women are burned at the stake for high treason, which is the fate of Mary Cleere in 1576. It is also the punishment for women guilty of petty treason; in 1590 a young woman is burned to death in St. George's Field, outside London, for poisoning her mistress.[22]

Peine forte et dure. When people stand mute in court and refuse to plead guilty or not guilty, they are sentenced to suffer *peine forte et dure* (strong and hard punishment). This means the victim is crushed to death beneath a board on which seven or eight hundredweight of stones are placed, one by one. In order to increase the suffering, a sharp stone is placed beneath the victim's spine. Astonishingly, some brave souls voluntarily choose this horrible death of their own free will. If a woman wishes to preserve an estate for her children, which will be confiscated if she is found guilty of a crime, she may refuse to offer a plea.[23] Margaret Clitherow is crushed to death in 1586, refusing to plead in order to save her children and fellow Catholics from being tortured to testify against her.

Imprisonment. People are normally locked up in jail only to restrain them until they can be brought to trial; as we have seen, fewer than 1 percent of assize cases result in a sentence of imprisonment. However, the privy council threatens people with imprisonment; in 1562 a royal proclamation stipulates that no one may speak of the falling value of money or else be imprisoned for three months and then pilloried.[24] Attempts to kill people with witchcraft and eating meat in Lent may also lead to periods of incarceration.

Imprisonment is generally the punishment used for debtors. If a man is accused of failing to pay another man a sum of money he owes, he is arrested by the constables or watchmen and consigned to prison, where he must remain until the debt is paid. In London this is the Fleet. The conditions therein are awful—fifty or so men in a room with bare boards and no furniture or blankets and with many inmates suffering from some disease or other. A debtor has to pay rent for his chamber if he does not wish to lie with the common criminals, and he also has to pay for his food. He is free to receive visitors and even to go out of the prison, if accompanied by a guard and as long as he pays the warden for the privilege. However, doing so only increases his debts. Many prisoners find themselves relegated from the chambers to the grim pit of the prison basement.

Bridewell Hospital in London is the place where people (mostly women) are locked up for vice crimes such as vagrancy, prostitution, and domestic disorders. It also has its own courts, where the master and governors can proceed without reference to any other external authority. The beds are filthy, the food is "fit for dogs," and the open sewer of the Fleet River runs beside it. Yet this is where poor Frances Palmer is sent in 1603. She has been twice made pregnant by menservants with whom she worked, has most recently given birth in the open street next to an alehouse—and both her children have died. Having been arrested for whoredom and vagrancy she is taken to Bridewell, where it is ordained that she be "punished," as if she needs further misery.[25]

Whipping. This is a common punishment generally used for vagabondage, theft, deceit, and sedition. Palliards and wild rogues looking for food and money often end up being whipped out of town before they can obtain either. Petty thieves who steal goods worth less than a shilling (petty larceny) are often sentenced to be whipped. Two men who remove lead from London's conduits, cutting off the city's water supply on November 30, 1560, are punished that way.[26] In 1561 a man is whipped through the streets of Westminster and then through London and across London Bridge to

Southwark for forging documents in the hand of the queen's master of horse.[27] In such cases the sentence is that the culprit be "whipped at a cart's arse." Tied to the back of a cart, he is stripped half naked and as he stumbles along, his back is lashed with leather whips "until he bleeds well." This is also a punishment meted out by JPs to couples who have an illegitimate child: the man and the woman are tied together, stripped half naked, and whipped as they are led twice through the parish.[28]

Certain other crimes entail whipping at a post. In 1561 a waterman is fastened to the whipping post at Queenhithe for uttering some seditious words against the magistrates.[29] A whipping post can also be found in many rural manors, complete with iron clasps for hands and legs to support the offender; it is used for such crimes as taking timber or firewood from the manor without permission, a crime known as "hedgebreaking."[30] Women and children are whipped too, both through the streets and at a whipping post. A woman heard denouncing Bridewell Hospital and its governors is "well-whipped" for her slander. A painter's wife is whipped so thoroughly that the gashes caused are deeper than her finger.[31] Young Fyndern Catesby steals a woman's kirtle, cloak, sheet, and some linen worth 31 shillings 4 pence, which is enough to warrant the gallows but because he is under the age of fourteen he is only whipped.[32] Even the mentally ill are whipped. In April 1561 a man released from Bedlam Hospital goes about professing that he is the risen Christ. Teaming up with a man released from the Marshalsea Prison by the name of Peter, the madman comes to believe that his companion is *Saint* Peter, which only confirms his conviction that he is Christ. Both men are whipped through the streets.[33]

The pillory. In the modern world, the pillory has become something of an object of amusement. But as you will see, it is anything but a light punishment. Just ask the man who started a fight in St. Paul's Cathedral in 1561. A special pillory is set up in the churchyard for him and, in the time-honored fashion, his ears are nailed to the wooden frame. Here he has to withstand the insults of the mob. And when the time comes for him to be released, his ears are sliced off.[34]

What crimes might lead you to the pillory? In short, almost anything that requires you to be humiliated. One Essex man who claimed that the queen has had two children by Robert Dudley is imprisoned for five months in 1580, then made to stand in the pillory, before being taken back to prison for three years. Two other Essex people spreading a similar rumor in 1590 (that Queen Elizabeth has four children by Lord Dudley, one of whom he killed by burning it in the fire in the chamber where it was born) also end up in the pillory, with paper notices stuck on their heads stating the nature of their crime. Selling rancid bacon or bad fish can also lead to being pilloried—with the foul-smelling food tied in front of your face.[35] The hundred court is supposed to maintain a pillory, and the court leet of a manor can also sentence people to stand in one for an hour or two: you'll find many country towns and parishes have pillories set up near the church or in the marketplace.

Other crimes that might result in you being pilloried include slander (especially against an officeholder), counterfeiting documents, conjuring, and spreading false rumors and news. A woman who declares that Queen Mary is dead on November 12, 1558—five days before she actually passes away—receives the pillory for sedition. If that seems harsh, in April 1563 a woman is pilloried for eating meat in Lent.[36] As the seriousness of the crime increases, so too does the severity of the pillorying. In July 1563 a schoolmaster called Penred is pilloried for beating a boy with a buckled leather belt so hard that he has torn all the skin off the boy's back. Watch what happens when Penred is punished in Cheapside. The boy is taken along to the pillory and his cloak is removed and his wounds are exhibited alongside the guilty schoolmaster. After he has been inspected in his pitiful state by the mayor and a great throng, Penred is whipped as he stands in the pillory until the blood flows freely and all the skin has been removed from his back too.[37]

Ironically it is the very severity of the pillory that allows it to be used as an instrument of clemency. The rumor-mongers who say Elizabeth has had children by Dudley would normally be drawn, hanged, and eviscerated; but if the sedition is treated as slander, a spell in the pillory might be deemed sufficient. In May 1560 a maidservant is set on the pillory for having tried to poison her master. Had he died, this would have been petty treason and she would have been burned at the stake. As things stand, she is lucky to be alive—being pilloried twice, losing one ear on each occasion, and being branded on the forehead.[38]

Cutting off hands. The cruelty of Elizabethan justice goes beyond evisceration, burning at the stake, branding, and cutting off ears. In a 1559 case of attempted poisoning that is nearly successful—the victims are saved only by the quick-wittedness of a woman who gives them olive oil to drink—the man and the woman who perpetrate the crime are pilloried twice, and have both their hands cut off as well as their ears.[39] According to William Harrison, malice aforethought should result in loss of hands prior to hanging; he adds that having your hands cut off is also the punishment for brawling in court. We have already heard about John Stubbs and his printer losing their right hands for publishing a tract that the queen does not like. By law, you can still have your hand cut off at the Standard in Cheapside for striking an alderman of the city of London, but whether anyone will impose this penalty is open to question. Given the number of hands that are lopped off for other reasons, you might be best advised to err on the side of caution.

Stocks. This is a frame containing a pair of wooden boards, like the pillory, but designed to hold two or three people by their legs. Stocks are to be found in both town and country: in towns they are frequently used for restraining people who do not obey an officer or watchman; in rural manors they are used in conjunction with fines for allowing animals to wander and break other people's crops, for failing to maintain a lane, or for a moral crime. But they are not limited to these crimes: a stranger coming into the city of London in 1561 is overheard saying that he is the "king of kings and lord of all lords," so he is set in the stocks; and some women caught eating meat on a fish day in 1563 are also placed in the stocks and left there all night.[40] Vagabonds and rogues are regularly placed in the stocks before being whipped out of the manor. Hedgebreaking is often punished by a 12-pence fine and a four-hour spell in the stocks.[41] If you see a man and a woman in the stocks together, the chances are that they have had a bastard child together and are spending twelve hours fastened by their legs.[42]

Cucking or *ducking stool.* In many rural manors and small towns there are customary punishments and bylaws. One of most common punishments, found almost everywhere in England, is the cucking or ducking stool. This is a seat on a long pole to which a woman is tied wearing nothing but her shift. She is then raised in the air and left there as an example to others, or she may be dipped in the water of a pond. Legally this punishment is reserved for "a troublesome and angry woman who, by her brawling and wrangling among her neighbors, doth break the public peace and beget, cherish and increase public discord."[43] It is not normally used for a first offense; there is a warning first, and the culprit is admonished in church before the stool is used. However, repeat offenders are punished in this way at every session of the court leet—until eventually they are pilloried. Interestingly, most women who are condemned to be ducked are married; you might guess from this that single women have less reason to be scolds. Men who similarly break the peace through brawling and wrangling are usually fined or put in the stocks.

Tumbrel. An alternative to the cucking stool is the tumbrel: a cart with wooden wheels in which the transgressor is placed and wheeled through the village or town. In 1571 the wife of the vicar of Epping is convicted in the court leet of being "garrulous to her neighbors" and placed in the tumbrel.[44] The same punishment is meted out to Londoners found guilty of immoral behavior. In December 1559 the wife of the goldsmith Henry Glyn is paraded through the city in a cart for selling the sexual services of her own daughter. The next month a baker is similarly paraded for multiple instances of fornication. In June 1560 a cart is drawn through the city exhibiting two men and three women:

> One man for he was the bawd, to bring women unto strangers, and one woman was the alewife of the Bell in Gracechurch Street, and another was the alewife of the Bull's Head by London Stone, and both were bawds and whores, and the other man and woman were brother and sister and were taken naked together.[45]

A few days later the cart is used again to exhibit the widow of Master Warner, late sergeant of the Admiralty, who is found guilty of being a bawd to her daughter and her maidservant, both of whom are unmarried and both of whom are pregnant. And on June 16, 1563, Dr. Christopher Langton, an Eton- and Cambridge-educated fellow of the College of Physicians, is carted through London in his best clothes—a gown of damask lined with velvet, and a coat and a cape made of velvet. Henry Machyn notes that he has a blue hood pinned on his cape and comes "through Cheapside on the market day . . . for he was taken with two young wenches at once."[46]

Fines. After all this dismemberment, killing, and ritualized humiliation it seems prosaic to inform you that the most common form of punishment in Elizabethan times is a fine. Manorial courts, hundred courts, and quarter sessions all operate on the basis of amercing people—fining them for wrongdoings or for failing to do their duty. Fines are levied for playing unlawful games, poaching, committing minor assaults, grazing too many cattle on the commons, driving away cattle, blocking drains, and so on.

Fines for petty larceny and theft are normally small—4 pence for the theft of a horseshoe, 12 pence for poaching a fish—but even these small sums can be onerous to pay if you are poor. Large fines of £5 or more are meted out to officers who fail to do their duty, or fail to respond to an instruction by a court. Manorial courts also use large fines as a threat: if a blocked stream is not unblocked quickly, the threat of a hefty fine of £2 usually prompts the offender to remedy the problem straightaway.

Getting Away with It, or the Process of Crime Detection

You might wonder how people are apprehended for crimes in the sixteenth century, an age with no forensic methods and no modern police force. The simple answer is that crimes are reported by the local community. The old system of the "hue and cry" is still in place, under which communities are sworn together as tithings (nominally groups of ten men) and are required to report each other's misdemeanors. If a crime is found to have been committed, the hue and cry is raised, and all those in the tithing are duty-bound to pursue the criminal and report the matter to the hundred constable. Depending on the severity of the case, the hundred court then passes the matter over either to the JPs at the quarter sessions or to the assize judges.

If a crime is brought to the attention of the constable, he will usually interview the witnesses. In cases involving a dead body, the coroner will be summoned. In 1577 Alice Neate is arrested on suspicion of having murdered her sister-in-law, whose throat has been slit as she lay in bed. The constable questions all the witnesses and potential suspects—everyone who has recently visited the cottage. One reports that Alice's husband exclaimed, "God save my wife," seemingly reflecting that he thought his wife had killed his sister. Others testify that Alice hated her sister-in-law because she believed that two of her children were murdered by the deceased woman. All of these other people can satisfactorily place themselves elsewhere on the night of the murder itself. Alice's daughter Abigail is then asked to give evidence. She admits she was sleeping in the same room as her murdered aunt that night, and maintains that it was not her mother who committed the deed. However, under intense questioning, her defense breaks down: she admits she was awake and saw her mother cut her aunt's throat. She further admits that her mother asked her to conceal what she saw. Alice Neate is imprisoned, and at the next jail delivery sentenced to hang.[47]

Alice Neate's case is relatively straightforward, showing that the systematic questioning of witnesses can produce results. However, many other cases are much more difficult. Crimes often go unreported. In small communities, where everyone knows who committed the deed, there is frequently a reluctance to hand the perpetrator over to the authorities. Similarly, when a crime is reported and an inquiry takes place, local people often say nothing. The constable, coroner, or JP may have to threaten them with a heavy fine of £5 or more if they will not give evidence. In such cases testimony is often fabricated, with the culprit falsely named as, for instance, "Richard Nemo" (Richard Nobody). In many parts of Essex, local communities attribute crimes to "John at Love," "John at Stile," or "John at Noke."[48] When a serving girl is beaten to death, the crime is often blamed on a fictitious person, because an employer has the right to chastise his servants. A husbandman one morning loses patience with his servant girl for taking too long to feed the pigs and strikes her in the face, making her nose bleed profusely. Six weeks later she dies. When the case comes to court he is not found guilty of murder; instead John at Stile is deemed to have killed her.[49]

The sense of natural justice underlying such lenient treatment affects other cases too. A pregnant servant in the house of a yeoman secretly delivers her baby herself and then hides it among her employer's pigs. When the yeoman finds the dead baby he reports his servant to the constable. At the subsequent trial the jury decides the child was already dead before it ended up in the pigsty. Another case concerns a woman who drowns a baby in a horsepond and submerges the corpse, weighed down with stones. She too is given the benefit of the doubt, and the jury decides it was stillborn.[50] Similarly a jury might be lenient on a man caught stealing a goose to feed his family and deliberately undervalue the animal so he is merely fined for petty larceny rather than hanged for theft.

Ecclesiastical Law

Perhaps the biggest difference between the law in Elizabethan times and in the modern world is its religious dimension. Some of the moral rules that apply to everyone in society have already been mentioned, such as the carting of bawds and incestuous couples through the streets of London. However, these few references do not even hint at the huge number of cases that are tried by the ecclesiastical courts. Essex has an adult population of about thirty-five thousand, rising to forty thousand by the end of the reign. At least fifteen thousand of these people—over a *third*—are arraigned for sexual offenses. Nor is this a peculiar feature of Essex. In the diocese of York, the proportion of those indicted for sexual offenses is even higher. It appears that people have a lot of sex and a great proportion of that sex is unlawful. Much of it is detected and reported by jealous husbands and wives, or revealed through the pregnancies of maidservants, girls, unmarried women, and widows. Even just being *suspected* of a sexual offense can result in your being summoned to appear and prove your innocence. While you might not treat ecclesiastical law as seriously as the common law—and many Elizabethan people don't treat it with much respect—its very ubiquity is a reminder that England is a deeply religious society.

If you are found to be living immorally or are in breach of any ecclesiastical law, the churchwardens of your parish will report you to the local archdeaconry court. You will then be summoned to appear by an apparitor on a certain date. If you are innocent, you need to arrange for a number of "compurgators"—upstanding, honest, and sober parishioners—to come to court with you and testify to that effect. The exact number of compurgators will be determined by the court; five or six is normal but for some offenses the court might ask for eight or nine. Men are required to produce male compurgators, women have to find other women (compurgatrices). If the archdeaconry court is twenty or thirty miles away you might well have to pay substantial expenses, including an overnight stay for all those accompanying you. If you are poor, therefore, you may find it impossible to produce compurgators in court. Moreover, if just one compurgator does not turn up, or fails to swear an oath on the Bible before testifying, then you will be found guilty and ordered to do penance.

The most usual form of penance ordered by the archdeaconry courts is to stand at the door of your parish church on Sunday in a white sheet, carrying a white wand, and to confess your fault to your fellow parishioners; you will also have to stand in front of the congregation during the service while the incumbent reads a suitable homily.[51] You may have to do penance on two or three Sundays in succession; you may also have to stand or kneel bareheaded and barefooted in the marketplace wearing a paper hat with the word "fornicator," "blasphemer," or "adulterer" written on it. Married women might have to do penance with their hair loose, emphasizing their wantonness. People who commit a sin involving two parishes or congregations have to do penance in both places. Such public humiliation is seen as both deterrent and punishment. Having said that, it is not an equitable system. If a couple is accused of adultery and the woman finds sufficient compurgatrices while the man fails to do so, he still has to go through the whole purgation ritual. Strangely his partner in crime may well be sitting in the congregation, having been found innocent, while the man confesses his adultery with her.

If you can't afford to travel to court with compurgators then you might well decide to let your reputation go to pieces and accept excommunication: four thousand people in Essex alone do exactly that during Elizabeth's reign.[52] There are two forms of excommunication. In its minor form it is simply suspension from church services and exclusion from the sacraments of marriage and communion. Major excommunication, however, is far more serious: it means that you will not be welcome in a Christian house, nor may your fellow Christians help you in any way; you cannot be represented or represent yourself in any court, ecclesiastical or secular, nor can you be buried in consecrated ground. If you are a truly morally offensive person, the archdeaconry court can apply to the bishop to seek royal assistance in having you imprisoned.[53] This is, however, very rare. Most people succumb after they have been punished with minor excommunication. Those who do not are regarded as beyond the pale by their fellow parishioners and have effectively excluded themselves from their community.

Moral Offenses

What sort of offenses will result in your being led to the archdeacon in shame? Failure to observe the rites of the church is a common reason. In fact, it is the second most common offense of all secular and ecclesiastical crimes and offenses (second only to unlawful sex).[54] Attendance at church is compulsory for everyone over the age of fourteen: you must go every Sunday and on nineteen saints' feast days, as well as the Feast of the Circumcision (January 1), Epiphany (January 6), the Annunciation of the Blessed Virgin Mary (March 25), Christmas Day, the Monday and Tuesday in Easter week, and the Monday and Tuesday in Whitsun week.[55] Failure to do so will lead to a fine—a shilling if you miss church just once, more if you are absent regularly. Children should be sent to church at least twice a month to be catechized. Failing to present a child for baptism is also an offense, as is opening a shop on a Sunday.

In Stratford-upon-Avon no fewer than thirty-seven tradesmen are accused of opening their shops on holy days in October 1592. When a Stratford woman is accused in court of brawling, being abusive, and failing to attend church, she replies, "God's wounds! A plague of God on you all, a fart of one's arse for you!"[56] Such a carefully thought-out theological position might well get her into further trouble: blasphemy is also likely to result in her being reported by the churchwardens. Even falling asleep during a sermon is a punishable offense. Considering sermons can last up to three hours, you can see why some people get a little bored. In 1593 Dorothy Richmond of Great Holland, Essex, is taken before the archdeaconry court for causing "disquietness" during a sermon. She "thrust a pin in Eddy Alefounder's buttocks."[57]

Defamation is the ecclesiastical equivalent of the secular crime of slander. Most derogatory speech is slanderous—or libelous if written down—but if it impugns the moral character of the victim, it is defamatory and dealt with by the archdeaconry court. If someone calls you "a whore and an arrant whore," you can report the person to the churchwarden and your accuser will have to answer for it in the archdeaconry courts. As a result, an archdeaconry court is rarely a boring place, enlivened by the language, stories, and invective. In 1586 John Worme prosecutes Helen Rand for defamation. A witness testifies that she was with Helen Rand and their husbands in the meadow at haymaking time when Helen declared that

> John Worme would have been naughty with her and would have laid her down upon a bed in her own house and before she could get rid of him she was fain to promise him the use of her body the next night. Worme did say unto Helen, when he would have had his pleasure upon her, that he could make as good a cunt of a lath and two coney skins as his wife had.[58]

The trouble with such cases is that it can be difficult to prove your innocence, as Helen Rand finds. Worse, the failure to prove your case might result in your being accused of defamation yourself. In July 1583 a Hertfordshire woman called Helen Burton suspects her husband is having an affair with Isabel Todd. One day she follows her husband to Isabel's house. She creeps in and bursts through the door of the bedchamber to see her husband holding Isabel up against the side of the bed without his shirt on. There is uproar and Helen is shoved out of the room. After the event, people round on Helen, telling her, "It is an evil bird that defileth its own nest." To add insult to injury, Isabel the adulteress then successfully prosecutes Helen for defamation.[59]

Drunkenness also might bring you face-to-face with the archdeacon. Of course, if you are violent or destructive in your drunkenness you will end up in the secular courts—but just *being* drunk can lead to being summoned to the ecclesiastical court. You can be charged for lying down in a field and sleeping it off, for being so drunk that you cannot stand up, and even for wetting your bed in your drunken state—although this mostly happens when it is someone else's bed. The offender normally has to do penance in church with a series of pint tankards arrayed before him as he kneels and confesses his transgression. In 1584 the sexton of a Colchester parish is reported as being "a railer, a blasphemer, a swearer and a slanderer, and suspected of drunkenness."[60] Whoever reported him to the churchwardens is leaving nothing to chance.

And then we come to sex, by far the most common form of moral offense. Like defamation, unlawful sex can be difficult to prove because most of the time there is no evidence available to the court that an offense has taken place—unless the woman becomes pregnant, or one of the parties confesses or contracts venereal disease. But even pregnancy does not indicate who is responsible. Hearsay, guilt, and moral outrage are therefore often the sum total of the "evidence." Of course, the loyalty of one's husband or wife is of such crucial importance that people are attentive to any signs of dishonor, and even to false rumors; but equally you will find men and women cover up their partners' sexual transgressions. Men especially do not want the neighborhood to know they have been cuckolded. Reputation is so important that many people will vigorously defend every accusation laid against them, whether true or not.

Unsurprisingly, adultery is the most common crime for which men and women are summoned to appear before the archdeaconry courts. Or, to be accurate, *suspicion* of adultery is. In 1591 a woman is seen to allow three men to enter her house at dusk. The authorities come to investigate and find all three men in separate beds and the woman sitting by the fire, wearing nothing but her smock. She is found guilty of acting lewdly and forced to do penance. In 1579 a widow persuades Henry Packer to spend the night in her house. He goes to sleep in a separate room but during the night he hears her sighing and goes to her. She asks him to warm her cold feet and he obliges. When the widow falls pregnant, the neighbors are convinced they know who is responsible. Both Henry Packer and the widow accordingly find themselves in court. The widow produces sufficient compurgatrices. Henry Packer, however, fails to gather enough support; instead he confesses and is ordered to do penance alone. You cannot help but see the irony—especially considering the common assumption that this is a man's world.

After listening to the proceedings in church courts for a while, you will come to think that the Church is more concerned about the crimes it deals with than about the victims. In regard to sexual misdemeanors, this is true. For example, both men and women can be presented to a church court for simply sheltering unmarried mothers. In the modern world, this would be seen as a charitable act. Not in Elizabethan England. In 1564 a man who gives shelter to a pregnant girl "for God's sake" is sentenced to do public penance in the marketplace and to give 2 shillings to the poor, even though there is no suggestion that he is in any part to blame for her pregnancy. In 1566, Agnes Rooke, a widow of West Ham, is brought before the archdeacon's court accused of harboring someone else's pregnant servant. She is let off only when the archdeacon is informed that the girl tried to drown herself and the kind widow saved her and took her in.[61]

It gets worse. If a female servant is raped and falls pregnant, and cannot persuade the secular courts to take action, she will be made to suffer for her "crime" by the church courts. Just before Christmas 1590 Joan Somers is in a field tending to her mistress's cattle when one Rice Evans comes up to her. He seizes her and violently rapes her, telling her that she can cry out as much as she wants, for there is no one to hear her. Joan is subsequently presented to the archdeacon for the sin of fornication.[62] A similar case is that of Jane Wright in 1579. She is a servant in the household of John Lawrence of Colne Engaine and his wife Joan. One night her master asks her to rub his back as he lies in bed. She refuses but her mistress Joan urges her to obey her husband. She is made to lie on the bed in her clothes rubbing his back until she feels tired and cold, at which point both John and Joan demand that she continue rubbing him under the covers. Jane later admits that she is then enticed by him and his wife that night as at other times also to come in bed naked with the two of them, at which times he has carnal knowledge of her, her said dame lying in bed with him and warranting her that she should have no harm and that the other maids used to do the like before.

Jane becomes pregnant and is reported to the archdeacon. She admits everything and is sentenced to stand in the church porch in a white sheet "and confess her fault penitently after the end of the sermon, praying God and the congregation to forgive her."[63] You cannot help but look toward John and Joan Lawrence as poor Jane makes her confession.

It is often said that society may be judged by the way it treats its most vulnerable members. In this respect, it is fair to say that Elizabethan England is not just a golden age but also a horrifyingly unjust one. Many of the injustices cannot be said to be politically expedient; they have nothing to do with Star Chamber or the necessity of ensuring the efficient functioning of society. They have nothing to do with the security of the realm. They are merely the results of people being unable to deal with their own natural inclinations, preferring to blame their weaknesses and lusts on their social inferiors, too proud to admit that these sins, which they publicly denigrate and punish in others, are in fact their own.

CHAPTER TWELVE

Entertainment

If any aspect of daily life were to be consistent across the ages, you would have thought it would be the things that people do to enjoy themselves. After all, we are all human, so the ways in which we gratify ourselves should be more or less the same. Or, to put it another way, if we enjoy doing something in one century, then the chances are that we will enjoy doing it in other centuries too. On the whole, this is true: sixteenth-century people are keen on the theater, playing chess, listening to music, making love, drinking wine and beer, reading books, and sightseeing. But they also enjoy things that we recoil from today. If you hear the shouts and look at the excited faces of the bloodthirsty crowd at a bull baiting, or hear the spectators' cheers as a traitor's entrails are sliced out and burned before his eyes, you might wonder how on earth Shakespeare's fellow Englishmen are able to understand the humanity of his writing.

Sightseeing

If you visit Elizabethan England you will want to go sightseeing, just as you do in the modern world. One of the most popular tourist destinations is Drake's famous ship, the *Golden Hind,* which is on display in Greenwich. Not only can you go aboard, you can also rent her as a banqueting house. Unfortunately she is slowly being dismantled because most visitors take a piece as a souvenir. If you want to see her in all her glory, go quickly: by 1618 only the keel will be left.[1]

The royal palaces are arguably the most attractive tourist destinations—not just Whitehall, Hampton Court, and Nonsuch Palace (Surrey) but also those farther afield, such as Woodstock Palace (Oxfordshire) and Windsor Castle (Berkshire). Not everyone can visit, of course. You will need to obtain the appropriate letters of introduction from well-connected friends and then hire horses or coaches to take you to these destinations. At Hampton Court you will be shown the royal apartments (including the king's and queen's bedchambers) with their woven tapestries and carpets, paintings, clocks, musical instruments, and royal furniture, as well as the royal library, chapel, and gardens. At Whitehall you will see the queen's collection of Dutch paintings, her wardrobe and jewels, and an "Indian bed" (Native American) with its "Indian" valance and an "Indian" table.[2]

At the Tower of London you will be shown around by a guide who will tell you about the large cannon and the armor of Henry VIII, both of which are on display there. Surprisingly your guide will even take you down to the dungeons to show you the instruments of torture used on Catholics. Don't believe everything he tells you—especially not that Julius Caesar built the White Tower and dined in the hall on the first floor. If you do the whole tour you will see the royal apartments, the royal mint, Traitors' Gate, the execution ax, and the royal menagerie (with its lions named after the Tudor kings and queens, "the last wolf in England," a tiger, and a porcupine). Bear in mind that you will have to pay a gratuity for every room you wish to see. When Thomas Platter and his two companions visit in 1599, they hand out eight gratuities of about 3s each. The total is the equivalent of twelve weeks' wages for a laborer, so you can understand why most native Londoners have not seen the Tower.

In London you can also visit houses which, in later centuries, will be referred to as cabinets of curiosities. Mr. Cope's house, for example, contains such exotic items as an African charm made of human teeth; the horn and tail of a rhinoceros; a unicorn's tail; a "thunder-bolt dug out of a mast which was hit at sea during a storm"; an embalmed child; "a round horn that grew on an English woman's forehead"; the baubles and bells of Henry VIII's fool; porcelain from China; a magnifying mirror; and an "Indian" (Native American) canoe and paddles, which hang from the ceiling in the center of the room.[3] As Shakespeare later puts it in *The Tempest*, "In England . . . when they will not give a doit to relieve a lame beggar, they will lay out ten to see a dead Indian." For those who cannot afford the entry fee to such houses, there are curios in the street. You can see a Dutch giant, over seven feet six inches high, and a dwarf, three feet high, in the city in 1581: the smaller man will walk straight beneath the legs of the giant. A fully grown live camel is to be seen in one of the houses on London Bridge in 1599. Claudius Hollyband even comes across a "makesport" or street entertainer, who swallows swords for a living.[4]

The most popular sights of a city, however, are the public ceremonies and processions. First and foremost has to be any event featuring the queen, such as the celebrations in London on January 14, 1559, the eve of her coronation, when she processes through the city to Westminster, with Londoners performing pageants, tableaux, and hymns. The day of her accession is also a great occasion, with bells ringing and bonfires and tables set up in the streets for feasting; within a few years it becomes traditional for courtiers to celebrate the anniversary of her accession by jousting before her on the tilting ground at Whitehall. Thousands turn up to watch Sir Philip Sidney and Sir Henry Lee joust against each other, or to watch the earl of Essex take on all comers in 1596 and break ninety-eight lances in the course of riding 108 courses against them. Chivalry might have had its day, and this ceremonial jousting may not be as violent as the tournaments of earlier centuries, but it is still a great spectacle.[5] Occasionally, when the queen goes on a royal progress, you will get to see firework displays, as at Kenilworth in 1575. For those living in the country, there are always the Mayday celebrations, when people go out into the fields and spend the night in pleasant frolics, returning the next morning with a Maypole. Unfortunately, the Puritans are keen to burn all Maypoles, regarding them as "stinking idols." They have already had their way with the great Maypole that used to be set up on Cornhill in London.

Alehouses and Taverns

Elizabethans do love their beer and wine, so alehouses, taverns, and "tippling houses" are all popular resorts. Indeed, they are the setting for the greatest array of indulgences, as in taverns you will be provided with food and drink, music, conversation, flirtation—and in some places much more than flirtation. Most taverns are simply the open halls of houses which are denoted by a sign hanging outside. They are all supposed to be licensed by the magistrates but many aren't. In London the better establishments have started placing partitions between the tables by 1599, affording their clientele greater privacy as they quaff wine sweetened with sugar and listen to the fiddlers perform.[6]

For many men, there is the added attraction of the tavern-cum-brothel; the usual charge is 6d a time to sleep with the house harlot. As you will have seen in the last chapter, a lot of prostitution is on a small scale and involves the sexual services of the alewife or one of her daughters. Joan Gwin of Clavering, Essex, for example, is the village prostitute and works at her mother's house, sleeping with those whom her mother admits.[7] But even such small-scale enterprises are not without trouble. Just before Christmas 1567 Henry Cooe's wife decides she has had enough of her husband's whoring and goes to the alehouse run by Widow Bowden in Chelmsford. It is dark, about six o'clock. When Henry hears his wife's shouting as she barges in, he hurriedly pulls up his hose and slips out of a back door. Failing to find her husband, Goodwife Cooe seizes Widow Bowden and her daughter (the house harlot) by the hair and starts to beat them. The daughter escapes into the street and raises the alarm. Eventually Henry Cooe, hiding in a garden, is apprehended by the constables. Pleasures in certain taverns can cost much more than 6d, even if you don't catch syphilis.[8] In Henry's case, his wife sounds far more fearsome than the penances imposed by the ecclesiastical courts.

The tavern is also where most people go to smoke. Brought to England from the New World in 1566, tobacco is exotic and fascinating. It appeals to most of the senses: there is the smell of it, the feeling of inhaling the smoke into the lungs, and the ethereal vision of it silently wafting in the candlelit air of the tavern or blown in smoke rings. Some people are of the opinion that "it makes your breath stink like the piss of a fox," but they are in the minority.[9] John Hawkins notices it being smoked in Florida in 1565 and probably introduces the practice to England on his return the following year.[10] William Harrison notes in his *Great Chronologie* of 1573:

In these days the taking-in of the Indian herb called "Tobaco" by an instrument formed like a little ladle, whereby it passeth from the mouth into the head and stomach, is greatly taken up and used in England, against rheums and other diseases engendered in the lungs and inward parts and not without effect.

If you are an addicted smoker you will want to visit England after this date. It is not a cheap habit, however: a quarter-ounce of tobacco will cost you 10 pence in a tavern. Consequently pipes have very small bowls and are often shared between the smokers. Note that the word "smoking" is not yet used to describe the new fad: at this time you "drink" the smoke. Women "drink" it too, often enjoying it with sweetened Spanish wine.

Not everyone is as certain as Harrison that tobacco is good for your health. A physician writing under the pen name "Philaretes" publishes a booklet entitled *Work for Chimny-sweepers or a warning for Tabacconists,* in 1602. Just like the future king of England, James I, who publishes his own anti-smoking tract, *A Counterblaste to Tobacco,* in 1604, Philaretes is keen to warn people away from the noxious herb. It is too dry to suit most people's health, he argues, especially being harmful for those of a choleric disposition. It is addictive and it causes sterility, indigestion, and colds. Moreover, it is also aesthetically unappealing:

> If any man be so far blinded with Tobacco that he will not admit for true that the vapor or fume thereof ascending to the brain is dark and swart of color, and of quality excessively dry, let him but cast his eyes on the smoke issuing forth from the nostrils of the Tobacconists, or the smoky tincture left in the tobacco pipe after the receipt thereof, and he shall easily reclaim his error.[11]

Thomas Platter seems to have talked with Philaretes or someone else inclined to liken smokers to chimneys. He notes in 1599 that the English

> carry the instrument [pipe] on them and light up on all occasions, at the play, in the taverns or elsewhere . . . and it makes them riotous and merry, and rather drowsy, just as if they were drunk, though the effect soon passes. And they use it so abundantly because of the pleasure it gives, that their preachers cry out on them for their self-destruction. And I am told the inside of one man's veins after death was found to be covered in soot just like a chimney.[12]

Games

If you accompany the Cornish gentleman William Carnsew around the county in the 1570s you will see that—when he is not attending to his estates, serving as a JP, or reading books—his pastimes are playing bowls, quoits, and card games with his friends.[13] All very innocent, you may think. However, playing these games is against the law for almost everyone. Ever since the Middle Ages kings have forbidden people from playing "unlawful games" in order to force them to practice archery. In 1542 Henry VIII re-issues legislation prohibiting all artificers, husbandmen, laborers, mariners, fishermen, watermen, servants, and apprentices from playing tables (back-gammon), cards, dice, football, bowls, tennis, quoits, ninepins, and shove-groat.[14] Carnsew is permitted to play these games only because he is a member of the gentry with an annual income of over £100. Everyone else can play them only at Christmas, and then only in their own homes. The penalty for every infringement is a heavy fine of £1.

For this reason you will be cautious about when and where you play games. There are bowling alleys in London and on greens across the coun-try but maintaining an unlicensed bowling alley can result in a fine of £2 per day for the proprietor and a 6 shilling 8 pence fine for anyone who plays there. Drake is famously playing bowls on Plymouth Hoe when the Ar-mada is sighted and declares that he has "enough time to win the game and beat the Spaniards." If any of his fellow mariners are playing with him they risk missing the great battle—for technically they should be taken off to face the magistrates at the quarter sessions. In reality, the fines levied are smaller than the law stipulates: men are sometimes fined just 40d by the magistrates in the hope that they will actually pay the more reasonable sum.[15] Even so, a fine of ten days' wages is enough to put off most working-men. The same penalties apply to people who maintain unlicensed tennis courts but you do not see people being arrested for playing tennis in the way that hundreds are for playing bowls. Although it is popular—£1,699 worth of tennis balls are imported in 1559–60—those who play it illegally do not build unlicensed tennis courts but play in the streets.[16] Tennis courts are the preserve of the aristocrats who play in private, and they are not sub-ject to these restrictions and fines.

Chess and tables are mostly played by gentlemen who bet on the out-come, but card games are played everywhere from alehouses to palaces. The most popular are gleek, primero, prima-vista, maw, cent or saint (like mod-ern picquet), one-and-thirty, new cut, and trumps (like modern whist).[17] The queen is very fond of her card games and bets huge amounts. Playing maw with Lord North in August 1577 she takes £33 from him, and when they play primero for double or quits he has to hand over another £33.[18] Shovegroat (shoveha'penny in later centuries) and dice are very popular with all classes; again, it is not the game that matters so much as the thrill of the betting. But do watch out for cheats. According to Gilbert Walker's *A Manifest Detection of Dice-play* (1552), fourteen different sorts of false dice are manufactured in the London prisons, such as "a bale of cinque-deuces" and "a bale of fullams," so you can roll a set of dice that will always be odd or even or always sixes. "Fullams" are weighted on one side with mercury or lead and "bristles" have tiny bristles set into one face so that they are unlikely ever to settle on that side.[19]

There is one form of gambling that the government wholeheartedly approves of: the lottery. This is first announced in 1567, when four thousand tickets are offered at 10 shillings each. The first prize is worth £5,000, of which £3,000 is in cash, £700 in silver and silver-gilt plate, and the rest in tapestry and linen. The second prize is £3,500 (£2,000 cash, £600 in plate, the rest in tapestry and linen). There are eleven more prizes, in descending value, down to £140; twelve prizes of £100; twenty-four prizes of £50; and so on, down to ten thousand prizes of 15 shillings.[20] You have to purchase your tickets by May 1, 1568, and the separate draws take place from January 11 to May 6, 1569, at the west door of St. Paul's Cathedral. It is not a great success: the ticket prices are just too high. The less ambitious three-day lottery of 1586 is more successful, but you may not want to take part in it: all the prizes are pieces of armor.

Outdoor Sports

As a result of the Archery Act of 1542 every man over the age of seventeen and under the age of sixty who is not lame or maimed, a nobleman, a clergyman, or a judge must keep a bow and four arrows in his house at all times or pay a fine of 6s 8d. Every father of a boy between the ages of seven and sixteen is also required to keep a bow for his son and two arrows, to train him to shoot. Bows made of elm, ash, or hazel have to be sold at 12 pence or less, and even the best yew bows cannot be sold for more than 3 shillings 4 pence. No bows or arrows may be exported, and no foreigners may practice with the bow in England. No man over twenty-four years should practice shooting at a mark less than 220 yards away (an eighth of a mile). Every man must shoot at the butts on every holy day, and parishes are to be fined if they do not keep their butts in good order. Englishmen cite the victories of Crécy, Poitiers, Agincourt, and Flodden as proof that the maintenance of archery is essential to the maintenance of English pride.[21] You can hardly doubt that archery is the national sport of England, not just a means of waging war.

Yet archery is slipping. Countrymen prefer crossbows for shooting coneys and game birds. Guns are more frequently employed when mustering for the militia, and they are growing increasingly cheaper (the average price is 8 shillings 3 pence in the 1560s).[22] In 1577 William Harrison opines, "Our strong shooting is decayed and laid in bed." Archery practice is dangerous—many archers and onlookers are killed at the butts—so why continue to practice in an age of guns?[23] Despite the queen's attempts to bolster her father's Archery Act by reissuing it in 1566 and 1571, the days of the longbow are approaching their end. In many places the butts are not kept in good order. At Purleigh in 1591 the manorial tenants confess they have not practiced shooting for ten months.[24] As the reign draws to a close fewer and fewer people observe the legislation. John Stow writes, "What should I speak of the ancient daily exercises in the longbow by the citizens of this city, now almost clean left off and forsaken?" Londoners now more frequently resort to bowling alleys than the butts.

The preferred sport of noblemen and gentlemen is hunting, mainly for deer, hares, and game birds. Spaniels are used to rouse the bird or beast and chase it out; hounds then continue the chase. "The spaniels and bloodhounds with their hanging ears seek out the game by smelling of soot of the foot," writes William Horman, adding, "A greyhound overtaketh the hare and catcheth him in his mouth." Many people scorn the hunting of hares with greyhounds as being too easy. Male red deer are the most highly valued quarry, especially stags and great stags (deer of four or five years) and, best of all, harts (six years or more). These make fine gifts for the park owner to offer to friends and relatives, or to make into venison pasties for visitors, being a mark of high status. If you want to witness a large hunt go by late in the afternoon of a hot summer's day, you will hear the baying of the hounds and the noise of the hunters' horns and see the hart dashing through the wood as it seeks safety. After a moment the pack will come into sight, chasing it toward water. As the deer plunges in and starts to swim away, with its antlers like the sails of a galleon, the hounds go after it, both along the bank and in the water. Then you will hear the galloping of hooves. The riders will appear, pulling on their reins as they twist and turn beneath the boughs. The footmen will come after them, running along in their leather jerkins. All are caught up in the thrill of the chase—and look forward to the feast at the end. As Robert Laneham writes in 1575, it is "a pastime delightful to so high a degree as for any person to take pleasure by most senses at once."[25]

One of the virtues of hunting in Elizabethan England is that it is almost the only physically demanding activity that men and women can enjoy together. The queen loves to hunt and so do many other English noblewomen, enthusiastically showing off their horsemanship in the chase. For those of a gentler disposition, hawking remains popular, as this too can be enjoyed by both sexes. Normally you will use a falcon or hawk to go after rabbits or other birds. A goshawk will cost you between 10 shillings and £1—albeit more for a very fine bird—but do not forget the greater costs of keeping it in meat and keeping it healthy and clean: contemporary treatises suggest they should be bathed every third day.[26]

The art of fishing is also practiced by both gentlemen and women, and enjoyed for the catching as well as the eating. But make sure you obtain permission: fishing on a river without the landowner's consent will see you indicted at the quarter sessions for poaching. Expert anglers use a rod and a selection of flies as well as the net. Books such as *The Arte of Angling* (1577) and William Gryndall's *Hawking, Hunting, Fouling and Fishing* (1596) will teach you the rudiments. The following comments appear in a dialogue book of the time:

> *First lady:* What a fair pond there is! . . . What fishes be in it?
> *Second lady [the owner of the pond]:* Truly, Madam, we put in a great store of fish, as of tench, bream, roach and carp; but I believe that the pirate-pikes have made good prize of the most part. The boat is at the other end but if it please you to set these gentlemen at work we will try to take some fish with the net.
> *First lady:* I had rather fish with the line.
> *First gentleman:* Here, Madam, is one all ready, that hath a good hook. I go to seek some bait. I beseech you, let me bait it for you. Now, cast your line in the water. I trust that the fishes will not be better able to keep themselves than so many brave hearts whom the sugar-sweet and forcible bait of your good grace and rare virtues do draw to himself. O happy hand! Draw, Madam, you have caught—but softly, for fear the line do break, for it is big.[27]

To which the second gentleman, who is as much a creep as the first, replies "O fish, thou hast had a happy destiny to be taken by so worthy a fisher. Thou couldst never have had a better end."

As noted in Chapter Four, gentlemen might take part in many other sports and games, including swimming, wrestling, athletics, horse riding, and fencing. This last art is most important. Even if you wear a sword only as a badge of status, you need to know how to use it—in case someone challenges you to a duel. For this reason go to one of the fencing schools in London; they are at Ely Place in Holborn, the Greyfriars within Newgate, Bridewell, the Artillery Gardens to the north of the city, Leadenhall, and Smithfield. There are also fencing schools at the larger inns where plays are performed, such as the Belle Savage on Ludgate Hill and the Bull in Bishopsgate Street, and at the Curtain Theatre, just to the north of the city.[28] Here certified members of the Corporation of Masters of the Noble Science of Defence will teach you how to use the rapier, the quarterstaff, and the broadsword. Students progress up the scale of learning from "scholar" (beginner) to "free scholar" (after seven years' training) and eventually may become "provost" (after another seven years).

Popular Sports

Wrestling is one of the most popular pastimes in the country. A ring is drawn out; the two competitors strip down to their breeches and attempt to throw each other to the ground and hold each other there—very much as in modern wrestling.[29] In London, competitions take place on Finsbury Fields in August, overseen by the lord mayor and the city's aldermen. In country towns, there is often wrestling on a market day or during a fair; the traditional prize for the victor is a ram. Gentlemen also wrestle but, of course, they do so only with other gentlemen and in private. No sport makes inroads into breaking down class barriers.

Elizabethan football has more in common with modern rugby than with soccer. There are no rules against picking up the ball and running with it or tripping up your opponent. There are also no limitations (other than local custom) on the number of players or the size of the pitch. You might be invited to join in a game in the streets of London; in the country it might be played across all the ground between two villages.[30] One of the very few innovations that sets the game apart from its medieval version is that it is now played with an inflated leather ball rather than a pig's bladder filled with peas; William Horman refers to playing football "with a ball full of wind" and Shakespeare describes a football as cased in leather in *The Comedy of Errors.*

Be careful, though: Elizabethan football is a far more violent game than its later incarnation. Sir Thomas Elyot dismisses it as nothing but "beastly fury and extreme violence whereof proceedeth hurt; and consequently rancor and malice do remain with them that be wounded...."[31] Philip Stubbes is of a like mind, declaring that football

> may rather be called a friendly kind of fight than a play or recreation; a bloody murdering practice than a fellowly sport or pastime. For doth not everyone lie in wait for his adversary, seeking to overthrow him and to pitch him on his nose, though it be upon hard stones, in ditch or dale, in valley or hill, or whatsoever place it be he careth not so he have him down.... By this means sometimes their necks are broken, sometimes their backs, sometimes their legs, sometimes their arms.... Sometimes their noses gush out with blood, sometimes their eyes start out.... And no marvel, for they have sleights to meet one betwixt two, to dash him against the heart with their elbows, to hit him under the short ribs with their gripped fists and with their knees to catch him upon the hip, and to pitch him upon his neck.... Is this murdering play now an exercise for the Sabbath day?[32]

Although deaths from football are nowhere near as common as those caused by practicing archery, Stubbes is not wholly exaggerating.[33] Henry Ingold, aged twenty-four, is killed after colliding with another player during a two-hour-long game between eight men of White Roothing and three men from Hatfield, on a March afternoon in 1567. In 1582 a Gosfield-versus-Bocking match results in a dead goalkeeper when Richard Elye collides with John Pye, who is defending Gosfield's goal. In a match at West Ham in April that same year a man is killed after being knocked down by an opponent. These incidents are treated as felonies: a game in which someone is killed ends up with all the players being reported to the coroner, tried for manslaughter, and fined for playing an illegal game. The courts do not usually hang the player responsible for the accident; that would be bad sportsmanship. Nevertheless sometimes a verdict of murder is returned by the coroner, and a certain "John at Stile" is found guilty instead of the named player.[34]

Today we associate hurling almost exclusively with Ireland but in the sixteenth century it is among the most popular sports played in Cornwall. There are two varieties: "hurling to goals" (played in east Cornwall) and "hurling to the country" (played in the west). The key difference between hurling and football is that the ball is always thrown, not kicked. Also, hurling to goals already has a set of rules. On each side there are fifteen, twenty, or thirty players, "stripped to their slightest apparel" and playing on a pitch that is 160 or two hundred yards in length, with a goal at each end. The players all pair off and mark each other, holding on to one another. When the referee puts the ball into the air, every man tries to jump for it, catch it, and carry it through his opponent's goal. "But therein lies one of the labors of Hercules," writes Richard Carew, "for he that is once possessed of the ball has his contrary mate waiting at inches and [trying] to lay hold on him. The other thrusteth him in the breast with his closed fist to keep him off, which they call butting. . . ." Note that his opponent may butt him only in the breast, not below the waist. If he is caught and held, he must pass the ball by throwing it to one of his teammates. He may not throw the ball forward to any of his teammates nearer to the opponents' goal than himself, only backward—an early offside rule. Hurling to goals, you might like to know, is commonly played at weddings.

Hurling to the country, the west Cornwall version, is almost entirely without rules. It is usually organized on holy days by two gentlemen who enlist teams of their tenants and set the goals as each gentleman's house. Hence "the hurlers take their way over hills, dales, hedges, ditches, yea, and through bushes, briars, mires, splashes and rivers whatsoever, so as you shall sometimes see twenty or thirty lying tugging together in the water, scrabbling and scratching for the ball." The gentlemen do not generally take part but provide the silver ball used and watch as their respective workers attempt to muscle it from one place to another. The gentleman whose team finally carries the ball to his house is given the ball as a "trophee" to keep— and everyone gets to drink his house dry of beer.[35]

You may wonder about that other great team game, cricket. If you attend some schools—such as Guildford Grammar School in Surrey—you will see boys playing a game with a bat and they do indeed call it "crecket," but as yet you will find it only sparingly mentioned and rarely played. As for golf, that game comes to England in the next reign. It is played in Scotland— it is banned as an unlawful game by the Scottish kings in 1457, 1471, and

1491, in favor of archery—but not yet in England. Mary, queen of Scots hits a round or two in her youth but it is one of the things she gives up when she comes south across the border.

Baiting Games

Baiting games reveal one of the most striking differences between sixteenth-century people and ourselves. Elizabethans are extraordinarily cruel to animals. It is not just the lower classes who take delight in seeing an animal in agony: almost everyone loves the sight of animal blood—except the Puritans, that is. Why is this? You might point to a deep-seated psychological connection between blood and food, so that animal blood is indicative of God's goodness in providing things to eat. Or you might think it is a respect for the nobility of the creatures to be killed, as with the modern Spanish bullfight. However, that second reason hardly applies to a cockfight: it is not the nobility of the chickens that engages the onlookers. Rather it is the huge bets that change hands. Life and death, money and chance—these are what captivate the audience.

Cockfighting, or cocking, is a regular Sunday occupation, with special celebratory fights taking place on Shrove Tuesday. Men spend considerable amounts—£5 or more—on purchasing a fighting bird and having it trained. Henry VIII builds a cockpit next to the Palace of Whitehall, alongside Birdcage Walk, but in Elizabeth's reign the most popular cockpits are in Jewin Street, in Shoe Lane, and at St. Giles in the Fields; the last of these will become the Drury Lane Theatre in the next reign. Thomas Platter describes the Shoe Lane cockpit in 1599:

> In the center of the floor stands a circular table covered with straw and with ledges round it, where the cocks are teased and incited to fly at one another, while those with wagers as to which cock will win sit around the circular disk. The spectators who are merely present on their entrance penny sit around higher up, watching with eager pleasure the fierce and angry fight between the cocks, as these wound each other to death with spurs and beaks.[36]

Entertainments can go on for four or five hours, with fight after fight leaving the straw all bloody. In the Shoe Lane establishment, strong spirits such

as *brandewijn* are given to the birds beforehand to enhance their vicious-
ness in fighting. Hundreds of pounds can be bet on each fight. Lord North
loses £13 on a cockfight in 1578.[37]

More exotic than cockfighting are the bear-baiting contests. In London
these take place on most days, including every Sunday, at Paris Garden in
Southwark. In 1570 a second theater is constructed so that there is one for
bears (the eastern one) and one for bulls (the western).[38] To watch the bear
baiting you will need to pay 1 pence for the stalls or 2 pence for the gallery.
The bear is brought in on a leash or chain and tied to the stake in the middle of the theater. Great English mastiffs are then set upon the bear:

> Now the excellence and fine temper of such mastiffs is shown for al-
> though they have been much struck and mauled by the bear, they do
> not give in but have to be pulled off by sheer force and their muzzles
> forced open with long sticks to which a broad iron piece is attached at
> the top. The bears' teeth are not sharp—they have them broken short
> so they cannot injure the dogs. When the first mastiffs grow tired,
> fresh ones are brought in to bait the bear. When the first bear is weary,
> another is supplied, and fresh dogs to bait him, first one at a time, then
> more and more as it lasts, till they have overpowered the bear.[39]

Thomas Platter is entertained by the display although his nose recoils at the
smell of the 120 mastiffs and thirteen bears in their cages and kennels beside the ring. The high value of the bears means that normally they are not
allowed to be killed by the dogs, although many dogs are killed by a bear
lashing out with its claws or grabbing a dog and "pinching" (crushing) it to
death. Some bears become celebrities. "Sackerson" is the most famous—so
famous that he is mentioned in Shakespeare's *The Merry Wives of Windsor*:
"I have seen Sackerson loose twenty times and have taken him by the
chain." Nevertheless you may be distressed at the sight of the bear enraged,
its mouth frothing with saliva, and its pelt red with its own blood and the
blood of the dogs it has killed. Robert Laneham writes of a bear baiting that

> If the dog would pluck the bear by the throat, the bear would claw him
> again by the scalp. . . . Thus with plucking and tugging, scratching and
> biting, by plain tooth and nail on one side and the other, such expense
> of blood and leather was there between them as a month's licking will

not recover. . . . It was a sport very pleasant of these beasts: to see the bear with his pink eyes leering after his enemy's approach, the nimbleness and watch of the dog to take his advantage, and the force and experience of the bear again to avoid the assaults. If he were bitten in one place how he would pinch in another to get free; that if he were taken once, then what shift with biting, with clawing, with roaring, tossing and tumbling he would work to wind himself from them; and when he was loose, to shake his ears twice or thrice with the blood and saliva about his face was a matter of goodly relief.[40]

Blind bears are whipped into a fury to entertain the crowds; they lash out and seize the whips, and cuff anyone who comes within range. However, some learn how to loosen their tethers and run amok about the crowd; Sackerson is by no means the only one to escape. In October 1565 at the abandoned church of the Austin Friars in Oxford, a twenty-four-year-old man is set upon by a runaway bear and killed. At Birling, Kent, in August 1563 a widow is mauled in Lord Bergavenny's house by his bear, it "biting and tearing her head, body and legs." In 1570, near Hereford, a bear breaks loose, enters a house, and kills a woman in her bed.[41]

Bear baiting is enjoyed in every part of the country and by all classes of people, men and women, young and old. In Shakespeare's *Twelfth Night,* Sir Andrew Aguecheek states he regrets spending so much time fencing, dancing, and bear baiting. In April 1559 the queen entertains the French ambassador with bear-baiting displays—and he is so taken with it that the very next day he goes to Paris Garden to see more animals tormented. Throughout her reign many visiting dignitaries are treated to a display of bear baiting: it seems to be one of the queen's personal delights. Robert Dudley provides displays for the queen at Kenilworth in 1575, and in 1599 she even attends the Paris Garden to watch the bloodshed.[42] (You may be surprised to learn that although she never goes to Southwark to visit the Globe Theatre, she does go to see the bear baiting.) Only the Puritans refuse to accept that it is suitable family entertainment, although most of them despise the baiting because it takes place on a Sunday, not because they feel sorry for the animal. A lone voice speaking against the cruelty is that of Philip Stubbes, who asks, "What Christian heart can take pleasure to see one poor beast rend, tear and kill another, and all for his foolish pleasure?"

There is also great enthusiasm for baiting bulls. Several mastiffs are released into the ring to challenge and bite a tethered animal. The bull lashes out with its horns and sends the dogs flying. Men with sticks break the dogs' fall so they can continue to fight. Eventually the large number of dogs set upon the bull will wear him down, but the fight continues until the surviving dogs have killed the bull or he is so badly injured that he is taken away to be slaughtered. What might surprise you is that it is actually against the law *not* to bait a bull. Every town has its "bull-ring" where the baiting takes place. Anyone slaughtering a bull without baiting it first is liable to be fined: the statutory penalty for selling meat from an animal killed without baiting it first is 3 shillings 4 pence per bull.[43]

The most distressing spectacle of this sort regularly to be seen in England is often the finale of a day of bull baiting. A monkey is placed in the saddle of an old horse and led into the ring. Half a dozen young dogs are then sent into the ring to attack the horse. In the words of Alessandro Magno, "It is a fine sight to see the horse run, kicking and biting, and the monkey grip the saddle tightly and scream, many times being bitten, in which baiting the horse is often left dead and removed by the attendants."[44]

Music and Dancing

Although no one has yet conclusively proved that music is the food of love, there is little doubt that Shakespeare himself thinks it is. More than 170 passages in his plays allude to music or musicians, airs or madrigals, and nearly all do so in a positive way. The words for many songs are reproduced verbatim in the plays.[45] Nor is Shakespeare alone in his passion for music: most Elizabethans are expected to play an instrument or at least to be able to sing. Barbers sometimes have a cittern or lute in their shops, which the customer is welcome to strum as he waits for his shave. The vast majority of taverns will have music played within, although the most commonly played instrument among working drinkers is still the bagpipes. In 1587 Stephen Gosson notes, "London is so full of unprofitable pipers and fiddlers that a man can no sooner enter a tavern than two or three cast of them hang at his heels to give him a dance ere he depart."[46]

There is just as great an aptitude for music at the top end of the social spectrum. Ever since the Middle Ages noblemen have maintained their own musicians to entertain them during meals and to perform at feasts. The royal family leads the way: Henry VIII maintained as many as fifty-eight musicians and Elizabeth has about thirty on the payroll of the royal household. The nobility themselves play music: all the members of the Willoughby family of Wollaton, for example, are trained to play the virginals.[47] The well-to-do ladies in Claudius Hollyband's dialogue book declare "our dancing master cometh at 9, our singing master and he that teacheth us to play on the virginals at 10, lute and viol de gamba at 4." The queen too plays the virginals, the lute, and the orpharion (a large cittern). The only difference between the aristocratic love of music and that of the common people is that noblemen and ladies are expected *never* to play in public, only in private. Elizabeth explains that she is fond of playing the virginals because it calms her down.

If you are keen to play along with the musicians of Elizabethan England, you will have plenty of opportunities to do so. However, it may not be as easy as you think. Music is not written or printed in the modern way: although the notes are depicted in more or less the same form, there are no bar marks. This makes it very difficult to play in time together—especially because music books are not printed with all the parts of a five-part piece on the same page. They are designed to be dismantled and handed out to the various players, who have only their own parts. Take a music book like Anthony Holborne's *Pavans, Galliards, Almains and Other Short Aeirs Both Grave and Light in Five Parts* (1599) and you will see that all the canto parts to all sixty-five pieces of music are printed in one section, all the alto parts in another, and all the "quinto," tenor, and bass parts in separate sections after that. Therefore you cannot see what the other parts are doing. Music stands are very rare; normally music is laid on a table.

The instruments also vary from their modern equivalents. A lute is not like a guitar. Its head is at a right angle to the neck, its gut strings are all in pairs or "courses," and it may have anything from six to ten courses, with the strings of lower courses tuned an octave apart from one another. The standard tuning is in fourths, with a major third between the central pair of courses; but there are many variations on this. Easier to play is the cittern, which generally has only four courses, a flat back, and an angled neck. Large bass versions are known as "bandoras," and intermediate ones as "orpharions." Instruments of the viol family, whether small ones the size and shape of a violin, or large ones the size of a cello, are strung with six strings, all made of gut. As for wind instruments, trumpets do not have valves. Flutes are made of wood. Keyboard instruments include the organ, the medieval hurdy-gurdy, and the harpsichord and its variants: the spinet and the virginals. As the virginals have keyboards that are not dissimilar to that of a modern piano, they will be among the easiest instruments for you to play.

Another reason you might have difficulty making your way as a musician in Elizabethan England is the low status of most performers. You would have thought that, with such a wide interest in music, players would be highly respected. However, musical ability is so common that many people place no great value on skill. A poor man with a musical instrument is first and foremost a poor man; his ability to play music does not make any difference to his status. In 1573 no fewer than fifty-six itinerant musicians are arrested for vagabondage in Essex.[48] Women cannot make money from music—paid positions are not open to them—and there are precious few opportunities for men to gain status or money as musicians. Puritans are hostile to singing and the playing of the organ in churches, and many parishes play it safe by not encouraging music at all. As a result musicians and composers are dependent on the court, the cathedrals, and the patronage of aristocrats and town corporations. Official groups of musicians called "waits," consisting of four or five men, are employed by many of the larger towns. Public performances are organized in the towns on Sundays—in London these take place at the Royal Exchange—and at official receptions and other functions. But being a town musician will not make you wealthy. Members of the Cambridge Waits in 1567 are paid just £2 per year; you will have to supplement this by playing at weddings and public celebrations, or by performing privately at the houses of noblemen if you are a virtuoso.

English music is not well known outside England in 1575 but that is all set to change: the last quarter of the century brings English music to the forefront of European critical attention. Religious music shows a strong recovery after the low point of the Reformation, when the choirs of abbeys and priories found themselves suddenly unemployed. Although many congregations sing only hymns and psalms, as allowed by the Religious Settlement of 1559, the cathedrals keep the tradition of religious music and polyphony alive. So too do noblemen's private chapels including, most important, the Chapel Royal and the chapels in Catholic households. Men start as choirboys and progress to being choirmasters or organists (or both), and then learn to compose their own music for the organ or the choir. The leading composers of the day, Thomas Tallis, William Byrd, and Dr. John Bull, are employed to perform in the Chapel Royal even though all three are Catholics. They continue to compose motets and masses, even though these cannot be performed in public. It is ironic that the greatest musical achievement of the reign, Tallis's motet *Spem in Alium,* one of the most famous pieces of polyphony of all time, has to be performed behind closed doors. To hear it in its full glory, sung by eight choirs, each of five voices, you will need to go to the Nonsuch Palace, where the Catholic earl of Arundel has it performed and where the music is kept in his library.

There are no such limitations on the singing of psalms. *The Whole Booke of Psalmes* by Thomas Sternhold and John Hopkins, printed by John Day in 1562, proves so popular that it remains in print for more than 250 years. Composers such as John Farmer, Giles Farnaby, Thomas Ravenscroft, Thomas Morley, and William Byrd are producing anthems, canticles, plainsong chants, and new settings for alternative versions. Some of this music will be familiar to you: Psalm 100, for example—"All people that on Earth do dwell"—is sung to the same tune as in the modern world, although the four-part setting by John Dowland might cause you some confusion.

In 1575 the queen grants an exclusive monopoly on printing music (for twenty-one years) to Thomas Tallis and William Byrd. Their initial joint publication of "sacred songs" is a disaster; they lose so much money that no further publications are planned in Thomas Tallis's lifetime. But after his death in 1585, William Byrd begins to realize the potential of his monopoly. He gets together with a new printer and, in the last eight years of his patent, oversees the publication of twenty books of music, four of them consisting of his own compositions. Soon everyone who has the ability to do so starts publishing new songs. And most of this new work is not remotely sacred. Indeed, secular music is another reason to call Elizabeth's reign "a golden age."

At the start of the reign most secular music composed for the court consists of dances, such as slow and stately pavanes or sprightly and energetic galliards. There are also scores of popular songs and ballads, many of which are collected in the four books published early in the next reign by Thomas Ravenscroft: you may be familiar with tunes such as "Three Blind Mice" and "Three Ravens." But everything changes in 1588, when a book of Italian madrigals with English lyrics, *Musica Transalpina,* appears. Many composers in England, including those who learned their music in a cathedral choir, are inspired to write madrigals for three to six voices. Even the Catholic court composer William Byrd is touched by this new fashion and writes a couple of madrigals in 1590. In 1601 Thomas Morley edits an anthology of twenty-five madrigals by the twenty-three leading composers of the day in honor of the queen, entitled *The Triumphs of Oriana*. The two men who command the greatest success in the genre of the madrigal are John Wilbye and Thomas Weelkes. They are chalk and cheese in terms of personality: Wilbye is a cautious and tidy man, whose music is exceedingly polished; he never offends his patron (Lady Kytson) and grows old in retirement. Thomas Weelkes is the nearest thing to an Elizabethan rock-and-roller, famous for his drunkenness, blasphemy, and bad behavior as much as for his brilliant musical achievements. On one occasion during evensong at Chichester Cathedral (where he is employed) he urinates from the organ loft on the dean below.

After madrigals it is the "air" that becomes the flavor of the moment. The craze for these single-voice songs accompanied by a lute is started by John Dowland, a brilliant lutenist in his own right, whose *First Booke of Songes or Ayres* appears in 1597. It is as influential as *Musica Transalpina*: now composers compete with each other in producing airs. Thomas Morley, in true "battle-of-the-bands" spirit, replies to Dowland's offering with his own *Canzonets or Little Short Aers* the same year.

Just as exciting is the growing demand for instrumental music, especially works for solo virginals and solo lute, and "consorts" (groups) of viols, flutes, and lutes. If you want to hear such pieces you should watch out for performances of lute music by John Dowland, virginals music by Giles Farnaby, William Byrd, and John Bull, or the court dances written for viol consorts by Bull, Byrd, Dowland, and Anthony Holborne. It is a glittering musical array—London will not be home to such a wealth of musical talent again for many centuries. It is very much a community of musicians too. In the 1590s Thomas Morley, William Byrd, John Bull, Giles Farnaby, and John Wilbye all live in the parish of St. Helen Bishopsgate; so does William Shakespeare. In fact, Thomas Morley sets two songs from Shakespeare's plays to music and publishes them: "O mistress mine" (from *Twelfth Night*) and "It was a lover and his lass" (from *As You Like It*). No wonder Shakespeare reflects on music so positively.

Dancing

Music and dancing go hand in hand in Elizabethan England. You have already heard how, on entering a tavern, you are likely to have a fiddler and bagpipe player entice you to dance. All physically able people dance, not just the young. You might come across folk dances such as "the satyr's dance," "the soldiers' dance," "the hay dance," "the shipmen's dance," "the children's dance," "the maidens' dance," "the old men's dance," "the winding dance," and "the barefoot dance"—all of which are mentioned by William Horman. These are intended to involve as many people as possible, so that every woman can dance with every man (and thus her favorite) within the social and moral security of the occasion. Thoinot Arbeau, who publishes a manual of dance in 1589, mentions several other country dances, such as the washerwomen's dance and the Scottish dance, referring to them collectively as "branles" or "brawls." They are very similar to medieval caroling, in which people hold hands and perform simple steps. Some of them include a special feature: in the "dance of the candlesticks," for instance, people light candles from one another as they pass between pairs.

One of the most common forms of dance is Morris dancing. Originating in fifteenth-century Moorish dancing, this is very much a spectacle—not for everyone to join in but to be performed by practiced troupes of dancers, with feathers in their hats, bells on their boots, and scarves tied to their wrists. In 1577 Lord North pays 2 shillings 6 pence for a group of Morris dancers with their accompaniment of fife and drum to entertain him and his household at Whitsun, the traditional time for Morris dancing in England.[49] It may be seen at other times of year too. In March 1559 Henry Machyn notes that the queen, after watching an artillery display and two bears baited at Mile End, is entertained by a troupe of Morris dancers.[50]

Much of the court music we encountered above is composed specifically for dances. Generally these can be divided into two sorts: *basse dance*, in which your feet stay on the ground, and *haute dance*, in which they do not. The original *basse dance* is still danced by old men and women, but according to Arbeau it has been unfashionable at court for forty years now. Instead newer forms of *basse dance* are in vogue: the pavane, a slow, stately processional dance, and the slightly faster almain. A gentleman wishing to ask a lady to dance should remove his hat with his left hand and offer the right hand to his partner to lead her out to dance. Most court dances presume that men and women will dance in pairs. Some slow dances allow a man to dance with two female partners, in which case he should lead his chosen women out in turn, one after the other, by the right hand. After the dance a gentleman should thank his partner (or each partner), bow to her, and escort her back to where he found her before the dance. In case you are wondering, ladies are permitted to ask gentlemen to dance. Note that it is bad manners to refuse an invitation.[51]

The galliard and coranto, both of which are types of *haute dance,* are more exciting than the slow processional dances. The pair dance around the hall a couple of times together to the quick tempo of the music and then they separate, so they can both show off their dancing skills with hops, half-steps, fast steps, twists, side steps, and leaps. Men might be seen to perform high kicks, jumps, and turns of 180 or even 360 degrees in midair. Ladies, encumbered by their skirts, cannot leap very high, and it would not be seemly for them to kick; but they are expected to keep up with the fast-moving men. Obviously you cannot improvise such moves: you will need to go to one of the many Italian dancing masters who have settled in London. Alternatively, after 1574 you can seek tuition in the various London dancing schools, which are now open again (having been closed down by Queen Mary in 1553). The queen dances galliards to keep fit, often completing six or seven of them in the morning. However, it is unlikely that you will see her dancing a variation on the galliard called "lavolta": in this fast dance, the gentleman lifts the lady by placing his left hand on her far hip and his right hand at the bottom of her corset, beneath her legs. It is no surprise that Philip Stubbes sharpens his quill and vents his spleen against "the horrible vice of pestiferous dancing in England.... What clipping, what culling, what kissing and bussing, what smouching and slabbering of one another: what filthy groping and unclean handling is not practiced everywhere in these dancings?" Stubbes would have women dance only with women and men dance only with men, "because otherwise it provoketh lust and the fire of lust, once conceived ... bursteth forth into the open action of whoredom and fornication." Despite such censure, even he has to acknowledge that dancing "in England ... is counted a virtue and an ornament to man, and the only way to attain promotion and advancement, as experience teacheth."[52]

A masque brings together music and dance. If invited to attend one you should wear a suitable costume, such as the dress of a foreigner or something fantastical. Moors and blackamoors are common subjects for masques, as are the ancient Roman gods and medieval knights and queens with their maidens. Torches will illuminate the night, and people will process in their costumes, with their faces covered. Sometimes there is scenery and actors are hired to play specific parts: don't worry, you won't be called upon to speak impromptu. Masques are always ceremonial and symbolic: they do not have moments of high drama and no serious acting is ever included. After the spoken parts are complete, the court dances begin; and after the dancing comes the banquet. At the end guests remove their masks to reveal their identities to the people with whom they have been dancing, speaking, and eating. Few things in Elizabethan England are certain but you can be wholly confident that your partner at a masque will not turn out to be Philip Stubbes.

Literature

The explosion in the number of books published over the course of the reign means that you will find reading material on almost every conceivable subject. And people do love to read. In 1576 William Carnsew records reading a history of the Turks, an account of the Protestant martyrs Ridley and Latimer, assorted sermons, Foxe's *Book of Martyrs,* Humphrey Gilbert's *A Discourse of a discoverie for a new passage to Cataia* (1576), an account of the acts of the Council of Basel, Calvin's letters, and *De Triplice Vita* by the Italian humanist Marsilio Ficino.[53] Well-educated people also love to read the ancient classics, such as Homer and Virgil, both in the original and in translation, and quite a few classic medieval works are now in print, such as Lord Berners's translation of *The Chronicles of Froissart* and Chaucer's *Canterbury Tales.* However, when it comes to contemporary creative writing, two forms dominate: poetry and writing for the stage.

Poetry

Almost every intelligent, well-educated person writes poetry—whether it be a short lyric on a special occasion or a pretty rhyme to amuse a potential lover. As a result, more than 440 volumes of verse are published during the reign (including reprints). But far more poetry is circulated in manuscript. Much of this is the work of gentlemen who do not wish to publish their private words. In some cases publication is quite out of the question—for instance, in the case of Chidiock Tichborne's moving poem written "on the eve of his execution" in 1586. The last stanza reads:

> I sought my death and found it in my womb,
> I looked for life and saw it was a shade,
> I trod the earth and knew it was my tomb
> And now I die, and now I was but made:
> My glass is full, and now my glass is run,
> And now I live, and now my life is done.

The queen herself is not too high for occasional versification; she writes a hauntingly sad poem on the departure of the duke of Anjou, her last suitor and her final potential groom of suitable rank, wit, and disposition. Entitled "On Monsieur's departure," it reads:

> I grieve and dare not show my discontent;
> I love, and yet am forced to seem to hate;
> I do, yet dare not say I ever meant;
> I seem stark mute, but inwardly do prate.
> I am, and not; I freeze and yet am burned,
> Since from myself another self I turned.
>
> My care is like my shadow in the sun—
> Follows me flying, flies when I pursue it,
> Stands, and lies by me, doth what I have done;
> His too familiar care doth make me rue it.
> No means I find to rid him from my breast,
> Till by the end of things it be suppressed.
>
> Some gentler passion slide into my mind,
> For I am soft, and made of melting snow;
> Or be more cruel, Love, and so be kind.
> Let me or float or sink, be high or low;
> Or let me live with some more sweet content,
> Or die, and so forget what love e'er meant.

With so much poetry being published and far more being written, how do you pick the finest? Perhaps the best guide is John Taylor, a waterman and poet in his own right, known to history as "the Water Poet." In his 1620 poem "The praise of hemp-seed," he lists those deceased English writers whose fame strikes him as well-deserved and secure:

> In paper, many a poet now survives
> Or else their lines had perish'd with their lives.
> Old Chaucer, Gower, and Sir Thomas More,
> Sir Philip Sidney, who the laurel wore,
> Spenser, and Shakespeare did in art excel,
> Sir Edward Dyer, Greene, Nashe, Daniel.
> Sylvester, Beaumont, Sir John Harington,
> Forgetfulness their works would over run
> But that in paper they immortally
> Do live in spite of death, and cannot die.

His reading list includes just three pre-Elizabethan writers: the two great medieval poets John Gower (d. 1408) and Geoffrey Chaucer (d. 1400), whose works are still read in Elizabethan times, and Sir Thomas More (d. 1540), Henry VIII's chancellor, who wrote *Utopia* and published various religious and historical works but is not actually known for his poetry. Few would deny that the next three writers really do "excel": Sir Philip Sidney, Edmund Spenser, and William Shakespeare. With the exception of the controversial poet and playwright Christopher Marlowe, no Elizabethan writer who dies in the century before 1620 comes anywhere near these three in terms of poetic skill, originality, and sustained achievement. Yet they all hail from different backgrounds and display varied ambitions.

Philip Sidney is an aristocrat, the grandson of the duke of Northumberland, educated at Oxford. A position at court is practically his birthright; traveling on the Continent—through Germany and Austria to Italy, Poland, and Hungary—is only to be expected of someone of his class. He is the epitome of the enlightened and educated courtier. But he is also proud and quick to defend himself. In August 1579, on the tennis court at Whitehall Palace, he challenges the earl of Oxford to a duel as they violently disagree about the merits of the queen's prospective marriage to the duke of Anjou. Elizabeth has to intervene to stop the bloodshed. Sidney then makes the mistake of presenting the queen with his argument against the marriage in written form; the queen is not amused and he hastily retreats from court. His ignominy does not last long, however; he is soon restored to favor, being knighted in 1582. Four years later he dies in battle, at the Siege of Zutphen, after receiving a bullet in the thigh. He never sees his thirty-second birthday but in his short life he revolutionizes English literature, composing a long pastoral romance, *Arcadia* (1590), remodeling the Petrarchan sonnet in his sequence *Astrophel and Stella* (1591), and robustly defending poetry against its critics in *The Defence of Poesy* (1595). To give you a taste of his poetic touch, the following is taken from *Arcadia:*

> My true-love hath my heart, and I have his,
> By just exchange one for the other given:
> I hold his dear, and mine he cannot miss;
> There never was a bargain better driven.
> His heart in me keeps me and him in one,
> My heart in him his thoughts and senses guides;
> He loves my heart for once it was his own;
> I cherish his because in me it bides.
> His heart his wound received from my sight;
> My heart was wounded with his wounded heart;
> For as from me on him his hurt did light,
> So still methought in me his hurt did smart:
> Both equal hurt, in this change sought our bliss,
> My true love hath my heart and I have his.

Edmund Spenser is the son of a London merchant. Educated at Cambridge, where he too translates Petrarch's sonnets, he meets and befriends Sidney in the household of the earl of Leicester. A friendship develops and Spenser dedicates his first book, *The Shepheardes Calender* (1579), to Sidney. Shortly afterward he travels to Ireland, where he pens his great work, *The Faerie Queene,* a series of courtly tales composed in a deliberately archaic style, celebrating Elizabeth and the Tudor dynasty. The first three books of this poem (he plans to write twenty-four) are published in 1590 and championed by Sir Walter Raleigh. Spenser travels to London to present them to the queen, hoping for a position at court; unfortunately Elizabeth does not oblige him. Disappointed, he returns to Ireland where he writes the next three books of *The Faerie Queene* and composes a sonnet sequence for his much-loved new bride, *Amoretti* (1594), followed by a poem that celebrates their marriage, *Epithalamion* (1595). Having attracted the hostility of the Irish, he is burned out of his home, Kilcolman Castle, by two thousand rebels in 1598 and forced to escape with his family by a secret underground passage. He returns to England and dies the following year at the age of forty-seven. This is Sonnet 75 from his *Amoretti*:

> One day I wrote her name upon the strand
> But came the waves and washed it away;
> Again I wrote it with a second hand
> But came the tide and made my pains his prey.
> Vain man, said she, that dost in vain assay
> A mortal thing so to immortalize,
> For I myself shall like to this decay
> And eke my name be wiped out likewise.
> Not so, quoth I, let baser things devise
> To die in dust, but you shall live by fame:
> My verse your virtues rare shall eternize
> And in the heavens write your glorious name
> Where when as death shall all the world subdue,
> Our love shall live, and later life renew.

By comparison with Sidney and Spenser, Shakespeare is of relatively humble background. Born in 1564, he does not attend a university but marries Anne Hathaway in 1582, when he is eighteen and she twenty-six. They have three children together before he is twenty-one, during which time he remains living at his father's house in Henley Street. But within six years he has moved to London, and begun writing and staging history plays. Despite early success as a playwright, his first published work is a poem, *Venus and Adonis,* which appears in 1593, when all the theaters are closed because of plague. You can pick up a copy from the stationers at St. Paul's for 1 shilling— as many people do, for it goes through reprint after reprint. The following year a second long poem, *The Rape of Lucrece,* is published. In 1595, when the theaters reopen, he appears on the payroll of the acting company known as the Lord Chamberlain's Men and thereafter devotes himself entirely to the stage. But quietly he is writing brilliant sonnets, building up a body of 154 poems, which is finally published in 1609. You will undoubtedly be familiar with many of these, such as "Shall I compare thee to a summer's day?" (Sonnet 18) and "Let me not to the marriage of true minds / admit impediment . . ." (Sonnet 116). But perhaps you are less familiar with Sonnet 78, one of the more obviously personal poems, in which he refers to his comparative lack of "learning" (i.e. his lack of a university education):

> So oft have I invoked thee for my Muse,
> And found such fair assistance in my verse
> As every alien pen hath got my use
> And under thee their poesy disperse.
> Thine eyes, that taught the dumb on high to sing
> And heavy ignorance aloft to fly,
> Have added feathers to the learned's wing
> And given grace a double majesty.
> Yet be most proud of that which I compile,
> Whose influence is thine, and born of thee:
> In others' works thou dost but mend the style,
> And arts with thy sweet graces graced be;
> But thou art all my art, and dost advance
> As high as learning, my rude ignorance.

The seven lesser poets on John Taylor's list have a collective wealth of ability, although not necessarily as much application as Sidney, Spenser, and Shakespeare. Sir Edward Dyer is a courtier who can turn an exquisite phrase and would be far more famous if only he put his pen to paper more often. He is well known as the author of the famous poem "My mind to me a kingdom is" and the even more touching "The lowest trees have tops." Robert Greene is a libertine, drunkard, and philanderer who writes extensively—poems and plays alike—but he is a jealous and conceited man who sees Shakespeare as a rival. Before things come to a head, Greene kills himself with red wine and pickled herring in 1592, at the age of thirty-four. Thomas Nashe, a clergyman's son from Suffolk, also manages to incur Greene's wrath but survives him to write a number of plays, satires, and poems as well as a notorious work of erotica, *The Choice of Valentines;* he too dies at the age of thirty-four. Samuel Daniel is of more sober stock: the son of a music master, he writes plays, masques, and poetry, including a series of sonnets to "Delia" (for which he is best known), the romance "The Complaint of Rosamond," and a history of medieval England in verse before he expires, aged fifty-six. Francis Beaumont is best known for collaborating on plays with John Fletcher but is also a friend of Ben Jonson and frequents the Mermaid Tavern in Cheapside. Sir John Harington has already been mentioned as a great wit, the inventor of the water closet and one of the queen's 102 godchildren. He is an epigrammatist of the first order but too risqué for his own good. Having incurred displeasure by translating some of Ariosto's *Orlando Furioso* in a very racy style, he is requested by his godmother to leave court and not return until he has translated the entire work in a more appropriate manner. This he does—to great acclaim. Apart from Shakespeare, Joshua Sylvester is the only sixteenth-century poet on Taylor's list who does not have a university education and the only one whose output is limited to translations (from the French), but he too is a highly accomplished wordsmith whose fame lasts for decades.

We should remember, however, that Taylor's poem only accounts for those poets who have died by 1620. In addition you have the poetry of Renaissance men like Thomas Campion, the physician and composer who dies in 1620, and Sir Walter Raleigh, the explorer, courtier, and historian who is executed in 1618. Then there are those poets who, like Shakespeare, also write plays, such as Ben Jonson and a young John Webster, but are only at the start of their careers; dedicated versifiers like the prodigious Michael Drayton, best known for *Poly-Olbion* and his historical poems "Agincourt" and *Mortimeriados;* and George Chapman, whose translations of Homer win the hearts of many readers. Although the young John Donne publishes nothing in Elizabeth's reign, his early amorous compositions date from this time. You also have the earliest female poets, including Emilia Lanier (whom we met in Chapter Two) and Sir Philip Sidney's remarkable sister, Mary, countess of Pembroke. Mary rewrites her brother's *Arcadia* for publication and presides over a worship of writers at Wilton House.

The Theater

In the modern world we have great admiration for Elizabethan theater. At the time, however, it is in the throes of a radical revolution. At the start of the reign the majority of productions are miracle plays—reconstructions of scenes from the Bible, performed as both civic and religious rituals. These go out of favor when the privy council decrees that they are too close to Catholicism and should stop. Those at York cease in 1569. In Chester the citizens defy the privy council and continue performing their play about Noah's Flood well into the 1570s. The Coventry mystery plays are finally suppressed in 1579, so this is the town to visit if you want to catch one later in the reign. The Guary miracle play in Cornwall continues for some years but is so amateurish it can hardly be seen as a threat. During its performances, a prompter goes to each actor in turn and whispers his speech to him, line by line.[54]

In their stead, people increasingly choose to see secular plays on historical and moral themes. These are performed up and down the country by theater companies called after lords, for example "Lord Sussex's Men," "Lord Strange's Men," "the Lord Admiral's Men," and "Lord Leicester's Men." The reason for these names is that, while unattached actors are liable to be arrested for vagrancy, the Act of 1572 specifically excludes players properly authorized by lords from being considered vagabonds. Note that the actors are all men: women do not perform on the stage in Elizabeth's reign. If there are any female parts, these are played by boys dressed as women. In London, performances take place in the afternoons in the yards of galleried inns, such as the Boar's Head Inn in Whitechapel High Street, the Bell Inn and the Cross Keys Inn (both on Gracechurch Street), the Belle Savage Inn (Ludgate Hill), and the Bull Inn (Bishopsgate Street). When on tour the theater companies are quite small, sometimes comprising just six or seven actors, each taking on a number of roles. They perform for the fee-paying public in provincial inns or privately in the houses of gentlemen. However, as the new theater proves more and more popular, actors, writers, and audiences become increasingly centered on the London playhouses.

The Elizabethan theater as we know it develops slowly. In 1562 the play *Gorboduc,* the first English play to include blank verse, is performed in front of the queen at the Inner Temple in London. This is written by two gentlemen, Thomas Sackville (the future earl of Dorset) and Thomas Norton, and leaves a lasting impression. Its tale of a kingdom torn between two heirs has great significance for the audience of the day. Other plays follow, drawing on classical themes as well as on ancient British and medieval history, written by (among others) John Heywood, John Pickering, and Lewis Wager. A sign of their success is the construction in 1567 of the first purpose-built theater, the Red Lion, built by John Brayne in Whitechapel. Unfortunately this is located too far from the city and it does not attract large audiences. Performances in the city inns, however, are flourishing—much to the annoyance of those who see them as uncouth and riotous establishments. In 1574 the city authorities are given powers to restrict playhouses, forcing the actors to find new premises in the suburbs. This becomes a golden opportunity for John Brayne and his brother-in-law, James Burbage, who in 1576 build a new theater, simply called The Theatre, at Shoreditch, just half a mile north of Bishopsgate. The following year a second theater, the Curtain, is built just two hundred yards away. Despite some heavy opposition from Puritan preachers and moralists, both theaters are successful.[55] New plays are written every year, courtesy of the new wave of playwrights: John Lyly, Thomas Preston, and Thomas Hughes. The queen continues to encourage dramatic art, personally attending performances at Gray's Inn, Greenwich Palace, and Whitehall Palace. In 1583 she establishes her own theater company, the Queen's Men, and leading actors flock to it. Puritans are enraged, and the following year the city authorities try to outlaw plays altogether, both within and outside the city walls. But now that drama has received royal approval, they don't stand a chance.[56]

In 1587 Thomas Kyd produces *The Spanish Tragedy,* and soon afterward Christopher Marlowe brings out the first part of *Tamburlaine the Great.* Kyd is the son of a London scrivener, born in 1558; Marlowe the son of a shoemaker from Canterbury, born in 1564 (the same year as Shakespeare), whose intellectual brilliance earns him a university education at Cambridge. They employ new verse forms, allowing different spoken rhythms, and compose bold speeches with greater resonance and meaning. The new conceptual framework of a revenge tragedy in particular allows them to portray powerful emotions voiced by strong characters. Suddenly it is possible to show so much more passion on the stage. The old narrative objectivity of the history play is replaced with a much more involved subjective experience, which excites and astounds audiences in equal measure. More theaters open their doors to the public. The Rose is built by Philip Henslowe at Southwark, not far from the bear-baiting and bull-baiting arenas, in 1587. Eight years later Francis Langley erects the Swan on a site nearby; and in 1596 Richard Burbage builds the Blackfriars Theatre, an indoor venue, although it does not open its doors until 1599. Most important of all, Shakespeare, Richard and Cuthbert Burbage, and their partners dismantle The Theatre and remove its beams to a new site at Southwark, where it is rebuilt in 1599 as the Globe. When Edward Alleyn builds the Fortune on the northern edge of the city in 1600, the array of Elizabethan theaters is complete.

Including the inn yards and the various other places where plays are still staged, London now has a dozen playhouses.

This exciting and rapidly expanding cultural melting pot—developing in parallel with the music and poetry of the 1590s—is the environment in which all the new plays are written. Over the last fifteen years of the reign, Shakespeare completes no fewer than twenty-five plays, including *Romeo and Juliet, A Midsummer Night's Dream,* the great historical cycle of *Richard II, Henry IV* (Parts 1 and 2), and *Henry V, The Merchant of Venice, As You Like It,* and *Hamlet.* Marlowe composes the second part of *Tamburlaine* and adds *The Jew of Malta, Doctor Faustus, Edward II,* and *The Massacre at Paris* to his oeuvre. George Peele writes all his plays (most notably *Edward I*), Robert Greene composes all his (including the comedy *Friar Bacon and Friar Bungay*), and John Marston completes his first five works. Thomas Nashe brings forth his masterpiece *Summers Last Will and Testament.* Thomas Dekker writes (or cowrites) his first twenty plays, some in conjunction with Michael Drayton, Henry Chettle, John Marston, and Robert Wilson. And Ben Jonson starts his headlong charge into English literature.

Alongside Marlowe and Shakespeare, Jonson is the third great dramatist of the age. Like Shakespeare, he does not go to university but, after schooling at Westminster, becomes a bricklayer and then a soldier. By the end of the reign he has married, had two children and lost one, tried to become an actor and failed, become a playwright, been arrested for a scurrilous play and released, killed another actor in a duel, been arrested again and put on trial for murder, and escaped hanging by pleading benefit of the clergy. The play for which he is arrested, *The Isle of Dogs,* coauthored with Thomas Nashe, is so slanderous and offensive that the privy council orders the closure not just of the play but of every theater in London. The following year, after most of the theaters open again, he has a blockbuster success with *Every Man in His Humour.* This he follows up with a sequel, *Every Man Out of His Humour,* and three more plays: *Cynthia's Revels, The Poetaster,* and *Sejanus: His Fall.* As with so many Elizabethan playwrights, he is prolific: by the age of twenty-nine, Jonson has completed at least six plays, comparable with Marlowe (at least six) and Shakespeare (at least seven).

With so many playwrights at work there are plenty of plays to choose from. Each theater shows twenty or thirty plays a year, changing the program every day. In 1594–95 the Lord Admiral's Men perform a total of thirty-eight plays, twenty-one of which are newly written. One in three adult Londoners sees a play every month.[57] It all adds up to a maelstrom of creative energy, theatrical delivery, and personal rivalry. But if you travel around England you will notice how all this is increasingly centered on London. Whereas in the 1550s and 1560s several companies tour the country, by 1590 the principal actors stay in the city. The burgeoning population of London provides them with large audiences, especially when they become established at their respective theaters: the Lord Admiral's Men at the Rose and the Lord Chamberlain's Men at the Globe. Only when the theaters are closed by the authorities because of the plague—in 1581–82, 1592–93, and 1603–4—do the London companies start to tour again, from Bath to Nottingham. Ironically, one place they do not play is Stratford-upon-Avon. Although many players visit Stratford in Shakespeare's youth, the town's corporation prohibits traveling actors from performing there in 1602.[58]

How do you decide which theater to go to? As with a modern production, you will be attracted to watch the best and most celebrated performers. Many Londoners flock to see the clowns. Richard Tarlton, who plays with the Queen's Men at the Curtain, is a crowd-puller; he can reduce the audience to tears simply by putting his head out between the curtains and pulling faces. Will Kempe, who performs first with the Lord Leicester's Men, becomes the clown with the Lord Chamberlain's Men and takes on roles such as Dogberry and Falstaff in Shakespeare's plays. Some gentlemen and ladies who regard the theater as brutish—and it has to be emphasized that many do see playhouses as lawless places infested with rogues, thieves, and prostitutes—will only go to see performances by the companies of boys drawn from the choristers of Chapel Royal and St. Paul's Cathedral. These companies are socially more elevated and their venues roofed over (so there is no danger of the audience getting wet). Nor are their plays inferior: Ben Jonson writes for them regularly. However, it is to the actors of the two main companies that you will be drawn. The Lord Chamberlain's Men have Richard Burbage, who takes the lead in many of Shakespeare's plays. The Lord Admiral's Men have Edward Alleyn: a very tall and powerful man who roars his part as he crosses the stage. With such actors in place, a playwright can compose the part to suit the actor's strengths. If you really want to see an all-star cast, go to the Curtain in 1598 to see the production of Ben Jonson's *Every Man in His Humour*. William Shakespeare is playing Kno'well, supported by the other leading men of the Lord Chamberlain's

Company, among them Richard Burbage, Augustine Phillips, John Heminges, Henry Condell, and Will Kempe.

Let's say you want to go to one of the theaters for an afternoon performance. If you are heading to the Swan, the Rose, or the Globe you will cross London Bridge or take a wherry across the river and then walk through Paris Garden. All sorts of people will be heading in the same direction: working men in groups, shop owners, gentlemen, householders' wives accompanied by their servants or husbands, foreign tourists, boys and girls. As you approach the theaters you will notice that they all seem to be round; in fact, they are polygonal—the Globe is twenty-sided, the Rose fourteen-sided. Whichever one you choose, you can expect to queue with two thousand other people to get in. You will see people standing in hats with pipes in hand, and women in their headdresses, all chatting, with an eye open for people they know. Entrance costs a penny: this allows you to stand in the yard in front of the stage, an uncovered area (hence the need for a hat). Around the yard are three galleries where you can stand or sit under cover. It costs an extra penny to stand here and another penny again for a place upstairs. If you are feeling very flash, you might hire a box for 6 pence. This gives you the best chance of seeing the stage and being seen by the crowd.

When the trumpets sound, most people quieten down, waiting for the play to begin. If you are sitting in the gallery you will have a clear view of the stage as it projects out from the far side of the round enclosure. Leading actors will come right out along this platform and deliver their soliloquies directly to the crowd. So too will a clown like Will Kempe, when he wishes to extemporize and make "a scurvy face." There are two large columns, both elaborately painted, which support the roof that covers the back of the stage. Behind them is the "tiring house," where the actors robe (or "attire") themselves. Above the tiring house is a gallery—useful for scenes such as the balcony scene in *Romeo and Juliet* but sometimes let out for those spectators who want to be seen. Note how few props are used: although *A Midsummer Night's Dream* cannot be performed without an ass's head, and *Titus Andronicus* requires a large pie, most of Shakespeare's plays are performed without props. The costumes, however, are splendid; many lords and merchants leave their best gowns to their servants who, being prohibited from wearing them by the sumptuary laws, sell them to the theatrical companies. As a result, the players are normally better dressed than the audience. There is a low murmur of voices throughout the play as women shoulder their way through the crowd, selling apples, nuts, and bottles of beer. People are constantly on the watch for cutpurses and pickpockets, and the chance encounter that might lead to an illicit liaison. Unlike your modern theater experience, you will find many people chatting away during the performance. Some speeches, however, do command universal attention and silence. At other points the report of a cannon or the sound of rolling thunder from above will make you jump. The latter effect is made by rolling cannonballs around the gallery roof.

As you sit there watching a performance of a Shakespeare, Jonson, or Marlowe play, the crowd will fade into the background. Instead you will be struck by the diction. There are words and phrases that you will not find funny but which will make the crowd roar with laughter. Your familiarity with the meanings of Shakespeare's words will rise and fall as you see and hear the actors' deliveries and notice the audience's reaction. That is the strange music of being so familiar with something that is not of your own time. What you are listening to in that auditorium is the genuine voice, something of which you have heard only distant echoes. Not every actor is perfect in his delivery—Shakespeare himself makes that quite clear in his *Hamlet*—but what you are hearing is the voice of the men for whom Shakespeare wrote his greatest speeches. Modern thespians will follow the rhythms or the meanings of these words but even the most brilliant will not always be able to follow both rhythm and meaning at once. If they follow the pattern of the verse they risk confusing the audience, who are less familiar with the sense of the words; if they pause to emphasize meanings, they lose the rhythm of the verse. Here, on the Elizabethan stage, you have a harmony of performance and understanding that will never quite be matched again in respect of any of these great writers.

It has been a long time in development but Elizabeth's reign sees the advent of a dramatic culture which has meaning for us in the modern world. Unlike their predecessors, the late Elizabethan playwrights are keen to explore the human condition. At the same time they have an awareness of the changing world that sets them wholly apart from the Middle Ages. Marlowe, Shakespeare, and Jonson know full well how novel their art is. Not for them the timeworn traditions of miracle plays, or the humility of writing only to please the wealthy. A great cultural wave is breaking here, on the Bankside shore of a Brave New World, sending up the spume of Marlowe's vitriolic atheism and Shakespeare's poetic and philosophical meditations amid the spray of madrigals and airs, scientific and geographic discoveries, a sense of history and Renaissance ideas. At a time of great discoveries, these wordsmiths are the spokesmen for the mass of newly educated townsmen who have never really known before what it is to have a voice. And Shakespeare above all others meets the challenge of the age by holding up a mirror to Mankind and showing people what they really are—and not what they think they are in the eyes of God. This is something truly original, and one of the reasons the rabble in the theater yard does fall quiet, and strains to hear the words of the great soliloquies and speeches; and, in so doing, becomes a little more like us.

Envoi

In Peter Erondell's dialogue book, *The French Garden*, a young girl listens to a caged bird singing. "I wish to God I had one of them," she exclaims. Her teacher replies: "What, Mistress, would you be so cruel as to deprive him of his liberty? O dear liberty! God grant me always the keys of the fields: I would like it better than to be in bondage in the fairest wainscoted or tapestried chamber."[1] It is a strikingly sympathetic and modern outlook—so different from the attitudes of the keepers of the cockpit birds, bloodied for a bet, and the bears licking their paws in cages in Southwark. The complete contrast suggests that society is at odds with itself, riddled with inconsistencies, full of both cruelty and sympathy. But as you struggle to make sense of it you realize that, not only can you not reconcile such contrasts, you do not need to try. It is by appreciating the contradictions and inconsistencies that exist within a society that you start to understand it.

Understanding a past society is not easy, however: your familiarity with it comes and goes like a tide. You may recognize the greetings, shouts, and insults of people in the street. You may understand the feelings, the smiles, and the tears. You may enjoy the laughter and music in the tavern, or see a sad death by candlelight, and feel so much a part of this old country. But then comes word of a Catholic priest who has been found hiding, who is to be pilloried and hanged, and you hear the anger in people's voices and see the hatred in their faces by light of burning torches. Or you see a boy in rags on the side of the road, his eyes drifting, starving, half blind. Here is a broken door hanging from a single hinge: inside a dozen people are living in a filthy room and the smell of ordure as you enter makes you retch. The tide of familiarity has receded. Sometimes the past will inspire you and sometimes it will leave you weeping.

For these reasons it would be foolish to describe Elizabeth's reign as "a golden age" and leave it at that. It certainly is "a golden age" in many respects—in poetry, drama, architecture, aristocratic fashion, and seafaring, to name just a few—but it is equally a "golden age" (if that term can be used) of religious hatred, political scare-mongering, superstition, racism, sexism, and class prejudice. There are dark shades as well as light here. Nor are these negatives merely modern perceptions: individuals truly suffer because of them. Modern readers, cushioned by the widespread acceptance of many forms of equality, might well balk at the hardships and inequalities of sixteenth-century life; but we should not close our eyes to them. Nor should we take our privileges for granted. Those who believe women and men naturally have equal "rights" will look back on the sixteenth century with horror. Everyone who has benefited from the more evenly distributed opportunities we enjoy in the modern world will realize how difficult it is to survive and thrive when those same chances are denied to the vast majority of people.

And yet our ancestors do survive and thrive. We are the descendants of the survivors. Elizabethans are not some distant, alien race but our families—they are *us*, in a manner of speaking—and they show us what human beings are capable of enduring. They cope with plague, low life expectancy, child mortality, endemic violence, superstition, harsh winters, and the taut rope of the law: humanity is remarkably resilient. More than that, our ancestors overcome their adversities to build, collect, and create. There might be a gnawing hunger in their bellies but they circumnavigate the world and sail to the Arctic, they laugh and sing, they cut topiary gardens and design banquets of sugar. They look to the stars and chart a new course that the Earth follows round the sun. They are afraid and, at the same time, they are excited and in love.

What is striking is that so many of the changes in society are made by individuals. In today's world even politicians elected by a landslide majority find it difficult to change a nation significantly. The leader's hand is the one on the tiller but it is not possible for him radically to change course. Civil servants stop him. The democratic process restrains him, and his political party never takes its hand off his shoulder. But in the sixteenth century some individuals *do* change the course of society. We think immediately of the queen. The shift to Protestantism is Elizabeth's doing, and the form of the new English religion is even more her personal design. She not only turns the tiller, she holds it firmly and never lets go, and shrugs off every hand placed on her shoulder. Elizabeth also deserves the credit for making herself splendidly visible to her people, even after the pope excommunicates her and puts her life at risk. It would be easy for her simply to hide away and keep herself safely; but then we would not have Gloriana, the regal symbol of English sovereign independence and national pride. She is loved by her people—not all of them, certainly, but by the majority—who have confidence in her as a God-chosen ruler. She decides not to marry, and while it is the correct political decision, she makes a huge personal sacrifice: much of her later life is tinged with loneliness and sadness. So many responsibilities lie on her shoulders that one cannot see her alone in her palace, putting on her wig, without hearing a whisper from Shakespeare's *Henry V:* "What infinite heart's ease must kings neglect that private men enjoy. And what have kings that privates have not too save ceremony, save general ceremony?"

Other, less eminent individuals also have a great impact on people's lives. You can hardly avoid the figure of Sir William Cecil, Lord Burghley, who carefully guides the queen's government and yet finds time to promote so many aspects of culture: art, architecture, gardening, mathematics, and astronomy. Then there are the heroes and pioneers—Grenville, Cavendish, and above all, Drake. And there are pioneers of another sort: Emilia Lanier for her railing against the misogynistic assumptions of society, John Leland for igniting the fires of historical inquiry, and Dr. John Dee for a mind open to the possibilities of both the past and the future. You have to admire those who rise above the hardships and fears of the time and set out to understand the universe, or search for new lands in spite of the huge risks. You have to take your hat off to those who apply themselves to the task of improving society, creating the Poor Law that saves hundreds of thousands of lives over the next centuries.

Then you have that singular genius who speaks with such authority about every condition of life: rich and poor, young and old, those in love and those in mourning. Shakespeare has given voice to so many of our feelings. Probably no other Englishman has been more influential. His influence is not militaristic or nationalistic, nor is it the discovery of a scientific phenomenon; it is simply that his writings are the biggest step ever taken along the path toward understanding the human condition. It is a path we are still following. Through his plays we can see that our ancestors are not inferior to us; they do not lack sophistication, subtlety, innovation, wit, or courage. In Shakespeare we can see that the Elizabethan creative intellect is equal to our own. His drive in attaining such heights becomes understandable when one sees what prejudices he has to overcome, as the son of a provincial glover. Through force of will and wit Shakespeare makes his way in society; he pays scant regard to the prejudices of nobles and gentlemen, always wanting to become one of them and yet always understanding what it is *not* to be one of them—not university-educated, never being able to take advantage of family connections. But at the end his social transformation is almost as complete as that of Francis Drake, and his kicking against contemporary prejudices every bit as revolutionary as that of Emilia Lanier. Again, we are reminded that it is through contrasts and contradictions that one becomes familiar with a society. In this case, it is by appreciating the exceptions to the norms, the hierarchies and prejudices, that one starts to understand Elizabethan England.

History is not really about the past; it is about understanding mankind over time. Within that simple, linear story of change and survival there are a thousand contrasts, and within each of those contrasts there is a range of experiences, and if we put our minds to it, we can relate to each one. Such a multidimensional picture of the human race is a far more profound one than an understanding based on a reading of today's newspapers: the image of mankind in the mirror of the moment is a relatively superficial one. Indeed, it is only through history that we can see ourselves as we really are. It is not enough to study the past for its own sake, to work out the facts; it is necessary to see the past in relation to ourselves. Otherwise studying the past is merely an academic exercise. Don't get me wrong: such exercises are important—without them we would be lost in a haze of uncertainty, vulnerable to the vagaries of well-meaning amateurs and prejudicial readings of historical evidence—but sorting out the facts is just a first step toward understanding humanity over time. If we wish to follow the old Delphic command, "Mankind, know thyself," then we need to look at ourselves over the course of history.

One last thought. It is often said of Shakespeare that he is "not of an age but for all time"—a line originally penned by Ben Jonson. But Shakespeare *is* of an age—Elizabethan England. It makes him. It gives him a stage, a language, and an audience. If Shakespeare is "for all time," then so too is Elizabethan England.

NOTES

ABBREVIATIONS USED IN NOTES

Airs, *TJCH*: Airs, *The Tudor and Jacobean Country House*

Beer, *TEO*: Beer, *Tudor England Observed*

BL: British Library

Black, *Reign*: Black, *The Reign of Elizabeth*

BRO: Berkshire Record Office, Reading, UK

CAHEW: Bowden, *Chapters from the Agrarian History of England and Wales*

Carew, *Survey*: Chynoweth et al., *The Survey of Cornwall by Richard Carew*

CKS: Centre for Kentish Studies, Maidstone, UK

Cressy, *BMD*: Cressy, *Birth, Marriage and Death*

Crisis: Clark and Slack, *Crisis and Order in English Towns*

CSPV: Brown and Bentinck, *Calendar State Papers Relating to English Affairs in the Archives on Venice*

CUH: Clark, *The Cambridge Urban History of Britain*

Dawson, *Jewel* (1587): Thomas Dawson, *The Good Huswife's Jewell* (1587)

Dawson, *Jewel*: Thomas Dawson (intro. Maggie Black), *The Good Housewife's Jewel* (1996)

DEEH: Fisher and Jurica, *Documents in English Economic History*

EHR: *The English Historical Review*

Emmison, *HWL*: Emmison, *Elizabethan Life: Home, Work and Land*

Girouard, *LECH*: Girourard, *Life in the English Country House*

Laslett, *WWHL*: Laslett, *The World We Have Lost*

Leland, *Itinerary*: Smith, *The Itinerary of John Leland*

Machyn, *Diary*: Nichols, *The Diary of Henry Machyn*

Magno: Barron et al., "The London Journal of Alessandro Magno"

Material London: Orlin, *Material London*

Morbus Gallicus: Clowes, *A Brief and Necessary Treatise touching the Cure of the Disease called Morbus Gallicus*

Mortimer, *D&D*: Mortimer, *The Dying and the Doctors*

Mortimer, *TTGME*: Mortimer, *The Time Traveler's Guide to Medieval England*

ODNB: *The Oxford Dictionary of National Biography*

OED: *The Oxford English Dictionary*

Pelling, *CL*: Pelling, *The Common Lot*

Platter, *Travels*: Williams, *Thomas Platter's Travels in England*

Port & Trade: Dietz, *The Port and Trade of Early Elizabethan London*

Scott, *EOaW*: Scott, *Every One a Witness*

Sh. Eng.: *Shakespeare's England*

Thomas, *RDM*: Thomas, *Religion and the Decline of Magic*

Treasurie: Anonymous, *The Good Hous-wife's Treasurie*

TRHS: *Transactions of the Royal Historical Society*

True bill (1603): Anonymous, *A true bill*
Wellcome Trust: Wellcome Trust Library and Archives, London

INTRODUCTION

1. The story of William Hacket is to be found in Richard Cosin, *A conspiracie for pretended reformation* (1592). I came to this piece after reading Alexandra Walsham's article on the events of July 16, 1591. See Walsham, "Hacket."
2. *Eliz. People*, p. 45, quoting Conyers Read, *Mr. Secretary Cecil and Queen Elizabeth* (1955), p. 124.
3. With reference to "the most powerful Englishwoman in history," Elizabeth personally ruled over England and had huge influence over the entire anti-Catholic community of Europe. This personal rule, not subject to the pope, is the reason for saying she was the most powerful woman in British history. While Anne, Victoria, and Elizabeth II all ruled over greater dominions, they were supported and controlled by a constitution that allowed them very little direct power. The power lay rather with the constitution that supported the monarchy, not in their own control of it. As for Margaret Thatcher, no elected secular politician can possibly have the authority of a hereditary and divinely appointed monarch, who can redirect the faith of the kingdom. A modern political leader simply has bigger bombs and better surveillance at her disposal.

CHAPTER ONE: The Landscape

1. These figures are based on an area of 50,337 square miles for England and the population estimate of 2,984,576 for 1561 in Wrigley & Schofield, p. 528. The modern population figure is the 2008 estimate by the Office for National Statistics of 51,460,000.
2. The regular layout of Stratford's center still reflects its charter of 1196, which stipulated that all the tenements or burgage plots should be a standard 3½ by 12 perches (57¾ by 198 feet). See Bearman, *Stratford*, p. 37.
3. Jones, *Family*, pp. 22–23.
4. Platt, *Rebuildings*, p. 20, quoting Harrison's *Description*.
5. Dyer, "Crisis," p. 90.
6. Wilson, "State," p. 11. For modern research into the number of market towns, see the "Gazetteer of Markets and Fairs in England and Wales to 1516: Full Introduction," table 2, maintained by the Centre for Metropolitan History, available online freely at http://www.history.ac.uk/cmh/gaz/gazweb2.html. This states that 675 of the 2,022 markets granted or functioning prior to 1516 were still active in 1600—one less than Wilson.
7. Vanessa Harding has suggested that the population, which most historians agree reached 55,000 in 1524 and 200,000 in 1600, could have reached 75,000 by 1550. See Harding, "London," p. 112.
8. Sacks, "Ports," p. 384, using table 7.1 in E. A. Wrigley, "Urban Growth and Agricultural Change: England and the Continent in the Early Modern Period," *Journal of Interdisciplinary History* 15 (1985).
9. England's coastline (not including any of its numerous islands) is about 5,581 miles, and Wales's, including Anglesey and Holyhead, is 1,680 miles, a combined total of 7,261 miles. The total coastline of the kingdom of Denmark and Norway is in the region of 20,000 miles. Greece and Italy, which both have long coastlines, were not political states in their own right in the sixteenth century, Greece being part of the

Ottoman Empire, and Italy then being a series of smaller states. Spain's coastline is about 3,100 miles, as is that of Iceland; France's is about 2,140 miles.

10. In addition to the 336,000 in the table, my own rough estimates are as follows. The next sixty largest towns (with 2,500–6,000 people in 1600, and an average of about 3,000) represent another 180,000 citizens. The next hundred towns (of 2,000–2,500, average 2,200) are home to another 220,000. About two hundred towns have populations between 1,000 and 2,000 (300,000); and the approximately three hundred remaining towns, with 500–1,000 inhabitants (average 700), represent about 210,000 more. This total means that 1.2 million people, out of a population of 4.11 million, were living in towns (29 percent). Checking this against the *Cambridge Urban History* figures, which are most detailed for the 1660s onward, even the rural southwest had achieved an overall proportion of 26 percent by 1660 (see Jonathan Barry, "South-West," in *CUH*, p. 68). A proportion of one in four is reasonable for 1600. For the medieval figures, see Mortimer, *TTGME*, p. 11 and note 3 on pp. 293–94. Note that the rise in urban populations was not a constant. In the early sixteenth century there was a significant downturn in the prosperity and size of the major towns.

11. Villenage still survived as a description of status in 1 percent of the population. See Black, *Reign*, p. 251. A rare example of it having legal force is published in *DEEH*, p. 126.

12. Wilson, "State," p. 11.

13. Hoskins, *Landscape*, p. 139.

14. For the role of towns in supplying their hinterlands, see Mortimer, "Marketplace."

15. *Tudor Tailor*, p. 9, quoting B. Fagan, *The Little Ice Age* (New York, 2000).

16. Dyer, "Crisis," p. 89.

17. M. A. Havinden, "Agricultural Progress in Open-Field Oxfordshire," *Agricultural History Review* 11 (1961), pp. 73–83, at p. 73; Mortimer, *Glebe*, pp. ix, xxviii; Ross Wordie, ed., *Enclosure in Berkshire 1485–1885*, Berkshire Record Society 5 (2000), p. xvii.

18. These figures are adapted from those of Gregory King, computed at the end of the seventeenth century, given in Thirsk, *Documents*, p. 779. Hoskins, *Landscape*, p. 139, calculated that the woodland in the early sixteenth century must have been a million acres greater than in King's day (a total of four million acres). The million acres of lost woodland were probably mostly put to pasture and parkland by 1695, so this area has been deducted from those totals. The amount of arable was probably within five hundred thousand acres of King's estimate, as that which had been turned into parkland by 1695 is very unlikely to have all been taken from arable. Besides, many enclosures of arable fields would have resulted in consolidated arable holdings, not just pasture, and thus be included as arable by King. The figure for Berkshire waste is from Hoskins, *Landscape*, p. 141.

19. Black, *Reign*, p. 237. The other major exports included in that 18.4 percent were lead, tin, corn, beer, coal, and fish.

20. This is the number estimated for the sheep population of England in 1500 (Hoskins, *Landscape*, p. 137).

21. Rowse, *Structure*, p. 97; Dawson, *Plenti & Grase*, p. 85. Thomas Platter notes that the heaviest sheep he sees on his journey weigh forty to sixty pounds (see Platter, *Travels*, p. 185).

22. Hoskins, *Landscape*, p. 138.

23. Damian Goodburn, "Woodworking Aspects of the Mary Rose," in Marsden, *Noblest Shippe,* p. 68.

24. For the acts, see 1 Elizabeth cap. 15; 23 Elizabeth cap. 5; 27 Elizabeth cap. 19. For prices, see Overton, "Prices," especially tables 6.1 (cupboards), 6.5 (bedsteads and coffers), 6.8 and 6.9 (coffers), and 6.11 (all wood).

25. Williams, *Life,* p. 40 (Warwickshire); Hoskins, *Landscape,* p. 154 (Leicestershire).

26. See Magno, especially p. 147.

27. Emmison, *HWL,* pp. 290–93.

28. Pound, *Census,* p. 10.

29. Platter, *Travels,* p. 153.

30. Machyn, *Diary,* p. 259.

31. For the prohibition of houses within three miles, see 35 Elizabeth I cap. 6. For the spread of housing: *DEEH,* p. 46.

32. Simon Thurley, "The Lost Palace of Whitehall," *History Today,* 48, 1 (January 1998).

33. Platter, *Travels,* pp. 153–54.

34. In the order they appear in Stow, *Survay,* these are: (1) Portsoken, (2) Tower Street, (3) Aldgate, (4) Lime Street, (5) Bishopsgate, (6) Broad Street, (7) Cornhill, (8) Langbourn, (9) Billingsgate, (10) Bridge Within, (11) Candlewick Street, (12) Walbrook, (13) Dowgate, (14) Vintry, (15) Cordwainer Street, (16) Cheap, (17) Coleman Street, (18) Basinghall, (19) Cripplegate, (20) Aldersgate, (21) Farringdon Within, (22) Bread Street, (23) Queenhithe, (24) Castle Baynard, (25) Farringdon Without, and (26) Bridge Without (including Southwark).

35. Schofield, "Topography," p. 300.

36. Magno, p. 142.

37. Machyn, *Diary,* p. 263.

38. 24 Henry VIII cap. 11 (Strand); 25 Henry VIII cap. 8 (Holborn High Street).

39. All the cries mentioned here are from plates 26 and 27 reproduced in Picard, *London.*

40. Nicoll, *Elizabethans,* p. 49, quoting W. Burton, "The Rowsing of the Sluggard."

41. Orlin, "Disputes," p. 347. Houses of six stories are visible in several early seventeenth-century woodcuts and engravings of the city and specified in Ralph Tresswell's surveys.

42. For sales of fish in Old St. Paul's, see Holmes, *London,* p. 41.

43. As often noted, the stories of the drinking club at the Mermaid attended by Shakespeare, Ben Jonson, John Donne, etc., are somewhat romantic. However, the landlord, William Johnson, was a friend and business partner of Shakespeare's, for they both took part in what proved to be Shakespeare's last property investment in 1613. See Schoenbaum, *Shakespeare,* p. 208.

CHAPTER TWO: **The People**

1. According to Wrigley & Schofield, p. 528, the greatest compound annual growth rate for the sixteenth century was 1.13 in 1581–86. This was not equaled until 1786–90, when it reached 1.20. By then the population was well in excess of seven million.

2. William Lambarde's charge at the commission for almshouses, etc., at Maidstone, January 17, 1594, in Conyers Read, ed., *William Lambarde and Local Government,* p. 182 (quoted in *Eliz. People,* p. 47).

3. Carew, *Survey,* f. 37v.

4. Wrigley & Schofield, pp. 229, 383, 399–400, 425, 477; Laslett, *WWHL,* p. 15. This model omits the factor of migration to the towns and the increase in real wages

caused by the increased manufacturing that accompanies increased urbanization, which is another reason for the rise in wage rates and the independence of men who otherwise would have been in service of some sort or other. See Wrigley & Schofield, especially p. 477.

5. Herbert Moller, "The Accelerated Development of Youth: Beard Growth as a Biological Marker," *Comparative Studies in Society and History* 29, 4 (October 1987), pp. 748–62.

6. Quoted in Picard, *London*, p. 174.

7. Harrison, "Description," quoted in Picard, *London*, p. 181.

8. Dyer, "Crisis," p. 92.

9. Wrigley & Schofield, p. 249. Half of those who died before the age of one died in the first month of life (see Wrigley & Schofield, p. 363). Child mortality grows even worse in the seventeenth and eighteenth centuries.

10. Pelling, "Old Age," p. 78.

11. Wrigley & Schofield, p. 250.

12. See G. E. Cokayne, revised by V. Gibbs, H. A. Doubleday, D. Warrand, Lord Howard de Walden, and Peter Hammond, eds., *The Complete Peerage of England, Scotland, Ireland, Great Britain and the United Kingdom Extant, Extinct or Dormant* (14 vols., 1910–98), iv, p. 250. Her husband was born in 1454 but his first wife was still living in 1505, so she did not marry him until after that date. He died aged eighty in 1534; if she married him when he was sixty, and if she was then in her early twenties (as most brides were), she was born about 1490, and so could have been a centenarian.

13. Pelling, *CL*, p. 74.

14. Carew, *Survey*, f. 63r.

15. See Harrison, *Description*, chapter one; Wilson, "State," p. 17.

16. Platter, *Travels*, p. 228.

17. Black, *Reign*, pp. 47–48 (Cecil); 223–24 (Parliament). For her dressing-down of an archbishop, see her rebuke of Edmund Grindal in 1577, in Black, *Reign*, p. 197.

18. The reasons for saying this are: England had Calais until 1558 and Gascony until 1453. The tenure of Gascony overlaps with the inheritance of Normandy, which was lost in 1204. Prior to 1066, Scandinavian kings played a major role in English affairs. One could even say that England had never before been so isolated, for prior to the Viking settlements the kingdom of England did not exist; England was a series of smaller kingdoms.

19. Rowse, *Structure*, p. 37; John J. Manning, ed., *The First and Second Parts of John Hayward's The Life and Raigne of King Henrie IIII*, Camden Fourth Series, 42 (1991), p. 1.

20. John Harington, *Nugae Antiquae* 1 (1804), p. 362, quoted in *Eliz. People*, p. 17.

21. Emmison, *Disorder*, p. 40.

22. Emmison, *Disorder*, pp. 40–43.

23. J. Bruce, ed., *Leycester Correspondence*, Camden Society, 27 (1844), p. 237.

24. Details of the royal processions 1550–63 are to be found in Machyn, *Diary*. See, for example, pp. 263–64.

25. Wilson, "State," pp. 26–29, gives a higher figure, £347,587, but this is generally thought to be an overestimate. Black, *Reign*, p. 366, suggests about £300,000. Hill, *Reformation*, p. 81, suggests £250,000 until 1588. The royal revenue was about £300,000 at the death of Henry VIII: £200,000 from the lands and rights acquired at the Reformation and Dissolution to add to the earlier royal income of £100,000;

but huge amounts of land, to the value of £1.5 million, were given away or sold under Edward VI (Hill, *Reformation*, p. 21).

26. The budget headings are from Wilson, "State," pp. 26–29.

27. Hill, *Reformation*, p. 81.

28. Black, *Reign*, p. 198.

29. According to Wilson, "State," pp. 2–8, the order of succession in 1600 was as follows: (1) James VI of Scotland, only son of Mary, queen of Scots, and great-grandson of Margaret Tudor, Henry VII's eldest daughter; (2) Arabella Stuart, cousin of James VI and also a great-grandchild of Margaret Tudor; (3) Edward Seymour, Lord Beauchamp, eldest son of the earl of Hertford, whose mother, Lady Catherine Grey, was a granddaughter of Mary Tudor, Henry VII's second daughter; (4) Thomas Seymour, younger son of the earl of Hertford, and another great-grandson of Mary Tudor; (5) the earl of Derby, second cousin of the Seymours and another great-grandson of Mary Tudor, through her younger daughter Eleanor. All five potential heirs were Elizabeth's first cousins twice removed.

30. Edward O. Smith Jr., "The Elizabethan Doctrine of the Prince as Reflected in the Sermons of the Episcopacy, 1559–1603," *Huntington Library Quarterly* 28, 1 (1964), pp. 1–17.

31. These were Oxford, Northumberland, Shrewsbury, Kent, Derby, Worcester, Rutland, Cumberland, Sussex, Huntingdon, Bath, Southampton, Bedford, Pembroke, Hertford, Essex, Lincoln, and Nottingham. The six Irish earls are not included in this total.

32. There was a third viscountcy, Hereford, but that was held by the earl of Essex.

33. This includes some titles whose holders were children but excludes titles that were in abeyance in 1600 awaiting a sole heiress to emerge (e.g., Ogle, Dacre, and Ros).

34. Dawson, *Plenti & Grase*, p. 30.

35. Wilson, "State," p. 22.

36. Gordon R. Batho, "The Finances of an Elizabethan Nobleman: Henry Percy, ninth earl of Northumberland (1564–1632)," *Economic History Review*, new ser., 9 (1957), pp. 433–450, at p. 436.

37. Hill, *Reformation*, pp. 33–34.

38. Various writers have commented on how difficult it is to enumerate the gentry. It depends on where one draws the line. If only counting those families that supplied the major offices for each county, such as JPs, deputy lieutenants, and sheriffs, then there were about a hundred families per county, or roughly four thousand gentry families in England. Mousley found eighty-seven such families for Sussex in his 1959 study of that county (J. E. Mousley, "The Fortunes of Some Gentry Families in Elizabethan Sussex," *Economic History Review* 11, 3 [1959], pp. 467–82). However, if we include all the armigerous families, the average per county in 1600 was probably in excess of 250, and so there were more than ten thousand gentry families. Shropshire had about 470 armigerous families in 1620, Devon a similar number in that year, having had about 250 in 1564. Thomas Wilson declared there were 16,000 such families in 1600 (Wilson, "State," p. 23) and this more or less tallies with Gregory King's total of 16,400 in 1688 (1400 baronets and knights, 3,000 esquires, and 12,000 gentlemen: see Thirsk, *Documents*, p. 780). It all depends where one draws the line as to what a "gentleman" is—a moot point now as well as in Elizabethan times.

39. Wilson, "State," p. 24.

40. *ODNB*, under "Howard, Thomas, fourth duke of Norfolk."

41. Schoenbaum, *Shakespeare*, p. 172.

42. For Bacon and Popham, see *ODNB*. For Coke, see Wilson, "State," p. 25.

43. The first surgeon to be knighted was Sir John Ayliffe (d. 1556). The first physician to be knighted was Sir William Butts (d. 1545).

44. Black, *Reign*, p. 236. Thomas Wilson in 1600 states that a few were worth £100,000 (Wilson, "State," p. 21). In 1600 Thomas Platter believed that the lord mayor of London had an *income* of £100,000—he cannot have been correct in this (see Platter, *Travels*, p. 157).

45. Wilson, "State," p. 20.

46. Hoskins, "Towns," p. 18.

47. Hoskins, "Towns," p. 9.

48. These proportions are based mainly on those established by Gregory King in his late seventeenth-century tract, "Natural and political observations upon the State and Condition of England," in Thirsk, *Documents*, p. 773. I have assumed for the sake of this exercise that the proportions of a larger provincial city's makeup did not alter substantially over the seventeenth century.

49. Rowe and Andrew M. Jackson, eds., *Exeter Freemen 1266–1967*, Devon and Cornwall Record Society, extra ser., 1 (1973), pp. 83–110.

50. These "other" are four town waits; a foreigner with letters of denizaton from the queen (1575); a city beadle (1588); the city sword-bearer (1590); one of the city sergeants (1592).

51. Herridge, *Inventories*, pp. 389–90.

52. CKS: PRC21/6/41; BRO: D/A1/212/194C.

53. Pound, *Census*, pp. 7, 10. Some of the statistics in what follows have been taken from Pelling, *CL*, p. 84.

54. Beier, "Vagrants," p. 9; Clark, "Migrant," p. 117.

55. Carew, *Survey*, f. 67r.

56. Hill, *Reformation*, p. 31.

57. Pound, *Census*, p. 23.

58. Pound, *Census*, p. 25.

59. Pound, *Census*, p. 35.

60. The details of Shipdams House are taken from Pound, *Census*, p. 36. For the boy and the blind man, and strategies for survival, see Pelling, *CL*, pp. 79–102, especially pp. 84–85. For wages of nurses, see Mortimer, *D&D*, p. 154.

61. Clark, "Migrant," p. 135.

62. Duffy, *Morebath*, p. 13.

63. Stubbes, *Anatomy*, p. 33.

64. I have taken this figure from Wrightson, *Earthly Necessities*, p. 34.

65. Clark, "Migrant," p. 127.

66. Beier, "Vagrants," p. 8.

67. 5 Elizabeth (1563) cap. 20.

68. 14 Elizabeth (1572) cap. 5.

69. 31 Elizabeth (1589) cap. 7. This enshrined in law what had long been the practice in many courts at much earlier dates. See Emmison, *HWL*, p. 268.

70. Emmison, *HWL*, p. 271.

71. 39 Elizabeth (1597), cap. 3.

72. Christopher Dyer, *Standards of Living in Medieval England* (Cambridge, rev. ed., 1989), p. 316; *Tudor Tailor*, p. 9.

73. Traister, *Notorious*, p. 135.

74. There were female churchwardens at Morebath, Kilmington, and St. Budeaux in

Devon, for instance. See Patricia Crawford, *Women and Religion in England 1500–1720* (1993), p. 220, n. 22; Duffy, *Morebath*, p. 124.

75. Mortimer, "Index," p. 110.
76. See D. A. Beaufort, "The Medical Practitioners of Western Sussex in the Early Modern Period: A Preliminary Survey," *Sussex Archaeological Collections* 131 (1948), pp. 427–39. Exeter too was a diocese in which the requirement to obtain a license to practice midwifery was resisted, judging from the paucity of such licenses sought.
77. Williams, *Life*, p.70.
78. Traister, *Notorious*, p. 154.
79. Laslett, *WWHL*, p. 95.
80. Laslett, *WWHL*, pp. 1–2.
81. Emmison, *HWL*, p. 111.
82. This appears in "De Conjugalibus," in Horman, *Vulgaria*.
83. William Shakespeare, *Romeo and Juliet*, act I, scene ii.
84. Laslett, *WWHL*, p. 88.
85. Wrigley & Schofield, p. 255.
86. Laslett, *WWHL*, p. 86. The data are for the period 1600–1625.
87. Laslett, *WWHL*, p. 103, says a quarter; Wrigley & Schofield, p. 190, suggest 30 percent.
88. Pelling, *CL*, p. 148.
89. Platter, *Travels*, p. 182. This seems to be a quotation from the duke of Württemberg's trip.
90. Quoted in *Eliz. People*, pp. 34–35.
91. Magno, p. 144.
92. Scott, *EOaW*, pp. 48–49, quoting Emanuel van Meteren, *Nederlandtsche Historie* (1575). It also appears in Rye, *England*, p. 73.
93. Platter, *Travels*, p. 170.
94. "Everie one in his calling is bound to doo somewhat to the furtherance of the holie building, but because great things by reason of my sex I may not doo, and that which I may I ought to doo, I have according to my duetie brought my poore basket of stones to the strengthning of the walles of that Jerusalem whereof (by grace) wee are all both citizens and members." Quoted in *ODNB*.
95. Emilia Lanier, "To the Reader," in *Salve Deus Rex Judaeorum* (1611).

CHAPTER THREE: **Religion**
1. Stubbes, *Anatomy*, p. 60.
2. Kocher, "Atheist," p. 231.
3. Kocher, "Atheist," p. 249.
4. *ODNB*, under "Black, David (c.1546–1603)."
5. Susanne S. Webb, "Raleigh, Hariot and Atheism in Elizabethan and Early Stuart England," *Albion* 1, 1 (1969), pp. 10–18, at pp. 11, 18.
6. *ODNB*, under "Marlowe."
7. *ODNB*, under "Marlowe." For the Buggery Act, see 5 Elizabeth I cap. xvii.
8. *CSPV*, p. 1.
9. *CSPV*, p. 2.
10. Duffy, *Morebath*, pp. 169–70.
11. Quoted in Scott, *EOaW*, p. 165.
12. Elizabeth's speech to the 1585 Parliament, quoted in *Eliz. People*, p. 115.
13. Its proper title is *Actes and monuments of these latter and perillous days, touching*

matters of the Church, wherein are comprehended and described the great persecu-tions and horrible troubles that have been wrought and practiced by the Romishe Prelates, specially in this realm of England and Scotland, from the year of our Lorde a thousand until the tyme now present . . . by Iohn Foxe (1st ed., 1563).

14. Marcia Lee Metzger, "Controversy and 'Correctness': English Chronicles and the Chroniclers, 1553–1568," *Sixteenth Century Journal* 27, 2 (1996), pp. 437–51, especially p. 450.

15. 23 Elizabeth I cap. 1.

16. Black, *Reign*, p. 181. As Patrick Collinson says, "Most 'Catholics' did not refuse to go to church" (Collinson, "The Mongrel Religion of Elizabethan England," in Doran, *Exhibition*, pp. 27–32, at p. 31).

17. Black, *Reign*, p. 188.

18. 35 Elizabeth I caps. 1, 2.

19. *Eliz. People*, p. 10. Black reckons that 250 Catholics were executed in twenty years (*Reign*, p. 188).

20. William Weston, *The Autobiography of an Elizabethan*, trans. Philip Caraman (1955), pp. 44–46.

21. Edward Peters, *Inquisition* (Berkeley, 1989), p. 141, quoting Edward Rishton.

22. Harrison, *Description*, chapter. 17.

23. Gerard, *Autobiography*, pp. 106–10.

24. Emmison, *Disorder*, p. 45.

25. Patrick Collinson, *The Elizabethan Puritan Movement* (Oxford, 1st ed., 1967; re-print 1990), pp. 432–33.

26. *Eliz. Home*, pp. 1, 10, 12, 111.

27. *Eliz. People*, pp. 71–72.

28. Beer, *TEO*, pp. 133–34.

29. Black, *Reign*, p. 205.

CHAPTER FOUR: **Character**

1. *CSPV*, p. 328.

2. 24 Henry VIII cap. 5; Emmison, *Disorder*, p. 150.

3. These cases are all from Emmison, *Disorder*, pp. 148–49.

4. Stoyle, "Witch," pp. 129–51.

5. Picard, *London*, p. 252, citing Edwin Green, "The Vintners' Lobby 1552–68," *Guildhall Studies in London History*, 2 (1974).

6. Charles G. Cruickshank, "Dead-Pays in the Elizabethan Army," *EHR*, 53 (1938), pp. 93–97.

7. Schoenbaum, *Shakespeare*, p. 152.

8. See the Essex examples noted in Emmison, *HWL*, p. 123.

9. *Sh. Eng.*, p. 222.

10. Figures taken from the online English Short-Title Catalogue (http://estc.bl.uk), maintained by the BL. The table of books published per decade includes books in English published abroad.

11. English Short-Title Catalogue.

12. Black, *Reign*, p. 64.

13. *Eliz. Home*, p. 4.

14. Black, *Reign*, p. 323, states that Greek was "taught only at Eton, Harrow, Westmin-ster, Shrewsbury and a few others." For Brownsword's syllabus, see Jonathan Bate, *The Genius of Shakespeare* (1997), pp. 8–9.

15. Black, *Reign,* p. 246.
16. David Armitage, "The Elizabethan Idea of Empire," *Transactions of the Royal Historical Society,* 6th ser., 14 (2004), pp. 269–77; Sian Flynn and David Spence, "Imperial Ambition and Elizabeth's Adventurers," in Doran, *Exhibition,* pp. 121–31.
17. Yeames, "Grand Tour," p. 107.
18. Yeames, "Grand Tour," p. 93.
19. Howard, "Women," p. 153.
20. Magno, p. 146.
21. Pollitt, "Refuge."
22. Lisa Ferraro Parmelee, "Printers, Patrons, Readers, and Spies: Importation of French Propaganda in Late Elizabethan England," *Sixteenth Century Journal* 25, 4 (1994), pp. 853–72.
23. Paul J. Hauben, "A Spanish Calvinist Church in Elizabethan London 1559–65," *Church History* 34, 1 (1965), pp. 50–56.
24. Pollitt, "Refuge," D1018.
25. Stow, *Survay,* pp. 209–10.
26. Emmison, *HWL,* pp. 306–8.
27. For prostitutes, see Howard, "Women," pp. 150–67; for courtiers, see Platter, *Travels,* p. 193.
28. In this and the next two paragraphs about English racism in literature, I have drawn heavily on an article by Alden T. Vaughan and Virginia Mason Vaughan, "Before Othello: Elizabethan Representations of Sub-Saharan Africans," *Willliam and Mary Quarterly,* 3rd ser., 54 (1997), pp. 19–44.
29. Doran, *Exhibition,* p. 150.
30. Arnold, *Wardrobe,* p. 106; Picard, *London,* p. 110.
31. Marika Sherwood, "Blacks in Tudor England," *History Today* 53, 10 (October 2003). The Plymouth references come from the Friends of Devon's Archives Web site, giving details of its project on black communities in Devon (http://www.foda.org.uk).
32. Kocher, "Old Cosmos," p. 104.
33. Leonard and Thomas Digges, *A prognostication everlasting of right good effect* (1583).
34. Thomas Blundeville, *M. Blundeville, his exercises* (1594), fol. 181, cited in Nicoll, *Elizabethans,* p. 14.
35. *ODNB,* under "Gilbert, William."
36. Gerard, *Herball,* p. 1338.
37. Madeleine Doran, "On Elizabethan 'Credulity': With Some Questions Concerning the Use of the Marvelous in Literature," *Journal of the History of Ideas* 1, 2 (1940), pp. 151–76, at p. 156.
38. Rowse, *Structure,* p. 28.
39. Iona Opie and Moira Tatem, *A Dictionary of Superstitions* (Oxford University Press, 1989), pp. 142, 165, 173.
40. As argued in the last chapter of Thomas, *RDM.*
41. Ecclesiasticus 38:4, quoted on the title page of Simon Kellwaye, *A Defensative against the Plague* (1593).
42. Ralph Houlbrooke, *Death, Religion and the Family in England 1480–1750* (Oxford, 1998), pp. 18–19.
43. Kocher, "Old Cosmos," p. 105.
44. Black, *Reign,* p. 310.

45. Traister, *Notorious*, pp. 59–62.
46. Sharpe, *Instruments*, p. 39.
47. Thomas Hill, "The Distinction of Dreams," in *The Most Pleasaunte Arte of the Interpretation of Dreames* (1576).
48. Thomas, *RDM*, p. 590; Platter, *Travels*, p. 174.
49. Both quotations come from Thomas, *RDM*, p. 177.
50. Alan MacFarlane, *Witchcraft in Tudor and Stuart England: A Regional and Comparative Study* (1970), p. 98.
51. Sharpe, *Instruments*, pp. 75–78.
52. Thomas, *RDM*, pp. 442–43.
53. Stoyle, "Witch."
54. Black, *Reign*, p. 331.
55. Sharpe, *Instruments*, p. 169.
56. Sir Henry Ellis, *Original Letters of Eminent Literary Men of the Sixteenth, Seventeenth, and Eighteenth Centuries*, Camden Society, 23 (1843), pp. 39–40.
57. Anon. [Richard Gough], "An Historical Account of the Origin and Establishment of the Society of Antiquaries," *Archaeologia* 1 (1770), pp. i–xxxix; Linda van Norden, "Sir Henry Spellman on the Chronology of the Elizabethan College of Antiquaries," *Huntington Library Quarterly* 13, 2 (1950), pp. 131–60; C. E. Wright, "The Elizabethan Society of Antiquaries and the Formation of the Cottonian Library," in F. Wormald and C. E. Wright, eds., *The English Library before 1700* (1958), pp. 176–212.
58. Michael Bennett, "Edward III's Entail and the Succession to the Crown, 1376–1471," *EHR* 113 (1998), pp. 580–609, at p. 606.
59. In 1582 Norton received a commission from Francis Walsingham to examine what the nation's history indicates for its future. He reported that the history of Britain undergoes a profound revolution approximately every five hundred years, the last of which took place in 1066. He predicted that England was due another revolution, and, looking back at the recent Reformation, suggested a transformation provoked by religion—an accurate prediction, given the events of Charles I's reign in the middle of the next century. See Barry Shaw, "Thomas Norton's 'Devices' for a Godly Realm: An Elizabethan Vision for the Future," *Sixteenth Century Journal* 22, 3 (Autumn 1991), pp. 495–509.

CHAPTER FIVE: **Basic Essentials**

1. David Crystal, "To Modernize or Not to Modernize: There Is No Question," *Around the Globe* 21 (2002), pp. 15–17.
2. Black, *Reign*, pp. 5, 364–65.
3. *Eliz. Home*, pp. 60, 69.
4. As in Harrison, *Description*, chapter 4: "No occupier shall have occasion to travel far off with his commodities."
5. Mortimer, "Machyn," pp. 981–98; Richard W. Bailey and Colette Moore, "Henry Machyn's English," in Christopher M. Cain and Geoffrey Russom, eds., *Studies in the English Language III* (2007), pp. 231–50; Derek Britton, "The Dialectal Origins of the Language of Henry Machyn," in Cain and Russon, *Studies in the English Language*, pp. 251–66.
6. P. Beresford Ellis, *The Cornish Language and Its Literature* (1974), p. 57, quoting Andrew Boorde, *Fyrst Boke of the Introduction of Knowledge* (1542).
7. Stoyle, *West Britons*, plate 2.

8. Stoyle, *West Britons*, pp. 35–39.

9. Carew, *Survey*, f. 56r.

10. Carew, Survey of Cornwall, f. 56r.

11. Hollyband, *Campo di Fior.*

12. Frances A. Yates, "Italian Teachers in Elizabethan England," *Journal of the War-burg Institute* 1 (1937), pp. 103–16, at pp. 103–4, quoting Bruno, *La Cena et la Ceneri* (1584), dialogue III, in G. Bruno, *Opere italiane*, ed. G. Gentile, i (1925), pp. 64–65.

13. Lawrence Stone, "Elizabethan Overseas Trade," *Economic History Review,* new ser. 2, 1 (1949), pp. 30–58, at p. 31.

14. The types of paper and wood used are taken from "De Scholasticus," in Horman's *Vulgaria.*

15. "Rules Made by E. B. for Children to Write By," quoted in Molly Harrison and O. M. Royston, *How They Lived*, vol. ii, *An Anthology of Original Accounts Written Between 1485 and 1700* (Oxford, 1963), p. 163.

16. Duffy, *Morebath*, p.14. Other examples are to be found in inventories: e.g., Havinden, *Inventories*, p. 150, and Herridge, *Inventories*, pp. 5, 8, 25.

17. The reference to chamber clocks is from Horman's *Vulgaria.* The price is from Stevenson, "Extracts," p. 301.

18. Doran, *Exhibition*, pp. 145–47.

19. Scott, *EOaW*, p. 50, quoting the letter of Robert Laneham.

20. 6 Henry VIII cap. 4 (1515). These hours are stated in the Statute of Artificers in 1563 (5 Elizabeth cap. 4).

21. Mortimer, "Machyn," p. 988.

22. Robert S. Dilley, "The Customary Acre: An Indeterminate Measure," *Agricultural History Review* 23 (1975), pp. 173–76, at p. 174.

23. Carew, *Survey*, f. 36r.

24. *Eliz. Home*, pp. 87, 93.

25. Platter, *Travels*, p. 175.

26. Hodgen, "Fairs," p. 391.

27. Emmison, *HWL*, p. 191.

28. Hoskins, *Exeter*, p. 59.

29. Wrightson, *Earthly Necessities*, p. 118. In London in 1560, basic foodstuffs, drink, and fuel are 75 percent more than they were twenty years earlier. See Dawson, *Plenti & Grase*, p. 34.

30. Wrightson, *Earthly Necessities*, p. 118; *CAHEW*, i, pp. 150–51; Overton, "Prices," p. 140.

31. Thirsk, *Documents*, pp. 599–601.

32. 5 Eliz. cap. 11.

33. For the horse-powered aspect of Mestrelle's press, see Magno, p. 142.

34. In stating this, it is acknowledged that a modern pair of sheets is a different commodity from the Elizabethan ones. The modern pair is manufactured by machine, it is a luxury item, and there are many cheaper artificial alternatives. In the 1590s the sheets represent many hours of labor and cheap artificial alternatives do not exist. Nevertheless, it is assumed here that they are comparable, for the sake of argument.

35. 13 Eliz. cap. 8. See also Peter Spufford, "Long-Term Rural Credit in Sixteenth and Seventeenth-Century England: The Evidence of Probate Accounts," in Arkell, *Death*, pp. 213–28; Emmison, *HWL*, p. 91; Mortimer, "Accounts."

36. Emmison, *HWL*, pp. 146, 165.

37. Hoskins, *Exeter*, p. 52.

38. Lawrence Stone, "An Elizabethan Coalmine," *Economic History Review*, new ser., 3, 1 (1950), pp. 97–106.

39. Mortimer, *Probate*, p. 25.

40. Emmison, *HWL*, p. 167.

41. Mortimer, *Probate*, p. 3.

42. Pelling, *CL*, p. 126. The causes of syphilis were well known at the time, so this reflects an expectation that the master would sleep with the servant.

43. *Eliz. Home*, pp. 4, 12, 20, 66, 72, 73, 80.

44. Magno, p. 146.

45. Platter, *Travels*, pp. 163, 183; Rye, *England;* Magno, p. 144.

CHAPTER SIX: **What to Wear**

1. Arnold, *Wardrobe*, p. 159, quoting Moryson's *Itinerary*, part one, p. 199. Most of the references to the queen's clothes in this chapter are from Arnold.

2. Scott, *EOaW*, p. 12.

3. Arnold, *Wardrobe*, pp. 7–10. The question of whether women can show their nipples is a matter of doubt—and of context. No Puritan would have thought it seemly. But in some artwork and in sculptures of women from the New World, the full breast is often depicted; and the French ambassador describes seeing "the whole breast."

4. *Eliz. People*, pp. 31–32.

5. For a 1568 case, see Emmison, *HWL*, p. 274.

6. *Tudor Tailor*, pp. 36–37.

7. *Tudor Tailor*, p. 38.

8. Arnold, *Wardrobe*, p. 90.

9. Schneider, "Colors," especially pp. 111–14. Her analysis of color having nationalistic overtones seems plausible, and I have followed it here; but she does not pay enough attention to the number of common women's petticoats and kirtles that are dyed with madder.

10. Arnold, *Wardrobe*, pp. 157–58. The practice of sending fashion dolls is mentioned in the correspondence between Marie de Medici and Henri II of France: "Fontenac tells me that you desired to have some models of the fashion of dress in France. I am sending you some dressed dolls and will send you with the Duc de Bellegarde a good tailor." (Quoted in Norris, *Costume*, ii, p. 667.) For the value of imports, see under "babies" in *Port & Trade*.

11. Thomas Dekker, *Seven Deadly Sins of London* (1606), quoted in Black, *Reign*, p. 268.

12. Arnold, *Wardrobe*, pp. 115, 125, 128, 135–36.

13. Arnold, *Wardrobe*, p. 4.

14. Stubbes, *Anatomy*, pp. 8, 33, 36.

15. Stubbes, *Anatomy*, p. 42.

16. Arnold, *Wardrobe*, pp. 4–5.

17. *Eliz. Home*, pp. 61–62.

18. *Tudor Tailor*, p. 36.

19. Cunnington, *Underclothes*, p. 47. The example cited there is recorded in the Much Wenlock parish register for 1547.

20. Arnold, *Wardrobe*, p. 208; Norris, *Costume*, ii, p. 545.

21. Holmes, *London*, p. 24; Schneider, "Colors," p. 119; Arnold, *Wardrobe*, pp. 206–10.

22. "Menstrual clouts" (cloths) are mentioned in the early English translations of the Bible (see *Tudor Tailor*, p. 24). Cunnington, *Underclothes*, p. 52, states that women do not wear drawers until the nineteenth century; but Pepys's wife does. See entries for May 15, 1663, and June 4, 1663.

23. *Tudor Tailor*, p. 20; Arnold, *Wardrobe*, p. 209.

24. Cunnington, *Underclothes*, p. 48.

25. Arnold, *Wardrobe*, pp. 144–47.

26. Arnold, *Wardrobe*, p. 154.

27. Cunnington, *Underclothes*, p. 49 (Kempe); *Tudor Tailor*, pp. 22, 40, 46.

28. Arnold, *Wardrobe*, p. 143.

29. Stubbes, *Anatomy*, pp. 44–45.

30. Holmes, *London*, p. 25.

31. Platter, *Travels*, p. 182.

32. Stubbes, *Anatomy*, p. 42.

33. Arnold, *Wardrobe*, pp. 122–23, 156–57.

34. Arnold, *Wardrobe*, pp. 213–14.

35. *Tudor Tailor*, p. 33.

36. Arnold, *Wardrobe*, p. 214.

37. Arnold, *Wardrobe*, p. 311, quoting BL Stowe 557, fol. 72.

38. Arnold, *Wardrobe*, p. 313, quoting BL Stowe 557, fol. 76.

39. Quoted in *Sh. Eng.*, ii, p. 97.

40. Quoted in Arnold, *Wardrobe*, p. 203.

41. Probate inventory of Alice Bates, http://www.the-orb.net/atherstone/inventory.html, downloaded June 10, 2011.

42. Havinden, *Inventories*, p. 120. Avis Gardner's clothes are a red petticoat (3s 4d), an old frieze cassock (2s), a waistcoat (8d), a flannel apron (6d), an old worsted apron (3d), two old linen aprons (4d), three smocks (1s 8d), seven kerchiefs (2s), an old rail [nightshift] (2d), seven partlets (1s 8d), an old pair of shoes (2d), and a hat (4d). The chest was worth 1s 8d.

43. Mortimer, *Probate*, pp. 15, 23, 25.

44. *Eliz. Home*, p. 62.

45. For the definition of "rubbers," see *OED*. The same source quotes as its earliest reference to hairbrushes Oswald Gaebelkhover, *The book of physicke*, trans. A. M. (1st ed., 1599). For a German illustration of a sixteenth-century maker of hairbrushes, see Arnold, *Wardrobe*, p. 233. Most gentlewomen used combs through the seventeenth and early eighteenth centuries. William Kent started manufacturing modern hairbrushes in 1777. Note that a high-quality hairbrush probably used for grooming was found on the *Mary Rose* (see *Before the Mast*, p. 354).

46. Stubbes, *Anatomy*, pp. 40–41.

47. Platter, *Travels*, p. 182.

48. 1 Corinthians 11:6; Stubbes, *Anatomy*, p. 40; *Tudor Tailor*, p. 28.

49. Arnold, *Wardrobe*, p. 325, quoting BL Stowe 557, f. 91.

50. Quoted in Norris, *Costume*, ii, p. 552. See also *Tudor Tailor*, p. 33.

51. This list is from the inventory of the glover William Hobday of Stratford, who died in 1601, quoted in Jeanne Jones, *Family Life in Shakespeare's England* (Stroud, 1996), pp. 80–81.

52. Arnold, *Wardrobe*, p. 332 (pelican); Doran, *Exhibition*, p. 107 (ship jewel).

53. *Eliz. Home*, p. 95.

54. Mortimer, *Probate*, p. 33. In saying this I am mindful especially of how very few probate inventories mention jewelry.
55. Stubbes, *Anatomy*, p. 42.
56. This apparently includes the queen. See Arnold, *Wardrobe*, p. 27 for her earrings being hung by pearls; look at almost all the painted portraits for her lack of piercings in her ears. However, the one by Federico Zuccaro, supposed to be of her at Sudeley Castle, clearly shows a pierced ear.
57. Stubbes, *Anatomy*, pp. 49–50.
58. Stubbes, *Anatomy*, p. 37.
59. Horman, "De Cubicularibus," in *Vulgaria*.
60. Quoted in Scott, *EOaW*, p. 81.
61. Doran, *Exhibition*, pp. 104–5.
62. A boxwood pomander was found on the *Mary Rose*. See *Before the Mast*, p. 161.
63. Quoted in Scott, *EOaW*, p. 80.
64. *Eliz. Home*, pp. 1–2.
65. *Tudor Tailor*, p. 16.
66. Cunnington, *Underclothes*, p. 39.
67. Phillis Cunnington and Catherine Lucas, *Occupational Costume in England* (1967, reprint 1968), p. 25.
68. *Tudor Tailor*, p. 39.
69. Stubbes, *Anatomy*, pp. 30–31; *Tudor Tailor*, p. 18; Norris, *Costume*, ii, 2, pp. 530, 542–44.
70. Cunnington, *Underclothes*, pp. 41, 44.
71. Andrew Boorde's advice to a youth was to wear a "petticoat" next to his shirt in winter, as was John Russell's. See Furnivall, ed., *Babees Book*, pp. 177, 247.
72. Cunnington, *Underclothes*, p. 41.
73. *Tudor Tailor*, pp. 18–19, 36.
74. Stubbes, *Anatomy*, p. 29.
75. Cunnington, *Underclothes*, p. 41; Stubbes, *Anatomy*, p. 26.
76. Leather jerkins were the most common garment on the *Mary Rose*. See *Before the Mast*, p. 18.
77. *Tudor Tailor*, pp. 18–20; Stubbes, *Anatomy*, p. 21; Picard, *London*, p. 128; Janet Arnold, *Patterns of Fashion: 1560–1620*, 3 (1985), p. 6.
78. Stubbes, *Anatomy*, p. 25.
79. Havinden, *Inventories*, p. 86; Herridge, *Inventories*, p. 421.
80. Claudius Hollyband, *The Italian Schoolmaster* (1597), n.p. (section on "familiar talks").
81. Stubbes, *Anatomy*, p. 18.
82. Combs were among the most common items found on the *Mary Rose*. See *Before the Mast*, p. 156.
83. Stevenson, "Extracts," p. 300 (lord's rapier, 1581); Herridge, *Inventories*, p. 268.
84. The armor quantifications are from Emanuel Green, ed., *Certificate of Musters in the County of Somerset, temp. Elizabeth 1569*, Somerset Record Society, 20 (1904), pp. 3–6.
85. See Arnold, *Wardrobe*, p. 139, for a nobleman wearing his damask nightgown to his execution.
86. Arnold, *Wardrobe*, pp. 139–40.
87. Quoted in Norris, *Costume*, ii, p. 617.
88. Arnold, *Wardrobe*, p. 7.

89. *OED*, quoting Wardr. Acc. Hen. VIII, in *Archaeologia*, 9 (1789), p. 245: "one dussen brushes, and one dussen and a halfe of rubbers delyvered to like use into oure saide warderobe of our roobis" [1536]; W. Warde translated by "Alessio," *Secretes* (1558), i. v. p. 90: "To die hogges brystels and other thinges, for to make rubbers and brusshes." See also the images in Arnold, *Wardrobe Unlock'd*, p. 233.

90. Arnold, *Wardrobe*, pp. 233–34.

91. Emmison, *HWL*, p. 98.

92. Dawson, *Jewel*, p. 151.

93. Stow, "Cordwainer Street Ward," in *Survay; Port & Trade*.

94. Stubbes, *Anatomy*, p. 31.

CHAPTER SEVEN: **Traveling**

1. Emmison, *Disorder*, p. 14.

2. Horman, "De Conjugalibus," in *Vulgaria*: "Maydens that carry gere upon theyr head putte a wrethe of haye between the vessel and theyr heed to stay it from goglynge."

3. Markland, "Carriages," p. 464.

4. Markland, "Carriages," p. 463; Holmes, *London*, p. 24.

5. Arnold, *Wardrobe*, p. 231; Markland, "Carriages," p. 463. Rippon made a coach for the earl of Rutland in 1564.

6. Arnold, *Wardrobe*, p. 232. Three hundred carts are mentioned by Von Wedel (Arnold, *Wardrobe*, p. 232), and four hundred by Harrison, *Description*, book 3, chapter 1.

7. Markland, "Carriages," p. 463.

8. Picard, *London*, p. 32.

9. Markland, "Carriages," pp. 458–59.

10. Markland, "Carriages," p. 469.

11. Markland, "Carriages," pp. 459, 462–63.

12. *Sh. Eng.*, i, p. 204.

13. Picard, *London*, p. 33, quoting T. R. Forbes, *Chronicle from Aldgate* (1971).

14. *Eliz. People*, p. 36, quoting John Stow.

15. Markland, "Carriages," p. 465.

16. Emmison, *HWL*, pp. 287–88.

17. For example, Black, *Reign*, p. 263.

18. Markland, "Carriages," p. 458.

19. 2 and 3 Philip and Mary, cap. 8 (1555); 5 Eliz cap. 13 (1563); 18 Eliz cap. 5 (1576); Emmison, *HWL*, pp. 242–43.

20. Emmison, *Disorder*, pp. 17–19.

21. Leland, *Itinerary*, i, pp. 221, 274. Eighty years later, Thomas Westcote described Devon in the same way, breaking the whole county up into rivers, and giving details of the towns and principal residences according to the river valley in which they are situated. See Thomas Westcote, *A View of Devonshire in MDCXXX*, eds. George Oliver and Pitman Jones (1845).

22. Emmison, *HWL*, p. 281.

23. The queen fails to repair several bridges in Essex. See Emmison, *HWL*, p. 281.

24. *Sh. Eng.*, i, p. 200.

25. Overton, "Prices," p. 130.

26. Havinden, *Inventories*, pp. 135, 140. A "lame old horse" is valued at 2s on p. 137.

27. Black, *Reign*, p. 264; Herbert Joyce, *The History of the Post Office from Its Establishment Down to 1836* (1893), pp. 2–5. The prices are from Black. I have read that the standard charge was 1 penny per mile as a result of an act of 1548, and I suspect that the 3 pence per mile was not introduced until James I's reign; but I cannot find any such act among Edward VI's statutes, and have therefore trusted Black.

28. Edward Watson, *The Royal Mail to Ireland* (1917), pp. 9–10.

29. Platter, *Travels*, p. 230.

30. *Sh. Eng.*, i, pp. 201–2.

31. Scott, *EOaW*, p. 180, quoting Claudius Hollyband, *French Littleton* (1576).

32. Magno, p. 149.

33. *Sh. Eng.*, i, p. 207. Black, *Reign*, p. 263, gives the same list.

34. Emmison, *Disorder*, pp. 271–77, 308–10.

35. Leland, *Itinerary*, i, p. 29.

36. Platter, *Travels*, p. 152.

37. Wilson, "State," p. 37.

38. Platter, *Travels*, p. 154.

39. Picard, *London*, p. 14.

40. Gerard, *Autobiography*, p. 132.

41. John Taylor "the Water Poet" describes their use in a poem about a sinking vessel.

42. Laughton, *Armada*, p. xlv; *Sh. Eng.*, i, p. li.

43. Laughton, *Armada*, pp. xliv–xlv; *Sh. Eng.*, i, pp. 156–57.

44. N. A. M. Rodger, *The Safeguard of the Sea: A Naval History of Britain*, vol. 1, 660–1649 (1997), p. 486; Harrison, "Description."

45. Wilson, "State," pp. 36–37.

46. Emmison, *HWL*, p. 62; Rose, "Navigation," p. 178.

47. Emmison, *HWL*, p. 59.

48. Laughton, *Armada*, pp. xliv–xlv; *Sh. Eng.*, i, p. 358.

49. Peter Earle, *The Last Fight of the Revenge* (1992), p. 56, quoting Dorothy O. Shilton and R. Holworthy, *High Court of Admiralty Examinations 1637–8* (1932), p. 18.

50. *Before the Mast*, p. 272.

51. *Before the Mast*, chapter six; Parry, *Reconnaissance*, chapters 5, 6.

52. Rose, "Mathematics"; Parry, *Reconnaissance*, pp. 94–95, 113.

53. These figures are from the bodies on the *Mary Rose*. See Marsden, *Noblest Shippe*, p. 155; *Before the Mast*, p. 520.

54. *Before the Mast*, p. 523.

55. *Before the Mast*, p. 615.

56. *Before the Mast*, pp. 520 (age), 564 (dogs). The survey of all the mariners in the southwest completed in the early seventeenth century records a large number of able sailors in their forties and fifties, but these men were operating fishing vessels or hoys and ketches along the coast or across the Channel; they were men who had left the navy, if ever they were in it. See Todd Gray, ed., *Early Stuart Mariners and Shipping: The Maritime Surveys of Devon and Cornwall, 1619–35*, Devon and Cornwall Record Soc. (1990).

57. *Before the Mast*, pp. 226–49.

58. Parry, *Reconnaissance*, p. 79.

59. Wilson, "State," pp. 40–41.

60. Laughton, *Armada*, p. 181.

61. This account of the circumnavigation has been taken largely from the entry for Drake in *ODNB* by Harry Kelsey.
62. Amilcar D'Avila de Mello, "Peter Carder's Strange Adventures Revealed," *Mariner's Mirror* 93, 3 (August 2007), pp. 1–8.

CHAPTER EIGHT: **Where to Stay**

1. Herridge, *Inventories*, pp. 38–40. There is no chamber above the hall mentioned; hence it is presumed that the hall was open to the roof and had a central hearth.
2. Herridge, *Inventories*, pp. 437–39.
3. Girouard, *Architecture*, p. 25.
4. Girouard, *Architecture*, p. 25.
5. Malcolm Airs, *The Tudor and Jacobean Country House* (1995), p. 97.
6. Sir Francis was £12,000 in debt by 1589, nine years after starting work. See Dawson, *Plenti & Grase*, p. 39.
7. Girouard, *Architecture*, p. 139.
8. Dawson, *Plenti & Grase*, p. 251.
9. Girouard, *LECH*, p. 101.
10. Dawson, *Plenti & Grase*, p. 43; Girouard, *LECH*, pp. 15, 138–39.
11. Dawson, *Plenti & Grase*, p. 43.
12. Dawson, *Plenti & Grase*, p. 49.
13. Girouard, *LECH*, p. 111.
14. Although rare, inventories of gentlemen's residences with glass do mention curtains and curtain rails. See Herridge, *Inventories*, pp. 43, 117, 218, 254 etc., for examples.
15. Doran, ed., *Exhibition*, p. 109.
16. An Elizabethan chest of drawers belonging to the corporation of Stratford is to be found in John Nash's house in Stratford. One is mentioned in the inventory of George Hocken of Totnes (see Margaret Cash, ed., *Devon Inventories of the Sixteenth and Seventeenth Centuries*, Devon and Cornwall Record Soc., new ser., 11 [1966], no. 37).
17. Girouard, *LECH*, pp. 94, 99–100.
18. Furnival, ed., *Babees Book*, p. 180.
19. Strong, *Garden*, p. 42.
20. Strong, *Garden*, pp. 32–43.
21. Strong, *Garden*, pp. 56–59.
22. The journal of the duke of Württemberg, quoted in Scott, *EOaW*, pp. 39–40.
23. Strong, *Garden*, pp. 52–55.
24. Hoskins, "Rebuilding," p. 45.
25. Havinden, *Inventories*, pp. 192–98.
26. Emmison, *HWL*, p. 6. These figures are based on houses in Maldon, Essex.
27. Hoskins, "Rebuilding," p. 46.
28. Herridge, *Inventories*, pp. 208–9.
29. Herridge, *Inventories*, pp. 356–57 (Jefferie); Havinden, *Inventories*, p. 21 (storage).
30. Carew, *Survey*, f. 66v.
31. Havinden, *Inventories*, pp. 91–94.
32. Herridge, *Inventories*, p. 233.
33. 31 Elizabeth I cap. 7; the exceptions were if it was in a borough or market town, or was built to house the poor. Havinden, *Inventories*, p. 14.
34. Havinden, *Inventories*, pp. 130–38; Dawson, *Plenti & Grase*, p. 111.

35. These included an anvil with a stock (13 shillings 4 pence), a pair of bellows (£1), two vises (£1), a bicorn with a stock (5 shillings), two sledgehammers, two hand hammers, and two nail hammers (8 shillings), two nail tools (2 shillings), fourteen files of various sizes (2 shillings), six pairs of tongs (4 shillings), weighing beams and scales (7 shillings), a wimble, a spring saw, a compass saw and a hand saw (2 shillings all four), three old chisels (6 pence), four board hammers (1 shilling 6 pence), two shoeing hammers and two pairs of pincers (2 shillings), two buttresses, a pairing knife and a clinching knife (1 shilling 6 pence), as well as various locks and keys, maundrils, axes, punches, chisels, candlesticks, shears, and twenty-six bushels of coal (the last being £1 6 shillings). (Havinden, *Inventories*, pp. 243–44.)

36. Herridge, *Inventories*, p. 116–17.

37. Dawson, *Plenti & Grase*, p. 79. Also see Horman, *Vulgaria:* "Water of the spring is better than well water." Boorde, *A Dyetary of Helthe,* also instructs his readers that they should site their houses in such a way as to use rainwater in preference to springwater, springwater in preference to well water, and well water in preference to river water.

38. "A great eel stopped the issue of the conduit that the water could not come out at the cocks" (William Horman, *Vulgaria*).

39. Charles Nicholl, *The Lodger: Shakespeare on Silver Street* (2007), p. 52.

CHAPTER NINE: **What to Eat and Drink**

1. The price of a house (£26 in the 1560s and £42 in the 1590s) is taken from Emmison, *HWL*, p. 6. The cost of a sheep was, on average, 3 shillings in the 1560s and 5 shillings in the 1590s, judging from Surrey probate accounts.

2. Dawson, *Plenti & Grase*, pp. 185–88, states that slaughtering went on as and when demand required it, rather than a mass cull at Martinmas; but his source materials (the Willoughby accounts) are the records of a family that could afford to feed their animals through the winter and needed fresh meat throughout the year for the sake of prestige entertainment.

3. Dyer, "Crisis," p. 93.

4. Emmison, *HWL*, pp. 185–87.

5. Laslett, *WWHL*, pp. 121–22. These details come from the 1623 famine entries, twenty years after Elizabeth's reign but are very much reminiscent of the conditions in 1594–97.

6. Emmison, *Disorder*, p. 252.

7. Black, *Reign*, pp. 252, 254.

8. Black, *Reign*, pp. 409–10.

9. C. J. Harrison, "Grain Price Analysis and Harvest Qualities, 1465–1634," *Agricultural History Review* 19, 2 (1971), pp. 135–55, especially pp. 149–50; *CAHEW*, pp. 150–51.

10. Thirsk, *Food*, p. 50.

11. *Treasurie*, n.p. [p. 31].

12. These lines about storing apples come from Horman's *Vulgaria* and partly from William Lawson as quoted in Dawson, *Plenti & Grase*, p. 183.

13. Dawson, *Plenti & Grase*, p. 222. The 1563 law is 5 Elizabeth I cap. 5, sections. 14–23.

14. Machyn, *Diary*, p. 249.

15. Drummond, *Food*, p. 64.

16. Thirsk, *Food*, p. 13; Williams, *Life*, p. 114, quoting Elyot's *Castel of Health.*

17. Wilson, *Food*, p. 338; Thirsk, *Food*, pp. 13–14.

18. Wilson, *Food,* p. 348; Gerard, *Herball,* pp. 275–76.
19. Dawson, *Plenti & Grase,* pp. 205–6; Platter, *Travels,* pp 148, 152.
20. *Eliz. Home,* p. 66.
21. Dawson, *Plenti & Grase,* p. 207 (Cogan); Picard, *London,* p. 159, quoting Hubert Hall, *Society in the Elizabethan Age* (1902).
22. Dawson, *Plenti & Grase,* p. 207.
23. Drummond, *Food,* p. 61. These household ordinances were first written down in 1512 but seem to have remained in force.
24. Dawson, *Plenti & Grase,* p. 207.
25. Dawson, *Jewel,* p. 66.
26. Drummond, *Food,* p. 54.
27. *Eliz. Home,* p. 99.
28. These dishes are adapted from the lists in *Cookrye,* ff. 2v–3r.
29. Drummond, *Food,* p. 59; *Eliz. Home,* p. 102.
30. Dawson, *Plenti & Grase,* p. 228.
31. Black, *Reign,* p. 273.
32. Stevenson, "Extracts," pp. 287–90. The number present with the queen is an assumption based on the consumption of beer and ale over the two days: 2,380 gallons. For the queen normally dining alone, see Roy Strong, *Feast: A History of Grand Eating* (2002) , pp. 202, 205; Platter, *Travels,* p. 195.
33. Dawson, *Jewel,* p. xv.
34. Herridge, *Inventories,* p. 255.
35. These items are provided by Lady Ri-Melaine at her dinner for a few friends in London. See *Eliz. Home,* p. 102.
36. Magno, p. 141.
37. Machyn, *Diary,* p. 237.
38. In the year 1559–60, £677 of nutmeg is brought into the port of London, along with £892 of cloves, £930 of mace, £2,333 of cinnamon, £2,848 of currants, £9,135 of raisins, £11,852 of pepper, and £18,237 of sugar. See *Port & Trade.*
39. Thirsk, *Food,* p. 34.
40. Thirsk, *Food,* p. 16.
41. *Cookrye,* p. 14.
42. Wilson, *Food,* p. 343.
43. Thirsk, *Food,* p. 289.
44. Thirsk, *Food,* p. 286; Wilson, *Food,* p. 340.
45. *DEEH,* p. 136; Wilson, *Food,* p. 363.
46. Thirsk, *Food,* p. 24; Gerard, *Herball,* p. 1384; Shakespeare, *The Tempest,* act V, scene i.
47. Drummond, *Food,* p. 59; *Eliz. Home,* p. 467.
48. Herridge, *Inventories,* p. 29.
49. Dawson, *Plenti & Grase,* p. 139, quoting Thomas Cogan.
50. Thirsk, *Food,* pp. 25, 50.
51. Dawson, *Plenti & Grase,* p. 216.
52. *Port & Trade.*
53. Doran, *Exhibition,* p. 98.
54. Herridge, *Inventories,* p. 491.
55. Doran, *Exhibition,* p. 98.
56. Quoted in Dawson, *Plenti & Grase,* p. 155.
57. Evan Jones, "The Economics Behind the Illicit Wine Trade in Elizabethan Bristol,"

downloaded from http://www.bris.ac.uk/Depts/History/Maritime/Sources/2008 sfpmallet.pdf.

58. Platter, *Travels,* pp. 158–59.
59. Magno, p. 146.
60. Harrison, *Description,* chapter vi.
61. Magno, p. 146.
62. Andrew Boorde, *The First Booke of Common Knowledge* (1547).

CHAPTER TEN: Hygiene, Illness, and Medicine
 1. Carew, *Survey,* p. 68a.
 2. Traister, *Notorious,* p. 119.
 3. Pepys records defecating twice in the chimney of a strange house in the 1660s (quoted in Andrew Wear, "Personal Hygiene," in W. F. Bynum and Roy Porter, eds., *Companion Encyclopedia of the History of Medicine* [Routledge, 2 vols., 1993], ii, pp. 1283–1308, at p. 1301).
 4. Quoted in Traister, *Notorious,* p. 159.
 5. Alain Corbin, in *The Foul and the Fragrant* (Leamington Spa, 1986), says that the eighteenth century sees a "lowering of olfactory tolerance." See Jenner, "Smell," p. 338.
 6. Schneider, "Colors," p. 112.
 7. Harington, *Ajax,* p. 84; Wright, *Clean,* pp. 71–73.
 8. Orlin, "Disputes," pp. 350–51.
 9. Hoskins, *Exeter,* p. 61.
 10. Jenner, "Smell," p. 340.
 11. Dawson, *Plenti & Grase,* p. 265.
 12. Pelling, *CL,* p. 82, quoting *Tudor Economic Documents,* ii, pp. 317–18.
 13. Bullein, *Government,* quoted in Smith, *Clean,* p. 209.
 14. Furnival, ed., *Babees Book,* p. 256.
 15. Furnival, *Babees Book,* p. 246, quoting Boorde, *Dyetary.*
 16. William Vaughan, "Fifteen Directions for Health" (1602), in Furnival, *Babees Book,* pp. 249–50.
 17. This idea is the main thrust of the early chapters of Vigarello, *Concepts.*
 18. Smith, *Clean,* p. 190.
 19. Smith, *Clean,* pp. 189–90 (Whitehall); Wright, *Clean,* p. 75 (Windsor).
 20. *Eliz. Home,* pp. 77–78.
 21. Information mentioned in a BBC article and personally communicated by Dr. Steven Gunn of Merton College, Oxford, to whom the author is most grateful.
 22. Bullein, *Government,* f. 22v.
 23. Anon., *A Description of a New Kinde of Artificial Bathes lately invented* (c. 1600). From the collections of the Society of Antiquaries.
 24. R. I. W. Evans, "Dentistry," in *Before the Mast,* at p. 554. This is from the *Mary Rose* sailors' skeletons; it is possible sailors had a higher degree of tooth loss than the general population, as scurvy results in a softening of the gums. However, they would have had a low-sugar diet compared with many people on land, so I suspect their teeth are representative of or better than those of the sugar-loving population in Elizabeth's reign.
 25. Scott, *EOaW,* p. 12 (quoting Hentzner); Wright, *Clean,* p. 245; Arnold, *Wardrobe,* p. 10.
 26. *Eliz. Home,* p. 17 (for manufacture of toothpicks); Arnold, *Wardrobe,* p. 111 (for quotation).

27. Boorde, *Breviary*, f. xvii.
28. Wright, *Clean*, p. 245.
29. John Partridge, *The Treasurie of Commodious Conceites* (1584), cap. 63.
30. Chrissie Freeth, "Ancient History of Trips to the Dentist," *British Archaeology* (April 1999), pp. 8–9, at p. 9.
31. Boorde, *Breviary*, f. 28r.
32. *CUH*, p. 51; Wrigley & Schofield, p. 337. According to the latter (Appendix 2.4), between August 1558 and May 1559 there were 180,766 burials. This equates to an annual crude burial rate of 216,919 at a time when the population had shrunk to fewer than three million because of the influenza of the previous year, roughly 72 per 1,000. The number of deaths in 1558 is given as 166,387 (53 per 1,000), and in 1559, 141,282 (47 per 1,000). The total, over 307,000, is roughly twice the "normal" total for two years, suggesting that influenza (and any other periodic killer diseases, such as plague) killed about 150,000–160,000 in these years. A normal year was 25 deaths per 1,000 at this time (Cressy, *BMD*, p. 380). The year 1569—chosen as representative of "normal"—experienced a death rate of 23.25 per thousand.
33. The generally accepted figure for 1918–19 is 228,000 deaths, at a time when the population was 43 million.
34. Mortimer, *D & D*, p. 33.
35. Dobson, *Contours*, pp. 288, 493.
36. Slack, *Impact*, p. 174, estimates that 658,000 died over the period of 1570–1670, or roughly 6,580 per year. If every year was equal, this would mean the forty-five years of Elizabeth's reign saw 296,100 deaths. There were some terrible plague years in this reign, 1563 being referred to as a great plague of London. Slack notes that major epidemics in Bristol became rarer after 1604, and in Devon they decreased in intensity over the period while in Essex they increased (p. 192). However, there were more plague years per decade in the provinces in Elizabeth's reign.
37. Slack, *Impact*, p. 128. The population of Norwich after the influx of foreign refugees and prior to the plague was about seventeen thousand.
38. Dyer, *Crisis*, p. 93.
39. Slack, *Impact*, p. 120.
40. Slack, *Impact*, pp. 85, 87, 90, 313.
41. Slack, *Impact*, pp. 84, 97, 120, 151; *True bill* (1603).
42. The figures for 1578 and 1593 are from Slack, *Impact*, p. 151. Those for 1563 and 1582 are from anon., *The Nvmber of all those that hath dyed in the Citie of London & the liberties of the same . . .* (1582). The 1603 figures are from *True bill* (1603); these include the figures for the city of Westminster and other parishes near London. The figures for London alone are 35,267 total dead, of whom the plague killed 29,402.
43. Slack, *Impact*, p. 11.
44. Traister, *Notorious*, p. 46.
45. Nicholas Bownd, *Medicines for the Plague* (1604), quoted in Slack, *Impact*, p. 22.
46. Mortimer, *D & D*, pp. 197–98.
47. Andrew Wear, "Caring for the Sick Poor in St. Bartholomew's Exchange, 1580–1676," in R. Porter and W. Bynum, eds., *Living and Dying in London* (suppl. to *Medical History*, xi [1991]), pp. 41–60; Mortimer, *D & Doctors*, p. 153; Pelling, *CL*, pp. 195–96.
48. Mortimer, *D & D*, pp. 154–56, 170.
49. The account of Thomas Smallbone is in Mortimer, *Probate*, pp. 70–72. It actually

dates from a little after Elizabeth's reign, from September 1608, but it may be considered representative of sealed households elsewhere at an earlier date.

50. Slack, *Impact*, p. 79. The last line states, "This he did, because he was a strong man and heavier than his said nephew and another wench were able to bury." John Dawson and the wench, a maidservant, also died and were buried near the house.

51. *Morbus Gallicus*, p. 1.

52. Edward Shorter, *A History of Women's Bodies* (1983), p. 98.

53. Dawson, *Jewell* (1587), p. 23v.

54. Dawson, *Jewell* (1587), p. 50r–v.

55. Mortimer, *D & D*, pp. 160–61.

56. Partridge, *Treasure*, n.p.

57. For the increase during Elizabeth's reign, it is worth noting that the diocese of Exeter granted 1.3 licenses per year in 1568–97 and 2.8 in 1610–27 (Mortimer, "Licensing," p. 51). Exeter had just eight freemen apothecaries in this reign and fifteen were granted their freedom in the years 1604–46. Similar changes are to be noted in other dioceses surveyed by Haggis (Wellcome Trust, MSS 5343-7, A. W. G. Haggis, typescript lists of medical licentiates). Arthur J. Willis, ed., *Canterbury Licenses (General) 1568–1646* (Phillimore, 1972), notes two licenses granted in the 1570s, five in the 1580s, fifteen in the 1590s, and twenty in the period 1600–1603. The minimum 2,000 for the country is estimated from (1) 500 in London in 1600 (as noted by Pelling, "Practitioners"); (2) the ratio of one licentiate per 8,000 population for Devon and Cornwall in the generation 1568–97; (3) the finding that there was at least one unlicensed practitioner for every licensed one, even in Kent (where many practitioners were licensed); (4) the much greater number of provincial practitioners clustered in the southeast; and (5) the number of provincial apothecaries. With regard to (2), the Devon and Cornwall ratio may be taken to be representative of the country, as most areas had a higher ratio of practitioners to population than this (Mortimer, *D & D*, pp. 42–44). With a population outside London of 3.9 million, there were at least 500 licensed and 500 unlicensed practitioners in the country. As the counties in the southeast seem to have had by 1620 a ratio of practitioners to population of 1:400, there must have been considerably more than 500 extra practitioners in these southeastern communities. In 1620 Canterbury Diocese alone (with a population of about 80,000) had 190 practitioners—170 more than suggested by the one licensed and one unlicensed practitioner per 8,000 population noted for the country as a whole. As the population of Kent, Sussex, Surrey, Oxfordshire, Berkshire, Bedfordshire, Buckinghamshire, and Essex was well in excess of 500,000 in 1570, the extra practitioners in the southeast outside London was (1/400–2/8,000) × 500,000 = 1,125. The real total for the kingdom, including all the empirics and apothecaries, was probably between 3,000 and 4,000.

58. Pelling, "Practitioners," p. 188.

59. Mortimer, *D & D*, pp. 61–63. In 2009, there were 246,181 names on the UK List of Registered Medical Practitioners for a population of 61.7 million.

60. Pelling, "Practitioners," p. 172.

61. Pelling, "Practitioners," p. 174. In addition older men with sufficient experience could join by paying a fee.

62. Mortimer, *D & D*, pp. 62–63.

63. *Morbus Gallicus*, f. 8r.

64. For example, Emmison, *HWL*, p. 138, wrote: "To most Elizabethans living outside

the big cities neither doctor nor hospital is normally available. . . ." See Mortimer, "Marketplace," pp. 69–87.

65. Pelling, "Practitioners"; Mortimer, *D & D*, pp. 37, 106, 213. The population figure of five thousand for Canterbury, given in Chapter One of this book, has been used rather than the estimate of six to seven thousand in *D&D*. The figure for people in towns seeking medical help when dying 1570–99 is 7.3 percent; those living more than a mile from town paid for medical help in 4.2 percent of cases.

66. Mortimer, *D & D*, pp. 43, 61–63; Mortimer, "Licensing." Exeter had only eight free-men apothecaries during the reign, and Devon and Cornwall between them had only thirty-eight licensed physicians and surgeons 1568–97, and a handful of university-trained physicians. In both counties there were probably no more than sixty apothecaries, fifty licentiates, twenty degree-holders, and an unknown number of itinerant physicians. The latter are likely to have outnumbered all the former, as there was a tradition of not applying for a license unless one had to, and then only later in one's career.

67. Lane, *John Hall*, pp. 138–42.

68. Lane, *John Hall*, pp. 40–41. For Plat, see Bee Wilson, review of Malcolm Thick, *Sir Hugh Plat: The Search for Useful Knowledge in Early Modern London* (Totnes, 2010), *TLS* (22 December 2010).

69. Thomas Gale, *Certaine Workes of Chirurgerie* (1563), f. 54r–v.

CHAPTER ELEVEN: **Law and Disorder**

1. Machyn, *Diary*, pp. 227–29, 253, 255, 261, 272, 275, 281.
2. Holmes, *London*, pp. 55–56.
3. Black, *Reign*, pp. 211–12.
4. Black, *Reign*, p. 209n.
5. Black, *Reign*, p. 143.
6. Philip Sugden, "Ratsey, Gamaliel (d. 1605), Highwayman," in *ODNB*.
7. These criminal types are all from Judges, *Underworld*.
8. Weiner, "Sex Roles," p. 39.
9. Weiner, "Sex Roles," p. 40.
10. Weiner, "Sex Roles," pp. 47–48.
11. Emmison, *Disorder*, p. 106.
12. Samaha, "Hanging," p. 763.
13. The selling of the girl is in Machyn, *Diary*, p. 228.
14. Platter, *Travels*, p. 174.
15. Machyn, *Diary*, pp. 251–52.
16. Holmes, *London*, p. 95, quoting Stow.
17. Machyn, *Diary*, p. 281. See Harrison, *Description*, chapter 17, for the three tides.
18. Emmison, *Disorder*, p. 319. Those "at large" have been excluded from this calculation, so the sample is 843 cases.
19. Pollitt, "Story," p. 152.
20. Note that "drawing" does not relate to the removal of the entrails. This is clearly noted in chapter 17 of Harrison, *Description*, and a number of other sixteenth-century and earlier sources, including Machyn, *Diary*, p. 63. See Ian Mortimer, "Why Do We Say 'Hanged, Drawn and Quartered," http://www.ianmortimer.com/essays/drawing.pdf.
21. Emmison, *Disorder*, pp. 40–41.
22. Quoted in Picard, *London*, p. 251. William Harrison emphasizes that women who

poison their husbands deserve to be punished in this way, although he believes that mass poisoning should still be punished by boiling to death.

23. For an example of a laborer suffering in this way, see Emmison, *Disorder*, p. 149.

24. Machyn, *Diary*, p. 279.

25. Beier, "Social Problems," p. 221.

26. Machyn, *Diary*, p. 246.

27. Machyn, *Diary*, p. 252.

28. Emmison, *HWL*, p. 231; Emmison, *Morals*, p. 31.

29. Machyn, *Diary*, p. 272.

30. Emmison, *HWL*, p. 257.

31. Griffiths, "Bridewell," pp. 285, 290.

32. Emmison, *Disorder*, p. 302.

33. Machyn, *Diary*, p. 255.

34. Machyn, *Diary*, p. 273.

35. For example, Machyn, *Diary*, p. 248.

36. Machyn, *Diary*, pp. 178 (Queen Mary dead), 196 (slander), 261 (conjuring), 251, 275 and 277 (all counterfeiting), 304 (meat).

37. Machyn, *Diary*, p. 311.

38. Machyn, *Diary*, p. 235. Another example appears on p. 236.

39. Machyn, *Diary*, pp. 196–97.

40. Machyn, *Diary*, pp. 255, 304 (eating meat).

41. Emmison, *Home, Work*, p. 257.

42. Emmison, *Morals*, p. 31.

43. Thomas, *RDM*, p. 528.

44. Emmison, *HWL*, p. 235.

45. Machyn, *Diary*, pp. 220, 223, 238.

46. Machyn, *Diary*, pp. 239, 309.

47. Samaha, "Hanging," p. 763.

48. Emmison, *Disorder*, p. 153.

49. Emmison, *Disorder*, p. 155.

50. Emmison, *Disorder*, p. 157.

51. Emmison, *Morals*, p. 282.

52. Emmison, *Morals*, p. 300.

53. Emmison, *Morals*, p. 304.

54. Alan MacFarlane, *Witchcraft in Tudor and Stuart England: A Regional and Comparative Study* (1970), p. 98.

55. Emmison, *Morals*, p. 79.

56. Hughes, "Godly," pp. 103, 105.

57. Emmison, *Morals*, p. 118.

58. Emmison, *Morals*, p. 59.

59. Wiener, "Sex Roles," p. 46.

60. Emmison, *Morals*, p. 71.

61. Emmison, *Morals*, p. 26.

62. Emmison, *Morals*, p. 45.

63. Emmison, *Morals*, p. 13.

CHAPTER TWELVE: **Entertainment**

1. Platter, *Travels*, p. 226; Holmes, *London*, p. 57.

2. Platter, *Travels*, pp. 163–65.

3. Platter, *Travels*, pp. 171–73.

4. Holmes, *London*, p. 57, quoting Stow (giant and dwarf); Hollyband, *Campo di Fior*, p. 19 (sword swallower); Platter, *Travels*, 173 (camel).

5. Black, *Reign*, p. 6; Doran, ed., *Exhibition*, p. 244; Frances A. Yates, "Elizabethan Chivalry: The Romance of the Accession Day Tilts," *Journal of the Warburg and Courtauld Institutes*, 20 (1957), pp. 4–25.

6. Platter, *Travels*, p. 189.

7. Emmison, *Morals*, pp. 22–23.

8. Emmison, *Disorder*, p. 26.

9. Picard, *London*, p. 229, quoting Dekker, *The Honest Whore*, act 2, scene i.

10. Charlton, "Tobacco," p. 103; Black, *Reign*, p. 274.

11. Charlton, "Tobacco," p. 109.

12. Platter, *Travels*, p. 171.

13. Rowse, *Tudor Cornwall*, pp. 426–33.

14. 33 Henry VIII, cap. 9.

15. Emmison, *HWL*, p. 238.

16. *Port & Trade*.

17. Judges, *Underworld*, p. 129; *Eliz. Home*, p. 110 (Trumps).

18. Stevenson, "Extracts," pp. 292–301.

19. Salgado, *Underworld*, p. 22; Judges, *Underworld*, pp. 27, 41.

20. William Bray, "Account of the Lottery of 1567, Being the First upon Record," *Archaeologia* 19 (1821), pp. 79–87.

21. Carew, *Survey*, f. 72v, mentions these four battles.

22. Gunn, "Archery," p. 78.

23. Gunn, "Archery," pp. 53–81.

24. Emmison, *HWL*, pp. 240–41.

25. Scott, *EOaW*, p. 111.

26. William Gryndall, *Hawking, Hunting Fouling and Fishing* (1596), n.p.

27. *Eliz. Home*, pp. 106–7.

28. *Sh. Eng.*, ii, p. 390.

29. Carew, *Survey*, ff. 75v–76r.

30. Holmes, *London*, p. 50.

31. Sim, *Pleasure*, p. 184, quoting Elyot, *The booke named the Governor*, p. 92.

32. Stubbes, *Anatomy*, pp. 138–39.

33. Gunn, "Archery," p. 65.

34. Emmison, *Disorder*, pp. 225–26.

35. Carew, *Survey*, ff. 73v–75v.

36. Platter, *Travels*, pp. 167–68.

37. Stevenson, "Extracts," p. 297.

38. *Sh. Eng.*, ii, p. 428.

39. Platter, *Travels*, pp. 168–69. The tense has been changed from the past to the present.

40. Scott, *EOaW*, quoting Robert Laneham's letter.

41. Information kindly supplied by Dr. Steven Gunn of Merton College, Oxford.

42. *Sh. Eng.*, ii, p. 431; Black, *Reign*, p. 354.

43. Emmison, *HWL*, p. 239.

44. Dawson, "Bull-Baiting," pp. 97–101.

45. *Sh. Eng.*, ii, p. 22.

46. *Sh. Eng.*, ii, p. 21.

47. Sim, *Pleasure*, p. 127.
48. Emmison, *HWL*, p. 169.
49. Stevenson, "Extracts," p. 296.
50. Machyn, *Diary*, p. 191.
51. Sim, *Pleasures*, p. 117.
52. Stubbes, *Anatomy*, pp. 114, 124.
53. Rowse, *Cornwall*, pp. 428–29.
54. Carew, *Survey*, f. 71v.
55. Ringler, "Attack," pp. 391–418.
56. Ringler, "Attack," p. 410.
57. Shapiro, *1599*, p. 10.
58. Hughes, "Godly," p. 103; *ODNB*.

ENVOI
1. *Eliz. Home*, p. 105.

FULL TITLES OF WORKS CITED IN THE NOTES

Airs, Malcolm. *The Tudor and Jacobean Country House* (Surrey, UK: Bramley Books, 1995).

Anonymous. *The Good Hous-wife's Treasurie* (1558).

Anonymous. *A true bill of the whole number that hath died in the Cittie of London* (1603).

Arkell, Tom, Nesta Evans, and Nigel Goose, eds. *When Death Do Us Part: Understanding and Interpreting the Probate Records of Early Modern England* (Oxford: Leopard's Head Press, 2000).

Arnold, Jane. *Queen Elizabeth's Wardrobe Unlock'd* (Leeds: Maney Publishing, 1998; repr. 2008).

Barron, Caroline, Christopher Coleman, and Claire Gobbi, eds. "The London Journal of Alessandro Magno 1562." *London Journal* 9, no. 2 (1983): 136–53.

Bearman, Robert, ed. *The History of an English Borough: Stratford-upon-Avon, 1196–1996* (Stroud, UK: Sutton Publishing, 1997).

Beer, Barrett L. *Tudor England Observed* (Stroud, UK: Sutton Publishing, 1998).

Beier, A. L. "Social Problems in Elizabethan London." *Journal of Interdisciplinary History* 9, no. 2 (1978): 203–21.

Beier, A. L. "Vagrants and the Social Order in Elizabethan England." *Past and Present* 64 (1974): 3–29.

Black, J. B. *The Reign of Elizabeth, 1558–1603*. 2nd ed. (Oxford: Oxford University Press, 1959).

Boorde, Andrew. *The Breuiary of Helthe, for all maner of syckenesses and diseases the whiche may be in man, or woman doth folowe* (1547).

Boorde, Andrew. *A Compendyous Regyment or a Dyetary of healthe made in Mountpyllyer* (1542).

Bowden, Peter J., ed. *Chapters from the Agrarian History of England and Wales, 1500–1750*. Vol. 1 (Cambridge: Cambridge University Press, 1990).

Brown, Rawdon, and G. Cavendish Bentinck, eds. *Calendar State Papers Relating to English Affairs in the Archives of Venice*. Vol. 7: 1558–1580 (1890).

Bullein, William. *The Government of Health* (1st ed. 1558; 1595 ed.).

Charlton, Ann. "Tobacco or Health 1602: An Elizabethan Doctor Speaks." *Health Education Research* 20, no. 1 (2005): 100–11.

Chynoweth, John, Nicholas Orne, and Alexandra Walsham, eds. *The Survey of Cornwall by Richard Carew* (Devon & Cornwall Record Society, New Series 47, 2004).

Clark, Peter, ed. *The Cambridge Urban History of Britain*. Vol. 2, 1540–1840 (Cambridge: Cambridge University Press, 2000).

Clark, Peter. "The Migrant in Kentish Towns, 1580–1640," in *Crisis*, eds. Peter Clark and Paul Slack, pp. 117–63.

Clark, Peter, and Paul Slack, eds. *Crisis and Order in English Towns, 1500–1700* (Oxford: Routledge, 1972).

Clowes, William. *A Brief and Necessary Treatise touching the Cure of the Disease called Morbus Gallicus* (1585).

Creighton, Charles. *A History of Epidemics in Britain*. 2 vols. (Cambridge: The University Press, 1891).

Cressy, David. *Birth, Marriage and Death* (Oxford: Oxford University Press, 1997).

Cunnington, C. Willett, and Phillis Cunnington. *The History of Underclothes* (London: Michael Joseph, 1951).

Dawson, Giles E. "London's Bull-Baiting and Bear-Baiting Arena in 1562." *Shakespeare Quarterly* 15 (1964): 97–101.

Dawson, Mark. *Plenti & Grase: Food and Drink in a Sixteenth-century Household* (Totnes, UK: Prospect Books, 2009).

Dawson, Thomas. *The Good Huswife's Jewell* (1587).

Dawson, Thomas. *The Good Housewife's Jewel*, with an introduction by Maggie Black (Sheffield, UK: Southover Press, 1996).

Dietz, Brian, ed. *The Port and Trade of Early Elizabethan London: Documents*, appendix III. Accessed through British History online.

Dobson, Mary. *Contours of Death and Disease in Early Modern England* (Cambridge: Cambridge University Press, 1997).

Doran, Susan, ed. *Elizabeth: The Exhibition at the National Maritime Museum* (London: Chatto & Windus, 2003).

Drummond, J. C., Anne Wilbraham, and Dorothy Hollingsworth. *The Englishman's Food: A History of Five Centuries of English Diet* (London: Jonathan Cape, 1958).

Duffy, Eamon. *The Voices of Morebath* (New Haven: Yale University Press, 2001).

Dyer, Alan. "Crisis and Resolution: Government and Society, 1540–1640," in *Stratford*, ed. Robert Bearman, pp. 80–96.

Emmison, F. G. *Elizabethan Life I: Disorder* (Chelmsford, UK: Essex Record Office, 1970).

Emmison, F. G. *Elizabethan Life: Home, Work, and Land* (Chelmsford, UK: Essex County Council, 1976).

Emmison, F. G. *Elizabethan Life II: Morals and the Church Courts* (Chelmsford, UK: Essex Record Office, 1973).

Fisher, F. J., ed. "The State of England Anno Dom. 1600 by Thomas Wilson." *Camden Miscellany* xvi, Camden Third Series 52 (1936): 1–43.

Fisher, H. E. S., and A. R. J. Juřica, eds. *Documents in English Economic History: England from 1000 to 1760* (repr., London: Collins Educational, 1984).

Furnivall, F. J. *The Babees Book* (repr., Suffolk, UK: Boydell and Brewer, 1997).

Gardiner, Julie, and Michael J. Allen, eds. *Before the Mast: Life and Death Aboard the Mary Rose*. Vol. 4 of *Archaeology of the Mary Rose* (Portsmouth, UK: Mary Rose Trust, 2005).

Gerard, John. *The Autobiography of an Elizabethan*. Trans. Philip Caraman (London: Longmans, 1951).

Gerard, John. *The Herball or Generall Historie of Plantes* (1597).

Girouard, Mark. *Elizabethan Architecture: Its Rise and Fall, 1540–1640* (New Haven: Yale University Press, 2009).

Girouard, Mark. *Life in the English Country House* (New Haven: Yale University Press, 1978).

Griffiths, Paul. "Contesting Bridewell, 1576–1580." *Journal of British Studies* 42, no. 3 (2003): 283–315.

Gunn, Steven. "Archery Practice in Tudor England." *Past and Present* 209 (2010): 53–81.

Harding, Vanessa. "The Population of London, 1550–1700: A Review of the Published Evidence." *London Journal* 15 (1990): 111–28.

Harington, Sir John. *A New Discourse of a Stale Subject Called the Metamorphosis of Ajax* (1586).

Harrison, William. *Description of England*, in Ralph Holinshed, *The Historie of England* (1577).

Havinden, M. A., ed. *Household and Farm Inventories in Oxfordshire, 1550–1590* (Historical Manuscript Society & H.M.S.O, 1965), p. 220.

Herridge, D. M., ed. *Surrey Probate Inventories, 1558–1603* (Surrey, UK: Surrey Record Society 39, 2005).

Hill, Christopher. *Reformation to Industrial Revolution* (London: Weidenfeld and Nicolson, 1967).

Hodgen, Margaret T. "Fairs of Elizabethan England." *Economic Geography* 18, no. 4 (1942): 389–400).

Hollyband, Claudius. *Campo di Fior, or the Flowery Field of Four Languages* (1583).

Holmes, Martin. *Elizabethan London* (London: Cassell, 1969).

Horman, William. *Vulgaria*. 2nd ed. (1530).

Hoskins, W. G. "The Rebuilding of Rural England, 1570–1640." *Past and Present* 4, no. 1 (1953): 44–59.

Hoskins, W. G. "English Provincial Towns in the Sixteenth Century." *Transactions of the Royal Historical Society* 5th ser. 6 (1956): 1–19.

Hoskins, W. G. *Two Thousand Years in Exeter* (Exeter: James Townsend & Sons, 1960).

Hoskins, W. G. *Making of the English Landscape* (1955; repr. London: Penguin Books, 1985).

Howard, Jean E. "Women, Foreigners and Urban Space in *Westward Ho*," in *Material London*, ed. Lena Cowen Orlin, pp. 150–67.

Hughes, Ann. "Building a Godly Town," in *Stratford*, ed. Bearman, pp. 97–109.

Hurstfield, Joel, and Alan G. R. Smith, eds. *Elizabethan People* (London: Arnold Publishing, 1972).

Jenner, Mark S. R. "Follow Your Nose? Smell, Smelling, and Their Histories." *American Historical Review* 116, no. 2 (2011): 335–51.

Jones, Jeanne. *Family Life in Shakespeare's England* (Stroud, UK: Sutton Publishing, 1996).

Joyce, Herbert. *The History of the Post Office from Its Establishment down to 1836* (London: R Bentley, 1893).

Judges, A. V. *The Elizabethan Underworld: A Collection of Tudor and Early Stuart Tracts and Ballads* (1930; repr. London: Routlege, 1965).

Kocher, Paul H. "The Physician as Atheist in Elizabethan England." *Huntington Library Quarterly* 10, no. 3 (1947): 229–49.

Kocher, Paul H. "The Old Cosmos: A Study in Elizabethan Science and Religion." *Huntington Library Quarterly* 15, no. 2 (1952): 101–21.

Lane, Joan. *John Hall and His Patients: The Medical Practice of Shakespeare's Son-in-law* (Stratford-upon-Avon: The Shakespeare Birthplace Trust, 1996).

Laslett, Peter. *The World We Have Lost* (repr. London: Methuen, 1979).

Laughton, John Knox, ed. *State Papers Relating to the Defeat of the Spanish Armada*. Vol. 1 (Navy Records Society, 1895).

Lee, Sidney. "Bearbaiting, bullbaiting, and cock-fighting," in *Shakespeare's England*.

Markland, J. H. "Remarks on the Early Use of Carriages." *Archaeologia* 20 (1894): 443–77.

Marsden, Peter, ed. Mary Rose *Your Noblest Shippe: Anatomy of a Tudor Warship*. Vol. 4 of *Archaeology of the* Mary Rose, vol. 2 (Portsmouth, UK: Mary Rose Trust, 2009).

Mikhalia, Ninya, and Jane Malcolm-Davies. *The Tudor Tailor: Reconstructing Sixteenth-Century Dress* (London: Batsford, 2006).

Mortimer, Ian. "Why Were Probate Accounts Made? Methodological Issues Concerning the Historical Use of Administrators' and Executors' Accounts." *Archives* 31 (2006): 2–17.

Mortimer, Ian. "Index of Medical Licentiates, Applicants, Referees and Examiners in the Diocese of Exeter, 1568–1783." *Transactions of The Devonshire Association* 136 (2004): 99–134.

Mortimer, Ian. "Diocesan Licensing and Medical Practitioners in South-West England." *Medical History* 48 (2004): 49–68.

Mortimer, Ian. "Tudor Chronicler or Sixteenth-century Diarist? Henry Machyn and the Nature of His Manuscript." *Sixteenth Century Journal* 33 (2002): 981–98.

Mortimer, Ian. "The Rural Medical Marketplace in Southern England c. 1570–1720," in *Med-*

icine and the Market in England and Its Colonies, c. 1450–1850, eds. Mark S. R. Jenner and Patrick Wallis (London: Palgrave Macmillan, 2007).

Mortimer, Ian. *The Dying and the Doctors* (Woodbridge, UK: The Royal Historical Society, 2009).

Mortimer, Ian, ed. *Berkshire Glebe Terriers, 1634.* Vol. 2 (Reading, UK: Berkshire Record Society, 1995).

Mortimer, Ian, ed. *Berkshire Probate Accounts, 1583–1712* (Reading, UK: Berkshire Record Society, 1995).

Mortimer, Ian. *The Time Traveler's Guide to Medieval England: A Handbook for Visitors to the Fourteenth Century* (London: Vintage, 2008).

Nichols, John Gough, ed. *The Diary of Henry Machyn* (London: Camden Society, 1848).

Nicoll, A. *The Elizabethans* (Cambridge: University Press, 1957).

Norris, Herbert. *Tudor Costume and Fashion.* Vol. 3 (London: J. M. Dent & Sons, 1938).

Orlin, Lena Cowen. "Boundary Disputes in Early Modern London," in *Material London*, ed. Lena Cowen Orlin, pp. 344–76.

Orlin, Lena Cowen, ed. *Material London ca. 1600* (Philadelphia: University of Pennsylvania Press, 2000).

Overton, Mark. "Prices from Inventories," in *Death*, ed. Tom Arkell, pp. 120–43.

The Oxford Dictionary of National Biography. Online edition; www. Oxforddnb.com.

The Oxford English Dictionary. Online edition; ww.oed.com.

Parry, J. H. *The Age of Reconnaissance* (Cleveland: World Publishing Company, 1963).

Partridge, John. *The Treasurie of Commodious Conceites* (1584).

Partridge, John. *The Widowes Treasure, plentifully furnished with sundry precious and approved secretes in Physick and Chirurgery for the health and pleasure of Mankind* (1588).

Pelling, Margaret. "Old Age, Poverty and Disability in Norwich," in *Life, Death, and the Elderly*, eds. Margaret Pelling and Richard M. Smith (London: Routledge, 1991), pp. 74–101.

Pelling, Margaret, and Charles Webster. "Medical Practitioners," in *Health, Medicine and Mortality in the Sixteenth Century*, ed. Charles Webster (Cambridge: Cambridge University Press, 1979), pp. 165–236.

Pelling, Margaret. *The Common Lot: Sickness, Medical Occupations, and the Urban Poor in the Early Modern England* (London: Longman, 1998).

Picard, Liza. *Elizabeth's London: Everyday Life in Elizabethan England* (London: Weidenfeld and Nicolson, 2003).

Platt, Colin. *The Great Rebuildings of Tudor and Stuart England* (London: Taylor and Francis, 1994).

Pollitt, Ronald. "'Refuge of the Distressed Nations': Perceptions of Aliens in Elizabethan England." *Journal of Modern History* 52, no. 1, on demand supplement (March 1980); D1001–D1019.

Pollitt, Ronald. "The Abduction of Doctor John Story and the Evolution of Elizabethan Intelligence Operations." *The Sixteenth Century Journal* 14, no. 2 (Summer 1983): 131–56.

Pound, John F., ed. *The Norwich Census of the Poor* (Norwich, UK: Norfolk Record Society, 1971).

Ringler, William. "The First Phase of an Elizabethan Attack on the Stage, 1558–1579." *Huntington Library Quarterly* 5, no. 4 (1942): 391–418.

Rose, Susan. "Mathematics and the Art of Navigation: The Advance of Scientific Seamanship in Elizabethan England." *Transactions of the Royal Historical Society* 6th ser. 14 (2004): 15–184.

Rowse, A. L. *Tudor Cornwall* (London: Jonathan Cape, 1941).

Rowse, A. L. *The England of Elizabeth: The Structure of Society* (New York: Macmillan, 1951).

Rye, W. B. *England as Seen by Foreigners in the Days of Elizabeth and James I* (London: J. R. Smith, 1865).

Sacks, David Harris, and Michael Lynch. "Ports 1540–1700," in *Cambridge Urban History of Britain*, ed. Peter Clark, chapter 12.

St. Clare Byrne, M., ed., *The Elizabethan Home*, 2nd ed. (London: Cobden-Sanderson, 1930).

Salgado, Gamini. *The Elizabethan Underworld* (1977, repr. Stroud, UK: Sutton Publishing, 1999).

Samaha, Joel B. "Hanging for Felony: The Rule of Law in Elizabethan Colchester." *The Historical Journal* 21, no. 4 (Dec. 1978): 763–82.

Schneider, Jane. "Fantastical Colors in Foggy London," in *Material London*, ed. Lena Cowen Orlin, pp. 109–27.

Schoenbaum, S. *William Shakespeare: A Documentary Life* (Oxford: Oxford University Press, 1975).

Schofield, John. "The Topography and Buildings of London," in *Material London*, ed. Lena Cowen Orlin, pp. 296–321.

Scott, A. F. *Every One a Witness: The Tudor Age* (Book Club Associates, 1975).

Shakespeare's England. (Oxford: Oxford University Press, 1917).

Shapiro, James. *1599: A Year in the Life of William Shakespeare* (London: HarperCollins, 2005).

Sharpe, James. *Instruments of Darkness: Witchcraft in Early Modern England* (Philadelphia: University of Pennsylvania Press, 1996).

Sim, Alison. *Pleasures and Pastimes in Tudor England* (Stroud, UK: The History Press, 2009).

Slack, Paul. *The Impact of Plague in Tudor and Stuart England* (Oxford: Clarendon Press, 1985).

Smith, Lucy Toulmin, ed. *The Itinerary of John Leland in or about the Years 1535–1543*. 5 vols. (London: G. Bell, 1907–10).

Smith, Virginia. *Clean: A History of Personal Hygiene and Purity* (Oxford: Oxford University Press, 2007).

Spufford, Peter. "Long-term Rural Credit in Sixteenth- and Seventeenth-Century England: The Evidence of Probate Accounts," in *Death*, ed. Tom Arkell, pp. 213–28.

Stevenson, William. "Extracts from the booke of the household charges and other payments laid out by the Lord North . . ." *Archaeologia* 19 (1821): 283–301.

Stow, John. *A Survey of London*, 2nd ed. (1603).

Stoyle, Mark. "'It is but an old witch gone': Prosecution and Execution for Witchcraft in Exeter, 1558–1610." *History* 96 (April 2011): 129–51.

Stoyle, Mark. *West Britons: Cornish Identities and the Early Modern British State* (Exeter, UK: University of Exeter Press, 2002).

Strong, Roy. *The Renaissance Garden in England* (1979; repr., London: Thames and Hudson, 1998).

Stubbes, Philip. *The Anatomy of Abuses*. 4th ed. (1595).

Thirsk, Joan. *Food in Early Modern England: Phases, Fads, and Fashions, 1500–1760* (London: Continuum, 2007).

Thirsk, Joan, and J. P. Cooper, eds. *Seventeenth-Century Economic Documents* (Oxford: Clarendon Press, 1972).

Thomas, Keith. *Religion and the Decline of Magic* (New York: Scribner, 1971).

Traister, Barbara Howard. *The Notorious Astrological Physician of London: Works and Days of Simon Forman* (Chicago: University of Chicago Press, 2001).

Vigarello, Georges. *Concepts of Cleanliness: Changing Attitudes in France since the Middle Ages*. J. Birrell trans. (Cambridge: Cambridge University Press, 1988).

W., A. *A book of Cookrye* (1591).

Walsham, Alexandra. "'Frantick Hacket': Prophecy, Sorcery, Insanity, and the Elizabethan Puritan Movement." *The Historical Journal* 41, no. 1 (1998): 27–66.

Weiner, Carol Z. "Sex Roles and Crime in Late Elizabethan Hertfordshire." *Journal of a Social History* 8, no. 4 (Summer 1975): 38–60.

Williams, Clare, ed. *Thomas Platter's Travels in England 1599* (London: Jonathan Cape, 1937).

Williams, Penry. *Life in Tudor England* (London: Batsford, 1964).

Wilson, C. Anne. *Food and Drink in Britain* (London: Constable, 1991).

Wright, Lawrence. *Clean and Decent* (London: Routledge & Paul, 1960).

Wrightson, Keith. *Earthly Necessities: Economic Lives in Early Modern Britain* (New Haven: Yale University Press, 2000).

Wrigley, E. A., and R. S. Schofield. *The Population History of England, 1541–1871: A Reconstruction* (London: Edward Arnold, 1981).

Yates, Frances A. "Elizabethan Chivalry: The Romance of the Accession Day Tilts." *Journal of the Warburg and Courtauld Institutes* 20 (1957): 4–25.

Yeames, A. H. S. "The Grand Tour of an Elizabethan." *Papers of the British School at Rome* 7 (1914): 92–113.

INDEX

Vital dates have been given where known, to aid identification. Flornit dates have been given only where the individual has an entry in *The Oxford Dictionary of National Biography*. Books have not been indexed—only their authors have—with the exception of Shakespeare's plays and anonymous works (indexed under Anon).